The Sociology of the Possible

SECOND EDITION

The Sociology of the Possible

Edited by

Richard Ofshe

UNIVERSITY OF CALIFORNIA, BERKELEY

PRENTICE-HALL, INC., ENGLEWOOD CLIFFS, NEW JERSEY 07632

Library of Congress Cataloging in Publication Data

Ofshe, Richard, comp.
The sociology of the possible.

(Prentice-Hall sociology series)
1. Sociology—Addresses, essays, lectures.
I. Title.
HM51.043 1977 301'.08 76-30853
ISBN 0-13-821595-2

Prentice-Hall Sociology Series
Neil J. Smelser, editor

Printed in the United States of America

10 9 8 7 6 5 4 3 2 1

Prentice-Hall International, Inc., *London*
Prentice-Hall of Australia Pty. Limited, *Sydney*
Prentice-Hall of Canada, Ltd., *Toronto*
Prentice-Hall of India Private Limited, *New Delhi*
Prentice-Hall of Japan, Inc., *Tokyo*
Prentice-Hall of Southeast Asia Pte. Ltd., *Singapore*

One ought to think about building a society in much the same manner as one builds a structure out of Tinker Toys. If a part doesn't quite go, chuck it out and try another.

Jason Peacock

Contents

Preface to the Second Edition

The purpose of this book is to provoke its readers into thinking about sociology in a certain fashion: how things could be or might become, rather than how they are and how they came to be that way. What is interesting, even exciting, about the subject matter of this book is what it can be used for and what it permits people to understand of the social forces that affect their lives.

Part of the task of teaching sociology is to help students apply the fact and theory they have learned to something they consider useful. That something might be an analysis and understanding of the effects of powerful variables such as social class or social norms on an individual's own life situation or an analysis of the consequences of some social change that an individual will live through. If students learning sociology are not more likely to attempt this sort of analysis as they learn more, and are not likely to make better bets about the consequences of this or that action, then they are lacking something in sociological training. Attempting this sort of activity as well as developing a skill at coming up with better answers is not easy. If I could be sure that I knew how to guarantee either one of these outcomes, I'd simply publish the method. I'm not sure and therefore all that I can do is provide a collection that seems to me to incorporate materials with which people can practice. In putting this book together I have attempted to collect materials that deal with the possible—not the future, just the possible. I did not intend this book to predict the future or even to speculate on the most likely possibilities. I have been concerned mainly with the value of the selections as treatments of social possibilities, independent of the probability of their being achieved. The selections are intended to provide a basis for exercises in sociological analysis and speculation and to illustrate the types of social arrangements that intelligent and creative persons have envisioned.

Some of the authors are first-rate sociologists. Their analyses of what would happen to a social system if some changes were introduced are perceptive, and the fictional societies that they create would probably function using the principles they set down. In other selections, the sociology seems quite naive. In all cases, however, it is possible to analyze why the predicted change would or would not come about, why the society would or would not function in the manner the designer expected, what unanticipated problems are inherent in the social structure of the created society, and why an individual would react to a situation as the writer expects.

My goal is to provide a context in which you may explore the conceptual consequences and, I hope, the possible real consequences of changes in the social order—a context in which you may *think* about the principles and possible applications of sociology in a creative fashion. One thing seems certain—whether the reference is to your personal life or to the society in which you live, if you want to find new solutions to old or recurring problems or more desirable ways to organize things, you cannot hope to succeed if you examine *only* existing solutions and study *only* existing forms of social organization. Something new must be attempted. The more practice you have at evaluating speculative sets of social arrangements, the more understanding you will have of any system's strengths and weaknesses. Perhaps you then will be more willing to consider changes and chance effecting those changes in the real world and in your own life.

January 1977
Fallon, California

The Sociology of the Possible

Designs for a Society: Introduction

In his ethnography of Erewhonian society, Samuel Butler[1] describes the principles of Erewhon's system of higher education. Although educational systems utilizing the same basic principles were in operation in Butler's own society and are clearly in evidence in most countries of today's world, the Erewhonians are the only people known to have extended these principles to the fullest and to have joined them with a set of concrete educational practices. Butler describes the organization of their system into two major lines of study:

> The main feature in their system is the prominence which they give to a study which I can only translate by the word "hypothetics." They argue thus—that to teach a boy merely the nature of the things which exist in the world around him, and about which he will have to be conversant during his whole life, would be giving him but a narrow and shallow conception of the universe, which it is urged might contain all manner of things which are not now to be found therein. To open his eyes to these possibilities, and so to prepare him for all sorts of emergencies, is the object of this system of hypothetics. To imagine a set of utterly strange and impossible contingencies, and require the youths to give intelligent answers to the questions that arise therefrom, is reckoned the fittest conceivable way of preparing them for the actual conduct of their affairs in after life (pp. 206–7).

The second major focus of Erewhonian educational practice was the study of unreason:

> The arguments in favor of the deliberate development of the unreasoning faculties were much more cogent. But here they depart from the principles on which they justify their study of hypothetics; for they base the importance which they assign to hypothetics upon the fact of their being a preparation for the extraordinary, while their study of Unreason rests upon its developing those faculties which are required for the daily conduct of affairs. Hence their professorships of Inconsistency and Evasion, in both of which studies the youths are examined before being allowed to proceed to their degree of

[1] Samuel Butler, *Erewhon,* first published in 1872 (New York: The Modern Library, 1933).

> hypothetics. The more earnest and conscientious students attain to a proficiency in these subjects which is quite surprising; there is hardly any inconsistency so glaring but they soon learn to defend it, or injunction so clear that they cannot find some pretext for disregarding it.
>
> Life, they urge, would be intolerable if men were to be guided in all they did by reason and reason only. Reason betrays men into the drawing of hard and fast lines, and to the defining by language—language being like the sun, which rears and then scorches. Extremes are alone logical, but they are always absurd; the mean is illogical, but an illogical mean is better than the sheer absurdity of an extreme. There are no follies and no unreasonableness so great as those which can apparently be irrefragably defended by reason itself, and there is hardly an error into which men may not easily be led if they base their conduct upon reason only (pp. 208–9).

Unfortunately, Butler's parody of English educational practices in the mid-1800s is a reasonable parody of the principles and practices of higher education today. The cry for relevance in education may do something to produce a change in the direction of introducing some correlation between what students are told to learn by their instructors, what is going on in the world around them, and what issues in that world need to be thought about.

Relevance in sociology takes two forms. On the one hand is the question of the structure of social reality as it now exists; on the other is the question of the nature of this (or any) social reality. On the one hand is a need to create in the minds of a society's members some realistic picture of their social world as it is now constituted, so that they may understand something of the true conditions of their environment. This kind of knowledge is immediately relevant, and like all descriptions of social systems it soon becomes an inadequate representation of current reality. On the other hand is a need to develop an understanding of, and to teach about, the principles by which social systems operate, so that members of a society may better understand how their environment is changing and, perhaps, act to shape it in a particular direction.

If this book is relevant, it is relevant in the second sense of the word. Sociology as a discipline has been concerned mainly with two issues: how a society arrived at a certain state, and how it functions now. Relatively little attention has been paid to the questions of how social systems might be constituted, whether certain sets of arrangements could be used, and what *advantages* and *disadvantages* inhere in drastically different forms of social organization. These questions are relevant to the future.

It is difficult to imagine a person who has not tried to devise a way of changing social arrangements that he feels need changing. The difficulty in such an endeavor is that selecting the best route to a certain social end requires the most sophisticated type of sociological knowledge. To succeed, a person must be able to predict with considerable accuracy whether the change he proposes will affect aspects of the social system that he does not wish to affect, and if it will do so, whether the main goal will be achieved and whether the net result will be a gain or a loss. To change an inefficient industrial system for an efficient system *and* a fascist government would probably constitute a net loss. To succeed at introducing change, moreover, a person must be able to gauge the extent to which individuals who enjoy advantages in the current state of affairs will object to losing them, and whether those who stand to gain by the change will recognize their interest in it and how much support they will give.

Thinking about sociological issues in this way should be a viable means of developing an understanding of the principles by which a system operates. It requires a person to apply what he believes to be true about the dynamics of society in a creative fashion. A plan for modification of a system or creation of an entirely new system can be examined in the light of what is known about how the social world operates. Thinking about sociological issues in this fashion should also serve at least to make students aware that, theoretically, there is no reason the social world must be organized in the manner in which they find it, that alternative forms of social organization are possible, and that they cannot be attained by fiat. The problem is not so much to design a social system that seems more humane, desirable, and fair; it is to figure out how to build it and to avoid destroying what is desirable about social life as we know it in the process of creating a "better world."

PART ONE
Interpersonal Behavior

I From Deviant to Deviant to Deviant

The status of social deviant is sometimes acquired when a person makes a more or less conscious choice; sometimes it is the result of a long sequence of minor actions that culminates in the person's moving into a subculture that has norms different from those of the larger society. A man who chooses to steal from his company in order to maintain or improve his standard of living is taking the first path to deviant status. In a currently fashionable example of the second pattern, a student is first introduced to and then becomes a member of a group whose practice it is to use marijuana and later finds that he no longer accepts the larger society's definition of pot as a substance to be suppressed.

Deviant status can be obtained in a third way. Unlike a deviant status that results from conscious choice or gradual movement, it is not an *achieved* status. It is *ascribed,* for it is a characteristic with which the individual is born. In the same sense that one's status as a male or a female is (usually) an ascribed status, some people are assigned at birth to certain categories of social deviance. The physically or mentally abnormal are social deviants in this sense. They are, to use Erving Goffman's term, *stigmatized.* The role of ascribed deviant is unusual, for it does not require that the individual reject society's norms, as do the thief, and the pot-head; the society rejects the deviant. Everyone else reacts to the stigmatized in terms of a set of norms different from those that typically govern interaction.

In his story, "Flowers for Algernon," Daniel Keyes views the world from the perspective of an ascribed deviant. The unique aspect of the story is that Keyes presents the deviant's view of the world from the bottom looking up, from the top looking down, and provides something of the experience of moving between the end points. Keyes's central character, Charlie, makes the transition from the status of idiot, with an IQ of 68, to that of genius and back again.

It seems appropriate to describe Charlie's mobility as a movement upward followed by a movement downward, as if one were describing the progress of a mountain climber. The significance of being at the bottom or the top is similar—you can see more and farther from the top than from the bottom. The worlds in which Charlie moves as an idiot and as a genius are no different physically, but they are vastly different psychologically. The difference is a function of Charlie's being able, as an idiot, to understand relatively little about how his physical and social worlds operate, and being able, as a genius, to understand a great deal about the dynamics of both worlds.

Keyes's story makes a particular point extraordinarily well and provides a stimulus that leads to the consideration of two interesting and frightening questions. Assume that it is reasonable to conceive an idiot's world in the manner Keyes has chosen. When reading the story you can easily understand Charlie's misperceptions of his social world, and therefore you can understand his actions. Consider the world from the perspective of a genius. Is it possible that this analogy is appropriate?—the world of a genius is to the world of a normal as the world of a normal is to the world of an idiot. If the analogy is appropriate, then relative to a genius, a man of normal intelligence must seem as pathetic as Charlie does to a normal man.

Consider a second point: to what extent is the account of the transition from genius to idiot a reasonable description of what it would be like to lose a substantial portion of your mental abilities? What would it be like to have an automobile accident and recover to find yourself able to function only in a manner equivalent to Charlie's ability level as an idiot?

Flowers for Algernon

Daniel Keyes

Progris Riport 1—Martch 5, 1965

Dr. Strauss says I shud rite down what I think and evrey thing that happins to me from now on. I dont know why but he says its importint so they will see if they will use me. I hope they use me. Miss Kinnian says maybe they can make me smart. I want to be smart. My name is Charlie Gordon. I am 37 years old and 2 weeks ago was my brithday. I have nuthing more to rite now so I will close for today.

Progris Riport 2—Martch 6

I had a test today. I think I faled it. and I think that maybe now they wont use me. What happind is a nice young man was in the room and he had some white cards with ink spillled all over them. He sed Charlie what do you see on this card. I was very skared even tho I had my rabits foot in my pockit because when I was a kid I always faled tests in school and I spillled ink to.

I told him I saw a inkblot. He said yes and it made me feel good. I thot that was all but when I got up to go he stopped me. He said now sit down Charlie we are not thru yet. Then I don't remember so good but he wantid me to say what was in the ink. I dint see nuthing in the ink but he said there was picturs there other pepul saw some picturs. I couldnt see any picturs. I reely tryed to see. I held the card close up and then far away. Then I said if I had my glases I could see better I usully only ware my glases in the movies or TV but I said they are in the closit in the hall. I got them. Then I said let me see that card agen I bet Ill find it now.

I tryed hard but I still couldnt find the pictures I only saw the ink. I told him maybe I need new glases. He rote somthing down on a paper and I got skared of faling the test. I told him it was a very nice inkblot with little points all around the eges. He looked very sad so that wasnt it. I said please let me try agen. Ill get it in a few minits becaus Im not so fast somtimes. Im a slow reeder too in Miss Kinnians class for slow adults but I'm trying very hard.

He gave me a chance with another card that had 2 kinds of ink spilled on it red and blue.

He was very nice and talked slow like Miss Kinnian does and he explaned it to me that it was a *raw shok.* He said pepul see things in the ink. I said show me where. He said think. I told him I think a inkblot but that wasnt rite eather. He said what does it remind you—pretend something. I closd my eyes for a long time to pretend. I told him I pretned a fowntan pen with ink leeking all over a table cloth. Then he got up and went out.

I dont think I passd the *raw shok* test.

Progris Report 3—Martch 7

. . . Some men in white coats took me to a difernt part of the hospitil and gave me a game to play. It was like a race with a white mouse. They called the mouse Algernon. Algernon was in a box with a lot of twists and turns like all kinds of walls and they gave me a pencil and a paper with lines and lots of boxes. On one side it said START and on the other end it said FINISH. They said it was *amazed* and that Algernon and me had the same *amazed* to do. I dont see how we could have the same *amazed* if Algernon had a box and I had a paper but I dint say nothing. Anyway there wasnt time because the race started.

One of the men had a watch he was trying to hide so I wouldnt see it so I tryed not to look and that made me nervous.

Anyway that test made me feel worser than all the others because they did it over 10 times with difernt *amazeds* and Algernon won every time. I dint know that mice were so smart. Maybe thats because Algernon is a white mouse. Maybe white mice are smarter than other mice.

Progris Riport 4—Mar 8

Their going to use me! Im so excited I can hardly write. Dr Nemur and Dr Strauss had a argament about it first. Dr Nemur was in the office when Dr

Strauss brot me in. Dr Nemur was worryed about using me but Dr Strauss told him Miss Kinnian rekemmended me the best from all the people who was teaching. I like Miss Kinnian becaus shes a very smart teacher. And she said Charlie your going to have a second chance. If you volenteer for this experament you mite get smart. They dont know if it will be perminint but theirs a chance. Thats why I said ok even when I was scared because she said it was an operashun. She said dont be scared Charlie you done so much with so little I think you deserv it most of all.

So I got scaird when Dr Nemur and Dr Strauss argud about it. Dr Strauss said I had something that was very good. He said I had a good *motor-vation.* I never even knew I had that. I felt proud when he said that not every body with an eye-q of 68 had that thing. I dont know what it is or where I got it but he said Algernon had it too. Algernons *motor-vation* is the cheese they put in his box. But it cant be that because I didnt eat any cheese this week.

Then he told Dr Nemur something I dint understand so while they were talking I wrote down some of the words.

He said Dr Nemur I know Charlie is not what you had in mind as the first of your new brede of intelek** (coudnt get the word) superman. But most people of his low ment** are host** and uncoop** they are usualy dull apath** and hard to reach. He has a good natcher hes intristed and eager to please.

Dr Nemur said remember he will be the first human beeng ever to have his intelijence trippled by surgicle meens.

Dr Strauss said exakly. Look at how well hes lerned to read and write for his low mentel age its as grate an acheve** as you and I lerning einstines therey of **vity without help. That shows the intenss motor-vation. Its comparat** a tremen* achev** I say we use Charlie.

I dint get all the words and they were talking to fast but it sounded like Dr Strauss was on my side and like the other one wasnt.

Then Dr Nemur nodded he said all right maybe your right. We will use Charlie. When he said that I got so excited I jumped up and shook his hand for being so good to me. I told him thank you doc you wont be sorry for giving me a second chance. And I mean it like I told him. After the operashun Im gonna try to be smart. Im gonna try awful hard.

Progris Ript—Mar 10

. . . I asked Dr Strauss if Ill beat Algernon in the race after the operashun and he said maybe. If the operashun works Ill show that mouse I can be as smart as he is. Maybe smarter. Then Ill be abel to read better and spell the words good and know lots of things and be like other people. I want to be smart like other people. If it works perminint they will make everybody smart all over the wurld.

They dint give me anything to eat this morning. I dont know what that eating has to do with getting smart. Im very hungry and Dr Nemur took away my box of candy. That Dr Nemur is a grouch. Dr Strauss says I can have it back after the operashun. You cant eat befor a operashun . . .

Progress Report 6—Mar 15

The operashun dint hurt. He did it while I was sleeping. They took off the bandijis from my eyes and my head today so I can make a PROGRESS REPORT. Dr Nemur who looked at some of my other ones sayd I spell PROGRESS wrong and he told me how to spell it and REPORT too. I got to try and remember that.

I have a very bad memary for spelling. Dr Strauss says its ok to tell about all the things that happin to me but he says I shoud tell more about what I feel and what I think. When I told him I dont know how to think he said try. All the time when the bandijis were on my eyes I tryed to think. Nothing happened. I dont know what to think about. Maybe if I ask him he will tell me how I can think now that Im suppose to get smart. What do smart people think about. Fancy things I suppose. I wish I knew some fancy things alredy.

Progress Report 7—mar 19

Nothing is happining. I had lots of tests and different kinds of races with Algernon. I hate that mouse. He always beats me. Dr Strauss said I got to play those games. And he said some time I got to take those tests over again. Thse inkblots are stupid. . . .

I got a headache from trying to think so much. I thot Dr Strauss was my frend but he dont help me. He dont tell me what to think or when Ill get smart. Miss Kinnian dint come to see me. I think writing these progress reports are stupid too.

Progress Report 8—Mar 23

Im going back to work at the factery. They said it was better I shud go back to work but I cant tell anyone what the operashun was for and I have to come to the hospitil for an hour evry night after work. They are gonna pay me mony every month for lerning to be smart.

Im glad Im going back to work because I miss my job and all my frends and all the fun we have there.

Dr Strauss says I shud keep writing things down but I dont have to do it every day just when I think of something or something speshul happins. He says dont get discoridged because it takes time and it happins slow. He says it took a long time with Algernon before he got 3 times smarter then he was before. That why Algernon beats me all the time because he had that operashun too. That makes me feel better. I coud probly do that *amazed* faster than a reglar mouse. Maybe some day Ill beat Algernon. Boy that would be something. So far Algernon looks like he mite be smart perminent.

Mar 25 (I dont have to write PROGRESS REPORT on top any more just when I hand it in once a week for Dr Nemur to read. I just have to put the date on. That saves time)

We had a lot of fun at the factery today. Joe Carp said hey look where Charlie had his operashun what did they do Charlie put some brains in. I was going to tell him but I remembered Dr Strauss said no. Then Frank Reilly said what did you do Charlie forget your key and open your door the hard way. That made me laff. Their really my friends and they like me.

Sometimes somebody will say hey look at Joe or Frank or George he really pulled a Charlie Gordon. I dont know why they say that but they always laff. This morning Amos Borg who is the 4 man at Donnegans used my name when he shouted at Ernie the office boy. Ernie lost a packige. He said Ernie for godsake what are you trying to be a Charlie Gordon. I dont understand why he said that. I never lost any packiges.

Mar 28 Dr Strauss came to my room tonight to see why I dint come in like I was suppose to. I told him I dont like to race with Algernon any more. He said I dont have to for a while but I shud come in. He had a present for me only it wasnt a present but just for lend. I thot it was a little television but it wasnt. He said I got to turn it on when I got to sleep. I said your kidding why shud I turn it on when Im going to sleep. Who ever herd of a thing like that. But he said if I want to get smart I got to do what he says. I told him I dont think I was going to get smart and he put his hand on my sholder and said Charlie you dont know it yet but your getting smarter all the time. You wont notice for a while. I think he was just being nice to make me feel good because I dont look any smarter. . . .

Mar 29 That crazy TV kept me up all night. How can I sleep with something yelling crazy things all night in my ears. And the nutty pictures. Wow. I dont know what it says when Im up so how am I going to know when Im sleeping.

Dr Strauss says its ok. He says my brains are lerning when I sleep and that will help me when Miss Kinnian starts my lessons in the hospitl (only I found out it isnt a hospitil its a labatory). I thinks its all crazy. If you can get smart when your sleeping why do people go to school. That thing I dont think will work. I use to watch the late show and the late late show on TV all the time and it never made me smart. Maybe you have to sleep while you watch it.

Progress Report 9—April 3

Dr Strauss showed me how to keep the TV turned low so now I can sleep. I dont hear a thing. And I still dont understand what it says. A few times I play it over in the morning to find out what I lerned when I was sleeping and I dont think so. Miss Kinnian says Maybe its another langwidge or something. But most times it sounds american. It talks so fast faster then even Miss Gold who was my teacer in 6 grade and I remember she talked so fast I coudnt understand her.

I told Dr Strauss what good is it to get smart in my sleep. I want to be smart when Im awake. He says its the same thing and I have two minds. Theres the *subconscious* and the *conscious* (that's how you spell it). And one dont tell the other one what its doing. They dont even talk to each other. Thats why I dream. And boy have I been having crazy dreams. Wow. Ever since that night TV. The late late late late late show.

I forgot to ask him if it was only me or if everybody had those two minds.

(I just looked up the word in the dictionary Dr Strauss gave me. The word is *subconscious. adj. Of the nature of mental operations yet not present in consciousness; as, subconscious conflict of desires.*) Theres more but I still dont know what it means. This isnt a very good dictionary for dumb people like me. . . .

April 6 I beat Algernon! I dint even know I beat him until Burt the tester told me. Then the second time I lost because I got so excited I fell off the chair before I finished. But after that I beat him 8 more times. I must be getting smart to beat a smart mouse like Algernon. But I dont feel smarter.

I wanted to race Algernon some more but Burt said thats enough for one day. They let me hold him for a minit. Hes not so bad. Hes soft like a ball of cotton. He blinks and when he opens his eyes their black and pink on the eges.

I said can I feed him because I felt bad to beat him and I wanted to be nice and make friends. But said no Algernon is a very specshul mouse with an operashun like mine, and he was the first of all the animals to stay smart so long. He told me Algernon is so smart that every day he has to solve a test to get his food. Its a thing like a lock on a door that changes every time Algernon goes in to eat so he has to lern something new to get his food. That made me sad because if he coudnt lern he would be hungry.

I dont think its right to make you pass a test to eat. How would Dr Nemur like it to have to pass a test every time he wants to eat. I think Ill be frends with Algernon.

April 10 Miss Kinnian teaches me to spell better. She says look at a word and close your eyes and say it over and over until you remember. I have lots of truble with *through* that you say *threw* and *enough* and *tough* that you dont say *new* and *tew.* You got to say *enuff* and *tuff.* Thats how I use to write it before I started to get smart. Im confused but Miss Kinnian says theres no reason in spelling.

April 15 Miss Kinnian says Im lerning fast. She read some of the Progress Reports and she looked at me kind of funny. She says Im a fine person and Ill show them all. I asked her why. She said never mind but I shoudnt feel bad if I find out that everybody isnt nice like I think. She said for a person who god gave so little to you done more then a lot of people with brains they never even used. I said all my frends are smart people but there good. They like me and they never did anything that wasnt nice. . . .

Apr 16 Today, I lerned, the *comma,* this is a comma (,) a period, with a tail, Miss Kinnian, says its importent, because, it makes writing, better, she said, somebody, could lose, a lot of money, if a comma, isnt, in the, right place, I dont have, any money, and I dont see, how a comma, keep you, from losing it,

But she says, everybody, uses commas, so Ill use, them too.

Apr 17 I used the comma wrong. Its punctuation. Miss Kinnian told me to look up long words in the dictionary to lern to spell them. I said whats the difference if you can read it anyway. She said its part of your education so now on Ill look up all the words Im not sure how to spell. It takes a long time to write that way but I think Im remembering. I only have to look up once and after that I get it right. Anyway thats how come I got the word *punctuation* right. (Its that way in the dictionary). Miss Kinnian says a period is punctuation too, and there are lots of other marks to lern. I told her I thot all the periods had to have tails but she said no.

You got to mix them up, she showed?me" how. to mix! them (up,. and now; I can! mix up all kinds" of punctuation, in! my writing? There, are lots! of rules? to lern; but I'm gettin'g them in my head.

One thing I? like about, Dear Miss Kinnian: (thats the way it goes in a business letter if I ever go into business) is she, always gives me' a reason" when—I ask. She's a gen'ius! I wish! I cou'd be smart" like, her;

(Punctuation, is; fun!)

April 18 What a dope I am! I didn't even understand what she was talking about. I read the grammar book last night and it explanes the whole thing. Then I saw it was the same way as Miss Kinnian was trying to tell me, but I didn't get it. I got up in the middle of the night, and the whole thing straightened out in my mind.

Miss Kinnian said that the TV working in my sleep helped out. She said I reached a plateau. Thats like the flat top of a hill.

After I figgered out how punctuation worked, I read over all my old Progress Reports from the beginning. Boy, did I have crazy spelling and punctuation! I told Miss Kinnian I ought to go over the pages and fix all the mistakes but she said, "No, Charlie, Dr. Nemur wants them just as they are. That's why he let you keep them after they were phototstated, to see your own progress. You're coming along fast, Charlie."

That made me feel good. After the lesson I went down and played with Algernon. We don't race any more.

April 20 I feel sick inside. Not sick like for a doctor, but inside my chest it feels empty like getting punched and a heartburn at the same time.

I wasn't going to write about it, but I guess I got to, because it's important. Today was the first time I ever stayed home from work.

Last night Joe Carp and Frank Reilly invited me to a party. There were lots of girls and some men from the factory. I remembered how sick I got last time I drank too much, so I told Joe I didn't want anything to drink. He gave me a plain Coke instead. It tasted funny, but I thought it was just a bad taste in my mouth.

We had a lot of fun for a while. Joe said I should dance with Ellen and she would teach me the steps. I fell a few times and I couldn't understand why because no one else was dancing besides Ellen and me. And all the time I was tripping because somebody's foot was always sticking out.

Then when I got up I saw the look on Joe's face and it gave me a funny feeling in my stomack. "He's a scream," one of the girls said. Everybody was laughing.

Frank said, "I ain't laughed so much since we sent him off for the newspaper that night at Muggsy's and ditched him."

"Look at him. His face is red."

"He's blushing. Charlie is blushing."

"Hey, Ellen, what'd you do to Charlie? I never saw him act like that before."

I didn't know what to do or where to turn. Everyone was looking at me and laughing and I felt naked. I wanted to hide myself. I ran out into the street and I threw up. Then I walked home. It's a funny thing I never knew that Joe and Frank and the others liked to have me around all the time to make fun of me.

Now I know what it means when they say "to pull a Charlie Gordon."

I'm ashamed.

Progress Report 11

April 21 Still didn't go into the factory. I told Mrs. Flynn my landlady to call and tell Mr. Donnegan I was sick. Mrs. Flynn looks at me very funny lately like she's scared of me.

I think it's a good thing about finding out how everybody laughs at me. I thought about it a lot. It's because I'm so dumb and I don't even know when I'm doing something dumb. People think it's funny when a dumb person can't do things the same way they can.

Anyway, now I know I'm getting smarter every day. I know punctuation and I can spell good. I like to look up all the hard words in the dictionary and I remember them. I'm reading a lot now, and Miss Kinnian says I read very fast. Sometimes I even understand what I'm reading about, and it stays in my mind. There are times when I can close my eyes and think of a page and it all comes back like a picture.

Besides history, geography, and arithmetic, Miss Kinnian said I should start to learn a few foreign languages. Dr. Strauss gave me some more tapes to play while I sleep. I still don't understand how that conscious and unconscious mind works, but Dr. Strauss says not to worry yet. He asked me to promise that when I start learning college subjects next week I wouldn't read any books on psychology—that is, until he gives me permission.

I feel a lot better today, but I guess I'm still a little angry that all the time people were laughing and making fun of me because I wasn't so smart. When I become intelligent like Dr. Strauss says, with three times my I.Q. of 68, then maybe I'll be like everyone else and people will like me and be friendly.

I'm not sure what an I.Q. is. Dr. Nemur said it was something that measured how intelligent you were—like a scale in the drugstore weighs pounds.

But Dr. Strauss had a big argument with him and said an I.Q. didn't weigh intelligence at all. He said an I.Q. showed how much intelligence you could get, like the numbers on the outside of a measuring cup. You still had to fill the cup up with stuff.

Then when I asked Burt, who gives me my intelligence tests and works with Algernon, he said that both of them were wrong (only I had to promise not to tell them he said so). Burt says that the I.Q. measures a lot of different things including some of the things you learned already, and it really isn't any good at all.

So I still don't know what I.Q. is except that mine is going to be over 200 soon. I didn't want to say anything, but I don't see how if they don't know *what* it is, or *where* it is—I don't see how they know *how much* of it you've got.

Dr. Nemur says I have to take a *Rorschach Test* tomorrow. I wonder what *that* is.

April 22 I found out what a *Rorschach* is. It's the test I took before the operation—the one with the inkblots on the pieces of cardboard. The man who gave me the test was the same one.

I was scared to death of those inkblots. I knew he was going to ask me to find the pictures and I knew I wouldn't be able to. I was thinking to myself, if only there was some way of knowing what kind of pictures were hidden there. Maybe there weren't any pictures at all. Maybe it was just a trick to see if I was dumb enough to look for something that wasn't there. Just thinking about that made me sore at him.

"All right, Charlie," he said, "you've seen these cards before, remember?"

"Of course I remember."

The way I said it, he knew I was angry, and he looked surprised. "Yes, of course. Now I want you to look at this one. What might this be? What do you see on this card? People see all sorts of things in these inkblots. Tell me what it might be for you—what it makes you think of."

I was shocked. That wasn't what I had expected him to say at all. "You mean there are no pictures hidden in those inkblots?"

He frowned and took off his glasses. "What?"

"Pictures. Hidden in the inkblots. Last time you told me that everyone could see them and you wanted me to find them too."

He explained to me that the last time he had used almost the exact same words he was using now. I didn't believe it, and I still have the suspicion that he misled me at the time just for the fun of it. Unless—I don't know any more—could I have been *that* feeble-minded?

We went through the cards slowly. One of them looked like a pair of bats tugging at something. Another one looked like two men fencing with swords. I imagined all sorts of things. I guess I got carried away. But I didn't trust him any more, and I kept turning them around and even looking on the back to see if there was anything there I was supposed to catch. While he was making his notes, I peeked out of the corner of my eye to read it. But is was all in code that looked like this:

$$WF + A\ DdF - Ad\ orig.\ WF - A\ SF + \text{obj}$$

The test still doesn't make any sense to me. It seems to me that anyone could make up lies about things that they didn't really see. How could he know I wasn't making a fool of him by mentioning things that I didn't really imagine? Maybe I'll understand it when Dr. Strauss lets me read up on psychology.

April 27 . . . Dr. Strauss and Dr. Nemur don't seem to be getting along so well. They're arguing all the time. This evening when I came in to ask Dr. Strauss [something] I heard him shouting. Dr. Nemur was saying that it was *his* experiment and *his* research, and Dr. Strauss was shouting back that he contributed just as much, because he found me through Miss Kinnian and he performed the operation. Dr. Strauss said that someday thousands of neurosurgeons might be using his technique all over the world.

Dr. Nemur wanted to publish the results of the experiment at the end of this month. Dr. Strauss wanted to wait a while longer to be sure. Dr. Strauss said that Dr. Nemur was more interested in the Chair of Psychology at Princeton than he was in the experiment. Dr. Nemur said that Dr. Strauss was nothing but an opportunist who was trying to ride to glory on *his* coattails.

When I left afterwards, I found myself trembling. I don't know why for sure, but it was as if I'd seen both men clearly for the first time. I remember hearing Burt say that Dr. Nemur had a shrew of a wife who was pushing him all the time to get things published so that he could become famous. Burt said that the dream of her life was to have a big-shot husband.

Was Dr. Strauss really trying to ride on his coattails?

Progress Report 12

April 30 I've quit my job with Donnegan's Plastic Box Company. Mr. Donnegan insisted that it would be better for all concerned if I left. What did I do to make them hate me so?

The first I knew of it was when Mr. Donnegan showed me the petition. Eight hundred and forty names, every one connected with the factory, except Fanny Girden. Scanning the list quickly, I saw at once that hers was the only missing name. All the rest demanded that I be fired.

Joe Carp and Frank Reilly wouldn't talk to me about it. No one else would either, except Fanny. She was one of the few people I'd known who set her mind to something and believed it no matter what the rest of the world proved, said, or did—and Fanny did not believe that I should have been fired. She had been against the petition on principle and despite the pressure and threats she'd held out.

"Which don't mean to say," she remarked, "that I don't think there's something mighty strange about you, Charlie. Them changes. I don't know. You used to be a good, dependable, ordinary man—not too bright maybe, but honest. Who knows what you done to yourself to get so smart all of a sudden. Like everybody around here's been saying, Charlie, it's not right."

"But how can you say that, Fanny? What's wrong with a man becoming intelligent and wanting to acquire knowledge and understanding of the world around him?"

She stared down at her work and I turned to leave. Without looking at me, she said: "It was evil when Eve listened to the snake and ate from the tree of knowledge. It was evil when she saw that she was naked. If not for that none of us would ever have to grow old and sick, and die."

Once again now I have the feeling of shame burning inside me. This intelligence has driven a wedge between me and all the people I once knew and loved. Before, they laughed at me and despised me for my ignorance and dullness; now, they hate me for my knowledge and understanding. What in God's name do they want of me?

They've driven me out of the factory. Now I'm more alone than ever before. . . .

May 15 Dr. Strauss is very angry at me for not having written any progress reports in two weeks. He's justified because the lab is now paying me a regular salary. I told him I was too busy thinking and reading. When I pointed out that writing was such a slow process that it made me impatient with my poor handwriting, he suggested that I learn to type. It's much easier to write now because I can type nearly seventy-five words a minute. Dr. Strauss continually reminds me of the need to speak and write simply so that people will be able to understand me.

I'll try to review all the things that happened to me during the last two weeks. Algernon and I were presented to the American Psychological Association sitting in convention with the World Psychological Association last Tuesday. We created quite a sensation. Dr. Nemur and Dr. Strauss were proud of us.

I suspect that Dr. Nemur, who is sixty—ten years older than Dr. Strauss—finds it necessary to see tangible results of his work. Undoubtedly the result of pressure by Mrs. Nemur.

Contrary to my earlier impressions of him, I realize that Dr. Nemur is not at all a genius. He has a very good mind, but it struggles under the spectre of self-doubt. He wants people to take him for a genius. Therefore, it is important for him to feel that his work is accepted by the world. I believe that Dr. Nemur was afraid of further delay because he worried that someone else might make a discovery along these lines and take the credit from him.

Dr. Strauss on the other hand might be called a genius, although I feel that his areas of knowledge are too limited. He was educated in the tradition of narrow specialization; the broader aspects of background were neglected far more than necessary—even for a neurosurgeon.

I was shocked to learn that the only ancient languages he could read were Latin, Greek, and Hebrew, and that he knows almost nothing of mathematics beyond the elementary levels of the calculus of variations. When he admitted this to me, I found myself almost annoyed. It was as if he'd hidden this part of himself in order to deceive me, pretending—as do many people I've discovered—to be what he is not. No one I've ever known is what he appears to be on the surface.

Dr. Nemur appears to be uncomfortable around me. Sometimes when I try to talk to him, he just looks at me strangely and turns away. I was angry at first when Dr. Strauss told me I was giving Dr. Nemur an inferiority complex. I thought he was mocking me and I'm oversensitive at being made fun of.

How was I to know that a highly respected psychoexperimentalist like Nemur was unacquainted with Hindustani and Chinese? It's absurd when you consider the work that is being done in India and China today in the very field of his study.

I asked Dr. Strauss how Nemur could refute Rahajamati's attack on his method and results if Nemur couldn't even read them in the first place. That strange look on Dr. Strauss' face can mean only one of two things. Either he doesn't want to tell Nemur what they're saying in India, or else—and this worries me—Dr. Strauss doesn't know either. I must be careful to speak and write clearly and simply so that people won't laugh.

May 20 I would not have noticed the new dishwasher, a boy of about sixteen, at the corner diner where I take my evening meals if not for the incident of the broken dishes.

They crashed to the floor, shattering and sending bits of white china under the tables. The boy stood there, dazed and frightened, holding the empty tray in his hand. The whistles and catcalls from the customers (the cries of "hey, there go the profits!" . . . "*Mazeltov!*" . . . and "well, *he* didn't work here very long . . ." which invariably seem to follow the breaking of glass or dishware in a public restaurant) all seemed to confuse him.

When the owner came to see what the excitement was about, the boy cowered as if he expected to be struck and threw up his arms as if to ward off the blow.

"All right! All right, you dope," shouted the owner, "don't just stand there! Get the broom and sweep that mess up. A broom . . . a broom, you idiot! It's in the kitchen. Sweep up all the pieces."

The boy saw that he was not going to be punished. His frightened expression disappeared and he smiled and hummed as he came back with the broom to sweep the floor. A few of the rowdier customers kept up the remarks, amusing themselves at his expense.

"Here, sonny, over here there's a nice piece behind you . . ."

"C'mon, do it again . . ."

"He's not so dumb. It's easier to break 'em than to wash 'em . . ."

And as his vacant eyes moved across the crowd of amused onlookers, he slowly mirrored their smiles and finally broke into an uncertain grin at the joke which he obviously did not understand.

I felt sick inside as I looked at his dull, vacuous smile, the wide, bright eyes of a child, uncertain but eager to please. They were laughing at him because he was mentally retarded.

And I had been laughing at him too.

Suddenly, I was furious at myself and all those who were smirking at him. I jumped up and shouted, "Shut up! Leave him alone! It's not his fault he can't understand! He can't help what he is! But for God's sake . . . he's still a human being!"

The room grew silent. I cursed myself for losing control and creating a scene. I tried not to look at the boy as I paid my check and walked out without touching my food. I felt ashamed for both of us.

How strange it is that people of honest feelings and sensibility, who would not take advantage of a man born without arms or legs or eyes—how such people think nothing of abusing a man born with low intelligence. It infuriated me to think that not too long ago I, like this boy, had foolishly played the clown.

And I had almost forgotten.

I'd hidden the picture of the old Charlie Gordon from myself because now that I was intelligent it was something that had to be pushed out of my mind. But today in looking at that boy, for the first time I saw what I had been. *I was just like him!*

Only a short time ago, I learned that people laughed at me. Now I can see that unknowingly I joined with them in laughing at myself. That hurts most of all.

I have often reread my progress reports and seen the illiteracy, the childish naivete, the mind of low intelligence peering from a dark room, through the keyhole, at the dazzling light outside. I see that even in my dullness I knew that I was inferior, and that other people had something I lacked—something denied me. In my mental blindness, I thought that it was somehow connected with the ability to read and write, and I was sure that if I could get those skills I would automatically have intelligence too.

Even a feeble-minded man wants to be like other men.

A child may not know how to feed itself, or what to eat, yet it knows of hunger.

This then is what I was like, I never knew. Even with my gift of intellectual awareness, I never really knew.

This day was good for me. Seeing the past more clearly, I have decided to use my knowledge and skills to work in the field of increasing human intelligence levels. Who is better equipped for this work? Who else has lived in both worlds? These are my people. Let me use my gift to do something for them.

Tomorrow, I will discuss with Dr. Strauss the manner in which I can work in this area. I may be able to help him work out the problems of widespread use of the technique which was used on me. I have several good ideas of my own.

There is so much that might be done with this technique. If I could be made into a genius, what about thousands of others like myself? What fantastic levels might be achieved by using this technique on normal people? On *geniuses?*

There are so many doors to open. I am impatient to begin.

Progress Report 13

May 23 It happened today. Algernon bit me. I visited the lab to see him as I do occasionally, and when I took him out of his cage, he snapped at my hand. I put him back and watched him for a while. He was unusually disturbed and vicious.

May 24 Burt, who is in charge of the experimental animals, tells me that Algernon is changing. He is less co-operative; he refuses to run the maze any more; general motivation has decreased. And he hasn't been eating. Everyone is upset about what this may mean.

May 25 They've been feeding Algernon, who now refuses to work the shifting-lock problem. Everyone identifies me with Algernon. In a way we're both the first of our kind. They're all pretending that Algernon's behavior is not necessarily significant for me. But it's hard to hide the fact that some of the other animals who were used in this experiment are showing strange behavior.

Dr. Strauss and Dr. Nemur have asked me not to come to the lab any more. I know what they're thinking but I can't accept it. I am going ahead with my plans to carry their research forward. With all due respect to both of these fine scientists, I am well aware of their limitations. If there is an answer, I'll have to find it out for myself. Suddenly, time has become very important to me.

May 29 I have been given a lab of my own and permission to go ahead with the research. I'm on to something. Working day and night. I've had a cot moved into the lab. Most of my writing time is spent on the notes which I keep in a separate folder, but from time to time I feel it necessary to put down my moods and my thoughts out of sheer habit.

I find the *calculus of intelligence* to be a fascinating study. Here is the place for the application of all the knowledge I have acquired. In a sense it's the problem I've been concerned with all my life.

May 31 Dr. Strauss thinks I'm working too hard. Dr. Nemur says I'm trying to cram a lifetime of research and thought into a few weeks. I know I should rest, but I'm driven on by something inside that won't let me stop. I've got to find the reason for the sharp regression in Algernon. I've go to know *if* and *when* it will happen to me.

June 4 Letter to Dr. Strauss *(copy)*
Dear Dr. Strauss:

Under separate cover I am sending you a copy of my report entitled, "The Algernon-Gordon Effect: A Study of Structure and Function of Increased Intelligence," which I would like to have you read and have published.

As you see, my experiments are completed. I have included in my report all of my formulae, as well as mathematical analysis in the appendix. Of course, these should be verified.

Because of its importance to both you and Dr. Nemur (and need I say to myself, too?) I have checked and rechecked my results a dozen times in the hope of finding an error. I am sorry to say the results must stand. Yet for the sake of science, I am grateful for the little bit that I here add to the knowledge of the function of the human mind and of the laws governing the artificial increase of human intelligence.

I recall your once saying to me that an experimental *failure* or the *disproving* of a theory was as important to the advancement of learning as a success would be. I know now that this is true. I am sorry, however, that my own contribution to the field must rest upon the ashes of the work of two men I regard so highly.

Yours truly,
Charles Gordon
encl.: rept.

June 5 I must not become emotional. The facts and the results of my experiments are clear, and the more sensational aspects of my own rapid climb cannot obscure the fact that the tripling of intelligence by the surgical technique developed by Drs. Strauss and Nemur must be viewed as having little or no practical applicability (at the present time) to the increase of human intelligence.

As I review the records and data on Algernon, I see that although he is still in his physical infancy, he has regressed mentally. Motor activity is impaired; there is a general reduction of glandular activity; there is an accelerated loss of co-ordination.

There are also strong indications of progressive amnesia.

As will be seen by my report, these and other physical and mental deterioration syndromes can be predicted with statistically significant results by the application of my formula.

The surgical stimulus to which we were both subjected has resulted in an intensification and acceleration of all mental processes. The unforeseen development, which I have taken the liberty of calling the *Algernon-Gordon Effect,* is the logical extention of the entire intelligence speed-up. The hypothesis here proven may be described simply in the following terms: Artificially increased intelligence deteriorates at a rate of time directly proportional to the quantity of the increase.

I feel that this, in itself, is an important discovery.

As long as I am able to write, I will continue to record my thoughts in these progress reports. It is one of my few pleasures. However, by all indications, my own mental deterioration will be very rapid.

I have already begun to notice signs of emotional instability and forgetfulness, the first symptoms of the burnout.

June 10 Deterioration progressing. I have become absent-minded. Algernon died two days ago. Dissection shows my predictions were right. His brain had decreased in weight and there was a general smoothing out of cerebral convolutions as well as a deepening and broadening of brain fissures.

I guess the same thing is or will soon be happening to me. Now that it's definite, I don't want it to happen.

I put Algernon's body in a cheese box and buried him in the back yard. I cried.

June 15 Dr. Strauss came to see me again. I wouldn't open the door and I told him to go away. I want to be left to myself. I have become touchy and irritable. I feel the darkness closing in. It's hard to throw off thoughts of suicide. I keep telling myself how important this introspective journal will be.

It's a strange sensation to pick up a book that you've read and enjoyed just a few months ago and discover that you don't remember it. I remembered how great I thought John Milton was, but when I picked up *Paradise Lost* I couldn't understand it at all. I got so angry I threw the book across the room.

I've got to try to hold on to some of it. Some of the things I've learned. Oh, God, please don't take it all away.

June 21 Why can't I remember? I've got to fight. I lie in bed for days and I don't know who or where I am. Then it all comes back to me in a flash. Fugues of amnesia. Symptoms of senility—second childhood. I can watch them coming on. It's so cruelly logical. I learned so much and so fast. Now my mind is deteriorating rapidly. I won't let it happen. I'll fight it. I can't help thinking of the boy in the restaurant, the blank expression, the silly smile, the people laughing at him. No—please—not that again.

June 22 I'm forgetting things that I learned recently. It seems to be following the classic pattern—the last things learned are the first things forgotten. Or is that the pattern? I'd better look it up again. . . .

I reread my paper on the *Algernon-Gordon Effect* and I get the strange feeling that it was written by someone else. There are parts I don't even understand.

Motor activity impaired. I keep tripping over things and it becomes increasingly difficult to type.

June 23 I've given up using the typewriter completely. My co-ordination is bad. I feel that I'm moving slower and slower. Had a terrible shock today. I picked up a copy of an article I used in my research, Krueger's *Uber psychische Ganzheit,* to see if it would help me understand what I had done. First I thought there was something wrong with my eyes. Then I realized I could no longer read German. I tested myself in other languages. All gone.

June 30 A week since I dared to write again. It's slipping away like sand through my fingers. Most of the books I have are too hard for me now. I get angry with them because I know that I read and understood them just a few weeks ago.

I keep telling myself I must keep writing these reports so that somebody will know what is happening to me. But it gets harder to form the words and remember spellings. I have to look up even simple words in the dictionary now and it makes me impatient with myself.

Dr. Strauss comes around almost every day, but I told him I wouldn't see or speak to anybody. He feels guilty. They all do. But I don't blame anyone. I knew what might happen. But how it hurts.

July 10 My landlady Mrs. Flynn is very worried about me. She says the way I lay around all day and don't do anything I remind her of her son before she threw him out of the house. She said she doesn't like loafers. If Im sick its one thing, but if Im a loafer thats another thing and she wont have it. I told her I think Im sick.

I try to read a little bit every day, mostly stories, but sometimes I have to read the same thing over and over again because I dont know what it means. And its hard to write. I know I should look up all the words in the dictionary but its so hard and Im so tired all the time.

Then I got the idea that I would only use the easy words instead of the long hard ones. That saves time. I put flowers on Algernons grave about once a week. Mrs Flynn thinks Im crazy to put flowers on a mouses grave but I told her that Algernon was special.

July 14 Its sunday again. I dont have anything to do to keep me busy now because my television set is broke and I dont have any money to get it fixed. (I think I lost this months check from the lab. I dont remember)

I get awful headaches and asperin doesnt help me much. Mrs Flynn knows Im really sick and she feels very sorry for me. Shes a wonderful woman whenever someone is sick.

July 22 Mrs Flynn called a strange doctor to see me. She was afraid I was going to die. I told the doctor I wasnt too sick and that I only forget sometimes. He asked me did I have any friends or relatives and I said no I dont have any. I told him I had a friend called Algernon once but he was a mouse and we used to run races together. He looked at me kind of funny like he thought I was crazy.

He smiled when I told him I used to be a genius. He talked to me like I was a baby and he winked at Mrs Flynn. I got mad and chased him out because he was making fun of me the way they all used to.

July 24 I have no more money and Mrs. Flynn says I got to go to work somewhere and pay the rent because I havent paid for over two months. I dont know any work but the job I used to have at Donnegans Plastic Box Company. I dont want to go back there because they all knew me when I was smart and maybe theyll laugh at me. But I dont know what else to do to get money.

July 27 Mr Donnegan was very nice when I came back and asked him for my old job of janitor. First he was very suspicious but I told him what happened to me then he looked very sad and put his hand on my shoulder and said Charlie Gordon you got guts.

Everybody looked at me when I came downstairs and started working in the toilet sweeping it out like I used to. I told myself Charlie if they make fun of you dont get sore because you remember their not so smart as you once thot they were. And besides they were once your friends and if they laughed at you that doesnt mean anything because they liked you too.

One of the new men who came to work there after I went away made a nasty crack he said hey Charlie I hear your a very smart fella a real quiz kid. Say something intelligent. I felt bad but Joe Carp came over and grabbed him by the shirt and said leave him alone you lousy cracker or Ill break your neck. I didnt expect Joe to take my part so I guess hes really my friend.

2 A Difference That Makes a Difference

The ways in which men of different races, cultures, ethnic groups, and statuses relate to one another and the varieties of belief systems and interaction patterns that develop in connection with relations between groups are subjects of considerable interest to social scientists and of considerable importance to the rest of the world's population. Clearly, conflicts drawn along lines of group identification have occurred frequently throughout recorded history. The fact that conflicts of this sort occur, generate effects that tend to endure, and frequently increase antipathy between groups is one of the more pathetic aspects of the human condition.

Accounting for the existence of hostilities between individuals who identify themselves as members of different groups, in any particular case, requires identifying the specific sociological variables and historical conditions that generated the antagonisms and tracing the changes in variables and historical events that determined whether the antagonisms grew or diminished. To explain why hostilities between groups come about in general—that is, to understand the phenomenon independent of any particular case—requires much more. The distinction between accounting for a particular instance of conflict and understanding the phenomenon in general is equivalent to the distinction between knowing history, being able to trace a sequence of events through time, and knowing sociology, understanding why a particular combination of social and historical conditions produced a certain outcome and being able to predict how changing any of the social or historical conditions would change the outcome.

To understand conflict between groups generally requires us not only to understand how social variables (such as economic competition) and historical events (such as the assassination of a certain individual) affect conflict, but also to construct a theory how stereotypes develop and how they are modified. A peculiar relationship seems to exist between the conditions necessary to generate hostilities between groups and the conditions necessary to maintain them. Unfortunately, the objective causes of antagonisms (such as competition for scarce goods between members of two groups) result in hostilities that typically give rise to stereotypes of the members of the opposing group. These stereotypes are consistent with the hostile feelings that exist between members of the two groups. Unfortunately, negative stereotypes tend to persist even after objective causes for antagonisms between groups cease to exist.

The sequence is something like this: Some realistic competition generates hostilities. In order to justify the hatred they feel for members of the opposing group, men convince themselves that their opponents are evil, dirty, uncivilized, cruel—that is, that they possess all the characteristics required of first-class villains. It is, after all, much easier to hate someone who is entirely despicable than someone who is only about as despicable as you are. The problem is that once this image of the members of another race, ethnic group, or social class has been created, it becomes a justification for treating these people differently from members of one's own group. The undesirable characteristics they are *known* to possess seem to justify treating members of the other group as essentially different from members of one's own group. The stereotype becomes the basis for maintaining hostility.

Hostilities between groups can come about for reasons far less understandable than competition for scarce resources or political domination. Hostilities can be the end-product of interactions between men of different groups who simply operate with reference to different norms and values.

Whether because of learned reaction or, as some zoologists claim, because of universal wariness of organisms that are substantially different in appearance or manner from oneself, interacting with a creature that is unfamiliar is anxiety-provoking. Its reactions, motivations, and desires cannot be assumed to be the same as one's own, and therefore its behavior cannot be predicted. A movement that would not provoke anxiety when made by a friend or even a casual acquaintance can provoke an extreme response when made by a stranger. Given that situations involving unknown quantities are inherently anxiety-provoking, it is relatively easy to understand how actions can be interpreted to mean something quite different from what the person who performed the act intended.

Accept for the moment the proposition that the greater the apparent physical or social distance between two individuals, the greater the inherent anxiety in their initial interactions. It therefore follows that the more the cultures of two persons differ, the greater will be the stress generated by their interaction. In the same manner, the more physically different two individuals are, the greater the potential fear of each other and the easier it is to generate misunderstandings. The range of variation across human cultures and the range of variation in physical characteristics of varieties of the human species are relatively so small that it may be difficult to detect easily in oneself the uneasiness that accompanies these differences. The possible variations between different species of intelligent life are, however, infinite. In "My Sister's Brother," Philip José Farmer proposes a situation in which the great cultural and physical differences between characters make it easier to detect the egocentrism of the human actor, his physical and cultural biases, and to follow the reasoning, motivations, and fears that lead him to act as he does.

My Sister's Brother

PHILIP JOSÉ FARMER

When he opened his eyes, he knew he was not alone. He saw a Martian.

A hole had appeared in the wall of the tube to his left. It was a round section about four feet across, and it had sunk in as if it were a plug being pulled inwards, as indeed it was.

A moment later a head popped out of the hole. The size of a Georgia watermelon, it was shaped like a football and was as pink as a baby's bottom. Its two eyes were as large as coffee cups and each was equipped with two vertical lids. It opened its two parrot-like beaks, ran out a very long tubular tongue, withdrew the tongue, and snapped the beak shut. Then it scuttled out from the hole to reveal a body also shaped like a football and only three times as large as its head. The pinkish body was supported three feet from the ground on ten spindly spidery legs, five on each side. Its legs ended in broad round pads on which it ran across the jellymire surface, sinking only slightly. Behind it streamed at least fifty others.

These picked up the little plants that Lane had upset in his struggles and licked them clean with narrow round tongues that shot out at least two feet. They also seemed to communicate by touching their tongues, as insects do with antennae.

As he was in the space between two rows, he was not involved in the setting up of the dislodged plants. Several of them ran their tongues over his helmet, but these were the only ones that paid him any attention. It was then that he began to stop dreading that they might attack him with their powerful looking beaks. Now he broke into a sweat at the idea that they might ignore him completely.

That was just what they did. After gently embedding the thin roots of the plantlets in the sticky stuff, they raced off towards the hole in the tube.

Lane, overwhelmed with despair, shouted after them, though he knew they couldn't hear him through his helmet and the thin air even if they had hearing organs.

"Don't leave me here to die!"

Nevertheless, that was what they were doing. The last one leaped through the hole, and the entrance stared at him like the round black eye of Death itself.

He struggled furiously to lift himself from the mire, not caring that he was only exhausting himself.

Abruptly, he stopped fighting and stared at the hole.

A figure had crawled out of it, a figure in a pressure-suit.

Now he shouted with joy. Whether the figure was Martian or not, it was built like a member of homo sapiens. It could be presumed to be intelligent and therefore curious.

He was not disappointed. The suited being stood up on two hemispheres of shiny red metal and began walking towards him in a sliding fashion.

Reaching him, it handed him the end of a plastic rope it was carrying under its arm.

He almost dropped it. His rescuer's suit was transparent. It was enough of a shock to see clearly the details of the creature's body, but the sight of the two heads within the helmet caused him to turn pale.

The Martian slidewalked to the tube from which Lane had leaped. It jumped lightly from the two bowls on which it had stood, landed on the three-foot high top of the tube, and began hauling Lane out from the mess. He came out slowly but steadily and soon was scooting forward, gripping the rope. When he reached the foot of the tube, he was hauled on up until he could get his feet in the two bowls. It was easy to jump from them to a place beside the biped.

It unstrapped two more bowls from its back, gave them to Lane, then lowered itself on the two in the garden. Lane followed it across the mire.

Entering the hole, he found himself in a chamber so low he had to crouch. Evidently, it had been constructed by the dekapeds and not by his companion for it, too, had to bend its back and knees.

Lane was pushed to one side by some dekapeds. They picked up the thick plug, made of the same grey stuff as the tube walls, and sealed the entrance with it. Then they shot out of their mouths strand after strand of grey spiderwebby stuff to seal the plug.

The biped motioned Lane to follow, and it slid down a tunnel which plunged into the earth at a forty-five degree angle. It illuminated the passage with a flashlight which it took from its belt. They came into a large chamber which contained all of the fifty dekapeds. These were waiting motionless. The biped, as if sensing Lane's curiosity, pulled off its glove and held it before several small vents in the wall. Lane removed his glove and felt warm air flowing from the holes.

Evidently this was a pressure chamber, built by the ten-legged things. But such evidence of intelligent engineering did not mean that these things had the individual intelligence of a man. It could mean group intelligence such as Terrestrial insects possess.

After a while, the chamber was filled with air. Another plug was pulled; Lane followed the dekapeds and his rescuer up another forty-five degree tunnel. He estimated that he would find himself inside the tube from which the biped had first come. He was right. He crawled through another hole into it.

And a pair of beaks clicked as they bit down on his helmet!

Automatically, he shoved at the thing, and under the force of his blow the dekaped lost its bite and went rolling on the floor, a bundle of thrashing legs.

Lane did not worry about having hurt it. It did not weigh much, but its body must be tough to be able to plunge without damage from the heavy air inside the tube into the almost-stratospheric conditions outside.

However, he did reach for the knife at his belt. But the biped put its hand on his arm and shook one of its heads.

Later, he was to find out that the seeming bite must have been an accident. Always—with one exception—the leggers were to ignore him.

He was also to find that he was lucky. The leggers had come out to inspect their garden because, through some unknown method of detection, they knew that the plantlets had been disturbed. The biped normally would not have accompanied them. However, today, its curiosity aroused because the leggers had gone out three times in three days, it had decided to investigate.

The biped turned out its flashlight and motioned to Lane to follow. Awkwardly, he obeyed. There was light, but it was dim, a twilight. Its source was the many creatures that hung from the ceiling of the tube. These were three feet long and six inches thick, cylindrical, pinkish-skinned, and eyeless. A dozen frondlike limbs waved continuously, and their motion kept air circulating in the tunnel.

Their cold firefly glow came from two globular pulsing organs which hung from both sides of the round loose-lipped mouth at the free end of the creature. Slime drooled from the mouth and dripped on to the floor or into a narrow channel which ran along the lowest part of the sloping floor. Water ran in the six-inch deep channel, the first native water he had seen. The water picked up the slime and carried it a little way before it was gulped up by an animal that lay on the bottom of the channel.

Lane's eyes adjusted to the dimness until he could make out the water-dweller. It was torpedo-shaped and without eyes or fins. It had two openings in its body; one obviously sucked in water, the other expelled it.

He saw at once what this meant. The water at the North Pole melted in the summertime and flowed into the far end of the tube system. Helped by gravity and by the pumping action of the line of animals in the channel, the water was passed from the edge of the Pole to the equator.

Leggers ran by him on mysterious errands. Several, however, halted beneath some of the downhanging organisms. They reared up on their hind five legs and their tongues shot out and into the open mouths by the glowing balls. At once the fireworm—as Lane termed it—its cilia waving wildly, stretched itself to twice its former length. Its mouth met the beak of the legger, and there was an exchange of stuff between their mouths.

Impatiently, the biped tugged at Lane's arm. He followed it down the tube. Soon they entered a section where pale roots came down out of holes in the ceiling and spread along the curving walls, gripping them, then becoming a network of many thread-thin rootlets that crept across the floor and into the water of the channel.

Here and there a dekaped chewed at a root and then hurried off to offer a piece to the mouths of the fire-worms.

After walking for several minutes, the biped stepped across the stream. It then began walking as closely as possible to the wall, meanwhile looking apprehensively at the other side of the tunnel, where they had been walking.

Lane also looked but could see nothing at which to be alarmed. There was a large opening at the base of the wall which evidently led into a tunnel. This tunnel, he presumed, ran underground into a room, or rooms, for many leggers dashed in and out of it. And about a dozen, larger than average, paced back and forth like sentries before the hole.

When they had gone about fifty yards past the opening, the biped relaxed. After it had led Lane along for ten minutes, it stopped. Its naked hand touched the wall. He became aware that the hand was small and delicately shaped, like a woman's.

A section of the wall swung out. The biped turned and bent down to crawl into the hole, presenting buttocks and legs femininely rounded, well shaped. It was then that he began thinking of it as a female. Yet the hips, though padded with fatty tissue, were not broad. The bones were not widely separated to make room to carry a child. Despite their curving, the hips were relatively as narrow as a man's.

Behind them, the plug swung shut. The biped did not turn on her flashlight, for there was illumination at the end of the tunnel. The floor and walls were not of the hard grey stuff nor of packed earth. They seemed vitrified, as if glassed by heat.

She was waiting for him when he slid off a three-foot high ledge into a large room. For a minute he was blinded by the strong light. After his eyes adjusted, he searched for the source of light but could not find it. He did observe that there were no shadows in the room.

The biped took off her helmet and suit and hung them in a closet. The door slid open as she approached and closed when she walked away.

She signalled that he could remove his suit. He did not hesitate. Though the air might be poisonous, he had no choice. His tank would soon be empty. Moreover, it seemed likely that the atmosphere contained enough oxygen. Even then he had grasped the idea that the leaves of the umbrella plants, which grew out of the top of the tubes, absorbed sunlight and traces of carbon dioxide. Inside the tunnels, the roots drew up water from the channel and absorbed the great quantity of carbon dioxide released by the dekapeds. Energy of sunlight converted gas and liquid into glucose and oxygen, which were given off in the tunnels.

Even here, in this deep chamber which lay beneath and to one side of the tube, a thick root penetrated the ceiling and spread its thin white web over the walls. He stood directly beneath the fleshy growth as he removed his helmet and took his first breath of Martian air. Immediately afterwards, he jumped. Something wet had dropped on his forehead. Looking up, he saw that the root was excreting liquid from a large pore. He wiped the drop off with his finger and tasted it. It was sticky and sweet. Well, he thought, the tree must normally drop sugar in water. But it seemed to be doing so abnormally fast, because another drop was forming.

Then it came to him that perhaps this was so because it was getting dark outside and therefore cold. The umbrella trees might be pumping the water in their trunks into the warm tunnels. Thus, during the bitter subzero night, they'd avoid freezing and swelling up and cracking wide open.

It seemed a reasonable theory.

He looked around. The place was half living quarters, half biological laboratory. There were beds and tables and chairs and several unidentifiable articles. . . .

The biped took a large green ceramic bowl from a cupboard and set it on a table. Lane eyed her curiously, wondering what she was going to do. By now he had seen that the second head belonged to an entirely separate creature. Its slim four foot length of pinkish skin was coiled about her neck and torso;

its tiny flat-faced head turned towards Lane; its snaky light blue eyes glittered. Suddenly its mouth opened and revealed toothless gums, and its bright red tongue, mammalian, not at all reptilian, thrust out at him.

The biped, paying no attention to the worm's actions, lifted it from her. Gently, cooing a few words in a soft many-vowelled language, she placed it in the bowl. It settled inside and looped around the curve, like a snake in a pit.

The biped took a pitcher from the top of a box of red plastic. Though the box was not connected to any visible power source, it seemed to be a stove. The pitcher contained warm water which she poured into the bowl, half filling it. Under the shower, the worm closed its eyes as if it were purring soundless ecstasy.

Then the biped did something that alarmed Lane.

She leaned over the bowl and vomited into it.

He stepped towards her. Forgetting the fact that she couldn't understand him, he said, 'Are you sick?'

She revealed human-looking teeth in a smile meant to reassure him, and she walked away from the bowl. He looked at the worm, which had its head dipped into the mess. Suddenly, he felt sick, for he was sure that it was feeding off the mixture. And he was equally certain that she fed the worm regularly with regurgitated food.

It didn't cancel his disgust to reflect that he shouldn't react to her as he would to a Terrestrial. He knew that she was totally alien and that it was inevitable that some of her ways would repel, perhaps even shock him. Rationally, he knew this. But if his brain told him to understand and forgive, his belly said to loathe and reject.

His aversion was not much lessened by a close scrutiny of her as she took a shower in a cubicle set in the wall. She was about five feet tall and slim as a woman should be slim, with delicate bones beneath rounded flesh. Her legs were human; in nylons and high heels they would have been exciting—other things being equal. However, if the shoes had been toeless, her feet would have caused much comment. They had four toes.

Her long beautiful hands had five fingers. These seemed nailless, like the toes, though a closer examination later showed him they did bear rudimentary nails.

She stepped from the cubicle and began towelling herself, though not before she motioned to him to remove his suit and also to shower. He stared intently back at her until she laughed a short embarrassed laugh. It was feminine, not at all deep. Then she spoke.

He closed his eyes and was hearing what he had thought he would not hear for years: a woman's voice. Hers was extraordinary: husky and honeyed at the same time.

But when he opened his eyes, he saw her for what she was. No woman. No man. What? It? No. The impulse to think *her, she,* was too strong.

This, despite her lack of mammaries. She had a chest, but no nipples, rudimentary or otherwise. Her chest was a man's, muscled under the layer of fat which subtly curved to give the impression that beneath it . . . budding breasts?

No, not this creature. She would never suckle her young. She did not even bear them alive, if she *did* bear. Her belly was smooth, undimpled with a navel.

Smooth also was the region between her legs, hairless, unbroken, as innocent of organ as if she were a nymph painted for some Victorian children's book.

It was that sexless joining of the legs that was so horrible. Like the white belly of a frog, thought Lane, shuddering.

At the same time, his curiosity became even stronger. How did this thing mate and reproduce?

Again she laughed and smiled with fleshy pale-red humanly everted lips and wrinkled a short, slightly uptilted nose and ran her hand through thick straight red-gold fur. It was fur, not hair, and it had a slightly oily sheen, like a water-dwelling animal's.

The face itself, though strange, could have passed for human, but only passed. Her cheekbones were very high and protruded upwards in an unhuman fashion. Her eyes were dark blue and quite human. This meant nothing. So were an octopus's eyes.

She walked to another closet, and as she went away from him he saw again that though the hips were curved like a woman's they did not sway with the pelvic displacement of the human female.

The door swung momentarily open, revealed the carcasses of several dekapeds, minus their legs, hanging on hooks. She removed one, placed it on a metal table, and out of the cupboard took a saw and several knives and began cutting.

Because he was eager to see the anatomy of the dekaped, he approached the table. She waved him to the shower. Lane removed his suit. When he came to the knife and axe he hesitated, but, afraid she might think him distrustful, he hung up the belt containing his weapons beside the suit. However, he did not take off his clothes because he was determined to view the inner organs of the animal. Later, he would shower.

The legger was not an insect, despite its spidery appearance. Not in the terrestrial sense, certainly. Neither was it a vertebrate. Its smooth hairless skin was an animal's, as lightly pigmented as a blond Swede's. But, though it had an endo-skeleton, it had no backbone. Instead, the body bones formed a round cage. Its thin ribs radiated from a cartilaginous collar which adjoined the back of the head. The ribs curved outwards, then in, almost meeting at the posterior. Inside the cage were ventral lung sacs, a relatively large heart, and liver-like and kidney-like organs. Three arteries, instead of the mammalian two, left the heart. He couldn't be sure with such a hurried examination, but it looked as if the dorsal aorta, like some terrestrial reptiles, carried both pure and impure blood.

There were other things to note. The most extraordinary was that, as far as he could discern, the legger had no digestive system. It seemed to lack both intestines and anus unless you would define as a intestine a sac which ran straight through from the throat half-way into the body. Further, there was nothing he could identify as reproductive organs, though this did not mean that it did not possess them. The creature's long tubular tongue, cut open by the biped, exposed a canal running down the length of tongue from its open tip to a bladder as its base. Apparently these formed part of the excretory system.

Lane wondered what enabled the legger to stand the great pressure differences between the interior of the tube and the Martian surface. At the same time he realized that this ability was no more wonderful than the biological mechanism which gave whales and seals the power to endure without harm the enormous pressures a half mile below the sea's surface.

The biped looked at him with round and very pretty blue eyes, laughed, and then reached into the chopped open skull and brought out the tiny brain.

"*Hauaimi,*" she said slowly. She pointed to her head, repeated. "*Hauaimi,*" and then indicated his head. "*Hauaimi.*"

Echoing her, he pointed at his own head. "*Hauaimi.* Brain."

"Brain," she said, and she laughed again.

She proceeded to call out the organs of the legger which corresponded to hers. Thus, the preparations for the meal passed swiftly as he proceeded from the carcass to other objects in the room. By the time she had fried the meat and boiled strips of the membranous leaf of the umbrella plant, and also added from cans various exotic foods, she had exchanged at least forty words with him. An hour later, he could remember twenty.

There was one thing yet to learn. He pointed to himself and said, "Lane."

Then he pointed to her and gave her a questioning look.

"Mahrseeya," she said.

"Martia?" he repeated. She corrected him, but he was so struck by the resemblance that always afterward he called her that. After a while, she would give up trying to teach him the exact pronunciation.

Martia washed her hands and poured him a bowlful of water. He used the soap and towel she handed him, then walked to the table where she stood waiting. On it was a bowl of thick soup, a plate of fried brains, a salad of boiled leaves and some unidentifiable vegetables, a plate of ribs with thick dark legger meat, hard-boiled eggs and little loaves of bread.

Martia gestured for him to sit down. Evidently her code did not allow her to sit down before her guest did. He ignored his chair, went behind her, put his hand on her shoulder, pressed down, and with the other hand slid her chair under her. She turned her head to smile up at him. Her fur slid away to reveal one lobeless pointed ear. He scarcely noticed it, for he was too intent on the half-repulsive, half-heartquickening sensation he got when he touched her skin. It had not been the skin itself that caused that, for she was soft and warm as a young girl. It had been the *idea* of touching her.

Part of that, he thought as he seated himself, came from her nakedness. Not because it revealed her sex but because it revealed her lack of it. No breasts, no nipples, no navel, no pubic fold or projection. The absence of these seemed wrong, very wrong, unsettling. It was a shameful thing that she had nothing of which to be ashamed.

That's a queer thought, he said to himself. And for no reason, he became warm in the face.

Martia, unnoticing, poured from a tall bottle a glassful of dark wine. He tasted it. It was exquisite, no better than the best Earth had to offer but as good.

Martia took one of the loaves, broke it into two pieces, and handed him one. Holding the glass of wine in one hand and the bread in the other, she bowed her head, closed her eyes, and began chanting.

He stared at her. This was a prayer, a grace-saying. Was it the prelude to a sort of communion, one so like Earth's it was startling?

Yet, if it were, he needn't be surprised. Flesh and blood, bread and wine: the symbolism was simple, logical, and might even be universal.

However it was possible that he was creating parallels that did not exist. She might be enacting a ritual whose origin and meaning were like nothing of which he had ever dreamed.

If so, what she did next was equally capable of misinterpretation. She nibbled at the bread, sipped the wine and then plainly invited him to do the same. He did so. Martia took a third and empty cup, spat a piece of wine-moistened bread into the cup and indicated that he was to imitate her.

After he did, he felt his stomach draw in on itself. For she mixed the stuff from their mouths with her finger and then offered it to him. Evidently, he was to put the finger in his mouth and eat from it.

So the action was both physical and metaphysical. The bread and the wine were the flesh and blood of whatever divinity she worshipped. More, she, being imbued with the body and the spirit of the god, now wanted to mingle hers and that of the god's with his. . . .

He took the proffered finger in his mouth and sucked the paste off it.

Then obeying her gestures, he dipped his own finger into the bowl and put it between her lips.

She closed her eyes and gently mouthed the finger. When he began to withdraw it, he was stopped by her hand on his wrist. He did not insist on taking the finger out, for he wanted to avoid offending her. Perhaps a long time interval was part of the rite.

But her expression seemed so eager and at the same time so ecstatic, like a hungry baby just given the nipple, that he felt uneasy. After a minute, seeing no indication on her part that she meant to quit, he slowly but firmly pulled the finger loose. She opened her eyes and sighed, but she made no comment. Instead, she began serving his supper.

The hot thick soup was delicious and invigorating. Its texture was somewhat like the plankton soup that was becoming popular on hungry Earth, but it had no fishy flavour. The brown bread reminded him of rye. The legger meat was like wild rabbit, though it was sweeter and had an unidentifiable tang. He took only one bite of the leaf salad and then frantically poured wine down his throat to wash away the burn. Tears came to his eyes, and he coughed until she spoke to him in an alarmed tone. He smiled back at her but refused to touch the salad again. The wine not only cooled his mouth, it filled his veins with singing. He told himself he should take no more. Nevertheless, he finished his second cup before he remembered his resolve to be temperate.

By then it was too late. The strong liquor went straight to his head; he felt dizzy and wanted to laugh. The events of the day, his near-escape from death, the reaction to knowing his comrades were dead, his realization of his present situation, the tension caused by his encounters with the dekapeds, and his unsatisfied curiosity about Martia's origin and the location of others of her kind, all these combined to produce in him a half-stupor, half-exuberance.

He rose from the table and offered to help Martia with the dishes. She shook her head and put the dishes in a washer. In the meantime, he decided that he needed to wash off the sweat, stickiness, and body odour left by two days of travel. On opening the door to the shower cubicle, he found that there wasn't room enough to hang his clothes in it. So, uninhibited by fatigue and wine also mindful that Martia, after all, was *not* a female, he removed his clothes.

Martia watched him, and her eyes became wider with each garment shed. Finally, she gasped and stepped back and turned pale.

"It's not that bad," he growled, wondering what had caused her reaction. "After all, some of the things I've seen around here aren't too easy to swallow."

She pointed with a trembling finger and asked him something in a shaky voice.

Perhaps it was his imagination, but he could swear she used the same inflection as would an English speaker.

"Are you sick? Are the growths malignant?"

He had no words with which to explain, nor did he intend to illustrate function through action. Instead, he closed the door of the cubicle after him and pressed the plate that turned on the water. The heat of the shower, and the feel of the soap, of grime and sweat being washed away, soothed him somewhat, so that he could think about matters he had been too rushed to consider.

First, he would have to learn Martia's language or teach her his. Probably both would happen at the same time. Of one thing he was sure. That was that her intentions toward him were, at least at present, peaceful. When she had shared communion with him, she had been sincere. He did not get the impression that it was part of her cultural training to share bread and wine with a person she intended to kill.

Feeling better, though still tired and a little drunk, he left the cubicle. Reluctantly, he reached for his dirty shorts. Then he smiled. They had been cleaned while he was in the shower. Martia, however, paid no attention to his smile of pleased surprise but, grim-faced, she motioned to him to lie down on the bed and sleep. Instead of lying down herself, however, she picked up a bucket and began crawling up the tunnel. He decided to follow her, and, when she saw him, she only shrugged her shoulders.

On emerging into the tube, Martia turned on her flashlight. The tunnel was in absolute darkness. Her beam, playing on the ceiling, showed that the glowworms had turned out their lights. There were no leggers in sight.

She pointed the light at the channel so he could see that the jetfish were still taking in and expelling water. Before she could turn the beam aside, he put his hand on her wrist and with his other hand lifted a fish from the channel. He had to pull it loose with an effort, which was explained when he turned the torpedo-shaped creature over and saw the colum of flesh hanging from its belly. Now he knew why the reaction of the propelled water did not shoot them backwards. The ventral-foot acted as a suction pad to hold them to the floor of the channel.

Somewhat impatiently, Martia pulled away from him and began walking swiftly back up the tunnel. He followed her until she came to the opening in the wall which had earlier made her so apprehensive. Crouching, she entered the opening, but before she had gone far she had to move a tangled heap of leggers to one side. They were the large great-beaked ones he had seen guarding the entrance. Now they were asleep at the post.

If so, he reasoned, then the thing they guarded against must also be asleep.

What about Martia? How did she fit into their picture? Perhaps she didn't fit into their picture at all. She was absolutely alien, something for which their instinctual intelligence was not prepared and which, therefore, they ignored. That would explain why they had paid no attention to him when he was mired in the garden.

Yet there must be an exception to that rule. Certainly Martia had not wanted to attract the sentinels' notice the first time she had passed the entrance.

A moment later he found out why. They stepped into a huge chamber which was at least two hundred feet square. It was as dark as the tube, but during the waking period it must have been very bright because the ceiling was jammed with glowworms.

Martia's flash raced around the chamber, showing him the piles of sleeping leggers. Then, suddenly it stopped. He took one look, and his heart raced, and the hairs on the back of his neck rose.

Before him was a worm three feet high and twenty feet long.

Without thinking, he grabbed hold of Martia to keep her from coming closer to it. But even as he touched her, he dropped his hand. She must know what she was doing.

Martia pointed the flash at her own face and smiled as if to tell him not to be alarmed. And she touched his arm with a shyly affectionate gesture.

For a moment he didn't know why. Then it came to him that she was glad because he had been thinking of her welfare. Moreover, her reaction showed she had recovered from her shock at seeing him unclothed.

He turned from her to examine the monster. It lay on the floor, asleep, its great eyes closed behind vertical slits. It had a huge head, football-shaped like those of the little leggers around it. Its mouth was big, but the beaks were very small, horny warts on its lips. The body, however, was that of a caterpillar worm's, minus the hair. Ten little useless legs stuck out of its side, too short even to reach the floor. Its sides bulged as if pumped full of gas.

Martia walked past the monster and paused by its posterior. Here she lifted up a fold of skin. Beneath it was a pile of a dozen leathery-skinned eggs, held together by a sticky secretion.

"Now I've got it," muttered Lane. "Of course. The egg-laying queen. She specializes in reproduction. That is why the others have no reproductive organs, or else they're so rudimentary I couldn't detect them. The leggers are animals, all right, but in some things they resemble terrestrial insects.

"Still, that doesn't explain the absence also of a digestive system."

Martia put the eggs in her bucket and started to leave the room. He stopped her and indicated he wanted to look around some more. She shrugged and began to lead him around. Both had to be careful not to step on the dekapeds, which lay everywhere.

They came to an open bin made of the same grey stuff as the walls. Its interior held many shelves, on which lay hundreds of eggs. Strands of the spiderwebby stuff kept the eggs from rolling off.

Nearby was another bin that held water. At its bottom lay more eggs. Above them minnow-sized torpedo shapes flitted about in the water.

Lane's eyes widened at this. The fish were not members of another genus but were the larvae of the leggers. And they could be set in the channel not only to earn their keep by pumping water which came down from the North Pole but to grow until they were ready to metamorphose into the adult stage.

However, Martia showed him another bin which made him partially revise his first theory. This bin was dry, and the eggs were laid on the floor. Martia picked one up, cut its tough skin open with her knife, and emptied its contents into one hand.

Now his eyes did get wide. This creature had a tiny cylindrical body, a suction pad at one end, a round mouth at the other, and two globular organs hanging by the mouth. A young glowworm.

Martia looked at him to see if he comprehended. Lane held out his hands and hunched his shoulders with an I-don't-get-it air. Beckoning, she walked to another bin to show him more eggs. Some had been ripped from within, and the little fellows whose hard beaks had done it were staggering around weakly on ten legs.

Energetically, Martia went through a series of charades. Watching her, he began to understand.

The embryos that remained in the eggs until they fully developed went through three main metamorphoses: the jetfish stage, the glowworm stage, and finally the baby dekaped stage. If the eggs were torn open by the adult nurses in one of the first two stages, the embryo remained fixed in that form, though it did grow larger.

What about the queen? he asked her by pointing to the monstrously egg-swollen body.

For answer, Martia picked up one of the newly-hatched. It kicked its many legs but did not otherwise protest, being, like all its kind, mute. Martia turned it upside down and indicated a slight crease in its posterior. Then she showed him the same spot on one of the sleeping adults. The adult's rear was smooth, innocent of the crease.

Martia made eating gestures. He nodded. The creatures were born with rudimentary sexual organs, but these never developed. In fact, they atrophied completely unless the young were given a special diet, in which case they matured into egg-layers.

But the picture wasn't complete. If you had females, you had to have males. It was doubtful if such highly developed animals were self-fertilizing or reproduced parthenogenetically.

Then he remembered Martia and began doubting. She gave no evidence of reproductive organs. Could her kind be self-producing? Or was she a Martian, her natural fulfillment diverted by diet?

It didn't seem likely, but he couldn't be sure that such things were not possible in her scheme of Nature.

Lane wanted to satisfy his curiosity. Ignoring her desire to get out of the chamber, he examined each of the five baby dekapeds. All were potential females.

Suddenly Martia, who had been gravely watching him, smiled and took his hand, and led him to the rear of the room. Here, as they approached another structure, he smelled a strong odour which reminded him of clorox.

Closer to the structure, he saw that it was not a bin but a hemispherical cage. Its bars were of the hard grey stuff, and they curved up from the floor to meet at a central point. There was no door. Evidently the cage had been built around the thing in it, and its occupant must remain until he died.

Martia soon showed him why this thing was not allowed freedom. It—he—was sleeping, but Martia reached through the bars and struck it on the head with her fist. The thing did not respond until it had been hit five more times. Then, slowly, it opened its sidewise lids to reveal great staring eyes, bright as fresh arterial blood.

Martia threw one of the eggs at the thing's head. Its beak opened swiftly, the egg disappeared, the beak closed, and there was a noisy gulp.

Food brought it to life. It sprang up on its ten long legs, clacked its beak, and lunged against the bars again and again.

Though in no danger, Martia shrank back before the killer's lust in the scarlet eyes. Lane could understand her reaction. It was a giant, at least two feet higher than the sentinels. Its back was on a level with Martia's; its beaks could have taken her head in between them.

Lane walked around the cage to get a good look at its posterior. Puzzled, he made another circuit without seeing anything of maleness about it except its wild fury like that of a stallion locked in a barn during the mating season. Except for its size, red eyes, and a cloaca, it looked like one of the guards.

He tried to communicate to Martia his puzzlement. By now, she seemed to anticipate his desires. She went through another series of pantomimes, some of which were so energetic and comical that he had to smile.

First, she showed him two eggs on a nearby ledge. These were larger than the others and were speckled with red spots. Supposedly, they held male embryos.

Then she showed him what would happen if the adult male got loose. Making a face which was designed to be ferocious but only amused him, clicking her teeth and clawing with her hands, she imitated the male running amok. He would kill everybody in sight. Everybody, the whole colony, queen, workers, guards, larvae, eggs, bite off their heads, mangle them, eat them all up, all, all. And out of the slaughterhouse he would charge into the tube and kill every legger he met, devour the jetfish, drag down the glowworms from the ceiling, rip them apart, eat them, eat the roots of the trees. Kill, kill, kill, eat, eat, eat!

That was all very well, sighed Lane. But how did. . . . ?

Martia indicated that, once a day, the workers rolled, literally rolled the queen across the room to the cage. There they arranged her so that she presented her posterior some few inches from the bars and the enraged male. And the male, though he wanted to do nothing but get his beak into her flesh and tear her apart, was not master of himself. Nature took over; his will was betrayed by his nervous system.

Lane nodded to show he understood. In his mind was a picture of the legger that had been butchered. It had had one sac at the internal end of the tongue. Probably the male had two, one to hold excretory matter, the other to hold seminal fluid.

Suddenly Martia froze, her hands held out before her. She had laid the flashlight on the floor so she could act freely; the beam splashed on her paling skin.

"What is it?" said Lane, stepping towards her.

Martia retreated, holding out her hands before her. She looked horrified.

"I'm not going to harm you," he said. However, he stopped so she could see he didn't mean to get any closer to her.

What was bothering her? Nothing was stirring in the chamber itself besides the male, and he was behind her.

Then she was pointing, first at him and then at the raging dekaped. Seeing this unmistakable signal of identification, he comprehended. She had perceived that he, like the thing in the cage, was male, and now she perceived structure and function in him.

What he didn't understand was why that should make her so frightened of him. Repelled, yes. Her body, its seeming lack of sex, had given him a feeling of distaste bordering on nausea. It was only natural that she should react similarly to his body. However, she had seemed to have got over her first shock.

Why this unexpected change, this horror of him?

Behind him, the beak of the male clicked as it lunged against the bars.

The click echoed in his mind.

Of course, the monster's lust to kill!

Until she had met him, she had known only one male creature. That was the caged thing. Now, suddenly, she had equated him with the monster. A male was a killer.

Desperately, because he was afraid that she was about to run in a panic out of the room, he made signs that he was not like this monster; he shook his head no, no, no. He wasn't, he wasn't, he wasn't!

Martia, watching him intently, began to relax. Her skin regained its pinkish hue. Her eyes became their normal size. She even managed a strained smile.

To get her mind off the subject, he indicated that he would like to know why the queen and her consort had digestive systems, though the workers did not. For answer, she reached up into the downhanging mouth of the worm suspended from the ceiling. Her hand, withdrawn, was covered with secretion. After smelling her fist, she gave it to him to sniff also. He took it, ignoring her slight and probably involuntary flinching when she felt his touch.

The stuff had an odour such as you would expect from predigested food.

Martia then went to another worm. The two light organs of this one were not coloured red, like the other, but had a greenish tint. Martia tickled its tongue with her finger and held out her cupped hands. Liquid trickled into the cup.

Lane smelled the stuff. No odour. When he drank the liquid, he discovered it to be a thick sugar water.

Martia pantomimed that the glowworms acted as the digestive system for the workers. They also stored food away for them. The workers derived part of their energy from the glucose excreted by the roots of the trees. The proteins and vegetable matter in their diet originated from the eggs and from the leaves of the umbrella plant. Strips of the tough membranous leaf were brought into the tubes by harvesting parties which ventured forth in the daytime. The worms partially digested the eggs, dead leggers, and leaves and gave it back in the form of a soup. The soup, like the glucose, was swallowed by the workers and passed through the walls of their throats or into the long straight sac which connected the throat to the larger blood vessels. The waste products were excreted through the skin or emptied through the canal in the tongue.

Lane nodded and then walked out of the room. Seemingly relieved, Martia followed him. When they had crawled back into her quarters, she put the eggs in a refrigerator and poured two glasses of wine. She dipped her finger in both, then touched the finger to her lips and to his. Lightly, he touched the tip with his tongue. This, he gathered, was one more ritual, perhaps a bedtime one, which affirmed that they were at one and at peace. It might be that it had an even deeper meaning, but if so, it escaped him.

Martia checked on the safety and comfort of the worm in the bowl. By now it had eaten all its food. She removed the worm, washed it, washed the bowl, half-filled it with warm sugar water, placed it on a table by the bed, and put the creature back in. Then she lay down on the bed and closed her eyes. She did not cover herself and apparently did not expect him to expect a cover. . . .

During their next period of wakefulness Lane and Mahrseeya establish a rudimentary form of communication. Lane discovers that Mahrseeya's species, the Eeltau, are not native Martians, that they have been observing Earth from Mars for a period of time, and that they have withdrawn their outpost from Mars in order not to be discovered by the explorers; he also learns the circumstances under which Mahrseeya was left behind. Lane convinces himself that Mahrseeya does not intend to permit his return to Earth.

As he fell asleep, he was thinking that perhaps Martia and he would be the two ambassadors to bring their people together in peace. After all, both of them were highly civilized, essentially pacifistic, and devoutly religious.

There was such a thing as the brotherhood, not only of man, but of all sentient beings throughout the cosmos, and . . .

Pressure on his bladder woke him up. He opened his eyes. The ceiling and walls expanded and contracted. His wristwatch was distorted. Only by extreme effort could he focus his eyes enough to straighten the arms on his watch. The piece, designed to measure the slightly longer Martian day, indicated midnight.

Groggily, he rose. He felt sure that he must have been drugged and that he would still be sleeping if the bladder pain hadn't been so sharp. If only he could take something to counteract the drug, he could carry out his plans now. But first he had to get to the toilet.

To do so, he had to pass close to Martia's bed. She did not move but lay on her back, her arms flung out and hanging over the sides of the bed, her mouth open wide.

He looked away, for it seemed indecent to watch when she was in such a position.

But something caught his eye—a movement, a flash of light like a gleaming jewel in her mouth.

He bent over her, looked, and recoiled in horror.

A head rose from between her teeth.

He raised his hand to snatch at the thing but froze in the posture as he recognized the tiny pouting round mouth and little blue eyes. It was the worm.

At first, he thought Martia was dead. The thing was not coiled in her mouth. Its body disappeared into her throat.

Then he saw her chest was rising easily and that she seemed to be in no difficulty.

Forcing himself to come close to the worm, though his stomach muscles writhed and his neck muscles quivered, he put his hand close to its lips.

Warm air touched his fingers, and he heart a faint whistling.

Martia was breathing through it!

Hoarsely, he said, "God!" and he shook her shoulder. He did not want to touch the worm because he was afraid that it might do something to injure her. In that moment of shock he had forgotten that he had an advantage over her, which he should use.

Martia's lids opened; her large grey-blue eyes stared blankly.

"Take it easy," he said soothingly.

She shuddered. Her lids closed, her neck arched back, and her face contorted.

He could not tell if the grimace was caused by pain or something else.

"What is this—this monster?" he said. "Symbiote? Parasite?"

He thought of vampires, of worms creeping into one's sleeping body and there sucking blood.

Suddenly she sat up and held out her arms to him. He seized her hands, saying, "What is it?"

Martia pulled him towards her at the same time lifting her face to his.

Out of her open mouth shot the worm, its head pointed towards his face, its little lips formed into an O.

It was reflex, the reflex of fear that made Lane drop her hands and spring back. He had not wanted to do that, but he could not help himself.

Abruptly, Martia came wide awake. The worm flopped its full length from her mouth and fell into a heap between her legs. There it thrashed for a moment before coiling itself like a snake, its head resting on Martia's thigh, its eyes turned upwards to Lane.

There was no doubt about it. Martia looked disappointed, frustrated.

Lane's knees, already weak, gave way. However, he managed to continue to his destination. When he came out, he walked as far as Martia's bed, where he had to sit down. His heart was thudding against his ribs and he was panting hard.

He sat behind her, for he did not want to be where the worm could touch him.

Martia made motions for him to go back to his bed and they would all sleep. Evidently, he thought, she found nothing alarming in the incident.

But he knew he could not rest until he had some kind of explanation. He handed her paper and pen from the bedside table and then gestured fiercely. Martia shrugged and began sketching while Lane watched over her shoulder. By the time she had used up five sheets of paper, she had communicated her message.

His eyes were wide, and he was even paler.

So—Martia *was* a female. Female at least in the sense that she carried eggs—and, at times, young—within her.

And there was the so-called worm. So called? What could he call it? It could not be designated under one category. It was many things in one. It was a larva. It was a phallus. It was also her offspring, of her flesh and blood.

But not of her genes. It was not descended from her.

She had given birth to it, yet she was not its mother. She was neither one of its mothers.

The dizziness and confusion he felt was not caused altogether by his sickness. Things were coming too fast. He was thinking furiously, trying to get this new information clear, but his thoughts kept going back and forth, getting nowhere.

"There's no reason to get upset," he told himself. "After all, the splitting of animals into two sexes is only one of the ways of reproduction tried on Earth. On Martia's planet Nature—God—has fashioned another method for the higher animals. And only He knows how many other designs for reproduction He has fashioned on how many other worlds."

Nevertheless, he was upset.

This worm, no, this larva, this embryo outside its egg and its secondary mother . . . well, call it, once and for all, larva, because it did metamorphose later.

This particular larva was doomed to stay in its present form until it died of old age.

Unless Martia found another adult of the Eeltau.

And unless she and this other adult felt affection for each other.

Then, according to the sketch she'd drawn, Martia and her friend, or lover, would lie down or sit together. They would caress and kiss as much as Terrestrial man and woman do. . . .

Then, unlike the Terran custom, a third would enter the union to form a highly desired and indeed indispensable and eternal triangle.

The larva, blindly, brainlessly obeying its instincts, aroused by mutual fondling by the two, would descend tail first into the throat of one of the two Eeltau. Inside the body of the lover a fleshy valve would open to admit the slim body of the larva. Its open tip would touch the ovary of the host. The larva, like an electric eel, would release a tiny current. The hostess would go into an ecstasy, its nerves stimulated electro-chemically. The ovary would release an egg no larger than a pencil dot. It would disappear into the open tip of the larva's tail, there to begin a journey up a canal towards the centre of its body, urged on by the contraction of muscle and whipping of cilia.

Then the larva slid out of the first hostess' mouth and went tail first into the other, there to repeat the process. Sometimes the larva garnered eggs, sometimes not, depending upon whether the ovary had a fully developed one to release.

When the process was successful, the two eggs moved towards each other but did not quite meet.

Not yet.

There must be other eggs collected in the dark incubator of the larva, collected by pairs, though not necessarily from the same couple of donors.

These would number anywhere from twenty to forty pairs.

Then, one day, the mysterious chemistry of the cells would tell the larva's body that it had gathered enough eggs.

A hormone was released, the metamorphosis begun. The larva swelled enormously, and the mother, seeing this, placed it tenderly in a warm place and fed it plenty of predigested food and sugar water.

Before the eyes of its mother, the larva then grew shorter and wider. Its tail contracted; its cartilaginous vertebrae, widely separated in its larval stage, shifted closer to each other and hardened. A skeleton formed, ribs, shoulders. Legs and arms budded and grew and took humanoid shape. Six months passed, and there lay in its crib something resembling a baby of homo sapiens.

From then until its fourteenth year, the Eeltau grew and developed much as its Terran counterpart.

Adulthood, however, initiated more strange changes. Hormone released hormone until the first pair of gametes, dormant these fourteen years, moved together.

The two fused, the chromatin of one uniting with the chromatin of the other. Out of the two—a single creature, wormlike, four inches long, released into the stomach of its hostess.

Then, nausea. Vomiting. And so, comparatively painlessly, the bringing forth of a genetically new being.

It was this worm that would be both foetus and phallus and would give ecstasy and draw into its own body the eggs of loving adults and would metamorphose and become infant, child, and adult.

And so on and so on.

He rose and shakily walked to his own bed. There he sat down, his head bowed, while he muttered to himself.

"Let's see now. Martia gave birth to, brought forth, or up, this larva. But the larva actually doesn't have any of Martia's genes. Martia was just the hostess for it.

"However, if Martia has a lover, she will, by means of this worm, pass on her heritable qualities. This worm will become an adult and bring forth, or up, Martia's child."

He raised his hands in despair.

"How do the Eeltau reckon ancestry? How keep track of their relatives? Or do they care? Wouldn't it be easier to consider your foster mother, your hostess, your real mother? As, in the sense of having borne you, she is?

"And what kind of sexual code do these people have? It can't, I would think, be much like ours. Nor is there any reason it should be.

"But who is responsible for raising the larva and child? Its pseudo-mother? Or does the lover share in the duties? And what about property and inheritance laws? And, and . . ."

Helplessly, he looked at Martia.

Fondly stroking the head of the larva, she returned his stare.

Lane shook his head.

"I was wrong. Eeltau and Terran couldn't meet on a friendly basis. My people would react to yours as to disgusting vermin. Their deepest prejudices would be aroused, their strongest taboos would be violated. They could not learn to live with you or consider you even faintly human.

"And as far as that goes, could you live with us? Wasn't the sight of me naked a shock? Is that reaction a part of why you don't make contact with us?"

Martia put the larva down and stood up and walked over to him and kissed the tips of his fingers. Lane, though he had to fight against visibly flinching, took her fingers and kissed them. Softly, he said to her, "Yet . . . individuals could learn to respect each other, to have affection for each other. And masses are made of individuals."

He lay back on the bed. The grogginess, pushed aside for a while by excitement, was coming back. He couldn't fight off sleep much longer.

"Fine noble talk," he murmured. "But it means nothing. The Eeltau don't think they should deal with us. And we are, unknowingly, pushing out towards them. What will happen when we are ready to make the interstellar jump? War? Or will they be afraid to let us advance even to that point and destroy us before then. After all, one cobalt bomb."

He looked again at Martia, at the not-quite-human yet beautiful face, the smooth skin of the chest, abdomen, and loins, innocent of nipple, navel, or labia. From far off she had come, from a possibly terrifying place across terrifying distances. About her, however, there was little that was terrifying and much that was warm, generous, companionable, attractive. . . .

He turned over so his back was to her, and he pounded his fist against the bed.

"Oh dear God why couldn't it be so?"

A long time he lay there, his face pressed into the mattress. Something had happened; the overpowering fatigue was gone; his body had drawn strength from some reservoir. Realizing this, he sat up and beckoned to Martia, smiling at the same time.

She rose slowly and started to walk to him, but he signalled that she should bring the larva with her. At first, she looked puzzled. Then her expression cleared, to be replaced by understanding. Smiling delightedly, she walked to him, and though he knew it must be a trick of his imagination, it seemed to him that she swayed her hips as a woman would.

She halted in front of him and then stooped to kiss him full on the lips. Her eyes were closed.

He hesitated for a fraction of a second. She—no, it, he told himself—looked so trusting, so loving, so womanly, that he could not do it.

He brought the edge of his palm hard against the side of her neck.

She crumpled forward against him, her face sliding into his chest. Lane caught her under the armpits and laid her face down on the bed. The larva, which had fallen from her hand to the floor, was writhing about as if hurt. Lane picked it up by its tail and, in a frenzy that owed its violence to the fear he might not be able to do it, snapped it like a whip. There was a crack as the head smashed into the floor, and blood spurted from its eyes and mouth. Lane placed his heel on the head and stepped down until there was a flat mess beneath his foot.

Then, quickly . . . , he ran to the cabinet. Snatching a narrow towel out of it, he ran back and gagged her. After that he tied her hands behind her back with the rope.

"Now, you bitch!" he panted. "We'll see who comes out ahead! You would do that with me, would you! You deserve this; your monster deserves to die!"

Furiously he began packing. In fifteen minutes he had the suits, helmets, tanks, and food rolled into two bundles. He searched for the weapon she had talked about and found something that might conceivably be it. It had a butt that fitted to his hand, a dial that might be a rheostat for controlling degrees of intensity of whatever it shot, and a bulb at the end. The bulb, he hoped, expelled the stunning and killing energy. Of course, he might be wrong. It could be fashioned for an entirely different purpose.

Martia had regained consciousness. She sat on the edge of the bed, her shoulders hunched, her head drooping, tears running down her cheeks and into the towel around her mouth. Her wide eyes were focused on the smashed worm by her feet.

Roughly, Lane seized her shoulder and pulled her upright. She gazed wildly at him, and he gave her a little shove. He felt sick within him, knowing that he had killed the larva when he did not have to do so and that he was handling her so violently because he was afraid, not of her, but of himself. If he had been disgusted because she had fallen into the trap he set for her, he was so because he, too, beneath his disgust, had wanted to commit that act of love. Commit, he thought, was the right word. It contained criminal implications.

Martia whirled around, almost losing her balance because of her tied hands. Her face worked, and sounds burst from the gag.

"Shut up!" he howled, pushing her again. She went sprawling and only saved herself from falling on her face by dropping on her knees. Once more, he pulled her to her feet, noting as he did so that her knees were skinned. The sight of the blood instead of softening him, enraged him even more.

"Behave yourself, or you'll get worse!" he snarled.

She gave him one more questioning look, threw back her head, and made a strange strangling sound. Immediately, her face took on a bluish tinge. A second later, she fell heavily on the floor.

Alarmed, he turned her over. She was choking to death.

He tore off the gag and reached into her mouth and grabbed the root of her tongue. It slipped away and he seized it again, only to have it slide away as if it were a live animal that defied him.

Then he had pulled her tongue out of her throat; she had swallowed it in an effort to kill herself. . . .

At that moment, hearing an unfamiliar noise, he looked up. There were two Eeltau in pressure suits standing there, and another crawling out of the tunnel. Each had a bulb-tipped handgun in her hand.

Desperately, Lane snatched at the weapon he carried in his belt. With his left hand he twisted the rheostat on the side of the barrel, hoping this would turn it on full force. Then he raised the bulb towards the group. . . .

He woke flat on his back, clad in his suit, except for the helmet, and strapped to a stretcher. His body was helpless, but he could turn his head. He did so, and saw many Eeltau dismantling the room. The one who had stunned him with her gun before he could fire was standing by him.

She spoke in English that held only a trace of foreign accent. "Settle down, Mr. Lane. You're in for a long ride. You'll be more comfortably situated once we're in our ship."

He opened his mouth to ask her how she knew his name but closed it when he realized she must have read the entries in the log at the base. And it was to be expected that some Eeltau would be trained in Earth languages. For over a century their sentinel spaceships had been tuning in to radio and TV.

It was then that Martia spoke to the captain. Her face was wild and reddened with weeping and marks where she had fallen. The interpreter said to Lane, "Mahrseeya asks you to tell her why you killed her . . . baby. She cannot understand why you thought you had to do so."

"I cannot answer," said Lane. His head felt very light, almost as if it were a balloon expanding. And the room began slowly to turn around.

"I will tell her why," answered the interpreter. "I will tell her that it is the nature of the beast."

"That is not so!" cried Lane. "I am no vicious beast. I did what I did because I had to! I could not accept her love and still remain a man! Not the kind of man. . . ."

"Mahrseeya," said the interpreter, "will pray that you be forgiven the murder of her child and that you will someday, under our teaching, be unable to do such a thing. She herself, though she is stricken with grief for her dead baby, forgives you. She hopes the time will come when you will regard her as a—sister. She thinks there is some good in you."

Lane clenched his teeth together and bit the end of his tongue until it bled while they put his helmet on. He did not dare to try to talk, for that would have meant he would scream and scream. He felt as if something had been planted in him and had broken its shell and was growing into something like a worm. It was eating him, and what would happen before it devoured all of him he did not know.

3 Can You Spare an Identity?

There is a broad distinction that cuts through almost all thinking about a fundamental understanding of the basic causal structure (important variables) of social life. It is the distinction between genetic and environmental causes of behavior, between the notion of a *primarily* genetically determined or a primarily socially determined "nature of man." For example, to what extent is the displayed intelligence of a "biologically normal"[1] individual at, say, age 12 attributable to a genetic factor or controlled by education and social experience during an individual's lifetime? Is there a maternal "instinct" that substantially determines the limits of a woman's role in social life, or is mothering largely a socially controlled and socially taught set of activities? Are there significant genetic predispositions that determine an individual's "personality" (e.g., are XYY males biologically biased toward violence)?

Though genetic and instinct arguments have proven to be not very helpful in understanding the social behavior of humans such arguments have not been completely abandoned. I suspect that this is largely due to the fact that there are obviously some human physical characteristics that are under genetic control; hence, the belief that *important* aspects of an individual's social behavior may also be genetically determined is sustained by analogy to the physical case.

There is a second level at which a variety of the interior-exterior controversy is found. This has to do with the extent to which a person's observable behavior is caused by powerful interior forces (usually called personality) and so can be said to be primarily determined by factors that are constants attached to the individual and are relatively permanent. The alternative formulation is that behavior is primarily under social control—that is, people are responding to the social stimuli they find within their environments and so will change as their environments change. Assertions that personality or heterosexual or homosexual sexual preference is determined by the time an individual reaches age two are examples of arguments that tend in the direction of the interior, fixed-state type. The argument that a behavior characteristic such as drug addiction is due to a combination of the reinforcing effects of drugs (pain relief or pleasure) and the social situation in which a potential addict finds himself rather than due to a "character defect" is an example of a primarily exterior causality theory of human behavior.

Most sociological thinking about the causes of an individual's behavior tends in the direction of external causality arguments. From this perspective the concept of

[1]By biologically normal I mean not having organic brain damage, not having been protein starved in infancy or early childhood etc.

role becomes a key element in understanding how society continually affects an individual's behavior and identity. In every society children are socialized to the norms—customs and patterns of life organization that are promoted by the traditions of the society into which they are born. Childhood may, therefore, be conceptualized as the first phase in the preparation of individuals to perform adult roles. All social life may, in the same manner, be conceptualized as the playing out of parts, learned as a child from these traditions and customs. It is as if individuals are handed a rough script by their societies and either permitted a choice or are assigned to parts in the play. From this point of view, an individual's unique identity can only be displayed through his or her interpretation of whatever character is to be portrayed. The script defines a good deal about the character's position in the play and specifies much about his activities. Although the actor is limited by these constraints, he has some freedom to choose the style with which the character goes about meeting the requirements of the script.

From a sociological perspective, it is difficult to conceptualize an individual as having an identity that is expressed independently of his social roles and one that is sustained out of interaction with others. That is, assume that an individual's personal style can only be inferred from the manner in which his interpretation of some character in the play differs from the manner in which others portray the same character. In this sense, individuality is variation in role performance and variability among the roles a person is able to perform. I can illustrate what I mean as follows: Whenever I find myself coming into contact with people who function in a role segregated social environment, I am always struck initially by the apparent similarity of the individuals I meet. By role segregated environment, I mean, groups such as professors living in a university dominated community, middle management executives who live in a middle class suburb, residents of an isolated farm community or members of a sect. On first contact, it seems that the people one meets are all interested in the same things and resemble one another to a remarkable degree. As one becomes more knowledgeable about the constraints placed on them by the requirements of their particular roles, one begins to perceive differences in their conduct that had previously been missed. As one becomes able to discriminate between what their roles require and the actions that are freely chosen (the individual's interpretation of his assigned character) one can begin to detect the outlines of the different identities of different people playing out simple roles. One also discovers that people play out a variety of different roles and that different identities are thereby supported.

If what I have argued above has any truth to it, the following statement should also be true. If you wish to know something of what you will be like at a point, say ten years in the future, observe a sample of individuals who are about ten years older than you and who currently occupy statuses with respect to major life activities such as occupation, marriage, and parenthood that you expect to occupy ten years from now. The chances are that you will appear to others seeing you ten years from now much as these individuals appear to you at present. Naturally, you will differ in many ways from any particular individual that you might observe just as any two of those persons you have observed differ from one another. It is likely, however, that you will share with them many of the characteristics of life organization and therefore identity that are common to the group you choose. The reason for this is that you will share with these individuals those role constraints that are attached to the statuses you expect to have in common with them. If you let things take their "natural" course, the chances are that what you observe to be true of the group you study will likely be true of you in the future.

The factor that makes role important for the shaping of identity is that the persons with whom one interacts sanction (reward or punish) one's behavior for adequate or inadequate and appropriate or inappropriate role performance. That is, they shape one's behavior much as an audience subtly shapes the behavior of an actor through responses such as laughter, gasps, appropriate silence and applause. Normally, when the *performance* is good, the audience behaves as it is supposed to and thereby rewards the actor. If *audiences* are good and discriminate in their responses to strengths and weaknesses in the actor's performance, they will shape and if not improve, certainly modify an actor's performance over time. In this way, an actor is affected by the quality of his audience. Since people generally share conceptions of appropriate behavior in normal social roles they are likely to be able to discriminate in their sanctioning and thereby affect the performer.

Consider the following example of identity shaping. It is often asserted that appropriate sex role behavior for women in American society is that they be relatively submissive and unassertive. This statement translates to the assertion that in American society women are positively reinforced for these behaviors and negatively reinforced for their opposites by those (both men and women) with whom they interact. We will call this the structure of support for traditional woman's identity. Research in behavior modification has shown that it is relatively easy to change reinforcements in controlled interaction and change the degree to which previously unassertive women make their wishes and ideas known. If, however, these same women return to traditional role relations in which they are merely not *approved* for their new behaviors and perhaps even mildly punished for no longer behaving like women with traditional identities, they are likely to either find their old identities being reborn or to seek new social situations in which their new identities are supported by those with whom they interact. The general presumption is that in order for behavior to continue to be displayed it is necessary for it to be socially supported.

One might argue that if an individual's behavior is largely determined by the reactions of others, that the reactions of others is largely determined by prevailing notions of acceptable social performance and that these controls are subtly and pervasively applied in all societies, then the individual is profoundly under social control and dependent upon social support. If this is true, and it probably is, then the choice of one's major social roles is in effect the only real choice an individual can make and, once having made it, relatively little room remains for interpretation of the role. An extreme case of both identity control and wise decision making given this fact of life is given by Kurt Vonnegut in his story "Who Am I This Time?"

Who Am I This Time?

KURT VONNEGUT

The North Crawford Mask and Wig Club, an amateur theatrical society I belong to, voted to do Tennessee Williams' *A Streetcar Named Desire* for the spring play. Doris Sawyer, who always directs, said she couldn't direct this time because her mother was so sick. And she said the club ought to develop some other directors anyway, because she couldn't live forever, even though she'd made it safely to seventy-four.

So I got stuck with the directing job, even though the only thing I'd ever directed before was the installation of combination aluminum storm windows and screens I'd sold. That's what I am, a salesman of storm windows and doors, and here and there a bathtub enclosure. As far as acting goes, the highest rank I ever held on stage was either butler or policeman, whichever's higher.

I made a lot of conditions before I took the directing job, and the biggest one was that Harry Nash, the only real actor the club has, had to take the Marlon Brando part in the play. To give you an idea of how versatile Harry is, inside of one year he was Captain Queeg in *The Caine Mutiny Court Martial,* then Abe Lincoln in *Abe Lincoln in Illinois* and then the young architect in *The Moon is Blue.* The year after that, Harry Nash was Henry the Eighth in *Anne of the Thousand Days* and Doc in *Come Back Little Sheba,* and I was after him for Marlon Brando in *A Streetcar Named Desire.* Harry wasn't at the meeting to say whether he'd take the part or not. He never came to meetings. He was too shy. He didn't stay away from meetings because he had something else to do. He wasn't married, didn't go out with women—didn't have any close men friends either. He stayed away from all kinds of gatherings because he never could think of anything to say or do without a script.

So I had to go down to Miller's Hardware Store, where Harry was a clerk, the next day and ask him if he'd take the part. I stopped off at the telephone company to complain about a bill I'd gotten for a call to Honolulu, I'd never called Honolulu in my life.

And there was this beautiful girl I'd never seen before behind the counter at the phone company, and she explained that the company had put in an automatic billing machine and that the machine didn't have all the bugs out of it yet. It made mistakes. "Not only did I not call Honolulu," I told her, "I don't think anybody in North Crawford ever has or will."

So she took the charge off the bill, and I asked her if she was from around North Crawford. She said no. She said she just came with the new billing machine to teach local girls how to take care of it. After that, she said, she would go with some other machine to someplace else. "Well," I said, "as long as people have to come along with the machines, I guess we're all right."

"What?" she said.

"When machines start delivering themselves," I said, "I guess that's when the people better start really worrying."

"Oh," she said. She didn't seem very interested in that subject, and I wondered if she was interested in anything. She seemed kind of numb, almost a machine herself, an automatic phone-company politeness machine.

"How long will you be in town here?" I asked her.

"I stay in each town eight weeks, sir," she said. She had pretty blue eyes, but there sure wasn't much hope or curiosity in them. She told me she had been going from town to town like that for two years, always a stranger.

And I got it in my head that she might make a good Stella for the play. Stella was the wife of the Marlon Brando character, the wife of the character I wanted Harry Nash to play. So I told her where and when we were going to hold tryouts, and said the club would be very happy if she'd come.

She looked surprised, and she warmed up a little. "You know," she said, "that's the first time anybody ever asked me to participate in any community thing."

"Well," I said, "there isn't any other way to get to know a lot of nice people faster than to be in a play with 'em."

She said her name was Helene Shaw. She said she might just surprise me—and herself. She said she just might come.

You would think that North Crawford would be fed up with Harry Nash in plays after all the plays he'd been in. But the fact was that North Crawford probably could have gone on enjoying Harry forever, because he was never Harry on stage. When the maroon curtain went up on the stage in the gymnasium of the Consolidated Junior-Senior High School, Harry, body and soul, was exactly what the script and the director told him to be.

Somebody said one time that Harry ought to go to a psychiatrist so he could be something important and colorful in real life, too—so he could get married anyway, and maybe get a better job than just clerking in Miller's Hardware Store for fifty dollars a week. But I don't know what a psychiatrist could have turned up about him that the town didn't already know. The trouble with Harry was he'd been left on the doorstep of the Unitarian Church when he was a baby, and he never did find out who his parents were.

When I told him there in Miller's that I'd been appointed director, that I wanted him in my play, he said what he always said to anybody who asked him to be in a play—and it was kind of sad, if you think about it.

"Who am I this time?" he said.

So I held the tryouts where they're always held—in the meeting room on the second floor of the North Crawford Public Library. Doris Sawyer, the woman who usually directs, came to give me the benefit of all her experience. The two of us sat in state upstairs, while the people who wanted parts waited below. We called them upstairs one by one.

Harry Nash came to the tryouts, even though it was a waste of time. I guess he wanted to get that little bit more acting in.

For Harry's pleasure, and our pleasure, too, we had him read from the scene where he beats up his wife. It was a play in itself, the way Harry did it, and Tennessee Williams hadn't written it all either. Tennessee Williams didn't write the part, for instance, where Harry, who weighs about one hundred forty-five, who's about five feet eight inches tall, added fifty pounds to his weight and four inches to his height by just picking up a playbook. He had a short little double-breasted bellows-back grade-school graduation suit coat on and a dinky little red tie with a horsehead on it. He took off the coat and tie, opened his collar, then turned his back to Doris and me, getting up steam for the part. There was a great big rip in the back of his shirt, and it looked like a fairly new shirt too. He'd ripped it on purpose, so he could be that much more like Marlon Brando, right from the first.

When he faced us again, he was huge and handsome and conceited and cruel. Doris read the part of Stella, the wife, and Harry bullied that old, old lady into believing that she was a sweet, pregnant girl married to a sexy gorilla who was going to beat her brains out. She had me believing it too. And I read the lines of Blanche, her sister in the play, and darned if Harry didn't scare me into feeling like a drunk and faded Southern belle.

And then, while Doris and I were getting over our emotional experiences, like people coming out from under ether, Harry put down the playbook, put on his coat and tie, and turned into the pale hardware-store clerk again.

"Was—was that all right?" he said, and he seemed pretty sure he wouldn't get the part.

"Well," I said, "for a first reading, that wasn't too bad."

"Is there a chance I'll get the part?" he said. I don't know why he always had to pretend there was some doubt about his getting a part, but he did.

"I think we can safely say we're leaning powerfully in your direction," I told him.

He was very pleased. "Thanks! Thanks a lot!" he said, and he shook my hand.

"Is there a pretty new girl downstairs?" I said, meaning Helene Shaw.

"I didn't notice," said Harry.

It turned out that Helene Shaw *had* come for the tryouts, and Doris and I had our hearts broken. We thought the North Crawford Mask and Wig Club was finally going to put a really good-looking, really young girl on stage, instead of one of the beat-up forty-year-old women we generally have to palm off as girls.

But Helene Shaw couldn't act for sour apples. No matter what we gave her to read, she was the same girl with the same smile for anybody who had a complaint about his phone bill.

Doris tried to coach her some, to make her understand that Stella in the play was a very passionate girl who loved a gorilla because she needed a gorilla. But Helene just read the lines the same way again. I don't think a volcano could have stirred her up enough to say, "Oo."

"Dear," said Doris, "I'm going to ask you a personal question."

"All right," said Helene.

"Have you ever been in love?" said Doris. "The reason I ask," she said, "remembering some old love might help you put more warmth in your acting."

Helene frowned and thought hard. "Well," she said, "I travel a lot, you know. And practically all the men in the different companies I visit are married and I never stay anyplace long enough to know many people who aren't."

"What about school?" said Doris. "What about puppy love and all the other kinds of love in school?"

So Helene thought hard about that, and then she said, "Even in school I was always moving around a lot. My father was a construction worker, following jobs around, so I was always saying hello or good-by to someplace, without anything in between."

"Um," said Doris.

"Would movie stars count?" said Helene. "I don't mean in real life. I never knew any. I just mean up on the screen."

Doris looked at me and rolled her eyes. "I guess that's love of a kind," she said.

And then Helene got a little enthusiastic. "I used to sit through movies over and over again," she said, "and pretend I was married to whoever the man movie star was. They were the only people who came with us. No matter where we moved, movie stars were there."

"Uh huh," said Doris.

"Well, thank you, Miss Shaw," I said. "You go downstairs and wait with the rest. We'll let you know.

So we tried to find another Stella. And there just wasn't one, not one woman in the club with the dew still on her. "All we've got are Blanches," I said, meaning all we had were faded women who could play the part of Blanche, Stella's faded sister. "That's life, I guess—twenty Blanches to one Stella."

"And when you find a Stella," said Doris, "it turns out she doesn't know what love is."

Doris and I decided there was one last thing we could try. We could get Harry Nash to play a scene along with Helene. "He just might make her bubble the least little bit," I said.

"That girl hasn't got a bubble in her," said Doris.

So we called down the stairs for Helene to come back on up, and we told somebody to go find Harry. Harry never sat with the rest of the people at tryouts—or at rehearsals either. The minute he didn't have a part to play, he'd disappear into some hiding place where he could hear people call him, but where he couldn't be seen. At tryouts in the library he generally hid in the reference room, passing the time looking at flags of different countries in the front of the dictionary.

Helene came back upstairs, and we were very sorry and surprised to see that she'd been crying.

"Oh, dear," said Doris. "Oh, my—now what on earth's the trouble, dear?"

"I was terrible, wasn't I?" said Helene, hanging her head.

Doris said the only thing anybody can say in an amateur theatrical society when somebody cries. She said, "Why, no dear—you were marvelous."

"No, I wasn't," said Helene. "I'm a walking icebox, and I know it."

"Nobody could look at you and say that," said Doris.

"When they get to know me, they can say it," said Helene. "When people get to know me, that's what they *do* say." Her tears got worse. "I don't want to be the way I am," she said. "I just can't help it, living the way I've lived all my life. The only experiences I've had have been in crazy dreams of movie stars. When I meet somebody nice in real life, I feel as though I were in some kind of big bottle, as though I couldn't touch that person, no matter how hard I tried." And Helene pushed on air as though it were a big bottle all around her.

"You ask me if I've ever been in love," she said to Doris. "No—but I want to be. I know what this play's about. I know what Stella's supposed to feel and why she feels it. I—I—I—" she said, and her tears wouldn't let her go on.

"You what, dear?" said Doris gently.

"I—" said Helene, and she pushed on the imaginary bottle again. "I just don't know how to begin," she said.

There was heavy clumping on the library stairs. It sounded like a deep-sea diver coming upstairs in his lead shoes. It was Harry Nash, turning himself into Marlon Brando. In he came, practically dragging his knuckles on the floor. And he was so much in character that the sight of a weeping woman made him sneer.

"Harry," I said, "I'd like you to meet Helene Shaw. Helene—this is Harry Nash. If you get the part of Stella, he'll be your husband in the play." Harry didn't offer to shake hands. He put his hands in his pockets, and he hunched over, and he looked her up and down, gave her looks that left her naked. Her tears stopped right then and there.

"I wonder if you two would play the fight scene," I said, "and then the reunion scene right after it."

"Sure," said Harry, his eyes still on her. Those eyes burned up clothes faster than she could put them on. "Sure," he said, "if Stell's game."

"What?" said Helene. She'd turned the color of cranberry juice.

"Stell—Stella," said Harry. "That's you. Stell's my wife."

I handed the two of them playbooks. Harry snatched his from me without a word of thanks. Helene's hands weren't working very well, and I had to kind of mold them around the book.

"I'll want something I can throw," said Harry.

"What?" I said.

"There's one place where I throw a radio out a window," said Harry. "What can I throw?"

So I said an iron paperweight was the radio, and I opened the window wide. Helene Shaw looked scared to death.

"Where you want us to start?" said Harry, and he rolled his shoulders like a prizefighter warming up.

"Start a few lines back from where you throw the radio out the window," I said.

"O.K., O.K.," said Harry, warming up, warming up. He scanned the stage directions. "Let's see," he said, "after I throw the radio, she runs off stage, and I chase her, and I sock her one."

"Right," I said.

"O.K., baby," Harry said to Helene, his eyelids drooping. What was about to happen was wilder than the chariot race in *Ben Hur*. "On your mark," said Harry. "Get ready, baby. Go!"

When the scene was over, Helene Shaw was as hot as a hod carrier, as limp as an eel. She sat down with her mouth open and her head hanging to one side. She wasn't in any bottle any more. There wasn't any bottle to hold her up and keep her safe and clean. The bottle was gone.

"Do I get the part or don't I?" Harry snarled at me.

"You'll do," I said.

"You said a mouthful!" he said. "I'll be going now. . . . See you around, Stella," he said to Helene, and he left. He slammed the door behind him.

"Helene?" I said. "Miss Shaw?"

"Mf?" she said.

"The part of Stella is yours," I said "You were great!"

"I was?" she said.

"I had no idea you had that much fire in you, dear," Doris said to her.

"Fire?" said Helene. She didn't know if she was afoot or on horseback.

"Skyrockets! Pinwheels! Roman candles!" said Doris.

"Mf," said Helene. And that was all she said. She looked as though she were going to sit in the chair with her mouth open forever.

"Stella," I said.

"Huh?" she said.

"You have my permission to go."

So we started having rehearsals four nights a week on the stage of the Consolidated School. And Harry and Helene set such a pace that everybody in the production was half crazy with excitement and exhaustion before we'd rehearsed four times. Usually a director has to beg people to learn their lines, but I had no such trouble. Harry and Helene were working so well together that everybody else in the cast regarded it as a duty and an honor and a pleasure to support them.

I was certainly lucky—or thought I was. Things were going so well, so hot and heavy, so early in the game that I had to say to Harry and Helene after one love scene, "Hold a little something back for the actual performance, would you please? You'll burn yourselves out."

I said that at the fourth or fifth rehearsal, and Lydia Miller, who was playing Blanche, the faded sister, was sitting next to me in the audience. In real life, she's the wife of Verne Miller. Verne owns Miller's Hardware Store. Verne was Harry's boss.

"Lydia," I said to her, "have we got a play or have we got a play?"

"Yes," she said, "you've got a play, all right." She made it sound as though I'd committed some kind of crime, done something just terrible. "You should be very proud of yourself."

"What do you mean by that?" I said.

Before Lydia could answer, Harry yelled at me from the stage, asked if I was through with him, asked if he could go home. I told him he could and, still Marlon Brando, he left, kicking furniture out of his way and slamming doors. Helene was left all alone on the stage, sitting on a couch with the same gaga look she'd had after the tryouts. That girl was drained.

I turned to Lydia again and I said, "Well—until now, I thought I had every reason to be happy and proud. Is there something going on I don't know about?"

"Do you know that girl's in love with Harry?" said Lydia.

"In the play?" I said.

"What play?" said Lydia. "There isn't any play going on now, and look at her up there." She gave a sad cackle. "You aren't directing this play."

"Who is?" I said.

"Mother Nature at her worst," said Lydia. "And think what it's going to do to that girl when she discovers what Harry really is." She corrected herself. "What Harry really isn't," she said.

I didn't do anything about it, because I didn't figure it was any of my business. I heard Lydia try to do something about it, but she didn't get very far.

"You know," Lydia said to Helene one night, "I once played Ann Rutledge, and Harry was Abraham Lincoln."

Helene clapped her hands. "That must have been heaven!" she said.

"It was, in a way," said Lydia. "Sometimes I'd get so worked up, I'd love Harry the way I'd love Abraham Lincoln. I'd have to come back to earth and remind myself that he wasn't ever going to free the slaves, that he was just a clerk in my husband's hardware store."

"He's the most marvelous man I ever met," said Helene.

"Of course, one thing you have to get set for, when you're in a play with Harry," said Lydia, "is what happens after the last performance."

"What are you talking about?" said Helene.

"Once the show's over," said Lydia, "whatever you thought Harry was just evaporates into thin air."

"I don't believe it," said Helene.

"I admit it's hard to believe," said Lydia.

Then Helene got a little sore. "Anyway, why tell me about it?" she said. "Even if it is true, what do I care?"

"I—I don't know," said Lydia, backing away. "I—I just thought you might find it interesting."

"Well, I don't," said Helene.

And Lydia slunk away, felling about as frowzy and unloved as she was supposed to feel in the play. After that nobody said anything more to Helene to warn her about Harry, not even when word got around that she'd told the telephone company that she didn't want to be moved around anymore, that she wanted to stay in North Crawford.

So the time finally came to put on the play. We ran it for three nights—Thursday, Friday, and Saturday—and we murdered those audiences. They believed every word that was said on stage, and when the maroon curtain came down they were ready to go to the nut house along with Blanche, the faded sister.

On Thursday night the other girls at the telephone company sent Helene a dozen red roses. When Helene and Harry were taking a curtain call together, I passed the roses over the footlights to her. She came forward for them, took one rose from the bouquet to give to Harry. But when she turned to give Harry the rose in front of everybody, Harry was gone. The curtain came down on that extra little scene—that girl offering a rose to nothing and nobody.

I went backstage, and I found her still holding that one rose. She'd put the rest of the bouquet aside. There were tears in her eyes. "What did I do wrong?" she said to me. "Did I insult him some way?"

"No," I said. "He always does that after a performance. The minute it's over, he clears out as fast as he can."

"And tomorrow he'll disappear again?"

"Without even taking off his makeup."

"And Saturday?" she said. "He'll stay for the cast party on Saturday, won't he?"

"Harry never goes to parties," I said. "When the curtain comes down on Saturday, that's the last anybody will see of him till he goes to work on Monday."

"How sad," she said.

Helene's performance on Friday night wasn't nearly so good as Thursday's. She seemed to be thinking about other things. She watched Harry take off after curtain call. She didn't say a word.

On Saturday she put on the best performance yet. Ordinarily it was Harry who set the pace. But on Saturday Harry had to work to keep up with Helene.

When the curtain came down on the final curtain call, Harry wanted to get away, but he couldn't. Helene wouldn't let go his hand. The rest of the cast and the stage crew and a lot of well-wishers from the audience were all standing around Harry and Helene, and Harry was trying to get his hand back.

"Well," he said, "I've got to go."

"Where?" she said.

"Oh," he said, "home."

"Won't you please take me to the cast party?" she said.

He got very red. "I'm afraid I'm not much on parties," he said. All the Marlon Brando in him was gone. He was tongue-tied, he was scared, he was shy—he was everything Harry was famous for being between plays.

"All right," she said. "I'll let you go—if you promise me one thing."

"What's that?" he said, and I thought he would jump out a window if she let go of him then.

"I want you to promise to stay here until I get you your present," she said.

"Present?" he said, getting even more panicky.

"Promise?" she said.

He promised. It was the only way he could get his hand back. And he stood there miserably while Helene went down to the ladies' dressing room for the present. While he waited, a lot of people congratulated him on being such a fine actor. But congratulations never made him happy. He just wanted to get away.

Helene came back with the present. It turned out to be a little blue book with a big red ribbon for a place marker. It was a copy of *Romeo and Juliet.* Harry was very embarrassed. It was all he could do to say "Thank you."

"The marker marks my favorite scene," said Helene.

"Um," said Harry.

"Don't you want to see what my favorite scene is?" she said.

So Harry had to open the book to the red ribbon.

Helene got close to him, and read a line of Juliet's. "'How cam'st thou hither, tell me, and wherefore?'" she read. "'The orchard walls are high and hard to climb, and the place death, considering who thou art, if any of my kinsmen find thee here.'" She pointed to the next line. "Now, look what Romeo says," she said.

"Um," said Harry.

"Read what Romeo says," said Helene.

Harry cleared his throat. He didn't want to read the line, but he had to. "'With love's light wings did I o'erperch these walls,'" he read out loud in his everyday voice. But then a change came over him. "'For stony limits cannot hold love out,'" he read, and he straightened up, and eight years dropped away from him, and he was brave and gay. "'And what love can do, that dares love attempt,'" he read, "'therefore thy kinsmen are no let to me.'"

"'If they do see thee they will murther thee,'" said Helene, and she started him walking toward the wings.

"'Alack!'" said Harry, "'there lies more peril in thine eye than twenty of their swords.'" Helene led him toward the backstage exit. "'Look thou but sweet,'" said Harry, "'and I am proof against their enmity.'"

"'I would not for the world they saw thee here,'" said Helene, and that was the last we heard. The two of them were out the door and gone.

They never did show up at the cast party. One week later they were married.

They seem very happy, although they're kind of strange from time to time, depending on which play they're reading to each other at the time.

I dropped into the phone company office the other day, on account of the billing machine was making dumb mistakes again. I asked her what plays she and Harry'd been reading lately.

"In the past week," she said, "I've been married to Othello, been loved by Faust and been kidnapped by Paris. Wouldn't you say I was the luckiest girl in town?"

I said I thought so, and I told her most of the women in town thought so too.

"They had their chance," she said.

"Most of 'em couldn't stand the excitement," I said. And I told her I'd been asked to direct another play. I asked if she and Harry would be available for the cast. She gave me a big smile and said, "Who are we this time?"

4 On the Effects of Improved Communication

One aspect of this story and the society it describes is the total absence of competition and conflict among members of the society. The implicit assumption of the story is that if people understood one another's feelings and perspectives, conflict would not occur. This story takes as a given a society that develops under this communication condition and tacitly accounts for the absence of conflict and competition as due to this cause. The sense of brotherhood felt between members of the society and the sense of self-satisfaction experienced by members of the society are attributed to the consequences of complete openness with respect to reactions by others to an individual. Social control operates perfectly because an individual has perfect access to the images others hold of him.

It is interesting to speculate on the consequences for social development of conditions of simultaneously having near "perfect communication" (at least a rule that one will verbalize one's responses, feelings, and thoughts about another's actions) and no political or economic competition or conflict within the society. It is perhaps even more interesting to consider what might happen in a world in which social conflict and value differences do exist, (as they do in real as opposed to romantic utopian worlds and are assumed in non-romantic utopian conceptions) and complete responsiveness is the norm. Even in the society Bellamy describes in the following story, those who are "less genially constituted than others" are so pained by knowledge of the reactions of others to them that they seek self-isolation. I suspect that in the real world those with whom one differs too frequently come thereby to be perceived as "less genially constituted" and that the open display would turn into intense social conflict with the socially powerful, either in number or position, causing the less powerful to either flee or abandon their positions.

In this case the mechanism of social control Bellamy postulates ceases to work effectively. If people constantly displayed reactions to one another that were caused by arbitrary and/or irreconcilable differences (such as strongly held religious beliefs) or an injustice believed to exist by one party and rejected by another (such as perceived unjust payment for performance of work) hostilities would probably tend to increase rather than decrease. Differences that might otherwise be ignored would be expressed and probably increased.

The fact that Bellamy's world presumes no meaningful differences between people, no reality based sources of conflict that are socially regulated, makes his world a romantic utopian vision rather than a social utopian one. If in reading this story you introduce the idea of an encounter group and have it function in the same manner that mind reading does in Bellamy's society (that is, to give each person an awareness of the position of every other person and a mirror to view the self) the story would become more interesting. One may then at least speculate on the conduct of Bellamy's society by imagining a group who's control is based on interpersonal communication or reputation rather than political procedures and explicit delineation of rights. I suspect that as in Bellamy's world if there is nothing about which people have serious disagreements an encounter polity would work. However, if there were meaningful social issues to be dealt with (such as unequal access to scarce and highly valued goods) and reasoned differences of position separating people, then the encounter polity would either be futile, or the majority would destroy the weaker position.

To Whom This May Come

EDWARD BELLAMY

It is now about a year since I took passage at Calcutta in the ship Adelaide for New York. We had baffling weather till New Amsterdam Island was sighted, where we took a new point of departure. Three days later, a terrible gale struck us. Four days we flew before it, whither, no one knew, for neither sun, moon, nor stars were at any time visible, and we could take no observation. Toward midnight of the fourth day, the glare of lightning revealed the Adelaide in a hopeless position, close in upon a low-lying shore, and driving straight toward it. All around and astern far out to sea was such a maze of rocks and shoals that it was a miracle we had come so far. Presently the ship struck, and almost instantly went to pieces, so great was the violence of the sea. I gave myself up for lost, and was indeed already past the worst of drowning, when I was recalled to consciousness by being thrown with a tremendous shock upon the beach. I had just strength enough to drag myself above the reach of the waves, and then I fell down and knew no more.

When I awoke, the storm was over. The sun, already halfway up the sky, had dried my clothing, and renewed the vigor of my bruised and aching limbs. On sea or shore I saw no vestige of my ship or my companions, of whom I appeared the sole survivor. I was not, however, alone. A group of persons, apparently the inhabitants of the country, stood near, observing me with looks of friendliness which at once freed me from apprehension as to my treatment at their hands. They were white and handsome people, evidently of a high order of civilization, though I recognized in them the traits of no race with which I was familiar.

Seeing that it was evidently their idea of etiquette to leave it to strangers to open conversation, I addressed them in English, but failed to elicit any response beyond deprecating smiles. I then accosted them successively in the French, German, Italian, Spanish, Dutch, and Portuguese tongues, but with no better results. I began to be very much puzzled as to what could possibly be the nationality of a white and evidently civilized race to which no one of the tongues of the great seafaring nations was intelligible. The oddest thing of all was the unbroken silence with which they contemplated my efforts to open communication with them. It was as if they were agreed not to give me a clue to their language by even a whisper; for while they regarded one another with looks of smiling intelligence, they did not once open their lips. But if this behavior suggested that they were amusing themselves at my expense, that presumption was negatived by the unmistakable friendliness and sympathy which their whole bearing expressed.

A most extraordinary conjecture occurred to me. Could it be that these strange people were dumb? Such a freak of nature as an entire race thus afflicted had never indeed been heard of, but who could say what wonders the unexplored vasts of the great Southern Ocean might thus far have hid from human ken? Now, among the scraps of useless information which lumbered my mind was an acquaintance with the deaf-and-dumb alphabet, and forthwith I began to spell out with my fingers some of the phrases I had already uttered to so little effect. My resort to the sign language overcame the last remnant of gravity in the already profusely smiling group. The small boys now rolled on the ground in convulsions of mirth, while the grave and reverend seniors, who had hitherto kept them in check, were fain momentarily to avert their faces, and I could see their bodies shaking with laughter. The greatest clown in the world never received a more flattering tribute to his powers to amuse than had been called forth by mine to make myself understood. Naturally, however, I was not flattered, but on the contrary entirely discomfited. Angry I could not well be, for the deprecating manner in which all, excepting of course the boys, yielded to their perception of the ridiculous, and the distress they showed at their failure in self-control, made me seem the aggressor. It was as if they were very sorry for me, and ready to put themselves wholly at my service, if I would only refrain from reducing them to a state of disability by being so exquisitely absurd. Certainly this evidently amiable race had a very embarrassing way of receiving strangers.

Just at this moment, when my bewilderment was fast verging on exasperation, relief came. The circle opened, and a little elderly man, who had evidently come in haste, confronted me, and, bowing very politely, addressed me in English. His voice was the most pitiable abortion of a voice I had ever heard. While having all the defects in articulation of a child's who is just beginning to talk, it was not even a child's in strength of tone, being in fact a mere alternation of squeaks and whispers inaudible a rod away. With some difficulty I was, however, able to follow him pretty nearly.

"As the official interpreter," he said, "I extend you a cordial welcome to these islands. I was sent for as soon as you were discovered, but being at some distance, I was unable to arrive until this moment. I regret this, as my presence would have saved you embarrassment. My countrymen desire me to intercede with you to pardon the wholly involuntary and uncontrollable mirth provoked by your attempts to communicate with them. You see, they understood you perfectly well, but could not answer you."

"Merciful heavens!" I exclaimed, horrified to find my surmise correct;

"can it be that they are all thus afflicted? Is it possible that you are the only man among them who has the power of speech?"

Again it appeared that, quite unintentionally, I had said something excrutiatingly funny; for at my speech there arose a sound of gentle laughter from the group, now augmented to quite an assemblage, which drowned the plashing of the waves on the beach at our feet. Even the interpreter smiled.

"Do they think it so amusing to be dumb?" I asked.

"They find it very amusing," replied the interpreter, "that their inability to speak should be regarded by any one as an affliction; for it is by the voluntary disuse of the organs of articulation that they have lost the power of speech, and, as a consequence, the ability even to understand speech."

"But," said I, somewhat puzzled by this statement, "didn't you just tell me that they understood me, though they could not reply, and are they not laughing now at what I just said?"

"It is you they understood, not your words," answered the interpreter. "Our speech now is gibberish to them, as unintelligible in itself as the growling of animals; but they know what we are saying, because they know our thoughts. You must know that these are the islands of the mind-readers."

Such were the circumstances of my introduction to this extraordinary people. The official interpreter being charged by virtue of his office with the first entertainment of shipwrecked members of the talking nations, I became his guest, and passed a number of days under his roof before going out to any considerable extent among the people. My first impression had been the somewhat oppressive one that the power to read the thoughts of others could be possessed only by beings of a superior order to man. It was the first effort of the interpreter to disabuse me of this notion. It appeared from his account that the experience of the mind-readers was a case simply of a slight acceleration, from special causes, of the course of universal human evolution, which in time was destined to lead to the disuse of speech and the substitution of direct mental vision on the part of all races. This rapid evolution of these islanders was accounted for by their peculiar origin and circumstances.

Some three centuries before Christ, one of the Parthian kings of Persia, of the dynasty of the Arsacidae, undertook a persecution of the soothsayers and magicians in his realms. These people were credited with supernatural powers by popular prejudice, but in fact were merely persons of special gifts in the way of hypnotizing, mind-reading, thought transference, and such arts, which they exercised for their own gain.

Too much in awe of the soothsayers to do them outright violence, the king resolved to banish them, and to this end put them, with their families, on ships and sent them to Ceylon. When, however, the fleet was in the neighborhood of that island, a great storm scattered it, and one of the ships, after being driven for many days before the tempest, was wrecked upon one of an archipelago of uninhabited islands far to the south, where the survivors settled. Naturally, the posterity of the parents possessed of such peculiar gifts had developed extraordinary psychical powers.

Having set before them the end of evolving a new and advanced order of humanity, they had aided the development of these powers by a rigid system of stirpiculture. The result was that, after a few centuries, mind-reading became so general that language fell into disuse as a means of communicating ideas. For many generations the power of speech still remained voluntary, but gradually the vocal organs had become atrophied, and for several hundred years the power of articulation had been wholly lost. Infants for a few months after birth did, indeed, still emit inarticulate cries, but at an age when in less advanced races these cries began to be articulate, the children of the mind-readers developed the power of direct vision, and ceased to attempt to use the voice.

The fact that the existence of the mind-readers had never been found out by the rest of the world was explained by two considerations. In the first place, the group of islands was small, and occupied a corner of the Indian Ocean quite out of the ordinary track of ships. In the second place, the approach to the islands was rendered so desperately perilous by terrible currents, and the maze of outlying rocks and shoals, that it was next to impossible for any ship to touch their shores save as a wreck. No ship at least had ever done so in the two thousand years since the mind-readers' own arrival, and the Adelaide had made the one hundred and twenty-third such wreck.

Apart from motives of humanity, the mind-readers made strenuous efforts to rescue shipwrecked persons, for from them alone, through the interpreters, could they obtain information of the outside world. Little enough this proved when, as often happened, the sole survivor of the shipwreck was some ignorant sailor, who had no news to communicate beyond the latest varieties of forecastle blasphemy. My hosts gratefully assured me that, as a person of some little education, they considered me a veritable godsend. No less a task was mine than to relate to them the history of the world for the past two centuries, and often did I wish, for their sakes, that I had made a more exact study of it.

It is solely for the purpose of communicating with shipwrecked strangers of the talking nations that the office of the interpreters exists. When, as from time to time happens, a child is born with some powers of articulation, he is set apart, and trained to talk in the interpreters' college. Of course the partial atrophy of the vocal organs, from which even the best interpreters suffer, renders many of the sounds of language impossible for them. None, for instance, can pronounce *v*, *f*, or *s;* and as to the sound represented by *th,* it is five generations since the last interpreter lived who could utter it. But for the occasional intermarriage of shipwrecked strangers with the islanders, it is probable that the supply of interpreters would have long ere this quite failed.

I imagine that the very unpleasant sensations which followed the realization that I was among people who, while inscrutable to me, knew my every thought, were very much what any one would have experienced in the same case. They were very comparable to the panic which accidental nudity causes a person among races whose custom it is to conceal the figure with drapery. I wanted to run away and hide myself. If I analyzed my feeling, it did not seem to arise so much from the consciousness of any particularly heinous secrets, as from the knowledge of a swarm of fatuous, ill-natured, and unseemly thoughts and half thoughts concerning those around me, and concerning myself, which it was insufferable that any person should peruse in however benevolent a spirit. But while my chagrin and distress on this account were at first intense, they were also very short-lived, for almost immediately I discovered that the very knowledge that my mind was overlooked by others operated to check thoughts that might be painful to them, and that, too, without more effort of the will than a kindly person exerts to check the utterance of disagreeable remarks. As a very few lessons in the elements of courtesy cures a decent person of inconsiderate speaking, so a brief experience among the mind-readers went far in my case to check inconsiderate thinking. It must not be supposed, however, that courtesy among the mind-readers prevents them from thinking pointedly and freely concerning one another upon serious occasions, any more than the finest courtesy among the talking races restrains them from speaking to one another with entire plainness when it is desirable to do so. Indeed, among the mind-readers, politeness never can extend to the point of insincerity, as among talking nations, seeing that it is always one another's real and inmost thought that they read. I may fitly mention here, though it was not till later that I fully understood why it must necessarily be so, that one need feel far less chagrin at the complete revelation of his weaknesses to a mind-reader than at the slightest betrayal of them to one of another race. For the very reason that the mind-reader reads all your thoughts, particular thoughts are judged with reference to the general tenor of thought. Your characteristic and habitual frame of mind is what he takes account of. No one need fear being misjudged by a mind-reader on account of sentiments or emotions which are not representative of the real character or general attitude. Justice may, indeed, be said to be a necessary consequence of mind-reading.

As regards the interpreter himself, the instinct of courtesy was not long needed to check wanton or offensive thoughts. In all my life before, I had been very slow to form friendships, but before I had been three days in the company of this stranger of a strange race, I had become enthusiastically devoted to him. It was impossible not to be. The peculiar joy of friendship is the sense of being understood by our friend as we are not by others, and yet of being loved in spite of the understanding. Now here was one whose every word testified to a knowledge of my secret thoughts and motives which the oldest and nearest of my former friends had never, and could never, have approximated. Had such a knowledge bred in him contempt of me, I should neither have blamed him nor been at all surprised. Judge, then, whether the cordial friendliness which he showed was likely to leave me indifferent.

Imagine my incredulity when he informed me that our friendship was not based upon more than ordinary mutual suitability of temperaments. The faculty of mind-reading, he explained, brought minds so close together, and so heightened sympathy, that the lowest order of friendship between mind-readers implied a mutual delight such as only rare friends enjoyed among other races. He assured me that later on, when I came to know others of his race, I should find, by the far greater intensity of sympathy and affection I should conceive for some of them, how true this saying was.

It may be inquired how, on beginning to mingle with the mind-readers in general, I managed to communicate with them, seeing that, while they could read my thoughts, they could not, like the interpreter, respond to them by speech. I must here explain that, while these people have no use for a spoken language, a written language is needful for purposes of record. They consequently all know how to write. Do they, then, write Persian? Luckily for me, no. It appears that, for a long period after mind-reading was fully developed, not only was spoken language disused, but also written, no records whatever having been kept during this period. The delight of the people in the newly found power of direct mind-to-mind vision, whereby pictures of the total mental state were communicated, instead of the imperfect descriptions of single thoughts which words at best could give, induced an invincible distaste for the laborious impotence of language.

When, however, the first intellectual intoxication had, after several generations, somewhat sobered down, it was recognized that records of the past were desirable, and that the despised medium of words was needful to preserve it. Persian had meanwhile been wholly forgotten. In order to avoid the prodigious task of inventing a complete new language, the institution of the interpreters was now set up, with the idea of acquiring through them a knowledge of some of the languages of the outside world from the mariners wrecked on the islands.

Owing to the fact that most of the castaway ships were English, a better knowledge of that tongue was acquired than of any other, and it was adopted as the written language of the people. As a rule, my acquaintances wrote slowly and laboriously, and yet the fact that they knew exactly what was in my mind rendered their responses so apt that, in my conversations with the slowest speller of them all, the interchange of thought was as rapid and incomparably more accurate and satisfactory than the fastest talkers attain to.

It was but a very short time after I had begun to extend my acquaintance among the mind-readers before I discovered how truly the interpreter had told me that I should find others to whom, on account of greater natural congeniality, I should become more strongly attached than I had been to him. This was in no wise, however, because I loved him less, but them more. I would fain write particularly of some of these beloved friends, comrades of my heart, from whom I first learned the undreamed-of possibilities of human friendship, and how ravishing the satisfactions of sympathy may be. Who, among those who may read this, has not known that sense of a gulf fixed between soul and soul which mocks love! Who has not felt that loneliness which oppresses the heart that loves it best! Think no longer that this gulf is eternally fixed, or is any necessity of human nature. It has no existence for the race of our fellowmen which I describe, and by that fact we may be assured that eventually it will be bridged also for us. Like the touch of shoulder to shoulder, like the clasping of hands, is the contact of their minds and their sensation of sympathy.

I say that I would fain speak more particularly of some of my friends, but waning strength forbids, and moreover, now that I think of it, another consideration would render any comparison of their characters rather confusing than instructive to a reader. This is the fact that, in common with the rest of the mind-readers, they had no names. Every one had indeed, an arbitrary sign for his designation in records, but it has no sound value. A register of these names is kept, so they can at any time be ascertained, but it is very common to meet persons who have forgotten titles which are used solely for biographical and official purposes. For social intercourse names are of course superfluous, for these people accost one another merely by a mental act of attention, and refer to third persons by transferring their mental pictures,—something as dumb persons might by means of photographs. Something so, I say, for in the pictures of one another's personalities which the mind-readers conceive, the physical aspect, as might be expected with people who directly contemplate each other's minds and hearts, is a subordinate element.

I have already told how my first qualms of morbid self-consciousness at knowing that my mind was an open book to all around me disappeared as I learned that the very completeness of the disclosure of my thoughts and motives was a guarantee that I would be judged with a fairness and a sympathy such as even self-judgment cannot pretend to, affected as that is by so many subtle reactions. The assurance of being so judged by every one might well seem an inestimable privilege to one accustomed to a world in which not even the tenderest love is any pledge of comprehension, and yet I soon discovered that open-mindedness had a still greater profit than this. How shall I describe the delightful exhilaration of moral health and cleanness, the breezy oxygenated mental condition, which resulted from the consciousness that I had absolutely nothing concealed! Truly I may say that I enjoyed myself. I think surely that no one needs to have had my marvelous experience to sympathize with this portion of it. Are we not all ready to agree that this having a curtained chamber where we may go to grovel, out of sight of our fellows, troubled only by a vague apprehension that God may look over the top, is the most demoralizing incident in the human condition? It is the existence within the soul of this secure refuge of lies which has always been the despair of the saint and the exultation of the knave. It is the foul cellar which taints the whole house above, be it never so fine.

What stronger testimony could there be to the instinctive consciousness that concealment is debauching, and openness our only cure, than the world-old conviction of the virtue of confession for the soul, and that the uttermost exposing of one's worst and foulest is the first step toward moral health? The wickedest man, if he could but somehow attain to writhe himself inside out as to his soul, so that its full sickness could be seen, would feel ready for a new life. Nevertheless, owing to the utter impotence of the words to convey mental conditions in their totality, or to give other than mere distortions of them, confession is, we must needs admit, but a mockery of that longing for self-revelation to which it testifies. But think what health and soundness there must be for souls among a people who see in every face a conscience which, unlike their own, they cannot sophisticate, who confess one another with a glance, and shrive with a smile! Ah, friends, let me now predict, though ages may elapse before the slow event shall justify me, that in no way will the mutual vision of minds, when at last it shall be perfected, so enhance the blessedness of mankind as by rending the veil of self, and leaving no spot of darkness in the mind for lies to hide in. Then shall the soul no longer be a coal smoking among ashes, but a star in a crystal sphere.

From what I have said of the delights which friendship among the mind-readers derive from the perfection of the mental rapport, it may be imagined how intoxicating must be the experience when one of the friends is a woman, and the subtle attractions and correspondences of sex touch with passion the intellectual sympathy. With my first venturing into society I had begun, to their extreme amusement, to fall in love with the women right and left. In the perfect frankness which is the condition of all intercourse among this people, these adorable women told me that what I felt was only friendship, which was a very good thing, but wholly different from love, as I should well know if I were beloved. It was difficult to believe that the melting emotions which I had experienced in their company were the result merely of the friendly and kindly attitude of their minds toward mine; but when I found that I was affected in the same way by every gracious woman I met, I had to make up my mind that they must be right about it, and that I should have to adapt myself to a world in which, friendship being a passion, love must needs be nothing less than rapture.

The homely proverb, "Every Jack has his Gill," may, I suppose, be taken to mean that for all men there are certain women expressly suited by mental and moral as well as by physical constitution. It is a thought painful, rather than cheering, that this may be the truth, so altogether do the chances preponderate against the ability of these elect ones to recognize each other even if they meet, seeing that speech is so inadequate and so misleading a medium of self-revelation. But among the mind-readers, the search for one's ideal mate is a quest reasonably sure of being crowned with success, and no one dreams of wedding unless it be; for so to do, they consider, would be to throw away the choicest blessing of life, and not alone to wrong themselves and their unfound mates, but likewise those whom they themselves and those undiscovered mates might wed. Therefore, passionate pilgrims, they go from isle to isle till they find each other, and, as the population of the islands is but small, the pilgrimage is not often long.

When I met her first we were in company, and I was struck by the sudden stir and the looks of touched and smiling interest with which all around turned and regarded us, the women with moistened eyes. They had read her thought when she saw me, but this I did not know, neither what was the custom in these matters, till afterward. But I knew, from the moment she first fixed her eyes on me, and I felt her mind brooding upon mine, how truly I had been told by those other women that the feeling with which they had inspired me was not love.

With people who become acquainted at a glance, and old friends in an hour, wooing is naturally not a long process. Indeed, it may be said that between lovers among mind-readers there is no wooing, but merely recognition. The day after we met, she became mine.

Perhaps I cannot better illustrate how subordinate the merely physical element is in the impression which mind-readers form of their friends than by mentioning an incident that occurred some months after our union. This was my discovery, wholly by accident, that my love, in whose society I had almost constantly been, had not the least idea what was the color of my eyes, or whether my hair and complexion were light or dark. Of course, as soon as I asked her the question, she read the answer in my mind, but she admitted that she had previously had no distinct impression on those points. On the other hand, if in the blackest midnight I should come to her, she would not need to ask who the comer was. It is by the mind, not the eye, that these people know one another. It is really only in their relations to soulless and inanimate things that they need eyes at all.

It must not be supposed that their disregard of one another's bodily aspect grows out of any ascetic sentiment. It is merely a necessary consequence of their power of directly apprehending mind, that whenever mind is closely associated with matter the latter is comparatively neglected on account of the greater interest of the former, suffering as lesser things always do when placed in immediate contrast with greater. Art is with them confined to the inanimate, the human form having, for the reason mentioned, ceased to inspire the artist. It will be naturally and quite correctly inferred that among such a race physical beauty is not the important factor in human fortune and felicity that it elsewhere is. The absolute openness of their minds and hearts to one another makes their happiness far more dependent on the moral and mental qualities of their companions than upon their physical. A genial temperament, a wide-grasping, godlike intellect, a poet soul, are incomparably more fascinating to them than the most dazzling combination conceivable of mere bodily graces.

A woman of mind and heart has no more need of beauty to win love in these islands than a beauty elsewhere of mind or heart. I should mention here, perhaps, that this race, which makes so little account of physical beauty, is itself a singularly handsome one. This is owing doubtless in part to the absolute compatibility of temperaments in all the marriages, and partly also to the reaction upon the body of a state of ideal mental and moral health and placidity.

Not being myself a mind-reader, the fact that my love was rarely beautiful in form and face had doubtless no little part in attracting my devotion. This, of course, she knew, as she knew all my thoughts, and, knowing my limitations, tolerated and forgave the element of sensuousness in my passion. But if it must have seemed to her so little worthy in comparison with the high spiritual communion which her race know as love, to me it became, by virtue of her almost superhuman relation to me, an ecstasy more ravishing surely than any lover of my race tasted before. The ache at the heart of the intensest love is the impotence of words to make it perfectly understood to its object. But my passion was without this pang, for my heart was absolutely open to her I loved. Lovers may imagine, but I cannot describe, the ecstatic thrill of communion into which this consciousness transformed every tender emotion. As I considered what mutual love must be where both parties are mind-readers, I realized the high communion which my sweet companion had sacrificed for me. She might indeed comprehend her lover and his love for her, but the higher satisfaction of knowing that she was comprehended by him and her love understood, she had foregone. For that I should ever attain the power of mind-reading was out of the question, the faculty never having been developed in a single lifetime.

Why my inability should move my dear companion to such depths of pity I was not able fully to understand until I learned that mind-reading is chiefly held desirable, not for the knowledge of others which it gives its possessors, but for the self-knowledge which is its reflex effect. Of all they see in the minds of others, that which concerns them most is the reflection of themselves, the photographs of their own characters. The most obvious consequence of the self-knowledge thus forced upon them is to render them alike incapable of self-conceit or self-depreciation. Every one must needs always think of himself as he is, being no more able to do otherwise than is a man in a hall of mirrors to cherish delusions as to his personal appearance.

But self-knowledge means to the mind-readers much more than this,—nothing less, indeed, than a shifting of the sense of identity. When a man sees himself in a mirror, he is compelled to distinguish between the bodily self he sees and his real self, which is within and unseen. When in turn the mind-reader comes to see the mental and moral self reflected in other minds as in mirrors, the same thing happens. He is compelled to distinguish between this mental and moral self which has been made objective to him, and can be contemplated by him as impartially as if it were another's, from the inner ego which still remains subjective, unseen, and indefinable. In this inner ego the mind-readers recognize the essential identity and being, the noumenal self, the core of the soul, and the true hiding of its eternal life, to which the mind as well as the body is but the garment of a day.

The effect of such a philosophy as this—which, indeed, with the mind-readers is rather an instinctive consciousness than a philosophy—must obviously be to impart a sense of wonderful superiority to the vicissitudes of this earthly state, and a singular serenity in the midst of the haps and mishaps which threaten or befall the personality. They did indeed appear to me, as I never dreamed men could attain to be, lords of themselves.

It was because I might not hope to attain this enfranchisement from the false ego of the apparent self, without which life seemed to her race scarcely worth living, that my love so pitied me.

But I must hasten on, leaving a thousand things unsaid, to relate the lamentable catastrophe to which it is owing that, instead of being still a resident of those blessed islands, in the full enjoyment of that intimate and ravishing companionship which by contrast would forever dim the pleasures of all other human society, I recall the bright picture as a memory under other skies.

Among a people who are compelled by the very constitution of their minds to put themselves in the places of others, the sympathy which is the inevitable consequence of perfect comprehension renders envy, hatred, and uncharitableness impossible. But of course there are people less genially constituted than others, and these are necessarily the objects of a certain distaste on the part of associates. Now owing to the unhindered impact of minds upon one another, the anguish of persons so regarded, despite the tenderest consideration of those about them, is so great that they beg the grace of exile, that, being out of the way, people may think less frequently upon them. There are numerous small islets, scarcely more than rocks, lying to the north of the archipelago, and on, these the unfortunates are permitted to live. Only one lives on each islet, as they cannot endure each other even as well as the more happily constituted can endure them. From time to time supplies of food are taken to them, and of course, any time they wish to take the risk, they are permitted to return to society.

Now, as I have said, the fact which, even more than their out-of-the-way location, makes the islands of the mind-readers unapproachable, is the violence with which the great antarctic current, owing probably to some configuration of the ocean bed, together with the innumerable rocks and shoals, flows through and about the archipelago.

Ships making the islands from the southward are caught by this current and drawn among the rocks, to their almost certain destruction; while, owing to the violence with which the current sets to the north, it is not possible to approach at all from that direction, or at least it has never been accomplished. Indeed, so powerful are the currents that even the boats which cross the narrow straits between the main islands and the islets of the unfortunate, to carry the latter their supplies, are ferried over by cables, not trusting to oar or sail.

The brother of my love had charge of one of the boats engaged in this transportation, and, being desirous of visiting the islets, I accepted an invitation to accompany him on one of his trips. I know nothing of how the accident happened, but in the fiercest part of the current of one of the straits we parted from the cable and were swept out to sea. There was no question of stemming the boiling current, our utmost endeavors barely sufficing to avoid being dashed to pieces on the rocks. From the first, there was no hope of our winning back to the land, and so swiftly did we drift that by noon—the accident having befallen in the morning—the islands, which are low-lying, had sunk beneath the southwestern horizon.

Among these mind-readers, distance is not an insuperable obstacle to the transfer of thought. My companion was in communication with our friends, and from time to time conveyed to me messages of anguish from my dear love; for, being well aware of the nature of the currents and the unapproachableness of the islands, those we had left behind, as well as we ourselves, knew well we should see each other's faces no more. For five days we continued to drift to the northwest, in no danger of starvation, owing to our lading of provisions, but constrained to unintermitting watch and ward by the roughness of the weather. On the fifth day my companion died from exposure and exhaustion. He died very quietly,—indeed, with great appearance of relief. The life of the mind-readers while yet they are in the body is so largely spiritual that the idea of an existence wholly so, which seems vague and chill to us, suggests to them a state only slightly more refined than they already know on earth.

After that I suppose I must have fallen into an unconscious state, from which I roused to find myself on an American ship bound for New York, surrounded by people whose only means of communicating with one another is to keep up while together a constant clatter of hissing, guttural, and explosive noises, eked out by all manner of facial contortions and bodily gestures. I frequently find myself staring open-mouthed at those who address me, too much struck by their grotesque appearance to bethink myself of replying.

I find that I shall not live out the voyage, and I do not care to. From my experience of the people on the ship, I can judge how I should fare on land amid the stunning Babel of a nation of talkers. And my friends,—God bless them! how lonely I should feel in their very presence! Nay, what satisfaction or consolation, what but bitter mockery, could I ever more find in such human sympathy and companionship as suffice others and once sufficed me,—I who have seen and known what I have seen and known! Ah, yes, doubtless it is far better I should die; but the knowledge of the things that I have seen I feel should not perish with me. For hope's sake, men should not miss the glimpse of the higher, sun-bathed reaches of the upward path they plod. So thinking, I have written out some account of my wonderful experience, though briefer far, by reason of my weakness, than fits the greatness of the matter. The captain seems an honest, well-meaning man, and to him I shall confide the narrative, charging him, on touching shore, to see it safely in the hands of some one who will bring it to the world's ear.

Note.—The extent of my own connection with the foregoing document is sufficiently indicated by the author himself in the final paragraph.

—E.B.

PART TWO
Institutional Arrangements

5 A Modified Stratification System

In *The Rise of the Meritocracy,* Michael Young writes from the perspective of a historical-sociologist in the year 2033. He describes a series of social changes that occur in England during the period 1870–2033 and result in the evolution of a stratification system in which a person's socioeconomic status is determined solely by merit. In the new society a person's merit is determined by combining two factors, his intelligence quotient and the amount of effort he willingly expends in putting that potential intelligence to work (IQ plus Effort equals Merit). Young calls the social order that develops during this period a *meritocracy*—that is, a social order in which rule is based on merit.

The need to make more efficient use of the fixed sum of talent available to British society, it is proposed, was the impetus for the social reforms that generated the meritocracy. Young makes two interesting points about using the talent base available to a society and the relationship between efficient use of talent and social development. He first argues that there is some fixed amount of talent upon which a society may draw—that is, some proportion of a society's population is born with the intellectual capacity of geniuses, some proportion is substantially talented, some proportion is rather dull, and so on. If we assume that the proportion of persons born with each degree of talent remains relatively stable across generations, it follows that the amount of potential talent available to any society will be fixed. To the extent that a society is successful in identifying talented individuals and making the best use of their abilities, it can be said to be making efficient use of its fixed resources.

Consider a person with an IQ of 180 who is prevented from attending college by his family's inability to pay for his education. With his level of intelligence he will probably be successful no matter what career he pursues. He might, for example, amass a fortune in the used-car business or end up as the most intelligent carpenter in the history of the world. However, in terms of any contribution to the social, scientific, or technological development of his society, his talent is wasted. Clearly, it is advantageous for a society to identify those of its members who possess unusual abilities, to make available to them the education they need to do the kinds of work that only relatively few are capable of attempting, and to offer them rewards that will motivate them to work on those problems the solution of which will benefit the society in general. Isaac Newton's IQ has been estimated at 180; it would have been unfortunate if he had spent his life as a farmer.

Young's second point is that in any society "the rate of social progress depends on the degree to which power is matched with ability" (p. 14). The movement toward a meritocracy in Britain between the years 1870 and 2033 can be conceptualized as a social revolution that brought about a relatively high correlation of ability with power throughout the society. During this period, Young reports, reform measures were adapted under which the barriers separating lower-class children from first-rate educations were removed, and advantages traditionally available to the children of the affluent were stripped away. Young also traces the spread of the equalization of talent and power from educational institutions through many important sectors of society.

In Young's social history one major obstacle to revolutionizing the social system turns out to be the institutionalized association of status and power with age. One major problem in making more efficient use of the products of a modernized educational system is the slowness with which the younger and better-trained move into positions of power in government and industry. The problem in work situations is to change the belief used to defend the association of age and seniority with power: that many years of experience are positively related to successful performance in important positions. Young suggests that through the careful perpetuation of this myth, senior men in an organization are able to prevent their replacement by the better-trained and more able who occupy junior positions. He also suggests that the juniors accept the myth because they realize that eventually *they* will be seniors in positions of power who need to protect themselves from their better-trained juniors.

The social reforms that Young outlines have tremendous positive effects on the society in which they occur. In many respects, the stratification system that emerges is very well suited to a social system in which economic development, technological improvement, and rapid movement toward an affluent society are desired.

The Rise of the Meritocracy

MICHAEL YOUNG

At the beginning of my special period, 1914, the upper classes had their fair share of geniuses and morons, so did the workers; or, I should say, since a few brilliant and fortunate working men always climbed up to the top despite having been subordinate in society, the inferior classes contained *almost* as high a proportion of superior people as the upper classes themselves. Intelligence was distributed more or less at random. Each social class was, in ability, the miniature of society itself; the part the same as the whole. The fundamental change of the last century, which was fairly begun before 1963, is that intelligence has been redistributed between the classes, and the nature of the classes changed. The talented have been given the opportunity to rise to the level which accords with their capacities, and the lower classes consequently reserved for those who are also lower in ability. The part is no longer the same as the whole.

The rate of social progress depends upon the degree to which power is matched with intelligence. The Britain of a century ago squandered its resources by condemning even talented people to manual work; and blocked the efforts of members of the lower classes to obtain just recognition for their abilities. But Britain could not be a caste society if it was to survive as a great nation, great, that is, in comparison with others. To withstand international competition the country had to make better use of its human material, above all, of the talent which was even in England, one might say always and everywhere, too scarce. Schools and industries were progressively thrown open to merit, so that the clever children of each generation had opportunity for ascent. The proportion of people with I.Q.s over 130 could not be raised—the task was rather to prevent a fall—but the proportion of such people in work which called upon their full capacities was steadily raised. For every Rutherford there have in modern times been ten such magnates, for every Keynes two, and even Elgar has had a successor. Civilization does not depend upon the stolid mass, the *homme moyen sensuel,* but upon the creative minority, the innovator who with one stroke can save the labour of 10,000, the brilliant few who cannot look without wonder, the restless elite who have made mutation a social, as well as a biological, fact. The ranks of the scientists and technologists, the artists and the teachers, have been swelled, their education shaped to their high genetic destiny, their power for good increased. Progress is their triumph; the modern world their monument.

The fundamental reform that began the movement toward a meritocracy was the general improvement of the grammar schools (in the British educational system, publicly supported elementary and high schools).

The Hitler war transformed the social composition of the grammar schools. Full employment and larger wages, fostering higher aspirations, made lower-class parents able and anxious to get better education for their children, and the 1944 Act helped by making secondary schools free. The consequences were dramatic. In the 1930s only a minority of able low-class children had more than the most primitive education; twenty years later practically all clever children were installed in the seats of learning. A sociological study of the 1950s was able to report that 'in very many, if not in most, parts of the country the chances of children at a given level of ability entering grammar schools are no longer dependent on their social origins'.

However, it was one thing for able children from the lower classes to enter grammar schools, another for them to stay there. Here prosperity was a handicap. Even against the wishes of their parents, many scholars were tempted by high wages to leave school early—and flocks of them did so at the minimum age. Prosperity did not create the problem, but it accentuated one of long-standing. In every decade children matured physically earlier than before. Constant shortening of childhood in the biological and social sense and constant lengthening of childhood in the educational sense posed a dilemma which was only resolved in the long run by treating grammar-school children as adults.

The superior classes took for granted that their children should enjoy higher education; the difficulty was not to get the able to stay at school, but to get the stupid to leave and put up with the manual jobs for which their intelligence fitted them. In the lower classes the situation was reversed. The higher the wages that could be earned at a machine by the children of manual workers, the more dreary seemed the school-desk. No age is more acquisitive than adolescence. The remedy was clear; the State had to prevent children from suffering for their cleverness by giving them and their parents a privileged status within the lower classes. The first step was to pay very much larger maintenance allowances—later scaled in ratio to intelligence—for grammar-school children staying the full course. But this was not enough. Inquiry showed that some irresponsible parents were spending the allowances on themselves, not on the children for whom they were intended. The obvious thing to do—eventually even to Ministers of Education—was to pay a learning wage direct to grammar-school pupils. At first it was equal to the average earnings of juveniles in ordinary industry; then the newly formed B.U.G.S.A. (the British Union of Grammar School Attenders) attacked the injustice of equality, rightly too, since the ability of the earner was usually so much lower than that of the pupil. In 1972 the government approved a learning wage on a sliding scale sixty per cent above industrial earnings. After that very few children left grammar schools prematurely for economic reasons. In modern times we could hardly imagine a grammar school without its weekly pay-day.

The universities paid wages to students (in the form of scholarships) long before grammar schools, but otherwise preserved some curious anachronisms of their own. Poorer parents were at a disadvantage in grammar schools, richer parents in universities. In the 1950s clever children of the middle-rich were deprived of grants because their parents were quite wrongly supposed to have enough money to pay, with the shocking result that some of them never got to university at all—surely a supreme example of the excesses of egalitarianism in its heyday! Closed 'scholarships' also gave pupils from certain public schools privileged entry to otherwise reputable colleges at Oxford and Cambridge; and in the middle of the century it was still not unknown for King's or Balliol to detect some special merit in sons whose father had been there before. Such barbaric practices were even excused in public from time to time by old-fashioned dons who declared it was better, educationally mind you, for the bright students to be mixed up with the dull. The dons had once again lost touch: the modern world no longer required the clever to mingle with the stupid, except when assigned to social intelligence work among the lower classes. When the die-hards died, universities came into line with national policy and selected all their entrants on merit properly tested in the examination-room. By 1972 public school-boys had either to compete openly with the Bradford Grammar School or seek "gringo admission" to South American universities. Few willingly incurred that stigma.

The learning wage and the universalization of university scholarships followed upon a change in the attitude of the State to spending on education, which itself reflected growing recognition that investment in brains is much more rewarding than investment in property. But politicians always wanted the impossible—the quick results education can never give. They kept tinkering with the top of the educational system instead of building securely from the bottom. They were as willing to spend on the universities as they were unwilling to spend on the primary schools. Politicians would not realize that the milk monitors were the future leaders of the nation. Faced with a shortage of engineers, the government said very well, spend more upon the engineering colleges. Of scientists, spend more upon the science faculties. Of technologists generally, then build more schools of technology. This was futile. For if the government attracted more promising youngsters into engineering, fewer were left behind for science. More for the civil service meant less for industry, more for laboratories less for teaching. The egalitarian doctrine that any man can be trained to substitute for any other was so deeply rooted that our ancestors only slowly came to appreciate the full significance of one simple fact: that all the professions were competing with each other for a limited supply of intelligence. It was not until well on into the last half of the century that the national scarcity of intellect became obvious to all those who had it. The government learned that the only way simultaneously to get more and better engineers, more and better physicists, more and better civil servants up to the limits set by Nature was to start with the three-year-olds, to ensure that from that age on no ability escaped through the net, and, most important, to make certain that the future physicists, psychologists, and the rest of the elite continuously had the best teaching they could get.

It did not matter so much about the defective, maladjusted, and delinquent upon whom up to 1972 England (as a sign of the times) spent more per head than upon the brilliant. It did not matter so much about the secondary modern schools. In an ideal world, not hampered by shortage of resources, the unfortunate could have large sums spent on them too. But it was not, has not been, nor ever will be, an ideal world. The choice was between priorities, and there was no doubt how the decision had to go. What mattered most were primary schools, where the pupils were being divided into the gifted and the ungifted; and, above all, the grammar schools where the gifted received their due. They had to have more generous endowments. And they got them.

From the moment that Sir Anthony Crosland was persuaded that the battle for national survival would be won or lost in the "A" streams all the way from nursery to grammar school, the money began to flow. Spending on education was still only 2.7 per cent of the gross national product in 1953; by 1963, 3.9 per cent; by 1982, after the "marvellous decade," it was 6.1 per cent. Most of the extra went on teachers. For more of them—it was still common in those grim middle years of the last century for one single teacher to have a mob of forty children in a class and who could she then be but a Joseph Lancaster! And for better ones. So far were teachers' salaries behind industry that in the early 1960s some grammar schools did not have a solitary physics teacher. At a time when the Atomic Energy Authority was clamouring for physicists! Many of the leading officials at the Ministry of Education and the Treasury, though they had read their Plato, had seemingly forgotten that none but the guardians themselves could be trusted to teach future guardians. Second-rate teachers, a second-rate elite: the meritocracy can never be better than its teachers. Things improved until at last the teachers attained their ideal of superiority of esteem. One of the wisest strokes of the marvellous decade was to put the salaries of science teachers on the same level as scientists in industry and all grammar-school teachers on the same level as their scientific colleagues. The schools could then attract good scientists; they got the very pick of other teachers.

The logic of the system can be portrayed in a simple table.

Distribution of Intelligence Between Types of Secondary School (1969)

Type of School	*IQ Level of Pupils*	*No. of Pupils per Teacher*	*IQ Level of Teachers*
E.S.N. (Educationally Subnormal) School	50–80	25	100–105
Secondary modern	81–115	20	105–110
Secondary grammar	116–180	10	135–180
Boarding grammar	125–180	8	135–180

The success of [educational] reforms depended upon continuous growth in the efficiency of selection methods. How pointless it would have been to set aside superior schools without the means of identifying the elect! Progress did not, of course, always proceed at the same pace on each of these complementary tasks. By and large, the seclusion of grammar schools went ahead more smoothly than selection of pupils. But the more widely recognized it was that better schools should be reserved for the more able, the greater the pressure upon the educational psychologists to improve their techniques. They responded. Necessity once again played its customary part.

Following 1944, there was a large increase in the demand for grammar school places without any corresponding expansion of supply. Competition was sharper; how were the winners to be picked? The value of intelligence tests as a guide to personnel selection in the Forces had been fully demonstrated during the war, and it was therefore natural to adopt the same kind of method for the peace-time purpose, especially in a stratified society prepared by habit of mind to recognize a hierarchy of intelligence as soon as it was pointed out. The results were remarkable: by 1950, merely a few years after the Act, most of the children in the country were taking these tests before they left their primary schools, and although older methods of examination were also used, high I.Q. was established as the chief qualification for entry to the elite. Educational psychology assumed a central place in pedagogy from which it was never later entirely dislodged. . . .

Progress was, as always, uneven, a period of stability being succeeded by a sudden jump forward. Man had to wait until 1989 for the leap of the century. Long before that the "cyberneticists" had realized that man would best understand his own brain when he could imitate it. As men became more like machines, machines became more like men, and when machines were built to mimic people, the ventriloquist at last understood himself. Modern mental capacity standards date from that year, a common unit of measurement being possible as soon as it was realized that a machine also can have its "intelligence" tested and scored as much as a human brain. "Pamela," Bird's pi-computer in the National Physiological Laboratory, with its constant I.Q. of 100, became the recognized national standard, and all the questions in the examination papers were first put to her before being distributed to the schools and other centres.

Well before 1989, psychologists had succeeded in identifying the problems which had to be solved. They realized that the brain was no more separable than the sexual organs from the biochemical economy of the individual, and the individual no more separable than his lungs from the environment, social as well as physical, in which he lived. Many people with high potential intelligence were prevented from making use of it by anxiety due to psychic disturbances. Some had lower intelligence, others higher, when the environment was unfavourable. Hence the I.Q. berserkers with an I.Q. of 140 at some times and 90 at others, and not only when in love or before breakfast—an affliction from which some leading members of the Technicians Party are alleged to suffer. Psychologists tackled the task of bringing the actual nearer to the potential. Advances in therapy were a beneficient by-product of educational selection.

The Spens Committee said in 1938 that it is 'possible at an early age to predict with some degree of accuracy the ultimate level of a child's intellectual powers'. That is true now; it was not true then. No wonder resentment was aroused when the main tests were given once, at eleven! A person's performance at that one age decided whether he went to a grammar school. If he failed he could, in theory, get a second chance later on. In practice he seldom did. Late developers were too late. A boy or girl whose capacity flowered even as young as fourteen was lucky indeed to get a transfer from a modern to a grammar school. He was usually stuck with the stupid, and classed with them for the rest of his life. That was a cruel injustice for the individual and a shocking waste for society—so much so that in a small way comprehensive schools actually did some good by making it easier for people to swim from one stream to another. People knew that in some people intelligence reached its height at twelve, in others it only came to full fruition at thirty—but they did not act as if they knew. As this truth was driven home, educators sought, with increasing success, to make intelligence assessment continuous throughout school life. I.Q.s were tested at seven, nine, eleven, thirteen, and fifteen, and at each stage a person whose score was higher than it had been previously was taken away from his inferiors and lodged with his equals. Yet the people whose ability developed only when they had left school escaped the net of selection altogether. Even in the 1980s, a man who suddenly came to his senses at the age of twenty-five had the greatest difficulty in securing proper recognition for his talents.

Here it is that the modern development of adult education has proved so vital. School came to last for life. By the end of the century the right of every person to be judged according to his ability was honoured in more than the breach. It was at last accepted that, as a matter of quite elementary justice, neither man nor child should be judged stupid until he was proved to be. The presumption was always of cleverness. So at *any* age *any* person became entitled, more than entitled, encouraged to apply every five years for re-test at a Regional Centre for Adult Education, and if his hopes were realized, then justice was invariably done. The copy of his National Intelligence card at H.Q. was destroyed, and a new card substituted containing the re-test score, so that no employer (or fiancee) who applied in the ordinary way for his I.Q. and aptitude scores would ever know about the lowlier status he had once had. It was also decided in the Courts that there was no obligation on anyone to put anything more than his current I.Q. in his *Who's Who* entry. A successful re-test was quite genuinely a fresh start.

No doubt this has led to difficulties. Some children have become excessively ambitious on behalf of their parents and have exerted too much pressure on them to strive for reclassification. Books on the care of parents have become too avidly studied. Some workmen have displayed jealousy when their elderly workmates have been sent away to university or gymnasium. But in the long interim period while methods of selection have been in process of improvement, the disadvantages have been far outweighed by the advantages. Now, of course, the psychologists have refined their methods to such a point that they can allow for most of the imponderables which delay development and forecast not only the I.Q. but the ages at which it will fructify. Exciting as the advance is to every scientifically-minded person, it has to be admitted that the discussions it has unloosed have been grist to the critics of the established order.

For a half-century schools were the target for reform, and quite rightly too, the achievement was brilliant. But the reformers were as always (perhaps had to be) too single-minded. They focused on schools to the exclusion of everything else, with the distressing result that for many years the efficiency with which manpower was used in industry lagged far behind the efficiency with which it was used in education. Our grandfathers did not fully realize that promotion of adults by merit, with all that it implied for industrial organization, was as necessary as promotion of children by merit. A society which acknowledged the claims of talent in the schools, but not in industry, was a house divided against itself. They did not fully understand that when castes were abolished, or rather converted into our modern kind of classes, there was still another category of people to circumvent—the class of old men. They did not fully appreciate that having the wrong man in a position of power merely because he was of superior age was every bit as wasteful as having the wrong man in a position of power merely because his parents were of a superior class. In an open society the few who are chosen out of the many who are called should be chosen on merit; age is as much an irrelevant criterion as birth.

Within the span of human history age has been the most enduring ruling class: once established, every aristocracy, every plutocracy, every bureaucracy has also been a gerontocracy; and even under democracy, government by the people, of the people, for the people, meant government by old people, of young people, for old people. In pre-industrial times the autocrat of the farm did not share his authority with any schoolmaster when his sons were young, and he retained his dominion over them when they were grown men, restrained only by the fear that if he irked his children overmuch his eventual fate might be that of King Lear. After the introduction of industry, fathers still did all they could to secure advancement for their own over other men's sons, but never over themselves, and to this end the solidarity of seniority made all fathers into a band of brothers. After the establishment of the new elite fathers could no longer gain privilege for their own sons, but they still continued to do all they could to ensure that other men's sons, however able, did not gain supremacy over themselves.

The meritocracy threatened, in short, to become yet another gerontocracy. Had this danger not been averted, the intellectual revolution would have been incomplete.

With education reformed, some people imagined they had matriculated to the millennium. The winners from school and university were inclined to lean upon their laurels. They entered, as if to a haven, professions still governed by a restrictive guild mentality. They accepted rule by elders of their profession. They comforted themselves that they would continue to make the same steady progression through the age-grades as they had done at school, until in proper season they became sacred elders in their turn. It was only the relentless facts of the modern world which roused people from their torpor and sent competition to storm industry as well as school. In order to combine the best of England, our regime for children, with the best of America, their regime for adults, competition had to last for the life.

Up till the Hitler war and for some years after, education determined prospects for promotion almost as much as it does in modern times. The manual worker who left school at the minimum age ordinarily remained a manual worker for life, the farthest he could go being to charge-hand and foreman, or, if he was lucky, by another route to general secretary of a trade union. The progress chaser taken away early from grammar school might climb to works manager, the payclerk to accountant. In most workplaces it was practically impossible to transfer from the ladder selected to start with according to the age at which the boy left school to another ladder which would take him higher; the foreman remained a foreman instead of beginning again on the ladder of works management, the accountant remained an accountant and was not in the running for director. Education decided the point of entry to industry, and the point of entry decided where one finished up.

This structure would have been well enough had the schools been rationalized. But when neither quality nor quantity of education were yet determined by intelligence, many clever children left school too soon, many stupid too late. A minority of more perceptive employers, following the civil service model which I have already described, set out to correct the injustices of the educational system and profit themselves at the same time. They gave their clever employees opportunities to rise within the firm in place of the opportunities they had missed at school. At its most complete (and to us most ridiculous), this practice made it possible for the tea-boy from the manual workers and the office-boy from the clerical to rise up to the board of directors. The first industries to be nationalized made some effort to do at least as well as the civil service. On British Railways a clerk could, for instance, if he moved off the lowest rungs when he was very young, transfer from the clerical ladder to one of the lower administrative posts. Electricity supply was more enlightened still.

Employees in the industry are considered to be on a common ladder, rising as openings occur, and in open competition according to experience and ability for the particular vacancy.

The statement is entertaining, practice not being quite like precept, because it shows how it was thought things should work. Some employers were so proud of their promotion schemes and ladder plans that they preferred to take on children straight from school and train them on the job than recruit university graduates. This attitude was regrettably common amongst the leading executives who had not been to university themselves; there were of course many such "self-made men" in those distant days. The school's shame was the factory's pride.

The beginning of the second phase, which has lasted until the present day, is usually put in the 1950s. The 1944 Act took ten to twenty years before its effect was generally felt in industry. Not many employers were as quick as the High Master to see its significance.

No longer, said Sir Eric, *will industry or commerce be able to recruit at fifteen or sixteen boys who, as in the past, are of a quality to work their way up to positions of the highest managerial responsibility.*

In the fullness of time only the most dim-witted employers failed to learn this lesson. The evidence came through the door at the end of every term. Whatever opportunities there might be for secondary modern children to climb the industrial ladder, the hard fact was that fewer and fewer of them had the ability to do so. The grammar schools were retaining the "likely lads" who in previous generations might have entered industry as fifteen-year-olds, and the cleverest of the clever were going on to the university. Since the only ladder plan that mattered was the educational one, the captains of industry had to fit in with that. Either they could attract a share of grammar school graduates, and a seasoning from the university; or their businesses would perish. To sustain top management they had to recruit cadets from higher education, even if it meant incurring the hostility of the trade unions to introducing outsiders, particularly well-educated outsiders. The union leaders claimed, in the interests of their own members, that a man who had "come up the hard way" by working his passage upwards was inherently superior to others of purely academic education. But that was before education came to be held in the high respect it later enjoyed. The view was obvious nonsense—there was no harder way of coming up than the grammar school.

Awareness that shortage of talent was more serious than any other fanned the competition between business executives. According to a contemporary report only a few years after 1944—

One young man in his second year at university had already been offered a post at 750 [pounds] by one large company for when he should graduate, and was being assiduously courted by another vast company, whose managing director entertained him to lunch.

This was nothing to what happened later; eventually every forward-looking company had its team of talent scouts combing the universities and grammar schools and most science masters and lecturers were offered retainers if they would regularly supply reports on promising students. Newspapers were filled with employers' appeals to scholars; college magazines grew larger and larger on the proceeds of advertisements. This hectic competition was sometimes unfair, as many trade associations alleged, and sometimes led to abuse. Some clever grammar school pupils were dissuaded from continuing into the sixth forms by offers of generous apprenticeships, and others from seeking admission to the university by glib scouts who promised them not only high salaries immediately but university education later at company expense. Retainers and assistance with research expenses were not the best way of augmenting science teachers' salaries.

The N.U.S. (National Union of Students) and B.U.G.S.A. had to protect their members and in 1969 the Ministry of Education and the Federation of British Industries drew up the Code of Fair Practice for Utilizing the Products of Higher Education. Although a worthy endeavour, this proved so ineffective in practice that government control over the allocation of intellectual resources became imperative. When it was instituted priorities could be generally enforced. Effective brain-power planning is not only necessary to end one of the kinds of competition between employers that is wasteful, but gives the government strategic power to control the whole economy.

Industry surrendered to teachers the function of selecting recruits for management with a good enough grace when it saw that surrender was essential to survival. From that time on most of those who at the ages of nineteen or twenty-three entered the higher reaches of industry, commerce, and the professions were the pick of their age-groups. Managerial cadets were chosen on merit through competitive selection in the schools. But there, in this transition period, free competition stopped. As soon as the newcomer arrived in factory or office, he no longer had the chance to pit his talents against all and sundry in the promotion stakes. He was no longer permitted, even after he had spent several years learning the business, to stand up in open competition with people much older than himself. While he was a *junior* man, whether he had the capacity of Henry Ford or Lord Nuffield it made no matter, he had to be content with being at best a *junior* executive. In all the most important jobs promotion was still by seniority, so much so that without exceptional luck even the best-educated could not hope to reach the top of the ladder until they were fifty or sixty. The story of the third and most recent phase is the story of the way in which the principle of seniority has gradually yielded to the principle of merit, and industry been modelled on the schools.

It is once again difficult for us to realize how strongly entrenched the old were in those days, especially in Britain. Status for age had once been linked with hereditary status, but it was far less easy to discredit. By the middle of last century it was extremely rare to hear anyone openly defending a hereditary system. Kinship connexions were no longer thought to confer merit on a man. But age was. The rights of the old did not have to be publicly acclaimed, they were so widely taken for granted. Age was accorded deference for no better reason than that, and people did not even have to acknowledge the existence of any dilemma when on the one hand they talked in favour of promotion by merit and on the other acted in favour of promotion by age. They resolved the dilemma before it was properly posed by enormously over-estimating the value of "experience" which was imagined to be the product purely of years. There was a mystique about it: people said, "Ah, yes, but he's got more experience," as though that was the last word. Respect for age was as much the rule of society as respect for the aristocracy from which it had grown.

Seniores priores—there is no stronger testament to its influence than the schools. They weakened their own progressive role by upholding the very principle with which they were fundamentally at loggerheads. Prefects were one of the most distinctive features of the old public schools. These prefects were older boys who exercised day-to-day government over their younger fellows, some of whom were selected as "fags" to perform the duties of servants. The maintenance of discipline was in large part the responsibility of the prefects, who had the power to secure obedience by beating any little boy who incurred their displeasure. The prefect system was unfortunately taken over by the grammar schools too. Consequently, the regard younger children always have for older was converted into an awe which often lasted for life. The old, by allowing the young to have authority when it was not a threat to themselves, helped to ensure that their own power would later go unchallenged. The abolition of prefects was an important reform which started in the "progressive" co-educational schools and later spread to the more orthodox.

I have no space to trace the subtle and individually infinitesimal changes which have combined to create a new spirit; all I can do is to pinpoint some of the counter-forces which have in the end proved too strong for the gerontocracy. I will deal briefly with each of them in turn.

Pressure from the young No solid progress could be made until the young had generated more confidence in themselves. As long as they accepted the dominance of the old there was no hope of a shift in the distribution of power, any more than there had been any hope of change while the superiority of the higher classes in a hereditary system was recognized by the lower. The right of the old to power had first to be questioned as strenuously as the legitimacy of inheritance, and for the same reason. Inheritance was denounced for the simple reason that a developing industrial country in competition with others could no longer afford second-rate leaders; the needs of the economy reshaped society. This campaign was not called off just because one victory had been won, but was turned against the old. Members of every fresh generation revolted against their elders; youth of mettle to oppose the pretensions of age instead of siding with it for the sake of favours to come. Some cried destruction on the established order, some tried, more constructively, to remove the blocks to their own advancement. The most rebellious knew instinctively that the fastest progress occurs anywhere when the old have to surrender their power before their span of life is complete—the essence of every social revolution is the earlier transfer of authority from one generation to another; the wisest knew that the surest progress is made by the mouse, by nibbling at the establishment instead of by taking arms against it. The best policy was to criticize the worth of individual old people in an empirical manner rather than the class as a whole.

The young succeeded as much as they did in opposing private practice because they had the resources of the public culture to support them. They declared that youth was generally entitled, on the grounds of merit, to more preferment than it received. They were quite right. In any rapidly changing society the young are more at home than the old: it is easier for them to learn for the first time than for the old to unlearn, and learn again, for a second or third time, especially when nostalgia for their own youth makes the old disinclined even to try. This is more than ever true when the schools are progressing even more rapidly than their host society. Then children not only learn different things, attuned to the needs of their own day (particularly when the teachers are also young); they also learn more because standards are higher and methods of pedagogy better. Compare the boy who learns physics today with an elderly man who was at the same university in the eighties before Shag was even born. The change is so dramatic, it is not really the same subject at all. Given the same native ability, there is no doubt which of them should obtain an important post in the laboratories, say at H.Q. in Eugenics House. I say "given the same native ability"—but of course this is implausible. The content of higher education has not only advanced; methods of selecting those to benefit from it have improved at least as fast. Each ten-year age-cohort of the elite has up till recently had more innate capacity than the previous one; the university alumnus of 2000 more talent, as well as better training, than the alumnus of 1990; of 2010 more than of 2000. . . .

Improvement of merit-rating Perhaps the greatest reason for the change in mental climate is that merit has become progressively more measurable. In the old days seniority had the splendid advantage of being an objective standard, even if it was irrelevant, whereas merit was still subjective even though relevant. Indeed, for a long time, "merit" was little more than a respectable disguise for nepotism. Fathers secured promotion for their relatives and friends, and pretended to themselves and to others they were doing nothing except give merit its due. But if they concealed their fault from themselves, others were not so easily deceived. The trade unions, in particular, were only too well aware of the pitfalls of selecting by "merit," when the father was his own judge and psychologist, and were justifiably suspicious that when outsiders were introduced into the line of promotion something less than justice had been done. They therefore stood by promotion by seniority, which was at least one better than vile nepotism. The world could see whether, according to this particular idea of fairness, right prevailed or not. If on any ladder, a man of thirty was given superiority over a man of forty (or rather a man with ten years' service preferred to a man with twenty), then all could see the miscarriage of justice.

This vicious circle—the vagueness of merit leading to its rejection—was only broken when the means of selection employed in the schools were adapted for use in the economy. Intelligence tests and aptitude tests were objective, and a good deal more reliable than the older forms of examination which they supplemented. The first stage, as we have seen, was for the level of performance achieved in the tests (when taken together with the level of education with which the test results were correlated) to determine the level of entry into industry. Once people were ready, it was then but a step to extend the sway of the tests until the markings controlled promotion as well as selection. To begin with, employers had to submit candidates to their own house-tests; yet such was the suspicion in industrial relations at that time, their impartiality was distrusted just because they were the employer's responsibility. The atmosphere was much sweetened when the government established its chain of Regional Adult Education Centres and community centres as a common service to industry, and, after a very long and acrimonious debate, gave employers access to the results of intelligence tests from the Centres as well as the schools. Employers now have as close an interest as employees in the quinquennial revaluations at the regional centres, and many of them show their appreciation on the Prize Days of their factories.

One thing the regional centres could not do. They could not measure the qualities of character expressed in effort expended by an employee in the course of his work. Intelligence and effort together make up merit (I + E = M). The lazy genius is not one. Here employers have made their own contribution to the cause of progress. "Scientific management" pioneered by Taylor, the Galbraiths, and Bedaux has led to modern time and motion study, and this in its turn to the measurement of effort. The art of work measurement has become more of a science, with the consequence that wages can be assessed, and related to effort, in a more and more precise manner. I shall return to this subject in a later chapter. Dr. Roskill's great contribution was to show how the principle of work study could be applied to mental processes. After that the employer had by him a Roskill chart as well as the scores from the education centres, and if he chose wrongly withal, it was high time he had a re-test himself.

In Young's future history the social reforms bring about not only results that are expected—rapid economic growth and affluence—but also certain unanticipated consequences. The procedures that are developed to identify those members of society who can best profit from intensive education eventually permit selections to be made early in a person's life. Although a person may be retested and qualify for training anytime in his life, the procedures used to make the initial measurements are quite good, and very infrequently are men found to have been incorrectly prevented from obtaining an education and joining the *meritocratic elite*. The accurate and early identification of talent permits the separation of the population into two large classes, the meritocratic elite and the lower class, with virtually no reason for a member of the lower class to expect to move into the elite during adult life.

This great distinction between segments of the society, coupled with the near-zero rate of adult mobility, created the conditions necessary for members of each class to recognize a commonality of self interest based on similarity in social position. Since the elite controlled legitimate power in the society, they could increase their share of the society's goods and services relative to the proportion allocated to the lower class. Large numbers of lower-class men found themselves in a position in which the ideology justifying the existing division of goods and services within the society doomed them to poverty relative to the elite and offered no hope of upward mobility. According to Young, they responded to this by rejecting the ideology on which the allocation of rewards was based and developing an alternate value system. The new values that emerge are similar to those on which the economic organization of Bellamy's utopia is based (see Chapter 20). At the close of Young's book, rebellion is beginning.

6 Equality for Its Own Sake

Elitest views (or viewers) of American society have a tendency to harp on a theme of social equality leading to lowest common denominator outcomes—that is, the results in which standards, values, and solutions are determined by the average performance or task, or the alternative, no matter how unsound, preferred by the masses. In one of the earliest commentaries on American society, Alexis de Tocqueville, saw little dissatisfaction in aristocratic societies despite great inequalities, because the people "get as much accustomed to poverty as the rich to opulence." He gave much attention to the great danger in democratic societies of the tyranny of the majority and the role of voluntary associations which protect against such tyranny. Presumably, voluntary associations are composed of those fit to exercise power.

Nostalgia for, or trust in the wise elite and fear of the mindless mass is the theme that keeps reappearing. Much of the modern carping about decay of standards in schools is probably better understood as the operation of elitist mythology rather than the detection of real change. For example, the great universities of this country were, until recently, the finishing schools for offspring of the wealthy who by and large wasted much of their years in school learning the social graces necessary to become gentlemen and gentlewomen (tea and whiskey drinking and a smattering of knowledge of the classics) and very little else. The modern student who is produced by one of the mass education institutions is probably as well, if not better educated on the average than the product of the pre-mass education system. Perhaps the only difference between what students learn today and what they learned in the past is the subject matter of what is learned, since it is hard to imagine that less is learned at present.

The following story illustrates, in classical satirical form, the sorts of equality run rampant of which elitist mythology warns.

Harrison Bergeron

KURT VONNEGUT

The year was 2081, and everybody was finally equal. They weren't only equal before God and the law. They were equal every which way. Nobody was smarter than anybody else. Nobody was better looking than anybody else. Nobody was stronger or quicker than anybody else. All this equality was due to the 211th, 212th, and 213th Amendments of the Constitution, and to the unceasing vigilance of agents of the United States Handicapper General.

Some things about living still weren't quite right, though. April, for instance, still drove people crazy by not being springtime. And it was in that clammy month that the H-G men took George and Hazel Bergeron's fourteen-year-old son, Harrison away.

It was tragic, all right, but George and Hazel couldn't think about it very hard. Hazel had a perfectly average intelligence, which meant she couldn't think about anything except in short bursts. And George, while his intelligence was way above normal, had a little mental handicap radio in his ear. He was required by law to wear it at all times. It was tuned to a government transmitter. Every twenty seconds or so, the transmitter would send out some sharp noise to keep people like George from taking unfair advantage of their brains.

George and Hazel were watching television. There were tears on Hazel's cheeks, but she'd forgotten for the moment what they were about.

On the television screen were ballerinas.

A buzzer sounded in George's head. His thoughts fled in panic, like bandits from a burglar alarm.

"That was a real pretty dance, that dance they just did," said Hazel.

"Huh?" said George.

"That dance—it was nice," said Hazel.

"Yup," said George. He tried to think a little about the ballerinas. They weren't really very good—no better than anybody else would have been, anyway. They were burdened with sashweights and bags of birdshot, and their faces were masked, so that no one, seeing a free and graceful gesture or a pretty face, would feel like something the cat drug in. George was toying with the vague notion that maybe dancers shouldn't be handicapped. But he didn't get very far with it before another noise in his ear radio scattered his thoughts.

George winced. So did two out of the eight ballerinas.

Hazel saw him wince. Having no mental handicap herself, she had to ask George what the latest sound had been.

"Sounded like somebody hitting a milk bottle with a ball peen hammer," said George.

"I'd think it would be real interesting, hearing all the different sounds," said Hazel, a little envious. "All the things they think up."

"Um," said George.

"Only, if I was Handicapper General, you know what I would do?" said

Hazel. Hazel, as a matter of fact, bore a strong resemblance to the Handicapper General, a woman named Diana Moon Glampers. "If I was Diana Moon Glampers," said Hazel, "I'd have chimes on Sunday—just chimes. Kind of in honor of religion."

"I could think, if it was just chimes," said George.

"Well—maybe make 'em real loud," said Hazel. "I think I'd make a good Handicapper General."

"Good as anybody else," said George.

"Who knows better'n I do what normal is?" said Hazel.

"Right," said George. He began to think glimmeringly about his abnormal son who was now in jail, about Harrison, but a twenty-one-gun salute in his head stopped that.

"Boy!" said Hazel, "that was a doozy, wasn't it?"

It was such a doozy that George was white and trembling, and tears stood on the rims of his red eyes. Two of the eight ballerinas had collapsed to the studio floor, were holding their temples.

"All of a sudden you look so tired," said Hazel. "Why don't you stretch out on the sofa, so's you can rest your handicap bag on the pillows, honeybunch." She was referring to the forty-seven pounds of birdshot in a canvas bag, which was padlocked around George's neck. "Go on and rest the bag for a little while," she said. "I don't care if you're not equal to me for a while."

George weighed the bag with his hands. "I don't mind it," he said. "I don't notice it any more. It's just a part of me."

"You've been so tired lately—kind of wore out," said Hazel. "If there was just some way we could make a little hole in the bottom of the bag, and just take out a few of them lead balls. Just a few."

"Two years in prison and two thousand dollars fine for every ball I took out," said George. "I don't call that a bargain."

"If you could just take a few out when you came home from work," said Hazel. "I mean—you don't compete with anybody around here. You just set around."

"If I tried to get away with it," said George, "then other people'd get away with it—and pretty soon we'd be right back to the dark ages again, with everybody competing against everybody else. You wouldn't like that, would you?"

"I'd hate it," said Hazel.

"There you are," said George. "The minute people start cheating on laws, what do you think happens to society?"

If Hazel hadn't been able to come up with an answer to this question, George couldn't have supplied one. A siren was going off in his head.

"Reckon it'd fall all apart," said Hazel.

"What would?" said George blankly.

"Society," said Hazel uncertainly. "Wasn't that what you just said?"

"Who knows?" said George.

The television program was suddenly interrupted for a news bulletin. It wasn't clear at first as to what the bulletin was about, since the announcer, like all announcers, had a serious speech impediment. For about half a minute, and in a state of high excitement, the announcer tried to say, "Ladies and gentlemen—"

He finally gave up, handed the bulletin to a ballerina to read.

"That's all right—" Hazel said of the announcer, "he tried. That's the big thing. He tried to do the best he could with what God gave him. He should get a nice raise for trying so hard."

"Ladies and gentlemen—" said the ballerina, reading the bulletin. She must have been extraordinarily beautiful, because the mask she wore was hideous. And it was easy to see that she was the strongest and most graceful of all the dancers, for her handicap bags were as big as those worn by two-hundred-pound men.

And she had to apologize at once for her voice, which was a very unfair voice for a woman to use. Her voice was a warm, luminous, timeless melody. "Excuse me—" she said, and she began again, making her voice absolutely uncompetitive.

"Harrison Bergeron, age fourteen," she said in a grackle squawk, "has just escaped from jail, where he was held on suspicion of plotting to overthrow the government. He is a genius and an athlete, is under-handicapped, and should be regarded as extremely dangerous."

A police photograph of Harrison Bergeron was flashed on the screen-upside down, then sideways, upside down again, then right side up. The picture showed the full length of Harrison against a background calibrated in feet and inches. He was exactly seven feet tall.

The rest of Harrison's appearance was Halloween and hardware. Nobody had ever born heavier handicaps. He had outgrown hindrances faster than the H-G men could think them up. Instead of a little ear radio for a mental handicap, he wore a tremendous pair of earphones, and spectacles with thick wavy lenses. The spectacles were intended to make him not only half blind, but to give him whanging headaches besides.

Scrap metal was hung all over him. Ordinarily, there was a certain symmetry, a military neatness to the handicaps issued to strong people, but Harrison looked like a walking junkyard. In the race of life, Harrison carried three hundred pounds.

And to offset his good looks, the H-G men required that he wear at all times a red rubber ball for a nose, keep his eyebrows shaved off, and cover his even white teeth with black caps at snaggle-tooth random.

"If you see this boy," said the ballerina, "do not—I repeat, do not—try to reason with him."

There was the shriek of a door being torn from its hinges.

Screams and barking cries of consternation came from the television set. The photograph of Harrison Bergeron on the screen jumped again and again, as though dancing to the tune of an earthquake.

George Bergeron correctly identified the earthquake, and well he might have—for many was the time his own home had danced to the same crashing tune. "My God—" said George, "that must be Harrison!"

The realization was blasted from his mind instantly by the sound of an automobile collision in his head.

When George could open his eyes again, the photograph of Harrison was gone. A living, breathing Harrison filled the screen.

Clanking, clownish, and huge, Harrison stood in the center of the studio. The knob of the uprooted studio door was still in his hand. Ballerinas, technicians, musicians, and announcers cowered on their knees before him, expecting to die.

"I am the Emperor!" cried Harrison. "Do you hear? I am the Emperor! Everybody must do what I say at once!" He stamped his foot and the studio shook.

"Even as I stand here—" he bellowed, "crippled, hobbled, sickened—I am a greater ruler than any man who ever lived! Now watch me become what I *can* become!"

Harrison tore the straps of his handicap harness like wet tissue paper, tore straps guaranteed to support five thousand pounds.

Harrison's scrap-iron handicaps crashed to the floor.

Harrison thrust his thumbs under the bar of the padlock that secured his head harness. The bar snapped like celery. Harrison smashed his headphones and spectacles against the wall.

He flung away his rubber-ball nose, revealed a man that would have awed Thor, the god of thunder.

"I shall now select my Empress!" he said, looking down on the cowering people. "Let the first woman who dares rise to her feet claim her mate and her throne!"

A moment passed, and then a ballerina arose, swaying like a willow.

Harrison plucked the mental handicap from her ear, snapped off her physical handicaps with marvelous delicacy. Last of all, he removed her mask.

She was blindingly beautiful:

"Now—" said Harrison, taking her hand, "shall we show the people the meaning of the word dance? Music! he commanded.

The musicians scrambled into their chairs, and Harrison stripped them of their handicaps, too. "Play your best," he told them, "and I'll make you barons and dukes and earls."

The music began. It was normal at first—cheap, silly, false. But Harrison snatched two musicians from their chairs, waved them like batons as he sang the music as he wanted it played. He slammed them back into their chairs.

The music began again and was much improved.

Harrison and his Empress merely listened to the music for a while—listened gravely, as though synchronizing their heartbeats with it.

They shifted their weights to their toes.

Harrison placed his big hands on the girl's tiny waist, letting her sense the weightlessness that would soon be hers.

And then, in an explosion of joy and grace, into the air they sprang!

Not only were the laws of the land abandoned, but the law of gravity and the laws of motion as well.

They reeled, whirled, swiveled, flounced, capered, gamboled, and spun.

They leaped like deer on the moon.

The studio ceiling was thirty feet high, but each leap brought the dancers nearer to it.

It became their obvious intention to kiss the ceiling.

They kissed it.

And then, neutralizing gravity with love and pure will, they remained suspended in air inches below the ceiling, and they kissed each other for a long, long time.

It was then that Diana Moon Glampers, the Handicapper General, came into the studio with a double-barreled ten-gauge shotgun. She fired twice, and the Emperor and the Empress were dead before they hit the floor.

Diana Moon Glampers loaded the gun again. She aimed it at the musicians and told them they had ten seconds to get their handicaps back on.

It was then that the Bergerons' television tube burned out.

Hazel turned to comment about the blackout to George. But George had gone out into the kitchen for a can of beer.

George came back in with the beer, paused while a handicap signal shook him up. And then he sat down again. "You been crying?" he said to Hazel.

"Yup," she said.

"What about?" he said.

"I forget," she said. "Something real sad on television."

"What was it?" he said.

"It's all kind of mixed up in my mind," said Hazel.

"Forget sad things," said George.

"I always do," said Hazel.

"That's my girl," said George. He winced. There was the sound of a rivetting gun in his head.

"Gee—I could tell that one was a doozy," said Hazel.

"You can say that again," said George.

"Gee—" said Hazel, "I could tell that one was a doozy."

7 Playing the System

Few sociologists would argue against the assertion that the development of the complex form of social organization called bureaucracy is the social form that dominates industrial society. Max Weber, a social theorist of major significance, regarded the spread of the bureaucratic form of social organization as a profound change in the structure of society. Currently, there are some sociologists who argue that in the long run the bureaucratic form of social organization will show itself to be a more powerful force on society than the mode of financing practiced in a society (e.g., capitalist, socialist, or communist economic organization). That is, they argue that it may make relatively *little* difference what style of money handling is practiced within a society compared to the fact that all industrial societies are developing their control structures along similar lines—we call this pattern of social organization bureaucracy.

To say that an organization is bureaucratic means that it may be described in terms of a set of positions connected to one another for the purpose of accomplishing the organization's work. Associated with the positions are powers and responsibilities distributed in what should be a sensible manner for getting the job done. Also associated with positions are office holders who actually conduct the actions defined by the organizational chart. A grossly oversimplified picture of a formally organized task group is therefore one in which the organization's activities are carried out in a set of discrete steps coordinated through a rational (sensible) plan in which the contribution of each unit of the organization is defined. In this manner responsibility for error and credit for satisfactory carrying out of responsibilities can be traced to the appropriate organizational unit. Within that unit, work can be organized in an efficient manner, and people can develop the skills necessary to complete their assigned jobs with relative efficiency since they get to know the requirements of the job and have considerable practice at doing it. The organization is constructed along lines of specialization, and clear cut delegation of responsibility at the level of both the organizational plan and individual action.

The factors that make bureaucracy a powerful form of social organization are that it permits tasks of any degree of complexity to be undertaken; the nature of its organization form at least permits, if not encourages, rational debate about the best way to accomplish the particular step in the work chain; the organization's structure and functioning are not wholly dependant upon the unique talents of the set of office holders who are present at the moment; and it can provide a degree of economic security and social freedom for its employees that can successfully *rival* the security offered through competing organizational forms. This last point may be a bit difficult to see in a society in which competing organizational forms are difficult to find. It is perhaps easier to understand if one contrasts holding a job in an organization (and therefore having a salary) with farming a small piece of land that has traditionally been worked by one's family. On the farm one is assured of survival (providing there is no drought) and assured of living under the traditional authority system (usually age graded and patriarchal) that is associated with this mode of social life. Working for a government or corporate bureaucracy may compare favorably to the prospects of working on the farm since the work-related authority system is separate from other aspects of an individual's life and there are relatively clearly articulated rules about the hours during which one works, the obligations of the position one holds, and the remuneration one can expect for labor.

That bureaucracy is a powerful force in society is beyond dispute. It is also agreed that a substantial part of the reason for this is due to the stability and efficiency gains that come through clearly defining responsibilities of office holders, coordinating activities to accomplish complex tasks, and having a work force that is practiced at its tasks. Bureaucracy in its societal pervasive form is, however, a new social phenomenon and its nature is still not clearly or widely understood. For example, if the administrative segment of an organization can expand more rapidly than the productive segment and it is the policy of an organization to seek expansion through diversification of productive function, then it follows that as the organization diversifies there will be an even faster rate of administrative expansion since management units will need more management units to manage the coordination of management. In theory, there is no reason why a system organized this way might not still compare favorably with a less organizationally complex arrangement. In theory, although the coordination of various units requires work, the saving in reduced duplication of effort within various units, reduced competition between units and greater ability to plan sensibly might still be yielding a net gain. On the other hand, if bureaucratic form fails to solve some of the problems it should in theory solve, or these problems reappear with increased magnitude, there may actually be a point beyond which each unit of expansion increases the disadvantages of the bureaucratic form of organization.

For example, in theory one of the advantages of a formal organization is that since job requirements can be defined, personnel can be selected on the basis of whether or not they have the abilities to carry out the work and promotion can be based on evaluation of past performance and whether or not an individual has the abilities necessary for a more desirable job. This looks quite sensible and probably makes sense when the job requires the ability to read and only 5% of the applicants have this ability. When 90% of the applicants have this ability and one must still make a choice, it becomes convenient to introduce other requirements that permit a decision maker to make a choice on the rule of law (the formal policy) if not on the rule of reason (being sensible). One of the most convenient rules is to tie job requirements to numbers of years of education, on the theory that education is somehow related to job performance. I'm sure that education is related to the performance of certain jobs—those for which people receive specific training. As a general requirement it may be related to job performance for the reason that numbers of years of education is related to the social class position of one's parents; therefore, years of education as a decision rule may work to increase the class homogeneity of the people who have access to certain jobs. How this criterion relates to superior job performance is unclear to say the least.

Again, in theory it should be possible to evaluate an individual's performance and reward for the right reasons—for actions that contribute to the success of the organization through making things work better or doing better work. If an organization loses the ability to distinguish superior performance from mediocre performance and superior performance that is related to greater organizational success (a better or cheaper product, a simpler way of handling things, etc.) from superior performance at pleasing the people to whom one reports, then it loses many advantages that are gained through a rationally arranged work and administrative system. One of the competitive advantages of a formal organization over older forms of social organization is thought to be that rationality and specification tends to protect people from the whims of petty tyrants (people in love with small amounts of absolute power) and therefore builds loyalty to the system or organization. If the system becomes a petty tyrant in the sense that its behavior can be described in the same terms as those used to describe the actions of human petty tyrants, I imagine it will generate the same effective reactions.

The purpose of having a rationally constructed organization is to permit more sensible control and therefore better planned and more efficient operation. This necessitates having good theories of how complex systems operate and how working in a complex system affects people. Systems can certainly be developed without well understood design rules and may work reasonably well. They may also work well for a while and then begin to reveal their internal strains and contradictions. One thing is certain, at present no one has a powerful theory of how to maximize organizational efficiency and human satisfaction within the same plan.

The following story illustrates something of life in a totally bureaucratically organized world in which the petty tyrant features of the system are extreme and give rise to alienation (the sense that one's life is externally controlled). It also illustrates the weaknesses of a system that is predicated on processing the usual and of the nature of a system that becomes so complex that all who live within it become hopelessly dependent upon its procedures. What this story illustrates about processing the usual concerns mere acceptance of decisions simply because they are supposedly planned and reliance upon the assumption that everyone else one encounters is carrying out their legitimate function. The second point is more important since it illustrates something central to the structure of large and very complex bureaucracies. What actually moves in a bureaucracy is information in the form of statistics, directives, requests, reports, and decisions. The consequence of this information flow is that action is directed. People come to depend upon this information flow, or at least are conditioned to be responsive to what it brings since they must coordinate their behavior with it. If this information system is flawed and the system is complex, it may be possible that no one will ever notice the flaw. My point will become clear as you read.

Dodkin's Job

JACK VANCE

The Theory of Organized Society (as developed by Kinch, Kolbig, Penton, and others) yields such a wealth of significant information, revealing manifold intricacies and portentous projections, that occasionally it is well to consider its deceptively simple major premise (here stated by Kolbig):

> When self-willed microunits combine to form and sustain a durable macrounit, certain freedoms of action are curtailed.
>
> This is the basic process of Organization.
>
> The more numerous and erratic the microunits, the more complex must be the structure and function of the macrounit—hence the more pervasive and restricting the details of Organization.
>
> —from LESLIE PENTON, *First Principles of Organization*

The general population of the City had become forgetful of curtailed freedoms, as a snake no longer remembers the legs of its forebears. Somewhere someone has stated, "When the discrepancy between the theory and practice of a culture is very great, this indicates that the culture is undergoing rapid change." By such a test the culture of the City was stable, if not static. The population ordered their lives by schedule, classification, and precedent, satisfied with the bland rewards of Organization.

But in the healthiest tissue bacteria exist, and the most negligible impurity flaws a critical crystallization.

Luke Grogatch was forty, thin and angular, dour of forehead, with a sardonic cast to his mouth and eyebrows and a sideways twist to his head as if he suffered from earache. He was too astute to profess nonconformity; too perverse to strive for improved status; too pessimistic, captious, sarcastic, and outspoken to keep the jobs to which he found himself assigned. Each new reclassification depressed his status; he disliked each new job with increasing fervor.

Finally, rated as *Flunky/Class D/Unskilled.* Luke was dispatched to the District 8892 Sewer Maintenance Department and from there ordered out as night-shift swamper on Tunnel Gang Number 3's rotary drilling machine.

Reporting for work, Luke presented himself to the gang foreman, Fedor Miskitman, a big, buffalo-faced man with flaxen hair and placid blue eyes. Miskitman produced a shovel and took Luke to a position close up behind the drilling machine's cutting head. Here, said Miskitman, was Luke's station. Luke would be required to keep the tunnel floor clean of loose rock and gravel. When the tunnel broke through into an old sewer, there would be scale and that detritus known as "wet waste" to remove. Luke was to keep the dust trap clean and in optimum adjustment. During the breaks he would lubricate those bearings isolated from the automatic lubrication system and he was to replace broken teeth on the cutting head whenever necessary.

Luke inquired if this was the extent of his duties, his voice strong with an irony the guileless Fedor Miskitman failed to notice.

"That is all," said Miskitman. He handed Luke the shovel. "Mostly it is the trash. The floor must be clean."

Luke suggested to the foreman a modification of the hopper jaws which would tend to eliminate the spill of broken rock; in fact, went Luke's argument, why bother at all? Let the rock lie where it fell. The concrete lining of the tunnel would mask so trivial a scatter of gravel.

Miskitman dismissed the suggestion out of hand: the rock must be removed. When Luke asked why, Miskitman told him, "That is the way the job is done."

Luke made a rude noise under his breath. He tested the shovel and shook his head in dissatisfaction. The handle was too long, the blade too short. He reported this fact to Miskitman, who merely glanced at his watch and signaled to the drill operator. The machine whined into revolution and with an ear-splitting roar made contact with the rock. Miskitman departed, and Luke went back to work.

During the shift he found that if he worked in a half-crouch most of the hot, dust-laden exhaust from the machine would pass over his head. Changing a cutting tooth during the first rest period he burned a blister on his left thumb. At the end of the shift a single consideration deterred Luke from declaring himself unqualified: he would be declassified from *Flunky/Class D/Unskilled* to *Junior Executive,* with a corresponding cut in expense account. Such a declassification would take him to the very bottom of the Status List, and so could not be countenanced; his present expense account was barely adequate, covering nutrition at a Type RP Victualing Service, sleeping space in a Sublevel 22 dormitory, and sixteen Special Coupons per month. He took Class 14 Erotic Processing, and was allowed twelve hours per month at his recreation club, with optional use of barbells, table-tennis equipment, two miniature bowling alleys, and any of the six telescreens tuned permanently to Band H. Luke often daydreamed of a more sumptuous life: AAA nutrition, a suite of rooms for his exclusive use, Special Coupons by the bale, Class 7 Erotic Processing, or even Class 6, or 5: despite Luke's contempt for the High Echelon he had no quarrel with High Echelon perquisites. And always as a bitter coda to the daydreams came the conviction that he might have been enjoying these good things in all reality. He had watched his fellows jockeying; he knew all the tricks and techniques: the beavering, the gregarization, the smutting, knuckling, and subuculation. . . . Why not make use of this knowledge?

"I'd rather be Class D Flunky," sneered Luke to himself.

Occasionally a measure of doubt would seep into Luke's mind. Perhaps he merely lacked the courage to compete, to come to grips with the world! And the seep of doubt would become a trickle of self-contempt. A Nonconformist, that's what he was—and he lacked the courage to admit it!

Then Luke's obstinacy would reassert itself. Why admit to Nonconformity when it meant a trip to the Disorganized House? A fool's trick—and Luke was no fool. Perhaps he was a Nonconformist in all reality; again, perhaps not—he had never really made up his mind. He presumed that he was suspected; occasionally he intercepted queer side-glances and significant jerks of the head among his fellow workers. Let them leer. They could prove nothing.

But now . . . he was Luke Grogatch, Class D Flunky, separated by a single status from the nonclassified sediment of criminals, idiots, children, and proved Nonconformists. Luke Grogatch, who had dreamed such dreams of the High Echelon, of pride and independence! Instead—Luke Grogatch, Class D Flunky. Taking orders from a hay-headed lunk, working with semi-skilled laborers with status almost as low as his own: Luke Grogatch, flunky.

Seven weeks passed. Luke's dislike for his job became a mordant passion. The work was arduous, hot, repellent. Fedor Miskitman turned an uncomprehending gaze on Luke's most rancorous grimaces, grunted and shrugged at Luke's suggestions and arguments. This was the way things were done—his manner implied—always had been done, and always would be done.

Fedor Miskitman received a daily policy directive from the works superintendent which he read to the crew during the first rest break of the shift. These directives generally dealt with such matters as work norms, team spirit, and cooperation; pleas for a finer polish on the concrete; warnings against off-shift indulgence which might dull enthusiasm and decrease work efficiency. Luke usually paid small heed, until one day Fedor Miskitman, pulling out the familiar yellow sheet, read in his stolid voice:

PUBLIC WORKS DEPARTMENT, PUBLIC UTILITIES DIVISION
AGENCY OF SANITARY WORKS, DISTRICT 8892
SEWAGE DISPOSAL SECTION

Bureau of Sewer Construction and Maintenance Office of Procurement

Policy Directive: 6511 Series BV96
Order Code: GZP—AAR—REG
Reference: G98—7542
Date Code: BT—EQ—LLT

Authorized: LL8—P—SC 8892
Checked: 48
Counterchecked: 92C

From: Lavester Limon, Manager, Office of Procurement
Through: All construction and maintenance offices
To: All construction and maintenance superintendents
Attention: All job foremen

Subject: Tool longevity, the promotion thereof
Instant of Application: Immediate
Duration of Relevance: Permanent
Substance: At beginning of each shift all hand-tools shall be checked out of District 8892 Sewer Maintenance Warehouse. At close of each shift all hand-tools shall be carefully cleaned and returned to District 8892 Sewer Maintenance Warehouse.

Directive reviewed and transmitted: BUTRY KEGHORN, General Superintendent of Construction, Bureau of Sewer Construction
CLYDE KADDO, Superintendent of Sewer Maintenance

As Fedor Miskitman read the "Substance" section, Luke expelled his breath in an incredulous snort. Miskitman finished, folded the sheet with careful movements of his thick fingers, looked at his watch. "That is the directive. We are twenty-five seconds over time; we must get back to work."

"Just a minute," said Luke. "One or two things about that directive I want explained."

Miskitman turned his mild gaze upon Luke. "You did not understand it?"

"Not altogether. Who does it apply to?"

"It is an order for the entire gang."

"What do they mean, 'hand-tools'?"

"These are tools which are held in the hands."

"Does that mean a shovel?"

"A shovel?" Miskitman shrugged his burly shoulders. "A shovel is a hand tool."

Luke asked in a voice of hushed wonder: "They want me to polish my shovel, carry it four miles to the warehouse, then pick it up tomorrow and carry it back here?"

Miskitman unfolded the directive, held it at arm's length, and read with moving lips. "That is the order." He refolded the paper and returned it to his pocket.

Luke again feigned astonishment. "Certainly there's a mistake."

"A mistake?" Miskitman was puzzled. "Why should there be a mistake?"

"They can't be serious," said Luke. "It's not only ridiculous, it's peculiar."

"I do not know," said Miskitman incuriously. "To work. We are late one minute and a half."

"I assume that all this cleaning and transportation is done on Organization time," Luke suggested.

Miskitman unfolded the directive, held it at arm's length, read. "It does not say so. Our quota is not different." He folded the directive and put it in his pocket.

Luke spat on the rock floor. "I'll bring my own shovel. Let 'em carry around their own precious hand-tools."

Miskitman scratched his chin and once more reread the directive. He shook his head dubiously. "The order says that all hand-tools must be cleaned and taken to the warehouse. It does not say who owns the tools."

Luke could hardly speak for exasperation. "You know what I think of that directive?"

Fedor Miskitman paid him no heed. "To work. We are over time."

"If I was general superintendent—" Luke began, but Miskitman rumbled roughly.

"We do not earn perquisites by talking. To work. We are late."

The rotary cutter started up; seventy-two teeth snarled into gray-brown sandstone. Hopper jaws swallowed the chunks, passing them down an epiglottis into a feeder gut which evacuated far down the tunnel into lift-buckets. Stray chips rained upon the tunnel floor, which Luke Grogatch must scrape up and return into the hopper. Behind Luke two reinforcement men flung steel hoops into place, flash-welding them to longitudinal bars with quick pinches of the fingers, contact-plates in their gauntlets discharging the requisite gout of energy. Behind came the concrete-spray man, mix hissing out of his revolving spider, followed by two finishers, nervous men working with furious energy, stroking the concrete into a glossy polish. Fedor Miskitman marched back and forth, testing the reinforcement, gauging the thickness of the concrete, making frequent progress checks on the chart to the rear of the rotary cutter, where an electronic device traced the course of the tunnel, guiding it through the system of conduits, ducts, passages, pipes, and tubes for water, air, gas, steam, transportation, freight, and communication which knit the City into an Organized unit.

The night shift ended at four o'clock in the morning. Miskitman made careful entries in his log; the concrete-spray man blew out his nozzles; the reinforcement workers removed their gauntlets, power packs, and insulating garments. Luke Grogatch straightened, rubbed his sore back, and stood glowering at the shovel. He felt Miskitman's ox-calm scrutiny. If he threw the shovel to the side of the tunnel as usual and marched off about his business, he would be guilty of disorganized conduct. The penalty, as Luke knew well, was declassification. Luke stared at the shovel, fuming with humiliation. Conform or be declassified. Submit—or become a Junior Executive.

Luke heaved a deep sigh. The shovel was clean enough; one or two swipes with a rag would remove the dust. But there was the ride by crowded man-belt to the warehouse, the queue at the window, the check-ins, the added distance to his dormitory. Tomorrow the process must be repeated. Why the necessity for this added effort? Luke knew well enough. An obscure functionary somewhere along the chain of bureaus and commissions had been at a loss for a means to display his diligence. What better method than concern for valuable City property? Consequently the absurd directive, filtering down to Fedor Miskitman and ultimately to Luke Grogatch, the victim. What joy to meet this obscure functionary face to face, to tweak his sniveling nose, to kick his craven rump along the corridors of his own office. . . .

Fedor Miskitman's voice disturbed his reverie. "Clean your shovel. It is the end of the shift."

Luke made token resistance. "The shovel is clean," he growled. "This is the most absurd antic I've ever been coerced into. If only I—"

Fedor Miskitman, in a voice as calm and unhurried as a deep river, said, "If you do not like the policy, you should put a petition in the suggestion box. That is the privilege of all. Until the policy is changed you must conform. That is the way we live. That is Organization, and we are Organized men."

"Let me see that directive," Luke barked. "I'll get it changed. I'll cram it down somebody's throat. I'll—"

"You must wait until it is logged. Then you may have it; it is useless to me."

"I'll wait," said Luke between clenched teeth.

With method and deliberation Fedor Miskitman made a final check of the job, inspecting machinery, the teeth of the cutter head, the nozzles of the spider, the discharge belt. He went to his little desk at the rear of the rotary drill, noted progress, signed expense account vouchers, finally registered the policy directive on minifilm. Then with a ponderous sweep of his arm he tendered the yellow sheet to Luke. "What will you do with it?"

"I'll find who formed this idiotic policy. I'll tell him what I think of it and what I think of him, to boot."

Miskitman shook his head in disapproval. "That is not the way such things should be done."

"How would you do it?" asked Luke with a wolfish grin.

Miskitman considered, pursing his lips, jerking his bristling eyebrows. At last with great simplicity of manner he said, "I would not do it."

Luke threw up his hands and set off down the tunnel. Miskitman's voice boomed against his back. "You must take the shovel!"

Luke halted. Slowly he faced about, glared back at the hulking figure of the foreman. Obey the policy directive or be declassified. With slow steps, with hanging head and averted eyes, he retraced his path. Snatching the shovel, he stalked back down the tunnel. His bony shoulder blades were exposed and sensitive; Fedor Miskitman's mild blue gaze, following him, seemed to scrape the nerves of his back.

Ahead the tunnel extended, a glossy pale sinus, dwindling back along the distance they had bored. Through some odd trick of refraction alternate bright and dark rings circled the tube, confusing the eye, creating a hypnotic semblance of two-dimensionality. Luke shuffled drearily into this illusory bull's-eye, dazed with shame and helplessness, the shovel a load of despair. Had he come to this—Luke Grogatch, previously so arrogant in his cynicism and barely concealed Nonconformity? Must he cringe at last, submit slavishly to witless regulations? . . . If only he were a few places farther up the list! Drearily he pictured the fine incredulous shock with which he would have greeted the policy directive, the sardonic nonchalance with which he would have let the shovel fall from his limp hands. . . . Too late, too late! Now he must toe the mark, must carry his shovel dutifully to the warehouse. In a spasm of rage he flung the blameless implement clattering down the tunnel ahead of him. Nothing he could do! Nowhere to turn! No way to strike back! Organization: smooth and relentless; Organization: massive and inert, tolerant of the submissive, serenely cruel to the unbeliever . . . Luke came to his shovel and, whispering an obscenity, snatched it up and half-ran down the pallid tunnel.

He climbed through a manhole and emerged upon the deck of the 1123rd Avenue Hub, where he was instantly absorbed in the crowds trampling between the man-belts, which radiated like spokes, and the various escalators. Clasping the shovel to his chest, Luke struggled aboard the Fontego manbelt and rushed south, in a direction opposite to that of his dormitory. He rode ten minutes to Astoria Hub, dropped a dozen levels on the Grimesby College Escalator, and crossed a gloomy dank area smelling of old rock to a local feeder-belt which carried him to the District 8892 Sewer Maintenance Warehouse.

Luke found the warehouse brightly lit, the center of considerable activity, with several hundred men coming and going. Those coming, like Luke, carried tools; those going went empty-handed.

Luke joined the line which had formed in front of the tool storeroom. Fifty or sixty men preceded him, a drab centipede of arms, shoulders, heads, legs, the tools projecting to either side. The centipede moved slowly, the men exchanging badinage and quips.

Observing their patience, Luke's normal irascibility asserted itself. Look at them, he thought, standing like sheep, jumping to attention at the rustle of an unfolding directive. Did they inquire about the reason for the order? Did they question the necessity for their inconvenience? No! The louts stood chuckling and chatting, accepting the directive as one of life's incalculable vicissitudes, something elemental and arbitrary, like the changing of the seasons. . . . And he, Luke Grogatch, was he better or worse? The question burned in Luke's throat like the aftertaste of vomit.

Still, better or worse, where was his choice? Conform or declassify. A poor choice. There was always the recourse of the suggestion box, as Fedor Miskitman, perhaps in bland jest, had pointed out. Luke growled in disgust. Weeks later he might receive a printed form with one statement of a multiple-choice list checked off by some clerical flunky or junior executive: "The situation described by your petition is already under study by responsible officials. Thank you for your interest." Or, "The situation described by your petition is temporary and may shortly be altered. Thank you for your interest." Or, "The situation described by your petition is the product of established policy and is not subject to change. Thank you for your interest."

A novel thought occurred to Luke: he might exert himself and reclassify *up* the list. . . . As soon as the idea arrived he dismissed it. In the first place he was close to middle age; too many young men were pushing up past him. Even if he could goad himself into the competition. . .

The line moved slowly forward. Behind Luke a plump little man sagged under the weight of a Velstro inchskip. A forelock of light brown floss dangled over his moony face; his mouth was puckered into a rosebud of concentration; his eyes were absurdly serious. He wore a rather dapper pink and brown coverall with orange ankle-boots and a blue beret with the three orange pompoms affected by the Velstro technicians.

Between shabby, sour-mouthed Luke and this short moony man in the dandy's overalls existed so basic a difference that an immediate mutual dislike was inevitable.

The short man's prominent hazel eyes rested on Luke's shovel, traveled thoughtfully over Luke's dirt-stained trousers and jacket. He turned his eyes to the side.

"Come a long way?" Luke asked maliciously.

"Not far," said the moon-faced man.

"Worked overtime, eh?" Luke winked. "A bit of quiet beavering, nothing like it—or so I'm told."

"We finished the job," said the plump man with dignity. "Beavering doesn't enter into it. Why spend half tomorrow's shift on five minute's work we could do tonight?"

"I know a reason," said Luke wisely. "To do your fellow man a good one in the eye."

The moon-faced man twisted his mouth in a quick uncertain smile, then decided that the remark was not humorous. "That's not my way of working," he said stiffly.

"That thing must be heavy," said Luke, noting how the plump little arms struggled and readjusted to the irregular contours of the tool.

"Yes," came the reply. "It is heavy."

"An hour and a half," intoned Luke. "That's how long its taking me to park this shovel. Just because somebody up the list has a nightmare. And we poor hoodlums at the bottom suffer."

"I'm not at the bottom of the list. I'm a Technical Tool Operator."

"No difference," said Luke. "The hour and a half is the same. Just for somebody's silly notion."

"It's not really so silly," said the moon-faced man. "I fancy there is a good reason for the policy."

Luke shook the shovel by its handle. "And so I have to carry this back and forth along the man-belt three hours a day?"

The little man pursed his lips. "The author of the directive undoubtedly knows his business very well. Otherwise he'd not hold his classification."

"Just who is this unsung hero?" sneered Luke. "I'd like to meet him. I'd like to learn why he wants me to waste three hours a day."

The short man now regarded Luke as he might an insect in his victual ration. "You talk like a Nonconformist. Excuse me if I seem offensive."

"Why apologize for something you can't help?" asked Luke and turned his back.

He flung his shovel to the clerk behind the wicket and received a check. Elaborately Luke turned to the moon-faced man and tucked the check into the breast pocket of the pink and brown coveralls. "You keep this; you'll be using that shovel before I will."

He stalked proudly out of the warehouse. A grand gesture, but—he hesitated before stepping on the man-belt—was it sensible? The technical tool operator in the pink and brown coveralls came out of the warehouse behind him, giving him a queer glance, and hurried away.

Luke looked back into the warehouse. If he returned now he could set things right, and tomorrow there'd be no trouble. If he stormed off to his dormitory, it meant another declassification. Luke Grogatch, Junior Executive. Luke reached into his jumper and took out the policy directive he had acquired from Fedor Miskitman: a bit of yellow paper, printed with a few lines of type, a trivial thing in itself—but it symbolized the Organization: massive force in irresistible operation. Nervously Luke plucked at the paper and looked back into the warehouse. The tool operator had called him a Nonconformist; Luke's mouth squirmed in a brief weary grimace. It wasn't true. Luke was not a Nonconformist; Luke was nothing in particular. And he needed his bed, his nutrition ticket, his meager expense account. Luke groaned quietly—almost a whisper. The end of the road. He had gone as far as he could go; had he ever thought he could defeat the Organization? Maybe he was wrong and everyone else was right. Possible, thought Luke without conviction. Miskitman seemed content enough; the technical tool operator seemed not only content but complacent. Luke leaned against the warehouse wall, eyes burning and moist with self-pity. Nonconformist. Misfit. What was he going to do?

He curled his lip spitefully, stepped forward onto the man-belt. Devil take them all! They could declassify him; he'd become a junior executive and laugh!

In subdued spirits Luke rode back to the Grimesby Hub. Here, about to board the escalator, he stopped short, blinking and rubbing his long sallow chin, considering still another aspect to the matter. It seemed to offer the chance of—but no. Hardly likely . . . and yet, why not? Once again he examined the directive. Lavester Limon, Manager of the District Office of Procurement, presumably had issued the policy; Lavester Limon could rescind it. If Luke could so persuade Limon, his troubles, while not dissipated, at least would be lessened. He could report shovel-less to his job; he could return sardonic grin for bland hidden grin with Fedor Miskitman. He might even go to the trouble of locating the moon-faced little technical tool operator with the inchskip. . . .

Luke sighed. Why continue this futile daydream? First Lavester Limon must be induced to rescind the directive—and what were the odds of this? . . . Perhaps not astronomical, after all, mused Luke as he rode the man-belt back to his dormitory. The directive clearly was impractical. It worked an inconvenience on many people, while accomplishing very little. If Lavester Limon could be persuaded of this, if he could be shown that his own prestige and reputation were suffering, he might agree to recall the ridiculous directive.

Luke arrived at his dormitory shortly after seven. He went immediately to the communication booth, called the District 8892 Office of Procurement. Lavester Limon, he was told, would be arriving at eight-thirty.

Luke made a careful toilet, and after due consideration invested four Special Coupons in a fresh set of fibers: a tight black jacket and blue trousers of somewhat martial cut, of considerably better quality than his usual costume. Surveying himself in the washroom mirror, Luke felt that he cut not so poor a figure.

He took his morning quota of nutrition at a nearby Type RP Victualing Service, then ascended to the Sublevel 14 and rode the man-belt to District 8892 Bureau of Sewer Construction and Maintenance.

A pert office girl, dark hair pulled forward over her face in the modish "robber baron" style, conducted Luke into Lavester Limon's office. At the door she glanced demurely backward, and Luke was glad that he had invested in new clothes. Responding to the stimulus, he threw back his shoulders and marched confidently into Lavester Limon's office.

Lavester Limon, sitting at his desk, bumped briefly to his feet in courteous acknowledgement—an amiable-seeming man of middle stature, golden-brown hair brushed carefully across a freckled and suntanned bald spot;

golden-brown eyes, round and easy; a golden-brown lounge jacket and trousers of fine golden-brown corduroy. He waved his arm to a chair. "Won't you sit down, Mr. Grogatch?"

In the presence of so much cordiality Luke relaxed his truculence, and even felt a burgeoning of hope. Limon seemed a decent sort; perhaps the directive was, after all, an administrative error.

Limon raised his golden-brown eyebrows inquiringly.

Luke wasted no time on preliminaries. He brought forth the directive. "My business concerns this, Mr. Limon: a policy which you seem to have formulated."

Limon took the directive, read, nodded. "Yes, that's my policy. Something wrong?"

Luke felt surprise and a pang of premonition: surely so reasonable a man must instantly perceive the folly of the directive!

"It's simply not a workable policy," said Luke earnestly. "In fact, Mr. Limon, it's completely unreasonable!"

Lavester Limon seemed not at all offended. "Well, well! And why do you say that? Incidentally, Mr. Grogatch, you're . . ." Again the golden-brown eyebrows arched inquiringly.

"I'm a flunky, Class D, on a tunnel gang," said Luke. "Today it took me an hour and a half to check my shovel. Tomorrow, there'll be another hour and a half checking the shovel out. All on my own time. I don't think that's reasonable."

Lavester Limon reread the directive, pursed his lips, nodded his head once or twice. He spoke into his desk phone. "Miss Rab, I'd like to see—" he consulted the directive's reference number—"Item seven-five-four-two, File G ninety-eight." To Luke he said in rather an absent voice: "Sometimes these things become a trifle complicated."

"But can you change the policy?" Luke burst out. "Do you agree that it's unreasonable?"

Limon cocked his head to the side, made a doubtful grimace. "We'll see what's on the reference. If my memory serves me . . ." His voice faded away.

Twenty seconds passed. Limon tapped his fingers on his desk. A soft chime sounded. Limon touched a button and his desk-screen exhibited the item he had requested: another policy directive similar in form to the first.

PUBLIC WORKS DEPARTMENT, PUBLIC UTILITIES DIVISION
AGENCY OF SANITARY WORKS, DISTRICT 8892
SEWAGE DISPOSAL SECTION

Director's Office

Policy Directive: 2888 Series BQ008
Order Code: GZP—AAR—REF
Reference: OP9 123
Date Code: BR—EQ—LLT
Authorized: JR D-SDS
Checked: AC
Counterchecked: CX McD

From: JUDIATH RIPP, Director
Through:
To: LAVESTER LIMON, Manager, Office of Procurement
Attention:
Subject: Economies of operation
Instant of Application: Immediate
Duration of Relevance: Permanent
Substance: Your monthly quota of supplies for disbursement Type A, B, D, F, H is hereby reduced 2.2%. It is suggested that you advise affected personnel of this reduction, and take steps to insure most stringent economies. It has been noticed that department use of supplies Type D in particular is in excess of calculated norm.

Suggestion: Greater care by individual users of tools, including warehouse storage at night.

"Type D supplies," said Lavester Limon wryly, "are hand-tools. Old Ripp wants stringent economies. I merely pass along the word. That's the story behind six-five-one-one." He returned the directive in question to Luke and leaned back in his seat. "I can see how you're exercised, but—" he raised his hands in a careless, almost flippant gesture— "that's the way the Organization works."

Luke sat rigid with disappointment. "Then you won't revoke the directive?"

"My dear fellow! How can I?"

Luke made an attempt at reckless nonchalance. "Well, there's always room for me among the junior executives. I told them where to put their shovel."

"Mmmf. Rash. Sorry I can't help." Limon surveyed Luke curiously, and his lips curved in a faint grin. "Why don't you tackle old Ripp?"

Luke squinted sideways in suspicion. "What good will that do?"

"You never know," said Limon breezily. "Suppose lightning strikes—suppose he rescinds his directive? I can't agitate with him myself; I'd get in trouble—but there's no reason why you can't." He turned Luke a quick knowing smile, and Luke understood that Lavester Limon's amiability, while genuine, served as a useful camouflage for self-interest and artful playing of the angles.

Luke rose abruptly to his feet. He played cat's-paw for no one, and he opened his mouth to tell Lavester Limon as much. In that instant a recollection crossed his mind: the scene in the warehouse, where he had contemptuously tossed the check for his shovel to the technical tool operator. Always Luke had been prone to the grand gesture, the reckless commitment which left him no scope for retreat. When would he learn self-control? In a subdued voice Luke asked, "Who is this Ripp again?"

"Judiath Ripp, Director of the Sewage Disposal Section. You may have difficulty getting in to see him; he's a troublesome old brute. Wait, I'll find if he's at his office."

He made inquiries into his desk phone. Information returned to the effect that Judiath Ripp had just arrived at the Section office on Sublevel 3, under Bramblebury Park.

Limon gave Luke tactical advice. "He's choleric—something of a barker. Here's the secret: pay no attention to him. He respects firmness. Pound the table. Roar back at him. If you pussyfoot he'll sling you out. Give him tit for tat and he'll listen."

Luke looked hard at Lavester Limon, well aware that the twinkle in the golden-brown eyes was malicious glee. He said, "I'd like a copy of that directive, so he'll know what I'm talking about."

Limon sobered instantly. Luke could read his mind: *Will Ripp hold it against me if I send up this crackpot? It's worth the chance.* "Sure," said Limon. "Pick it up from the girl."

Luke ascended to Sublevel 3 and walked through the pleasant trilevel arcade below Bramblebury Park. He passed the tall, glass-walled fishtank open to the sky and illuminated by sunlight, boarded the local man-belt, and after a ride of two or three minutes alighted in front of the District 8892 Agency of Sanitary Works.

The Sewage Disposal Section occupied a rather pretentious suite off a small courtyard garden. Luke walked along a passage tiled with blue, gray, and green mosaic and entered a white room furnished in pale gray and pink. A long mural of cleverly twisted gold, black, and white tubing decorated one wall; another was swathed in heavy green leaves growing from a chest-high planter. At a desk sat the receptionist, a plump pouty blonde girl with a simulated bone through her nose and a shark's-tooth necklace dangling around her neck. She wore her hair tied up over her head like a sheaf of wheat, and an amusing black and brown primitive symbol decorated her forehead.

Luke explained that he wished a few words with Mr. Judiath Ripp, Director of the Section.

Perhaps from uneasiness, Luke spoke brusquely. The girl, blinking in surprise, examined him curiously. After a moment's hesitation she shook her head doubtfully. "Won't someone else do? Mr. Ripp's day is tightly scheduled. What did you want to see him about?"

Luke, attempting a persuasive smile, achieved instead a leer of sinister significance. The girl was frankly startled.

"Perhaps you'll tell Mr. Ripp I'm here," said Luke. "One of his policy directives—well, there have been irregularities, or rather a misapplication—"

"Irregularities?" The girl seemed to hear only the single word. She gazed at Luke with new eyes, observing the crisp new black and blue garments with their quasi-military cut. Some sort of inspector? "I'll call Mr. Ripp," she said nervously. "Your name, sir, and status?"

"Luke Grogatch. My status—" Luke smiled once more, and the girl averted her eyes. "It's not important."

"I'll call Mr. Ripp, sir. One moment, if you please." She swung around, murmured anxiously into her screen, looked at Luke, and spoke again. A thin voice rasped a reply. The girl swung back around and nodded at Luke. "Mr. Ripp can spare a few minutes. The first door, please."

Luke walked with stiff shoulders into a tall, wood-paneled room, one wall of which displayed green-glowing tanks of darting red and yellow fish. At the desk sat Judiath Ripp, a tall, heavy man, himself resembling a large fish. His head was narrow, pale as mackeral, and rested backward-tilting on his shoulders. He had no perceptible chin; the neck ran up to his carplike mouth. Pale eyes stared at Luke over small round nostrils; a low brush of hair thrust up from the rear of his head like dry grass over a sand dune. Luke remembered Lavester Limon's verbal depiction of Ripp: "choleric." Hardly appropriate. Had Limon a grudge against Ripp? Was he using Luke as an instrument of mischievous revenge? Suspecting as much, Luke felt uncomfortable and awkward.

Judiath Ripp surveyed him with cold unblinking eyes. "What can I do for you, Mr. Grogatch? My secretary tells me you are an investigator of some sort."

Luke considered the situation, his narrow black eyes fixed on Ripp's face. He told the exact truth. "For several weeks I have been working in the capacity of a Class D Flunky on a tunnel gang."

"What the devil do you investigate on a tunnel gang?" Ripp asked in chilly amusement.

Luke made a slight gesture, one signifying much or nothing, as the other might choose to take it. "Last night the foreman of this gang received a policy directive issued by Lavester Limon of the Office of Procurement. For sheer imbecility this policy caps any of my experience."

"If it's Limon's doing, I can well believe it," said Ripp between his teeth.

"I sought him out in his office. He refused to accept the responsibility and referred me to you."

Ripp sat a trifle straighter in his chair. "What policy is this?"

Luke passed the two directives across the desk. Ripp read slowly, then reluctantly returned the directives. "I fail to see exactly—" He paused. "I should say, these directives merely reflect instructions received by me which I have implemented. Where is the difficulty?"

"Let me cite my personal experience," said Luke. "This morning—as I say, in my temporary capacity as a flunky—I carried a shovel from tunnel head to warehouse and checked it. The operation required an hour and a half. If I were working steadily on a job of this sort, I'd be quite demoralized."

Ripp appeared untroubled. "I can only refer you to my superiors." He spoke aside into his desk phone. "Please transmit File OR nine, Item one-two-three." He turned back to Luke. "I can't take responsibility, either for the directive or for revoking it. May I ask what sort of investigation takes you down into the tunnels? And to whom you report?"

At a loss for words at once evasive and convincing, Luke conveyed an attitude of contemptuous silence.

Judiath Ripp contracted the skin around his blank round eyes in a frown. "As I consider this matter I become increasingly puzzled. Why is this subject a matter for investigation? Just who—"

From a slot appeared the directive Ripp had requested. He glanced at it, then tossed it to Luke. "You'll see that this relieves me totally of responsibility," he said curtly.

The directive was the standard form:

PUBLIC WORKS DEPARTMENT, PUBLIC UTILITIES DIVISION

Office of The Commissioner of Public Utilities

Policy Directive: 449 Series UA-14-G2
Order Code: GZP—AAR—REF
Reference: TQ9—1422
Date Code: BP—EQ—LLT
Authorized: PU-PUD-Org.
Checked: G. Evan
Counterchecked: Hernon Klanech

From: Parris deVicker, Commissioner of Public Utilities
Through: All District Agencies of Sanitary Works
To: All Department Heads
Attention:

Subject: The urgent need for sharp and immediate economies in the use of equipment and consumption of supplies.

Instant of Application: Immediate
Duration of Relevance: Permanent
Substance: All department heads are instructed to initiate, effect, and enforce rigid economies in the employment of supplies and equipment, especially those items comprised of or manufactured from alloy metals or requiring the functional consumption of same in those areas in which official authority is exercised. A decrement of 2% will be considered minimal. Status augmentation will in some measure be affected by economies achieved.

Directive reviewed and transmitted: LEE JON SMITH, District Agent of Sanitary Works 8892

Luke rose to his feet, concerned now only to depart from the office as quickly as possible. He indicated the directive. "This is a copy?"

"Yes."

"I'll take it, if I may." He included it with the previous two.

Judiath Ripp watched with a faint but definite suspicion. "I fail to understand whom you represent."

"Sometimes the less one knows the better," said Luke.

The suspicion faded from Judiath Ripp's piscine face. Only a person secure in his status could afford to use language of this sort to a member of the low High Echelon. He nodded slightly. "Is that all you require?"

"No," said Luke, "but it's all I can get here."

He turned toward the door, feeling the rake of Ripp's eyes on his back.

Ripp's voice cut at him suddenly and sharply. "Just a moment."

Luke slowly turned.

"Who are you? Let me see your credentials."

Luke laughed coarsely. "I don't have any."

Judiath Ripp rose to his feet, stood towering with knuckles pressed on the desk. Suddenly Luke saw that, after all, Judiath Ripp *was* choleric. His face, mackeral-pale, became suffused with salmon-pink. "Identify yourself," he said throatily, "before I call the watchman."

"Certainly," said Luke. "I have nothing to hide. I am Luke Grogatch. I work as Class D Flunky on Tunnel Gang Number Three, out of the Bureau of Sewer Construction and Maintenance."

"What are you doing here, misrepresenting yourself, wasting my time?"

"Where did I misrepresent myself?" demanded Luke in a contentious voice. "I came here to find out why I had to carry my shovel to the warehouse this morning. It cost me an hour and a half. It doesn't make sense. You've been ordered to economize two per cent, so I spend three hours a day carrying a shovel back and forth."

Judiath Ripp stared at Luke for a few seconds, then abruptly sat down. "You're a Class D Flunky?"

"That's right."

"Hmm. You've been to the Office of Procurement. The manager sent you here?"

"No. He gave me a copy of his directive, just as you did."

The salmon-pink flush had died from Ripp's flat cheeks. The carplike mouth twitched in infinitesimal amusement. "No harm in that, certainly. What do you hope to achieve?"

"I don't want to carry that blasted shovel back and forth. I'd like you to issue orders to that effect."

Judiath Ripp spread his pale mouth in a cold drooping smile. "Bring me a policy directive to that effect from Parris deVicker and I'll be glad to oblige you. Now—"

"Will you make an appointment for me?"

"An appointment?" Ripp was puzzled. "With whom?"

"With the Commissioner of Public Utilities."

"Pffah!" Ripp waved his hand in cold dismissal. "Get out."

Luke stood in the blue mosaic entry seething with hate for Ripp, Limon, Miskitman, and every intervening functionary. If he were only chairman of the board for a brief two hours (went the oft-repeated daydream), how they'd quickstep! In his mind's eye he saw Judiath Ripp shoveling wads of wet waste with a leaden shovel while a rotary driller, twice as noisy and twice as violent, blew back gales of hot dust and rock chips across his neck. Lavester Limon would be forced to change the smoking teeth of the drill with a small and rusty monkey wrench, while Fedor Miskitman, before and after the shift, carried shovel, monkey wrench, and all the worn teeth to and from the warehouse.

Luke stood moping in the passage for five minutes, then escalated to the surface, which at this point, by virtue of Bramblebury Park, could clearly be distinguishable as the surface and not just another level among coequal levels. He walked slowly along the gravel paths, ignoring the open sky for the immediacy of his problems. He faced a dead end. There was no further scope of action. Judiath Ripp had mockingly suggested that he consult the Commissioner of Public Utilities. Even if by some improbable circumstance he secured an appointment with the Commissioner, what good would ensue? Why should the Commissioner revoke a policy directive of such evident importance? Unless he could be persuaded—by some instrumentality Luke was unable to define or even imagine—to issue a special directive exempting Luke from the provision of the policy . . . Luke chuckled hollowly, a noise which alarmed the pigeons strutting along the walk. Now what? Back to the dormitory. His dormitory privileges included twelve hours use of his cot per day, and he was not extracting full value from his expense account unless he made use of it. But Luke had no desire for sleep. As he glanced up at the perspective of the towers surrounding the park he felt a melancholy exhilaration. The sky, the wonderful clear open sky, blue and brilliant! Luke shivered, for the sun here was hidden by the Morgenthau Moonspike, and the air was brisk.

Luke crossed the park, thinking to sit where a band of hazy sunlight slashed down between the towers. The benches were crowded with blinking old men and women, but Luke presently found a seat. He sat looking up into the sky, enjoying the mild natural sun warmth. How seldom did he see the sun! In his youth he had frequently set forth on long cross-city hikes, rambling high along the skyways, with space to right and left, the clouds near enough for intimate inspection, the sunlight sparkling and stinging his skin. Gradually the hikes had spread apart, coming at ever longer intervals, and now he could hardly remember when last he'd tramped the wind-lanes. What dreams he had had in those early days, what exuberant visions! Obstacles seemed trivial; he had seen himself clawing up the list, winning a good expense account, the choicest of perquisites, unnumbered Special Coupons! He had planned to have a private air-car, unrestricted nutrition, an apartment far above the surface, high and remote. . . . Dreams. Luke had been victimized by his tongue, his quick temper, his obstinacy. At heart, he was no Nonconformist—no, cried Luke, never! Luke had been born of tycoon stock, and through influence, a word here, a hint there, had been launched into the Organization on a high status. But circumstances and Luke's chronic truculence had driven him into opposition with established ways, and down the Status List he had gone: through professional scholarships, technical trainee appointments, craft apprenticeships, all the varieties of semiskills and machine operation. Now he was Luke Grogatch, flunky, unskilled, Class D, facing the final declassification. But still too vain to carry a shovel. No: Luke corrected himself. His vanity was not at stake. Vanity he had discarded long ago, along with his youthful dreams. All he had left was pride, his right to use the word "I" in connection with himself. If he submitted to Policy Directive 6511 he would relinquish this right; he would be absorbed into the masses of the Organization as a spatter of foam falls back and is absorbed into the ocean. . . . Luke jerked nervously to his feet. He wasted time sitting here. Judiath Ripp, with conger-like malice, had suggested a directive from the Commissioner of Public Utilities. Very Well, Luke would obtain that directive and fling it down under Ripp's pale round nostrils.

How?

Luke rubbed his chin dubiously. He walked to a communication booth and checked the directory. As he had surmised, the Commission of Public Utilities was housed in the Organization Central Tower, in Silverado, District 3666, ninety miles to the north.

Luke stood in the watery sunlight, hoping for inspiration. The aged idlers, huddling on the benches like winterbound sparrows, watched him incuriously. Once again Luke was obscurely pleased with his purchase of new clothes. A fine figure he cut, he assured himself.

How? wondered Luke. How to gain an appointment with the Commissioner? How to persuade him to change his views?

No inkling of a solution presented itself.

He looked at his watch: it was still only mid-morning. Ample time to visit Organization Central and return in time to report for duty . . . Luke grimaced wanly. Was his resolution so feeble, then? Was he, after all, to slink back into the tunnel tonight carrying the hated shovel? Luke shook his head slowly. He did not know.

At the Bramblebury Interchange Luke boarded an express highline northbound for Silverado Station. With a hiss and a whine, the shining metal worm darted forward, sliding up to the 13th Level, flashing north at great speed in and out of the sunlight, through tunnels, across chasms between towers, with far below the nervous seethe of the City. Four times the express sighed to a halt: at IBM University, at Braemar, at Great Northern Junction, and finally, thirty minutes out of Bramblebury, at Silverado Central Luke disembarked; the express slid away through the towers, lithe as an eel through waterweed.

Luke entered the tenth-level foyer of the Central Tower, a vast cave of marble and bronze. Throngs of men and women thrust past him: grim, striding tycoons, stamped with the look of destiny, High Echelon personnel, their assistants, the assistants to their assistants, functionaries on down the list, all dutifully wearing high-status garments, the lesser folk hoping to be mistaken for their superiors. All hurried, tense-faced and abrupt, partly from habit, partly because only a person of low status had no need to hurry. Luke thrust and elbowed with the best of them, and made his way to the central kiosk where he consulted a directory.

Parris deVicker, Commissioner of Public Utilities, had his office on the 59th Level. Luke passed him by and located the Secretary of Public Affairs, Mr. Sewell Sepp, on the 81st Level. No more underlings, thought Luke. This time I'm going to the top. If anyone can resolve this matter, it's Sewell Sepp.

He put himself aboard the lift and emerged into the lobby of the Department of Public Affairs—a splendid place, glittering with disciplined color and ornament after that mock-antique décor known as Second Institutional. The walls were of polished milk glass inset with medallions of shifting kaleidoscopic flashes. The floor was diapered in blue and white sparklestone. A dozen bronze statues dominated the room, massive figures symbolizing the basic public services: communication, transport, education, water, energy, and sanitation. Luke skirted the pedestals and crossed to the reception counter, where ten young women in handsome brown and black uniforms stood with military precision, each to her six feet of counter top. Luke selected one of these girls, who curved her lips in an automatic empty smile.

"Yes sir?"

"I want to see Mr. Sepp," said Luke brazenly.

The girl's smile remained frozen while she looked at him with startled eyes. "Mr. who?"

"Sewell Sepp, the Secretary of Public Affairs."

The girl asked gently, "Do you have an appointment, sir?"

"No."

"It's impossible, sir."

Luke nodded sourly. "Then I'll see Commissioner Parris deVicker."

"Do you have an appointment to see Mr. deVicker?"

"No, I'm afraid not."

The girl shook her head with a trace of amusement. "Sir, you can't just walk in on these people. They're extremely busy. Everyone must have an appointment."

"Oh, come now," said Luke. "Surely it's conceivable that—"

"Definitely not, sir."

"Then," said Luke, "I'll make an appointment. I'd like to see Mr. Sepp some time today, if possible."

The girl lost interest in Luke. She resumed her manner of impersonal courtesy. "I'll call the office of Mr. Sepp's appointment secretary."

She spoke into a mesh, then turned back to Luke. "No appointments are open this month, sir. Will you speak to someone else? Some under-official?"

"No," said Luke. He gripped the edge of the counter for a moment, started to turn away, then asked, "Who authorizes these appointments?"

"The secretary's first aide, who screens the list of applications."

"I'll speak to the first aide, then."

The girl sighed. "You need an appointment, sir."

"I need an appointment to make an appointment?"

"Yes, sir."

"Do I need an appointment to make an appointment for an appointment?"

"No, sir. Just walk right in."

"Where?"

"Suite Forty-two, inside the rotunda, sir."

Luke passed through twelve-foot crystal doors and walked down a short hall. Scurrying patterns of color followed him like shadows along both the walls, grotesque cubistic shapes parodying the motion of his body: a whimsey which surprised Luke and which might have pleased him under less critical circumstances.

He passed through another pair of crystal portals into the rotunda. Six levels above, a domed ceiling depicted scenes of legend in stained glass. Behind a ring of leather couches doors gave into surrounding offices; one of these doors, directly across from the entrance, bore the words:

Offices of the Secretary
Department of Public Affairs

On the couches, half a hundred men and women waited with varying degrees of patience. The careful disdain with which they surveyed each other suggested that their status was high; the frequency with which they consulted their watches conveyed the impression that they were momentarily on the point of departure.

A mellow voice sounded over a loudspeaker: "Mr. Artur Coff, please, to the Office of the Secretary." A plump gentleman threw down the periodical he had fretfully been examining and jumped to his feet. He crossed to the bronze and black glass door and passed through.

Luke watched him enviously, then turned aside through an arch marked *Suite 42*. An usher in a brown and black uniform stepped forward: Luke stated his business and was conducted into a small cubicle.

A young man behind a metal desk peered intently at him. "Sit down, please." He motioned to a chair. "Your name?"

"Luke Grogatch."

"Ah, Mr. Grogatch. May I inquire your business?"

"I have something to say to the Secretary of Public Affairs."

"Regarding what subject?"

"A personal matter."

"I'm sorry, Mr. Grogatch. The Secretary is more than busy. He's swamped with important Organization business. But if you'll explain the situation to me, I'll recommend you to an appropriate member of the staff."

"That won't help," said Luke, "I want to consult the Secretary in relation to a recently issued policy directive."

"Issued by the Secretary?"

"Yes."

"You wish to object to this directive?"

Luke grudgingly admitted as much.

"There are appropriate channels for this process," said the aide decisively. "If you will fill out this form—not here, but in the rotunda—drop it into the suggestion box to the right of the door as you go out—"

In sudden fury Luke wadded up the form and flung it down on the desk. "Surely he has five minutes free—"

"I'm afraid not, Mr. Grogatch," the aide said in a voice of ice. "If you will look through the rotunda you will see a number of very important people who have waited, some of them for months, for five minutes with the Secretary. If you wish to fill out an application, stating your business in detail, I will see that it receives due consideration."

Luke stalked out of the cubicle. The aide watched him go with a bleak smile of dislike. The man obviously had Nonconformist tendencies, he thought . . . probably should be watched.

Luke stood in the rotunda, muttering, "What now? What now? What now?" in a half-mesmerized undertone. He stared around the rotunda, at the pompous High Echelon folk, arrogantly consulting their watches and tapping their feet. "Mr. Jepper Prinn!" called the mellow voice over the loudspeaker. "The Office of the Secretary, if you please." Luke watched Jepper Prinn walk to the bronze and black glass portal.

Luke slumped into a chair, scratched his long nose, looked cautiously around the rotunda. Nearby sat a big, bull-necked man with a red face, protruding lips, a shock of rank blond hair—a tycoon, judging from his air of absolute authority.

Luke rose and went to a desk placed for the convenience of those waiting. He took several sheets of paper with the Tower letterhead and unobtrusively circled the rotunda to the entrance into Suite 42. The bull-necked tycoon paid him no heed.

Luke girded himself, closing his collar, adjusting the set of his jacket. He took a deep breath, then, when the florid man glanced in his direction, came forward officiously. He looked briskly around the circle of couches, consulting his papers: then catching the eye of the tycoon, frowned, squinted, walked forward.

"Your name, sir?" asked Luke in an official voice.

"I'm Hardin Arthur," rasped the tycoon. "Why?"

Luke nodded, consulted his paper. "The time of your appointment?"

"Eleven-ten. What of it?"

"The Secretary would like to know if you can conveniently lunch with him at one-thirty?"

Arthur considered. "I suppose it's possible," he grumbled. "I'll have to rearrange some other business. . . . An inconvenience—but I can do it, yes."

"Excellent," said Luke. "At lunch the Secretary feels that he can discuss your business more informally and at greater length than at eleven-ten, when he can only allow you seven minutes."

"Seven minutes!" rumbled Arthur indignantly. "I can hardly spread my plans out in seven minutes."

"Yes sir," said Luke. "The Secretary realizes this, and suggests that you lunch with him."

Arthur petulantly hauled himself to his feet. "Very well. Lunch at one-thirty, correct?"

"Correct, sir. If you will walk directly into the Secretary's office at that time."

Arthur departed the rotunda, and Luke settled into the seat Arthur had vacated.

Time passed very slowly. At ten minutes after eleven the mellow voice called out, "Mr. Hardin Arthur, please. To the Office of the Secretary."

Luke rose to his feet, stalked with great dignity across the rotunda, and went through the bronze and black glass door.

Behind a long black desk sat the Secretary, a rather undistinguished man with gray hair and snapping gray eyes. He raised his eyebrows as Luke came forward: Luke evidently did not fit his preconception of Hardin Arthur.

The Secretary spoke. "Sit down, Mr. Arthur. I may as well tell you bluntly and frankly that we think your scheme is impractical. By 'we' I mean myself and the Board of Policy Evaluation—who of course have referred to the Files. First, the costs are excessive. Second, there's no guarantee that you can phase your program into that of our other tycoons. Third, the Board of Policy Evaluation tells me that Files doubts whether we'll need that much new capacity.

"Ah," Luke nodded wisely. "I see. Well, no matter. It's not important."

"Not important?" The Secretary sat up in his chair, stared at Luke in wonder. "I'm surprised to hear you say so."

Luke made an airy gesture. "Forget it. Life's too short to worry about these things. Actually there's another matter I want to discuss with you."

"Ah?"

"It may seem trivial, but the implications are large. A former employee called the matter to my attention. He's now a flunky on one of the sewer maintenance tunnel gangs, an excellent chap. Here's the situation. Some idiotic jack-in-office has issued a directive which forces this man to carry a shovel back and forth to the warehouse every day, before and after work. I've taken the trouble to follow up the matter and the chain leads here." He displayed his three policy directives.

Frowningly the Secretary glanced through them. "These all seem perfectly regular. What do you want me to do?"

"Issue a directive clarifying the policy. After all, we can't have these poor devils working three hours overtime for tomfoolishness."

"Tomfoolishness?" The Secretary was displeased. "Hardly that, Mr. Arthur. The economy directive came to me from the Board of Directors, from the Chairman himself, and if—"

"Don't mistake me," said Luke hastily. "I've no quarrel with economy; I merely want the policy applied sensibly. Checking a shovel into the warehouse—where's the economy in that?"

"Multiply that shovel by a million, Mr. Arthur," said the Secretary coldly.

"Very well, multiply it," argued Luke. "We have a million shovels. How many of these million shovels are conserved by this order? Two or three a year?"

The Secretary shrugged. "Obviously in a general directive of this sort, inequalities occur. So far as I'm concerned, I issued the directive because I was instructed to do so. If you want it changed you'll have to consult the Chairman of the Board."

"Very well. Can you arrange an appointment for me?"

"Let's settle the matter even sooner," said the Secretary. "Right now. We'll talk to him across the screen, although, as you say, it seems a trivial matter. . . ."

"Demoralization of the working force isn't trivial, Secretary Sepp."

The Secretary shrugged, touched a button, spoke into a mesh. "The Chairman of the Board, if he's not occupied."

The screen glowed. The Chairman of the Board of Directors looked out at them. He sat in a lounge chair on the deck of his penthouse at the pinnacle of the tower. In one hand he held a glass of pale effervescent liquid; beyond him opened sunlight and blue air and a wide glimpse of the miraculous City.

"Good morning, Sepp," said the Chairman cordially, and nodded toward Luke. "Good morning to you, sir."

"Chairman, Mr. Arthur here is protesting the economy directive you sent down a few days ago. He claims that strict application is causing hardship among the labor force: demoralization, actually. Something to do with shovels."

The Chairman considered. "Economy directive? I hardly recall the exact case."

Secretary Sepp described the directive, citing code and reference numbers, explaining the provisions, and the Chairman nodded in recollection. "Yes, the metal shortage thing. Afraid I can't help you, Sepp, or you, Mr. Arthur. Policy Evaluation sent it up. Apparently we're running short of minerals; what else can we do? Cinch in the old belts, eh? Hard on all of us. What's this about shovels?"

"It's the whole matter," cried Luke in sudden shrillness, evoking startled glances from Secretary and Chairman. "Carrying a shovel back and forth to the warehouse—three hours a day! It's not economy, it's a disorganized farce!"

"Come now, Mr. Arthur," the Chairman chided humorously. "So long as you're not carrying the shovel yourself, why the excitement? It works the very devil with one's digestion. Until Policy Evaluation changes its collective mind—as it often does—then we've got to string along. Can't go counter to Policy Evaluation, you know. They're the people with the facts and figures."

"Neither here nor there," mumbled Luke. "Carrying a shovel three hours—"

"Perhaps a bit of bother for the men concerned," said the Chairman with a hint of impatience, "but they've got to see the thing from the long view. Sepp, perhaps you'll lunch with me? A marvelous day, lazy weather."

"Thank you, Mr. Chairman. I'll be pleased indeed."

"Excellent. At one or one-thirty, whenever it's convenient for you."

The screen went blank. Secretary Sepp rose to his feet. "There it is, Mr. Arthur. I can't do any more."

"Very well, Mr. Secretary," said Luke in a hollow voice.

"Sorry I can't be of more help in that other matter, but as I say—"

"It's inconsequential."

Luke turned, left the elegant office, passed through the bronze and black glass doors into the rotunda. Through the arch into Suite 42 he saw a large, bull-necked man, tomato-red in the face, hunched forward across a counter. Luke stepped forward smartly, leaving the rotunda just as the authentic Mr. Arthur and the aide came forth, deep in agitated conversation.

Luke stopped by the information desk. "Where is the Policy Evaluation Board?"

"Twenty-ninth Level, sir, this building."

In Policy Evaluation on the 29th Level Luke talked with a silk-mustached young man, courtly and elegant, with the status classification *Plan Coordinator*. "Certainly!" exclaimed the young man in response to Luke's question. "Authoritative information is the basis of authoritative organization. Material from Files is collated and digested in the Bureau of Abstracts, and sent up to us. We shape it and present it to the Board of Directors in the form of a daily précis."

Luke expressed interest in the Bureau of Abstracts, and the young man quickly became bored. "Grubbers among the statistics, barely able to compose an intelligible sentence. If it weren't for us . . ." His eyebrows, silken as his mustache, hinted of the disasters which in the absence of Policy Evaluation would overtake the Organization. "They work in a suite down on the Sixth Level."

Luke descended to the Bureau of Abstracts, and found no difficulty gaining admission to the general office. In contrast to the rather nebulous intellectualism of Policy Evaluation, the Bureau of Abstracts seemed workaday and matter-of-fact. A middle-aged woman, cheerfully fat, inquired Luke's business, and when Luke professed himself a journalist, conducted him about the premises. They went from the main lobby, walled in antique cream-colored plaster with gold scrollwork, past the small fusty cubicles, where clerks sat at projection-desks scanning ribbons of words. Extracting idea-sequences, emending, excising, condensing, cross-referring, finally producing the abstract to be submitted to Policy Evaluation. Luke's fat and cheerful guide brewed them a pot of tea; she asked questions which Luke answered in general terms, straining his voice and pursing his mouth in the effort to seem agreeable and hearty. He himself asked questions.

"I'm interested in a set of statistics on the scarcity of metals, or ores, or something similar, which recently went up to Policy Evaluation. Would you know anything about this?"

"Heavens, no!" the woman responded. "There's just too much material coming in—business of the entire Organization."

"Where does this material come from? Who sends it to you?"

The woman made a humorous little grimace of distaste. "From Files, down on Sublevel Twelve. I can't tell you much, because we don't associate with the personnel. They're low status: clerks and the like. Sheer automatons."

Luke expressed an interest in the source of the Bureau of Abstract's information. The woman shrugged, as if to say, everyone to his own taste. "I'll call down to the Chief File Clerk; I know him, very slightly."

The Chief File Clerk, Mr. Sidd Boatridge, was self-important and brusque, as if aware of the low esteem in which he was held by the Bureau of Abstracts. He dismissed Luke's questions with a stony face of indifference. "I really have no idea, sir. We file, index, and cross-index material into the Information Bank, but we concern ourselves very little with outgoing data. My duties in fact are mainly administrative. I'll call in one of the under-clerks; he can tell you more than I can."

The under-clerk who answered Boatridge's summons was a short, turnip-faced man with matted red hair. "Take Mr. Grogatch into the outer office," said the Chief File Clerk testily. "He wants to ask you a few questions."

In the outer office, out of the Chief File Clerk's hearing, the under-clerk became rather surly and pompous, as if he had divined the level of Luke's status. He referred to himself as a "line-tender" rather than as a file clerk, the latter apparently being a classification of lesser prestige. His "line-tending" consisted of sitting beside a panel which glowed and blinked with a thousand orange and green lights. "The orange lights indicate information going down into the Bank," said the file clerk. "The green lights show where somebody up-level is drawing information out—generally at the Bureau of Abstracts."

Luke observed the orange and green flickers for a moment. "What information is being transmitted now?"

"Couldn't say," the file clerk grunted. "It's all coded. Down in the old office we had a monitoring machine and never used it. Too much else to do."

Luke considered. The file clerk showed signs of restiveness. Luke's mind worked hurriedly. He asked, "So—as I understand it—you file information, but have nothing further to do with it?"

"We file it and code it. Whoever wants information puts a program into the works and the information goes out to him. We never see it, unless we went and looked in the old monitoring machine."

"Which is still down at your old office?"

The file clerk nodded. "They call it the staging chamber now. Nothing there but input and output pipes, the monitor, and the custodian."

"Where is the staging chamber?"

"Way down the levels, behind the Bank. Too low for me to work. I got more ambition." For emphasis he spat on the floor.

"A custodian is there, you say?"

"An old junior executive named Dodkin. He's been there a hundred years."

Luke dropped thirty levels aboard an express lift, then rode the down escalator another six levels to Sublevel 46. He emerged on a dingy landing with a low-perquisite nutrition hall to one side, a lift-attendants' dormitory to the other. The air carried the familiar reek of the deep underground, a compound of dank concrete, phenol, mercaptans, and a discreet but pervasive human smell. Luke realized with bitter amusement that he had returned to familiar territory.

Following instructions grudgingly detailed by the under-file clerk, Luke stepped aboard a chattering man-belt labeled *902—Tanks.* Presently he came to a brightly lit landing marked by a black and yellow sign: *Information Tanks. Technical Station.* Inside the door a number of mechanics sat on stools, dangling their legs, lounging, chaffering.

Luke changed to a side-belt, even more dilapidated, almost in a state of disrepair. At the second junction—this one unmarked—he left the man-belt and turned down a narrow passage toward a far yellow bulb. The passage was silent, almost sinister in its dissociation from the life of the City.

Below the single yellow bulb a dented metal door was daubed with a sign:

Information Tanks—Staging Chamber
No Admittance

Luke tested the door and found it locked. He rapped and waited.

Silence shrouded the passage, broken only by a faint sound from the distant man-belt.

Luke rapped again, and now from within came a shuffle of movement. The door slid back and a pale placid eye looked forth. A rather weak voice inquired, "Yes, sir?"

Luke attempted a manner of easy authority. "You're Dodkin the custodian?"

"Yes, sir, I'm Dodkin."

"Open up, please, I'd like to come in."

The pale eye blinked in mild wonder. "This is only the staging room sir. There's nothing here to see. The storage complexes are around to the front; if you'll go back to the junction—"

Luke broke into the flow of words. "I've just come down from the Files; it's you I want to see."

The pale eye blinked once more; the door slid open. Luke entered the long, narrow, concrete-floored staging room. Conduits dropped from the ceiling by the thousands, bent, twisted, and looped, and entered the wall, each conduit labeled with a dangling metal tag. At one end of the room was a grimy cot where Dodkin apparently slept; at the other end was a long black desk: the monitoring machine? Dodkin himself was small and stooped, but moved nimbly in spite of his evident age. His white hair was stained but well brushed; his gaze, weak and watery, was without guile, and fixed on Luke with an astronomer's detachment. He opened his mouth, and words quavered forth in spate, with Luke vainly seeking to interrupt.

"Not often do visitors come from above. Is something wrong?"

"No, nothing wrong."

"They should tell me if aught isn't correct, or perhaps there's been new policies of which I haven't been notified."

"Nothing like that, Mr. Dodkin. I'm just a visitor—"

"I don't move out as much as I used to, but last week I—"

Luke pretended to listen while Dodkin maundered on in obbligato to Luke's bitter thoughts. The continuity of directives leading from Fedor Miskitman to Lavester Limon to Judiath Ripp, bypassing Parris deVicker to Sewell Sepp and the Chairman of the Board, then returning down the classifications, down the levels, through the Policy Evaluation Board, the Bureau of Abstracts, the File Clerk's Office—the continuity had finally ended; the thread he had traced with such forlorn hope seemed about to lose itself. Well, Luke told himself, he had accepted Miskitman's challenge; he had failed, and now was faced with his original choice. Submit, carry the wretched shovel back and forth to the warehouse, or defy the order, throw down his shovel, assert himself as a free-willed man, and be declassified, to become a junior executive like old Dodkin—who, sucking and wheezing, still rambled on in compulsive loquacity.

". . . Something incorrect, I'd never know, because who ever tells me? From year end to year end I'm quiet down here, and there's no one to relieve me, and I only get to the up-side rarely, once a fortnight or so, but then once you've seen the sky, does it ever change? And the sun, the marvel of it, but once you've seen a marvel—"

Luke drew a deep breath. "I'm investigating an item of information which reached the File Clerk's Office. I wonder if you can help me."

Dodkin blinked his pale eyes. "What item is this, sir? Naturally I'll be glad to help in any way, even though—"

"The item dealt with economy in the use of metals and metal tools."

Dodkin nodded. "I remember the item perfectly."

It was Luke's turn to stare. "You *remember* this item?"

"Certainly. It was, if I say so, one of my little interpolations. A personal observation which I included among the other material."

"Would you be kind enough to explain?"

Dodkin would be only too pleased to explain. "Last week I had occasion to visit an old friend over by Claxton Abbey, a fine conformist, well adapted and cooperative, even if, alas, like myself, a junior executive. Of course, I mean no disrespect to good Davy Evans, like myself about ready for the pension—though little enough they allow nowadays—

"The interpolation?"

"Yes, indeed. On my way home along the man-belt—on Sublevel Thirty-two, as I recall—I saw a workman of some sort—perhaps an electrical technician—toss several tools into a crevice on his way off-shift. I thought, now there's a slovenly act—disgraceful! Suppose the man forgot where he had hidden his tools? They'd be lost! Our reserves of raw metallic ore are very low—that's common knowledge—and every year the ocean water becomes weaker and more dilute. That man had no regard for the future of Organization. We should cherish our natural resources, do you not agree, sir?"

"I agree, naturally. But—"

"In any event, I returned here and added a memorandum to that effect into the material which goes up to the Assistant File Clerk. I thought that perhaps he'd be impressed and say a word to someone with influence—perhaps the Head File Clerk. In any event, there's the tale of my interpolation. Naturally I attempted to give it weight by citing the inevitable diminution of our natural resources."

"I see," said Luke. "And do you frequently include interpolations into the day's information?"

"Occasionally," said Dodkin, "and sometimes, I'm glad to say, people more important than I share my views. Only three weeks ago I was delayed several minutes on my way between Claxton Abbey and Kittsville on Sublevel Thirty. I made a note of it, and last week I noticed that construction has commenced on a new eight-lane man-belt between the two points, a really magnificent and modern undertaking. A month ago I noticed a shameless group of girls daubed like savages with cosmetic. What a waste, I told myself; what vanity and folly! I hinted as much in a little message to the Under-File Clerk. I seem to be just one of the many with these views, for two days later a general order discouraging these petty vanities was issued by the Secretary of Education."

"Interesting," Luke muttered. "Interesting indeed. How do you include these—interpolations—into the information?"

Dodkin hobbled nimbly to the monitoring machine. "The output from the tanks comes through here. I print a bit on the typewriter and tuck it in where the Under-Clerk will see it."

"Admirable," sighed Luke. "A man with your intelligence should have ranked higher in the Status List."

Dodkin shook his placid old head. "I don't have the ambition nor the ability. I'm fit for just this simple job, and that only barely. I'd take my pension tomorrow, only the Chief File Clerk asked me to stay on a bit until he could find a man to take my place. No one seems to like the quiet down here."

"Perhaps you'll have your pension sooner than you think," said Luke.

Luke strolled along the glossy tube, ringed with alternate pale and dark refractions like a bull's-eye. Ahead was motion, the glint of metal, the mutter of voices. The entire crew of Tunnel Gang Number 3 stood idle and restless.

Fedor Miskitman waved his arm with uncharacteristic vehemence. "Grogatch! At your post! You've held up the entire crew!" His heavy face was suffused with pink. "Four minutes already we're behind schedule."

Luke strolled closer.

"Hurry!" bellowed Miskitman. "What do you think this is, a blasted promenade?"

If anything Luke slackened his pace. Fedor Miskitman lowered his big head, staring balefully. Luke halted in front of him.

"Where's your shovel?" Fedor Miskitman asked.

"I don't know," said Luke. "I'm here on the job. It's up to you to provide tools."

Fedor Miskitman stared unbelievingly. "Didn't you take it to the warehouse?"

"Yes," said Luke. "I took it there. If you want it go get it—"

Fedor Miskitman opened his mouth. He roared, "Get off the job!"

"Just as you like," said Luke. "You're the foreman."

"Don't come back!" bellowed Miskitman. "I'll report you before the day is out. You won't gain status from me, I tell you that!"

"Status?" Luke laughed. "Go ahead. Cut me down to junior executive. Do you think I care? No. And I'll tell you why. There's going to be a change or two made. When things seem different to you, think of me."

Luke Grogatch, Junior Executive, said good-by to the retiring custodian of the staging chamber. "Don't thank me, not at all," said Luke. "I'm here by my own doing. In fact—well, never mind all that. Go up-side, sit in the sun, enjoy the air."

Finally Dodkin, in mingled joy and sorrow, hobbled for the last time down the musty passageway to the chattering man-belt.

Luke was alone in the staging chamber. Around him hummed the near-inaudible rush of information. From behind the wall came the sense of a million relays clicking, twitching, meshing; of cylinders and trace-tubes and memory-lakes whirring with activity. At the monitoring machine the output streamed forth on a reel of yellow tape. Nearby rested the typewriter.

Luke seated himself. His first interpolation: what should it be? Freedom for the Nonconformists? Tunnel gang foremen to carry tools for the entire crew? A higher expense account for junior executives?

Luke rose to his feet and scratched his chin. Power . . . to be subtly applied. How should he use it? To secure rich perquisites for himself? Yes, of course, this he would accomplish, by devious means. And then—what? Luke thought of the billions of men and women living and working in the Organization. He looked at the typewriter. He could shape their lives, change their thoughts, disorganize the Organization. Was this wise? Or right? Or even amusing?

Luke sighed. In his mind's eye he saw himself standing on a high terrace overlooking the city. Luke Grogatch, Chairman of the Board. Not impossible, quite feasible. A little at a time, the correct interpolations . . . Luke Grogatch, Chairman of the Board, Yes. This for a starter. But it was necessary to move cautiously, with great delicacy.

Luke seated himself at the typewriter and began to pick out his first interpolation.

8 I Forgot About That

Predicting the consequences of a planned intervention in the normal state of affairs of an ongoing social system is an exceedingly difficult feat to accomplish. Some of the reasons for this are the complexity of the situation that one is attempting to control, the likelihood that there are more variables affecting the outcome than are recognized, the fact that some of the causal variables are not under one's control and the fact that some of the people whose behavior one wishes to control may desire different outcomes than intended and so may respond differently than is expected.

If, for the moment, we eliminate from consideration the involvement of people in the prediction of effects of interference in the operation of an ongoing system, it turns out that both physical and social scientists frequently face the same problems of lack of adequate knowledge of causal variables and lack of adequate control over causal variables when they attempt to control the actions of normal systems. Controlling the weather and controlling the economy might be thought of as problems of about the same magnitude of difficulty for physical and social scientists. Both problems involve the management of extremely complex systems about which relatively little is understood, and both systems are markedly affected by variables that no one knows how to control at the present.

If one looks carefully, it turns out that the great successes of physical science (where success means doing something that has a consequence that people value) are not in the area of controlling "natural" systems. For example, no one knows how to change weather patterns so that adequate rainfall will permit farming in a naturally arid region. The typical solution to this sort of problem is to invent something that does not exist in the "natural" environment—an irrigation system. Perhaps physical scientists learned long ago that they don't know enough to play god in a big way. What they can do is play god in a small way by putting together in a new fashion bits and pieces of the world to produce things that people need that did not come about "naturally."

Social scientists have failed to learn that they don't know enough to plan to control "natural" systems. Instead of trying to control well developed "natural" systems it might be wise to attempt to build something new. Katherine Maclean's story "The Snowball Effect" illustrates what might happen if one were to go about introducing some small changes in the normal state of affairs.

The Snowball Effect

KATHERINE MACLEAN

"All right," I said, "what is sociology good for?"

Wilton Caswell, Ph.D., was head of my Sociology Department, and right then he was mad enough to chew nails. On the office wall behind him were three or four framed documents in Latin, but I didn't care at that moment if he papered the walls with his degrees. I had been appointed dean and president to see to it that the university made money. I had a job to do, and I meant to do it.

He bit off each word with great restraint: "Sociology is the study of social institutions, Mr Halloway."

I tried to make him understand my position. "Look, it's the big-money men who are supposed to be contributing to the support of this college. To them, sociology sounds like socialism—nothing can sound worse than that—and an institution is where they put Aunt Maggy when she began collecting Wheaties in a stamp album. We can't appeal to them that way. Come on now." I smiled condescendingly, knowing it would irritate him. "What are you doing that's worth anything?"

He glared at me, his white hair bristling and his nostrils dilated like a war horse about to whinny. I can say one thing for them—these scientists and professors always keep themselves well under control. He had a book in his hand and I was expecting him to throw it, but he spoke instead:

"This department's analysis of institutional accretion, by the use of open system mathematics, has been recognized as an outstanding and valuable contribution to—"

The words were impressive, whatever they meant, but this still didn't sound like anything that would pull in money. I interrupted, "Valuable in what way?"

He sat down on the edge of his desk thoughtfully, apparently recovering from the shock of being asked to produce something solid for his position, and ran his eyes over the titles of the books that lined his office walls.

"Well, sociology has been valuable to business in initiating worker efficiency and group motivation studies, which they now use in management decisions. And, of course, since the depression, Washington has been using sociological studies of employment, labour, and standards of living as a basis for its general policies of—"

I stopped him with both hands raised. "Please, Professor Caswell! That would hardly be a recommendation. Washington, the New Deal and the present Administration are somewhat touchy subjects to the men I have to deal with. They consider its value debatable, if you know what I mean. If they got the idea that sociology professors are giving advice and guidance—No, we have to stick to brass tacks and leave Washington out of this. What, specifically, has the work of this specific department done that would make it as worthy to receive money as—say, a heart disease research fund?"

He began to tap the corner of his book absently on the desk, watching me. "Fundamental research doesn't show immediate effects, Mr Halloway, but its value is recognized."

I smiled and took out my pipe. "All right, tell me about it. Maybe I'll recognize its value."

Prof. Caswell smiled back tightly. He knew his department was at stake. The other departments were popular with donors and pulled in gift money by scholarships and fellowships, and supported their professors and graduate students by research contracts with the government and industry. Caswell had to show a way to make his own department popular—or else.

He laid down his book and ran a hand over his ruffled hair. "Institutions—organizations, that is—" his voice became more resonant: like most professors, when he had to explain something he instinctively slipped into his platform lecture mannerisms, and began to deliver an essay—"have certain tendencies built into the way they happen to have been organized, which cause them to expand or contract without reference to the needs they were founded to serve."

He was becoming flushed with the pleasure of explaining his subject. "All through the ages, it has been a matter of wonder and dismay to men that a simple organization—such as a church to worship in, or a delegation of weapons to a warrior class merely for defence against an outside enemy—will either grow insensately and extend its control until it is a tyranny over their whole lives, or, like other organizations set up to serve a vital need, will tend to repeatedly dwindle and vanish, and have to be painfully rebuilt.

"The reason can be traced to little quirks in the way they were organized, a matter of positive and negative power feedbacks. Such simple questions as, "Is there a way a holder of authority in this organization can use the power available to him to increase his power?" provide the key. But it still could not be handled until the complex questions of interacting motives and long-range accumulations of minor effects could somehow be simplified and formulated. In working on the problem, I found that the mathematics of open system, as introduced to biology by Ludwig von Bertalanffy and George Kreezer, could be used as a base that would enable me to develop a specifically social mathematics, expressing the human factors of intermeshing authority and motives in simple formulas.

"By these formulations, it is possible to determine automatically the amount of growth and period of life of any organization. The UN, to choose an unfortunate example, is a shrinker type organization. Its monetary support is not in the hands of those who personally benefit by its governmental activities, but, instead, in the hands of those who would personally lose by any extension and encroachment of its authority on their own. Yet by the use of formula analysis—"

"That's theory," I said. 'How about proof?'

"My equations are already being used in the study of limited-size Federal corporations. Washington—"

I held up my palm again. "Please, not that nasty word again. I mean, where else has it been put into operation? Just a simple demonstration, something to show that it works, that's all."

He looked away from me thoughtfully, picked up the book and began to tap it on the desk again. It had some unreadable title and his name on it in gold letters. I got the distinct impression again that he was repressing an urge to hit me with it.

He spoke quietly. "All right. I'll give you a demonstration. Are you willing to wait six months?"

"Certainly, if you can show me something at the end of that time."

Reminded of time, I glanced at my watch and stood up.

"Could we discuss this over lunch?" he asked.

"I wouldn't mind hearing more, but I'm having lunch with some executors of a millionaire's will. They have to be convinced that by, 'furtherance of research into human ills,' he meant that the money should go to research fellowships for postgraduate biologists at the university, rather than to a medical foundation."

"I see you have your problems, too," Caswell said, conceding me nothing. He extended his hand with a chilly smile. "Well, good afternoon, Mr Halloway. I'm glad we had this talk."

I shook hands and left him standing there, sure of his place in the progress of science and the respect of his colleagues, yet seething inside because I, the president and dean, had boorishly demanded that he produce something tangible.

My job isn't easy. For a crumb of favourable publicity and respect in the newspapers and an annual ceremony in a silly costume, I spend the rest of the year going hat in hand, asking politely for money at everyone's door, like a well-dressed panhandler, and trying to manage the university on the dribble I get. As far as I was concerned, a department had to support itself or be cut down to what student tuition pays for, which is a handful of overcrowded courses taught by an assistant lecturer. Caswell had to make it work or get out.

But the more I thought about it, the more I wanted to hear what he was going to do for a demonstration.

At lunch, three days later, while we were waiting for our order, he opened a small notebook. "Ever hear of feedback effects?"

"Not enough to have it clear."

"You know the snowball effect, though."

"Sure, start a snowball rolling downhill and it grows."

"Well, now—" He wrote a short line of symbols on a blank page and turned the notebook around for me to inspect it. "Here's the formula for the snowball process. It's the basic general growth formula—covers everything."

It was a row of little symbols arranged like an algebra equation. One was a concentric spiral going up, like a cross-section of a snowball rolling in snow. That was a growth sign.

I hadn't expected to understand the equation, but it was almost as clear as a sentence. I was impressed and slightly intimidated by it. He had already explained enough so that I knew that, if he was right, here was the growth of the Catholic Church and the Roman Empire, the conquests of Alexander and the spread of the smoking habit and the change and rigidity of the unwritten law of styles.

"Is it really as simple as that?" I asked.

"You notice," he said, "that when it becomes too heavy for the cohesion strength of snow, it breaks apart. Now in human terms—"

The chops and mashed potatoes and peas arrived.

"Go on," I urged.

He was deep in the symbology of human motives and the equations of human behaviour in groups. After running through a few different types of grower and shrinker type organizations, we came back to the snowball, and decided to run the test by making something grow.

"You add the motives," he said, "and the equation will translate them into organization."

"How about a good selfish reason for the ins to drag others into the group—some sort of bounty on new members, a cut of their membership fee?" I suggested uncertainly, feeling slightly foolish. "And maybe a reason why the members would lose if any of them resigned, and some indirect way they could use to force each other to stay in."

"The first is the chain letter principle," he nodded. "I've got that. The other . . ." He put the symbols through some mathematical manipulation so that a special grouping appeared in the middle of the equation. "That's it."

Since I seemed to have the right idea, I suggested some more, and he added some, and juggled them around in different patterns. We threw out a few that would have made the organization too complicated, and finally worked out an idyllically simple and deadly little organization set-up where joining had all the temptation of buying a sweepstakes ticket, going in deeper was as easy as hanging around a race track, and getting out was like trying to pull free from a Malayan thumb trap. We put our heads closer together and talked lower, picking the best place for the demonstration.

"Abington?"

"How about Watashaw? I have some student sociological surveys of it already. We can pick a suitable group from that."

"This demonstration has got to be convincing. We'd better pick a little group that no one in his right mind would expect to grow."

"There should be a suitable club—"

"Ladies," said the skinny female chairman of the Watashaw Sewing Circle. "Today we have guests." She signalled for us to rise, and we stood up, bowing to polite applause and smiles. "Professor Caswell, and Professor Smith." (My alias.) "They are making a survey of the methods and duties of the clubs of Watashaw."

We sat down to another ripple of applause and slightly wider smiles, and then the meeting of the Watashaw Sewing Circle began. In five minutes I began to feel sleepy.

There were only about thirty people there, and it was a small room, not the halls of Congress, but they discussed their business of collecting and repair ing second-hand clothing for charity with the same endless boring parliamentary formality.

I pointed out to Caswell the member I thought would be the natural leader, a tall, well-built woman in a green suit, with conscious gestures and a resonant, penetrating voice, and then went into a half doze while Caswell stayed awake beside me and wrote in his notebook. After a while the resonant voice roused me to attention for a moment. It was the tall woman holding the floor over some collective dereliction of the club. She was being scathing.

I nudged Caswell and murmured, "Did you fix it so that a shover has a better chance of getting into office than a nonshover?"

"I think there's a way they could find for it," Caswell whispered back, and went to work on his equation again. "Yes, several ways to bias the elections."

"Good. Point them out tactfully to the one you select. Not as if she'd use such methods, but just as an example of the reason why only *she* can be trusted with initiating the change. Just mention all the personal advantages an unscrupulous person could have."

He nodded, keeping a straight and sober face as if we were exchanging admiring remarks about the techniques of clothes repairing, instead of conspiring.

After the meeting, Caswell drew the tall woman in the green suit aside and spoke to her confidentially, showing her the diagram of organization we had drawn up. I saw the responsive glitter in the woman's eyes and knew she was hooked.

We left the diagram of organization and our typed copy of the new by-laws with her and went off soberly, as befitted two social science experimenters. We didn't start laughing until our car passed the town limits and began the climb for University Heights.

If Caswell's equations meant anything at all, we had given that sewing circle more growth drives than the Roman Empire.

Four months later I had time out from a very busy schedule to wonder how the test was coming along. Passing Caswell's office, I put my head in. He looked up from a student research paper he was correcting.

"Caswell, about that sewing club business—I'm beginning to feel the suspense. Could I get an advance report on how it's coming?"

"I'm not following it. We're supposed to let it run the full six months."

"But I'm curious. Could I get in touch with that woman—what's her name?"

"Searles. Mrs George Searles."

Would that change the results?"

"Not in the slightest. If you want to graph the membership rise, it should be going up in a log curve, probably doubling every so often."

I grinned. "If it's not rising, you're fired."

He grinned back. "If it's not rising, you won't have to fire me—I'll burn my books and shoot myself."

I returned to my office and put in a call to Watashaw.

While I was waiting for the phone to be answered, I took a piece of graph paper and ruled it off into six sections, one for each month. After the phone had rung in the distance for a long time, a servant answered with a bored drawl:

"Mrs Searles' residence."

I picked up a red gummed star and licked it.

"Mrs Searles, please."

"She's not in just now. Could I take a message?"

I placed the star at the thirty line in the beginning of the first section. Thirty members they'd started with.

"No, thanks. Could you tell me when she'll be back?"

"Not until dinner. She's at the meetin'."

"The sewing club?" I asked.

No, *sir,* not that thing. There isn't any sewing club anymore, not for a long time. She's at the Civic Welfare meeting."

Somehow I hadn't expected anything like that.

"Thank you," I said and hung up, and after a moment noticed I was holding a box of red gummed stars in my hand. I closed it and put it down on top of the graph of membership in the sewing circle. No more members . . .

Poor Caswell. The bet between us was ironclad. He wouldn't let me back down on it even if I wanted to. He'd probably quit before I put through the first slow move to fire him. His professional pride would be shattered, sunk without a trace. I remembered what he said about shooting himself. It had seemed funny to both of us at the time, but . . . What a mess that would make for the university.

I had to talk to Mrs Searles. Perhaps there was some outside reason why the club had disbanded. Perhaps it had not just died.

I called back. "This is Professor Smith," I said, giving the alias I had used before. "I called a few minutes ago. When did you say Mrs Searles will return?"

"About six-thirty or seven o'clock."

Five hours to wait.

And what if Caswell asked me what I had found out in the meantime? I didn't want to tell him anything until I had talked it over with that woman Searles first.

"Where is this Civic Welfare meeting?"

She told me.

Five minutes later, I was in my car, heading for Watashaw, driving considerably faster than usual and keeping a careful watch for highway patrol cars as the speedometer climbed.

The town meeting hall and theatre was a big place, probably with lots of small rooms for different clubs. I went in through the centre door and found myself in the huge central hall where some sort of rally was being held. A political-type rally—you know, cheers and chants, with bunting already down on the floor, people holding banners, and plenty of enthusiasm and excitement in the air. Someone was making a speech up on the platform. Most of the people there were women.

I wondered how the Civic Welfare League could dare hold its meeting at the same time as a political rally that could pull its members away. The group with Mrs Searles was probably holding a shrunken and almost memberless meeting somewhere in an upper room.

There probably was a side door that would lead upstairs.

While I glanced around, a pretty girl usher put a printed bulletin in my hand, whispering, "Here's one of the new copies." As I attempted to hand it back, she retreated. "Oh, you can keep it. It's the new one. Everyone's supposed to have it. We've just printed up six thousand copies to make sure there'll be enough to last."

The tall woman on the platform had been making a driving, forceful speech about some plans for rebuilding Watashaw's slum section. It began to penetrate my mind dimly as I glanced down at the bulletin in my hands.

"Civic Welfare League of Watashaw. The United Organization of Church and Secular Charities." That's what it said. Below began the rules of membership.

I looked up. The speaker, with a clear, determined voice and conscious, forceful gestures, had entered the home-stretch of her speech, an appeal to the civic pride of all citizens of Watashaw.

"With a bright and glorious future—potentially without poor and without uncared-for ill—potentially with no ugliness, no vistas which are not beautiful—the best people in the best-planned town in the country—jewel of the United States."

She paused and then leaned forward intensely, striking her clenched hand on the speaker's stand with each word for emphasis.

"All we need is more members. Now, get out there and recruit!"

I finally recognized Mrs Searles, as an answering sudden blast of sound half deafened me. The crowd was chanting at the top of its lungs: "Recruit! Recruit!"

Mrs Searles stood still at the speaker's table and behind her, seated in a row of chairs, was a group that was probably the board of directors. It was mostly women, and the women began to look vaguely familiar, as if they could be members of the sewing circle.

I put my lips close to the ear of the pretty usher while I turned over the stiff printed bulletin on a hunch. "How long has the League been organized?" On the back of the bulletin was a constitution.

She was cheering with the crowd, her eyes sparkling. "I don't know," she answered between cheers. "I only joined two days ago. Isn't it wonderful?"

I went into the quiet outer air and got into my car with my skin prickling. Even as I drove away, I could hear them. They were singing some kind of organization song with the tune of "Marching through Georgia."

Even at the single glance I had given it, the constitution looked exactly like the one we had given the Watashaw Sewing Circle.

All I told Caswell when I got back was that the sewing circle had changed its name and the membership seemed to be rising.

Next day, after calling Mrs Searles, I placed some red stars on my graph for the first three months. They made a nice curve, rising more steeply as it reached the fourth month. They had picked up their first increase in membership simply by amalgamating with all the other types of charity organizations in Watashaw, changing the club name with each fusion, but keeping the same constitution—the constitution with the bright promise of advantages as long as there were always new members being brought in.

By the fifth month, the League had added a mutual baby-sitting service and had induced the local school board to add a nursery school to the town service, so as to free more women for League activity. But charity must have been completely organized by then, and expansion had to be in other directions.

Some real estate agents evidently had been drawn into the whirlpool early, along with their ideas. The slum improvement plans began to blossom and take on a tinge of real estate planning later in the month.

The first day of the sixth month, a big two-page spread appeared in the local paper of a mass meeting which had approved a full-fledged scheme for slum clearance of Watashaw's shack-town section, plus plans for rehousing, civic building, and re-zoning. And good prospects for attracting some new industries to the town, industries which had already been contacted and seemed interested by the privileges offered.

And with all this, an arrangement for securing and distributing to the club members *alone* most of the profit that would come to the town in the form of a rise in the price of building sites and a boom in the building industry. The profit distributing arrangement was the same one that had been built into the organization plan for the distribution of the small profits of membership fees and honorary promotions. It was becoming an openly profitable business. Membership was rising more rapidly now.

By the second week of the sixth month, news appeared in the local paper that the club had filed an application to incorporate itself as the Watashaw Mutual Trade and Civic Development Corporation, and all the local real estate promoters had finished joining en masse. The Mutual Trade part sounded to me as if the Chamber of Commerce was on the point of being pulled in with them, ideas, ambitions, and all.

I chuckled while reading the next page of the paper, on which a local politician was reported as having addressed the club with long flowery oration on their enterprise, charity, and civic spirit. He had been made an honorary member. If he allowed himself to be made a *full member* with its contractual obligations and its lures, if the politicians went into this, too . . .

I laughed, filing the newspaper with the other documents on the Watashaw test. These proofs would fascinate any businessman with the sense to see where his bread was buttered. A businessman is constantly dealing with organizations, including his own, and finding them either inert, cantankerous, or both. Caswell's formula could be a handle to grasp them with. Gratitude alone would bring money into the university in car-load lots.

The end of the sixth month came. The test was over and the end reports were spectacular. Caswell's formulas were proven to the hilt.

After reading the last newspaper reports, I called him up.

"Perfect, Wilt, *perfect!* I can use this Watashaw thing to get you so many fellowships and scholarships and grants for your department that you'll think it's snowing money!"

He answered somewhat uninterestedly, "I've been busy working with students on their research papers and marking tests—not following the Watashaw business at all, I'm afraid. You say the demonstration went well and you're satisfied?"

He was definitely putting on a chill. We were friends now, but obviously he was still peeved whenever he was reminded that I had doubted that his theory could work. And he was using its success to rub my nose in the realization that I had been wrong. A man with a string of degrees after his name is just as human as anyone else. I had needled him pretty hard that first time.

"I'm satisfied," I acknowledged. "I was wrong. The formulas work beautifully. Come over and see my file of documents on it if you want a boost for your ego. Now let's see the formula for stopping it."

He sounded cheerful again. "I didn't complicate that organization with negatives. I wanted it to *grow.* It falls apart naturally when it stops growing for more than two months. It's like the great stock boom before an economic crash. Everyone in it is prosperous as long as the prices just keep going up and new buyers come into the market, but they all know what would happen if it stopped growing. You remember, we built in as one of the incentives that the members know they are going to lose if membership stops growing. Why, if I tried to stop it now, they'd cut my throat."

I remembered the drive and frenzy of the crowd in the one early meeting I had seen. They probably would.

"No," he continued. "We'll just let it play out to the end of its tether and die of old age."

"When will that be?"

"It can't grow past the female population of the town. There are only so many women in Watashaw, and some of them don't like sewing."

The graph on the desk before me began to look sinister. Surely Caswell must have made some provision for—

"You underestimate their ingenuity," I said into the phone. "Since they wanted to expand, they didn't stick to sewing. They went from general charity to social welfare schemes to something that's pretty close to an incorporated government. The name is now the Watashaw Mutual Trade and Civic Development Corporation, and they're filing an application to change it to Civic Property Pool and Social Dividend, membership contractual, open to all. That social dividend sounds like a Technocrat climbed on the band wagon, eh?"

While I spoke, I carefully added another red star to the curve above the thousand member level, checking with the newspaper that still lay open on my desk. The curve was definitely some sort of log curve now, growing more rapidly with each increase.

"Leaving out practical limitations for a moment, where does the formula say it will stop?" I asked.

"When you run out of people to join it. But after all, there are only so many people in Watashaw. It's a pretty small town."

"They've opened a branch office in New York," I said carefully into the phone, a few weeks later.

With my pencil, very carefully, I extended the membership curve from where it was then.

After the next doubling, the curve went almost straight up and off the page.

Allowing for a lag of contagion from one nation to another, depending on how much their citizens intermingled, I'd give the rest of the world about twelve years.

There was a long silence while Caswell probably drew the same graph in his own mind. Then he laughed weakly. "Well, you asked me for a demonstration."

That was as good an answer as any. We got together and had lunch in a bar, if you can call it lunch. The movement we started will expand by hook or by crook, by seduction or by bribery or by propaganda or by conquest, but it will expand. And maybe a total world government will be a fine thing—until it hits the end of its rope in twelve years or so.

What happens then, I don't know.

But I don't want anyone to pin that on me. From now on, if anyone asks me, I've never heard of Watashaw.

9 Shitwork

In the following story Isaac Asimov creates a situation that poses, in a highly dramatic fashion, questions of moral responsibility, the realities of choice, and the consequences of action in an ongoing society. Less dramatic instances of the same general issues Asimov addresses are commonplace occurrences in any society. Obvious injustices are not corrected because the social costs of change are seen as too great by those who have the power to produce change, and because those who give their token support for a just cause end up acting as enemies, by accepting passively the status quo, while thinking themselves to be friends.

One of the advantages of using science fiction as a medium for considering sociological problems is that it illuminates a situation in which social variables are isolated and highlighted, or new social structures are constructed to illustrate the effects of certain processes that are obscured in "real societies." In "Strikebreakers," Asimov creates a world in which an arbitrary custom is defended to what appears to be an absurd degree. A reader might be struck with the obviousness of the reasonable solution to the problem that Asimov creates and wonder why reasonable people would not also see the answer and act accordingly. In the story, it is implied that the reason the inhabitants of Elsevere do not act as sensible people would is that their culture does not permit them to consider the wise solution. The idea in the story that culture dominates reason may at first seem strange. But reflect upon our own society where people die because adequate medical care is denied them, people are sent to jail for permitting adults to see pornographic films, and people spend their lives trying to change any one of a thousand obvious wrongs, which are determined by "culture."

The position of the main character in Asimov's story is a superb illustration of the position of the well educated, reasonable, wishy-washy liberal. He is afraid to support demands for the sort of change that he recognizes to be justified and necessary, and ends up acting as an agent of the powers of cultural inflexibility and stupidity.

Strikebreaker

ISAAC ASIMOV

Elvis Blei rubbed his plump hands and said, "Self-containment is the word." He smiled uneasily as he helped Steven Lamorak of Earth to a light. There was uneasiness all over his smooth face with its small wide-set eyes.

Lamorak puffed smoke appreciatively and crossed his lanky legs. His hair was powdered with gray and he had a large and powerful jawbone. "Home grown?" he asked, staring critically at the cigarette. He tried to hide his own disturbance at the other's tension.

"Quite," said Blei.

"I wonder," said Lamorak, "that you have room on your small world for such luxuries."

(Lamorak thought of his first view of Elsevere from the spaceship visiplate. It was a jagged, airless planetoid, some hundred miles in diameter—just a dust-gray rough-hewn rock, glimmering dully in the light of its sun, 200,000,000 miles distant. It was the only object more than a mile in diameter that circled that sun, and now men had burrowed into that miniature world and constructed a society in it. And he himself, as a sociologist, had come to study the world and see how humanity had made itself fit into that queerly specialized niche.)

Blei's polite fixed smile expanded a hair. He said, "We are not a small world, Dr. Lamorak; you judge us by two-dimensional standards. The surface area of Elsevere is only ¾ that of the State of New York, but that's irrelevant. Remember, we can occupy, if we wish, the entire interior of Elsevere. A sphere of 50 miles radius has a volume of well over half a million cubic miles. If all of Elsevere were occupied by levels 50 feet apart, the total surface area within the planetoid would be 56,000,000 square miles, and that is equal to the total land area of Earth. And none of these square miles, Doctor, would be unproductive."

Lamorak said, "Good Lord," and stared blankly for a moment. "Yes, of course you're right. Strange I never thought of it that way. But then, Elsevere is the only thoroughly exploited planetoid world in the Galaxy; the rest of us simply can't get away from thinking of two-dimensional surfaces, as you pointed out. Well, I'm more than ever glad that your Council has been so cooperative as to give me a free hand in this investigation of mine."

Blei nodded convulsively at that.

Lamorak frowned slightly and thought: He acts for all the world as though he wished I had not come. Something's wrong.

Blei said, "Of course, you understand that we are actually much smaller than we could be; only minor portions of Elsevere have as yet been hollowed out and occupied. Nor are we particularly anxious to expand, except very slowly. To a certain extent we are limited by the capacity of our pseudo-gravity engines and Solar energy converters."

"I understand. But tell me, Councillor Blei—as a matter of personal curiosity, and not because it is of prime importance to my project—could I view some of your farming and herding levels first? I am fascinated by the thoughts of fields of wheat and herds of cattle inside a planetoid."

"You'll find the cattle small by your standards, Doctor, and we don't have much wheat. We grow yeast to a much greater extent. But there will be some wheat to show you. Some cotton and tobacco, too. Even fruit trees."

"Wonderful. As you say, self-containment. You recirculate everything, I imagine."

Lamorak's sharp eyes did not miss the fact that this last remark twinged Blei. The Elseverian's eyes narrowed to slits that hid his expression.

He said, "We must recirculate, yes. Air, water, food, minerals—everything that is used up—must be restored to its original state; waste products are reconverted to raw materials. All that is needed is energy, and we have enough of that. We don't manage with one hundred percent efficiency, of course; there is a certain seepage. We import a small amount of water each year; and if our needs grow, we may have to import some coal and oxygen."

Lamorak said, "When can we start our tour, Councillor Blei?"

Blei's smile lost some of its negligible warmth. "As soon as we can, Doctor. There are some routine matters that must be arranged."

Lamorak nodded, and having finished his cigarette, stubbed it out.

Routine matters? There was none of this hesitancy during the preliminary correspondence. Elsevere had seemed proud that its unique planetoid existence had attracted the attention of the Galaxy.

He said, "I realize I would be a disturbing influence in a tightly-knit society," and watched grimly as Blei leaped at the explanation and made it his own.

"Yes," said Blei, "we feel marked off from the rest of the Galaxy. We have our own customs. Each individual Elseverian fits into a comfortable niche. The appearance of a stranger without fixed caste is unsettling."

"The caste system does involve a certain inflexibility."

"Granted," said Blei quickly; "but there is also a certain self-assurance. We have firm rules of intermarriage and rigid inheritance of occupation. Each man, woman and child knows his place, accepts it, and is accepted in it; we have virtually no neurosis or mental illness."

"And are there no misfits?" asked Lamorak.

Blei shaped his mouth as though to say no, then clamped it suddenly shut, biting the word into silence; a frown deepened on his forehead. He said, at length, "I will arrange for the tour, Doctor. Meanwhile, I imagine you would welcome a chance to freshen up and to sleep."

They rose together and left the room, Blei politely motioning the Earthman to precede him out the door.

Lamorak felt oppressed by the vague feeling of crisis that had prevaded his discussion with Blei.

The newspaper reinforced that feeling. He read it carefully before getting into bed, with what was at first merely a clinical interest. It was an eight-page tabloid of synthetic paper. One quarter of its items consisted of "personals":

births, marriages, deaths, record quotas, expanding habitable volume (not area! three dimensions!). The remainder included scholarly essays, educational material, and fiction. Of news, in the sense to which Lamorak was accustomed, there was virtually nothing.

One item only could be so considered and that was chilling in its incompleteness.

It said, under a small headline: *DEMANDS UNCHANGED: There has been no change in his attitude of yesterday. The Chief Councillor, after a second interview, announced that his demands remain completely unreasonable and cannot be met under any circumstances.*

Then, in parenthesis, and in different type, there was the statement: *The editors of this paper agree that Elsevere cannot and will not jump to his whistle, come what may.*

Lamorak read it over three times. *His* attitude. *His* demands. *His* whistle.

Whose?

He slept uneasily, that night.

He had no time for newspapers in the days that followed; but spasmodically, the matter returned to his thoughts.

Blei, who remained his guide and companion for most of the tour, grew ever more withdrawn.

On the third day, (quite artificially clock-set in an Earth-like twenty-four hour pattern), Blei stopped at one point, and said, "Now this level is devoted entirely to chemical industries. That section is not important—"

But he turned away a shade too rapidly, and Lamorak seized his arm. "What are the products of that section?"

"Fertilizers. Certain organics," said Blei stiffly.

Lamorak held him back, looking for what sight Blei might be evading. His gaze swept over the close-by horizons of lined rock and the buildings squeezed and layered between the levels.

Lamorak said, "Isn't that a private residence there?"

Blei did not look in the indicated direction.

Lamorak said, "I think that's the largest one I've seen yet. Why is it here on a factory level?" That alone made it noteworthy. He had already seen that the levels on Elsevere were divided rigidly among the residential, the agricultural and the industrial.

He looked back and called, "Councillor Blei!"

The councillor was walking away and Lamorak pursued him with hasty steps. "Is there something wrong, sir?"

Blei muttered, "I am rude, I know. I am sorry. There are matters that prey on my mind—" He kept up his rapid pace.

"Concerning *his* demands."

Blei came to a full halt. "What do *you* know about that?"

"No more than I've said. I read that much in the newspaper."

Blei muttered something to himself.

Lamorak said, "Ragusnik? What's that?"

Blei sighed heavily. "I suppose you ought to be told. It's humiliating, deeply embarrassing. The Council thought that matters would certainly be arranged shortly and that your visit need not be interfered with, that you need not know or be concerned. But it is almost a week now. I don't know what will happen and, appearances notwithstanding, it might be best for you to leave. No reason for an Outworlder to risk death."

The Earthman smiled incredulously. "Risk death? In this little world, so peaceful and busy. I can't believe it."

The Elseverian councillor said, "I can explain. I think it best I should." He turned his head away. "As I told you, everything on Elsevere must recirculate. You understand that."

"Yes."

"That includes—uh, human wastes."

"I assumed so," said Lamorak.

"Water is reclaimed from it by distillation and absorption. What remains is converted into fertilizer for yeast use; some of it is used as a source of fine organics and other by-products. These factories you see are devoted to this."

"Well?" Lamorak had experienced a certain difficulty in the drinking of water when he first landed on Elsevere, because he had been realistic enough to know what it must be reclaimed from; but he had conquered the feeling easily enough. Even on Earth, water was reclaimed by natural processes from all sorts of unpalatable substances.

Blei, with increasing difficulty, said, "Igor Ragusnik is the man who is in charge of the industrial processes immediately involving the wastes. The position has been in his family since Elsevere was first colonized. One of the original settlers was Mikhail Ragusnik and he—he—"

"Was in charge of waste reclamation."

"Yes. Now that residence you singled out is the Ragusnik residence; it is the best and most elaborate on the planetoid. Ragusnik gets many privileges the rest of us do not have; but, after all—" Passion entered the Councillor's voice with great suddenness, "we cannot *speak* to him."

"What?"

"He demands full social equality. He wants his children to mingle with ours, and our wives to visit— Oh!" It was a groan of utter disgust.

Lamorak thought of the newspaper item that could not even bring itself to mention Ragusnik's name in print, or to say anything specific about his demands. He said, "I take it he's an outcast because of his job."

"Naturally. Human wastes and—" words failed Blei. After a pause, he said more quietly, "As an Earthman, I suppose you don't understand."

"As a sociologist, I think I do." Lamorak thought of the Untouchables in ancient India, the ones who handled corpses. He thought of the position of swineherds in ancient Judea.

He went on, "I gather Elsevere will not give in to those demands."

"Never," said Blei, energetically. "Never."

"And so?"

"Ragusnik has threatened to cease operations."

"Go on strike, in other words."

"Yes."

"Would that be serious?"

"We have enough food and water to last quite a while; reclamation is not essential in that sense. But the wastes would accumulate; they would infect the planetoid. After generations of careful disease control, we have low natural resistance to germ diseases. Once an epidemic started—and one would—we would drop by the hundred."

"Is Ragusnik aware of this?"

"Yes, of course."

"Do you think he is likely to go through with his threat, then?"

"He is mad. He has already stopped working; there has been no waste reclamation since the day before you landed." Blei's bulbous nose sniffed at the air as though it already caught the whiff of excrement.

Lamorak sniffed mechanically at that, but smelled nothing.

Blei said, "So you see why it might be wise for you to leave. We are humiliated, of course, to have to suggest it."

But Lamorak said, "Wait; not just yet. Good Lord, this is a matter of great interest to me professionally. May I speak to the Ragusnik?"

"On no account," said Blei, alarmed.

"But I would like to understand the situation. The sociological conditions here are unique and not to be duplicated elsewhere. In the name of science—"

"How do you mean, speak? Would image-reception do?"

"Yes."

"I will ask the Council," muttered Blei.

They sat about Lamorak uneasily, their austere and dignified expressions badly marred with anxiety. Blei, seated in the midst of them, studiously avoided the Earthman's eyes.

The Chief Councillor, gray-haired, his face harshly wrinkled, his neck scrawny, said in a soft voice, "If in any way you can persuade him, sir, out of your own convictions, we will welcome that. In no case, however, are you to imply that we will, in any way, yield."

A gauzy curtain fell between the Council and Lamorak. He could make out the individual councillors still, but now he turned sharply toward the receiver before him. It glowed to life.

A head appeared in it, in natural color and with great realism. A strong dark head, with massive chin faintly stubbled, and thick, red lips set into a firm horizontal line.

The image said, suspiciously, "Who are you?"

Lamorak said, "My name is Steven Lamorak; I am an Earthman."

"An Outworlder?"

"That's right. I am visiting Elsevere. You are Ragusnik?"

"Igor Ragusnik, at your service," said the image, mockingly. "Except that there is no service and will be none until my family and I are treated like human beings."

Lamorak said, "Do you realize the danger that Elsevere is in? The possibility of epidemic disease?"

"In twenty-four hours, the situation can be made normal, if they allow me humanity. The situation is theirs to correct."

"You sound like an educated man, Ragusnik."

"So?"

"I am told you're denied of no material comforts. You are housed and clothed and fed better than anyone on Elsevere. Your children are the best educated."

"Granted. But all by servo-mechanism. And motherless girl-babies are sent us to care for until they grow to be our wives. And they die young for loneliness. Why?" There was sudden passion in his voice. "Why must we live in isolation as if we were all monsters, unfit for human beings to be near? Aren't we human beings like others, with the same needs and desires and feelings. Don't we perform an honorable and useful function—?"

There was a rustling of sighs from behind Lamorak. Ragusnik heard it, and raised his voice. "I see you of the Council behind there. Answer me: Isn't it an honorable and useful function? It is *your* waste made into food for *you*. Is the man who purifies corruption worse than the man who produces it?—Listen, Councillors, I will *not* give in. Let all of Elsevere die of disease—including myself and my son, if necessary—but I will not give in. My family will be better dead of disease, than living as now."

Lamorak interrupted. "You've led this life since birth, haven't you?"

"And if I have?"

"Surely you're used to it."

"Never. Resigned, perhaps. My father was resigned, and I was resigned for a while; but I have watched my son, my only son, with no other little boy to play with. My brother and I had each other, but my son will never have anyone, and I am no longer resigned. I am through with Elsevere and through with talking."

The receiver went dead.

The Chief Councillor's face had paled to an aged yellow. He and Blei were the only ones of the group left with Lamorak. The Chief Councillor said, "The man is deranged; I do not know how to force him."

He had a glass of wine at his side; as he lifted it to his lips, he spilled a few drops that stained his white trousers with purple splotches.

Lamorak said, "Are his demands so unreasonable? Why can't he be accepted into society?"

There was momentary rage in Blei's eyes. "A dealer in excrement." Then he shrugged. "You are from Earth."

Incongruously, Lamorak thought of another unacceptable, one of the numerous classic creations of the medieval cartoonist, Al Capp. The variously-named "inside man at the skonk works."

He said, "Does Ragusnik really deal with excrement? I mean, is there physical contact? Surely, it is all handled by automatic machinery."

"Of course," said the Chief Councillor.

"Then exactly what is Ragusnik's function?"

"He manually adjusts the various controls that assure the proper functioning of the machinery. He shifts units to allow repairs to be made; he alters functional rates with the time of day; he varies end production with demand." He added sadly, "If we had the space to make the machinery ten times as complex, all this could be done automatically; but that would be such needless waste."

"But even so," insisted Lamorak, "all Ragusnik does he does simply by pressing buttons or closing contacts or things like that."

"Yes."

"Then his work is no different from any Elseverian's."

Blei said, stiffly, "You don't understand."

"And for that you will risk the death of your children?"

"We have no other choice," said Blei. There was enough agony in his voice to assure Lamorak that the situation was torture for him, but that he had no other choice indeed.

Lamorak shrugged in disgust. "Then break the strike. Force him."

"How?" said the Chief Councillor. "Who would touch him to or go near him? And if we kill him by blasting from a distance, how will that help us?"

Lamorak said, thoughtfully, "Would you know how to run his machinery?"

The Chief Councillor came to his feet. "I?" he howled.

"I don't mean *you*," cried Lamorak at once. "I used the pronoun in its indefinite sense. Could *someone* learn how to handle Ragusnik's machinery?"

Slowly, the passion drained out of the Chief Councillor. "It is in the handbooks, I am certain—though I assure you I have never concerned myself with it."

"Then couldn't someone learn the procedure and substitute for Ragusnik until the man gives in?"

Blei said, "Who would agree to do such a thing? Not I, under any circumstances."

Lamorak thought fleetingly of Earthly taboos that might be almost as strong. He thought of cannibalism, incest, a pious man cursing God. He said, "But you might have made provision for vacancy in the Ragusnik job. Suppose he died."

"Then his son would automatically succeed to his job, or his nearest other relative," said Blei.

"What if he had no adult relatives? What if all his family died at once?"

"That has never happened; it will never happen."

The Chief Councillor added, "If there were danger of it, we might, perhaps, place a baby or two with the Ragusniks and have it raised to the profession."

"Ah. And how would you choose that baby?"

"From among children of mothers who died in childbirth, as we choose the future Ragusnik bride."

"Then choose a substitute Ragusnik now, by lot," said Lamorak.

The Chief Councillor said, "*No! Impossible!* How can you suggest that? If we select a baby, that baby is brought up to the life; it knows no other. At this point, it would be necessary to choose an adult and subject him to Ragusnikhood. No, Dr. Lamorak, we are neither monsters nor abandoned brutes."

No use, thought Lamorak helplessly. *No use, unless—*

He couldn't bring himself to face that *unless* just yet.

That night, Lamorak slept scarcely at all. Ragusnik asked for only the basic elements of humanity. But opposing that were thirty thousand Elseverians who faced death.

The welfare of thirty thousand on one side; the just demands of one family on the other. Could one say that thirty thousand who would support such injustice deserved to die? Injustice by what standards? Earth's? Elsevere's? And who was Lamorak that he should judge?

And Ragusnik? He was willing to let thirty thousand die, including men and women who merely accepted a situation they had been taught to accept and could not change if they wished to. And children who had nothing at all to do with it.

Thirty thousand on one side; a single family on the other.

Lamorak made his decision in something that was almost despair; in the morning he called the Chief Councillor.

He said, "Sir, if you can find a substitute, Ragusnik will see that he has lost all chance to force a decision in his favor and will return to work."

"There can be no substitute," sighed the Chief Councillor; "I have explained that."

"No substitute among the Elseverians, but I am not an Elseverian; it doesn't matter to me. *I* will substitute."

They were excited, much more excited than Lamorak himself. A dozen times they asked him if he was serious.

Lamorak had not shaved, and he felt sick, "Certainly, I'm serious. And any time Ragusnik acts like this, you can always import a substitute. No other world has the taboo and there will always be plenty of temporary substitutes available if you pay enough."

(He was betraying a brutally exploited man, and he knew it. But he told himself desperately: *Except for ostracism, he's very well treated. Very well.*)

They gave him the handbooks and he spent six hours, reading and re-reading. There was no use asking questions. None of the Elseverians knew anything about the job, except for what was in the handbook; and all seemed uncomfortable if the details were as much as mentioned.

"Maintain zero reading of galvanometer A-2 at all times during red signal of the Lunge-howler," read Lamorak.

"Now what's a Lunge-howler?"

"There will be a sign," muttered Blei, and the Elseverians looked at each other hang-dog and bent their heads to stare at their finger-ends.

They left him long before he reached the small rooms that were the central headquarters of generations of working Ragusniks, serving their world. He had specific instructions concerning which turnings to take and what level to reach, but they hung back and let him proceed alone.

He went through the rooms painstakingly, identifying the instruments and controls, following the schematic diagrams in the handbook.

There's a Lunge-howler, he thought, with gloomy satisfaction. The sign did indeed say so. It had a semi-circular face bitten into holes that were obviously designed to glow in separate colors. Why a "howler" then?

He didn't know.

Somewhere, thought Lamorak, *somewhere wastes are accumulating, pushing against gears and exits, pipelines and stills, waiting to be handled in half a hundred ways. Now they just accumulate.*

Not without a tremor, he pulled the first switch as indicated by the handbook in its directions for "Initiation." A gentle murmur of life made itself felt through the floors and walls. He turned a knob and lights went on.

At each step, he consulted the handbook, though he knew it by heart; and with each step, the rooms brightened and the dial-indicators sprang into motion and a humming grew louder.

Somewhere deep in the factories, the accumulated wastes were being drawn into the proper channels.

A high-pitched signal sounded and startled Lamorak out of his painful concentration. It was the communications signal and Lamorak fumbled his receiver into action.

Ragusnik's head showed, startled; then slowly, the incredulity and outright shock faded from his eyes. "*That's* how it is, then."

"I'm not an Elseverian, Ragusnik; I don't mind doing this."

"But what business is it of yours? Why do you interfere?"

"I'm on your side, Ragusnik, but I must do this."

"Why, if you're on my side? Do they treat people on your world as they treat me here?"

"Not any longer. But even if you are right, there are thirty thousand people on Elsevere to be considered."

"They would have given in; you've ruined my only chance."

"They would *not* have given in. And in a way, you've won; they know now that you're dissatisfied. Until now, they never dreamed a Ragusnik could be unhappy, that he could make trouble."

"What if they know? Now all they need do is hire an Outworlder anytime."

Lamorak shook his head violently. He had thought this through in these last bitter hours. "The fact that they know means that the Elseverians will begin to think about you; some will begin to wonder if it's right to treat a human so. And if Outworlders are hired, they'll spread the word that this goes on upon Elsevere and Galactic public opinion will be in your favor."

"And?"

"Things will improve. In your son's time, things will be much better."

"In my son's time," said Ragusnik, his cheeks sagging. "I might have had it now. Well, I lose. I'll go back to the job."

Lamorak felt an overwhelming relief. "If you'll come here now, sir, you may have your job and I'll consider it an honor to shake your hand."

Ragusnik's head snapped up and filled with a gloomy pride. "You call me 'sir' and offer to shake my hand. Go about your business, Earthman, and leave me to my work, for I would not shake yours."

Lamorak returned the way he had come, relieved that the crisis was over, and profoundly depressed, too.

He stopped in surprise when he found a section of corridor cordoned off, so he could not pass. He looked about for alternate routes, then startled at a magnified voice above his head. "Dr. Lamorak, do you hear me? This is Councillor Blei."

Lamorak looked up. The voice came over some sort of public address system, but he saw no sign of an outlet.

He called out, "Is anything wrong? Can you hear me?"

"I hear you."

Instinctively, Lamorak was shouting. "Is anything wrong? There seems to be a block here. Are there complications with Ragusnik?"

"Ragusnik has gone to work," came Blei's voice. "The crisis is over, and you must make ready to leave."

"Leave?"

"Leave Elsevere; a ship is being made ready for you now."

"But wait a bit." Lamorak was confused by this sudden leap of events. "I haven't completed my gathering of data."

Blei's voice said, "This cannot be helped. You will be directed to the ship and your belongings will be sent after you by servo-mechanisms. We trust—we trust—"

Something was becoming clear to Lamorak. "You trust *what?*"

"We trust you will make no attempt to see or speak directly to any Elseverian. And of course we hope you will avoid embarrassment by not attempting to return to Elsevere at any time in the future. A colleague of yours would be welcome if further data concerning us is needed."

"I understand," said Lamorak, tonelessly. Obviously, he had himself become a Ragusnik. He had handled the controls that in turn had handled the wastes; he was ostracized. He was a corpse-handler, a swineherd, an inside man at the skonk works.

He said, "Good-bye."

Blei's voice said, "Before we direct you, Dr. Lamorak—. On behalf of the Council of Elsevere, I thank you for your help in this crisis."

"You're welcome," said Lamorak, bitterly.

10 A Possible Educational System

So far only one revolution of truly major proportions has changed how education is carried out. The revolutionary event was the introduction of written supplements to an instructor's oral teachings. When ideas could be recorded in an enduring form, it was possible to carry out instruction in either oral or a written fashion. Obviously, this revolution is not a recent event.

Educational procedures introduced since the invention of writing have all been attempts to find the most efficient manner of using oral and written matter to educate people, or to produce certain characteristics in those who are being educated or both. There have been attempts to educate people in ways that foster or even teach creativity; special techniques have been developed to educate students of limited intelligence and those of exceptional brillance, students with little motivation and those with a great passion for learning. Each new procedure simply recombines and reapportions oral and written instruction and makes some attempt to tailor the procedure to the special needs of students.

As modern psychology has come to know something of the principles of learning, alternative schedules for presenting ideas and alternative techniques for facilitating learning have become feasible. This research, together with the development of powerful computers that can process many problems and administer and control many projects simultaneously (through time-sharing systems), make possible computerized instruction. This technique could be the closest thing to a major revolution in education since the invention of writing. The departure from traditional techniques is that a computer-based method permits individualized instruction of large numbers of students in a manner designed to maximize the speed and ease with which a student acquires information. If programs for computerized instruction develop to a level of true sophistication, many desirable aspects of the one-to-one student-teacher relationship will be possible; the "teacher" will be adept at sensing when a student has understood a particular problem, and moving on to the next level, or choosing to step backward in order to correct faulty learning that is affecting present performance.

Even computerized instruction, however, as it is now practiced, falls within the definition of education. At best it will make available an extraordinarily talented teacher who can give individual attention to each student. In a story called

"Profession," Isaac Asimov considers a truly revolutionary educational system. The excerpts from the story describe something of the social conditions that fostered the development of this system and something of the experience of being educated under it.

Profession

ISAAC ASIMOV

There was a time, four or five thousand years ago when mankind was confined to the surface of Earth. Even then, his culture had grown quite technological and his numbers had increased to the point where any failure in technology would have meant mass starvation and disease. To maintain the technological level and advance it in the face of an increasing population, more and more technicians and scientists had to be trained, and yet, as science advanced, it took longer and longer to train them.

As first interplanetary and then interstellar travel was developed, the problem grew more acute. In fact, actual colonization of extra-Solar planets was impossible for about fifteen hundred years because of a lack of properly trained men.

The turning point came when the mechanics of the storage of knowledge within the brain was worked out. Once that had been done, it became possible to devise Educational tapes that would modify the mechanics in such a way as to place within the mind a body of knowledge ready-made, so to speak. . . .

Once that was done, trained men could be turned out by the thousands and millions, and we could begin what someone has since called the "Filling of the Universe." There are now fifteen hundred inhabited planets in the Galaxy and there is no end in sight.

Do you see all that is involved? Earth exports Education tapes for low-specialized professions and that keeps the Galactic culture unified. For instance, the Reading tapes insure a single language for all of us. . . .

Earth also exports highly specialized professionals and keeps its own population at an endurable level. Since they are shipped out in a balanced sex ratio, they act as self-reproductive units and help increase the populations on the Outworlds where an increase is needed. Furthermore, tapes and men are paid for in material which we much need and on which our economy depends.

For most of the first eighteen years of his life, George Platen had headed firmly in one direction, that of Registered Computer Programmer. There were those in his crowd who spoke wisely of Spationautics, Refrigeration Technology, Transportation Control, and even Administration. But George held firm.

He argued relative merits as vigorously as any of them, and why not? Education Day loomed ahead of them and was the great fact of their existence. It approached steadily, as fixed and certain as the calendar—the first day of November of the year following one's eighteenth birthday.

After that day, there were other topics of conversation. One could discuss with others some detail of the profession, or the virtues of one's wife and children. . . .

Before Education Day, however, there was only one topic that unfailingly and unwearyingly held everyone's interest, and that was Education Day.

"What are you going for? Think you'll make it? That's no good. Look at the records; quota's been cut. Logistics now—"

Or Hypermechanics now— Or Communications— Or Gravitics now—

Especially Gravitics at the moment. Everyone had been talking about Gravitics in the few years just before George's Education Day because of the development of the Gravitic power engine.

Any world within ten light-years of a dwarf star, everyone said, would give its eyeteeth for any kind of Registered Gravitics Engineer.

The thought of that never bothered George. Sure it would; all the eyeteeth it could scare up. But George had also heard what had happened before in a newly developed technique. Rationalization and simplification followed in a flood. New models each year; new types of gravitic engines; new principles. Then all those eyeteeth gentlemen would find themselves out of date and superseded by later models with later educations. The first group would then have to settle down to unskilled labour or ship out to some backwoods world that wasn't quite caught up yet.

Now Computer Programmers were in steady demand year after year, century after century. The demand never reached wild peaks; there was never a howling bull market for Programmers; but the demand climbed steadily as new worlds opened up and as older worlds grew more complex.

He had argued with Trevelyan about that constantly. As best friends, their arguments had to be constant and vitriolic and, of course, neither ever persuaded or was persuaded.

But then Trevelyan had had a father who was a Registered Metallurgist and had actually served on one of the Outworlds, and a grandfather who had also been a Registered Metallurgist. He himself was intent on becoming a Registered Metallurgist almost as a matter of family right and was firmly convinced that any other profession was a shade less than respectable.

"There'll always be metal," he said, "and there's an accomplishment in moulding alloys to specification and watching structures grow. Now what's a Programmer going to be doing. Sitting at a coder all day long, feeding some fool machine."

Even at sixteen, George had learned to be practical. He said simply, "There'll be a million Metallurgists put out along with you."

"Because it's good. A good profession. The best."

"But you get crowded out, Stubby. You can be way back in line. Any world can tape out its own Metallurgists, and the market for advanced Earth models isn't so big. And it's mostly the small worlds that want them. You know what percent of the turnout of Registered Metallurgists get tabbed for worlds with a Grade A rating. I looked it up. It's just 13.3 percent. That means you'll have seven chances in eight of being stuck in some world that just about has running water. You may even be stuck on Earth; 2.3 percent are."

Trevelyan said belligerently, "There's no disgrace in staying on Earth. Earth needs technicians, too. Good ones." His grandfather had been an Earthbound Metallurgist, and Trevelyan lifted his finger to his upper lip and dabbed at an as yet non-existent moustache.

George knew about Trevelyan's grandfather and, considering the Earthbound position of his own ancestry, was in no mood to sneer. He said diplomatically, "No intellectual disgrace. Of course not. But it's nice to get into a Grade A world, isn't it?

"Now you take Programmers. Only the Grade A worlds have the kind of computers that really need first-class Programmers so they're the only ones in the market. And Programmer tapes are complicated and hardly any one fits. They need more Programmers than their own population can supply. It's just a matter of statistics. There's one first-class Programmer per million, say. A world needs twenty and has a population of ten million, they have to come to Earth for five to fifteen Programmers. Right?

"And you know how many Registered Computer Programmers went to Grade A planets last year? I'll tell you. Every last one. If you're a Programmer, you're picked man. Yes, sir.

Trevelyan frowned. "If only one in a million makes it, what makes you think *you*'ll make it?"

George said guardedly, "I'll make it."

He never dared tell anyone; not Trevelyan; not his parents; of exactly what he was doing that made him so confident. But he wasn't worried. He was simply confident. . . .

He was as blandly confident as the average eight-year old kid approaching Reading Day—that childhood preview of Education Day.

Of course, Reading Day had been different. Partly, there was the simple fact of childhood. A boy of eight takes many extraordinary things in his stride. One day you can't read and the next day you can. That's just the way things are. Like the sun shining.

And then not so much depended upon it. There were no recruiters just ahead, waiting and jostling for the lists and scores. . . .A boy or girl who goes through the Reading Day is just someone who has ten more years of undifferentiated living upon Earth's crawling surface; just someone who returns to his family with one new ability.

By the time Education Day came, ten years later, George wasn't even sure of most of the details of his own Reading Day.

Most clearly of all, he remembered it to be a dismal September day with a mild rain falling. . . George had dressed by the wall lights, with his parents far more excited than he himself was. His father was a Registered Pipe Fitter and had found his occupation on earth. This fact had always been a humiliation to him, although, of course, as anyone could see plainly, most of each generation must stay on Earth in the nature of things.

There had to be farmers and miners and even technicians on Earth. It was only the late-model, high-specialty professions that were in demand on the Outworlds, and only a few millions a year out of Earth's eight billion population could be exported. Every man and woman on Earth couldn't be among that group.

But every man and woman could hope that at least one of his children could be one, and Platen, Senior, was certainly no exception. It was obvious to him (and, to be sure, to others as well) that George was notably intelligent and quick-minded. He would be bound to do well and he would have to, as he was an only child. If George didn't end on an Outworld, they would have to wait for grandchildren before a next chance would come along, and that was too far in the future to be much consolation.

Reading Day would not prove much, of course, but it would be the only indication they would have before the big day itself. Every parent on Earth would be listening to the quality of reading when his child came home with it; listening to the quality for any particularly easy flow of words and building that into certain omens of the future. There were few families that didn't have at least one hopeful who, from Reading Day on, was the great hope because of the way he handled his trisyllabics.

Dimly, George was aware of the cause of his parents' tension, and if there was any anxiety in his young heart that drizzly morning, it was only the fear that his father's hopeful expression might fade out when he returned home with his reading.

The children met in the large assembly room of the town's Education hall. All over Earth, in millions of local halls, throughout that month, similar groups of children would be meeting. George felt depressed by the greyness of the room and by the other children, strained and stiff in unaccustomed finery.

Automatically, George did as all the rest of the children did. He found the small clique that represented the children on his floor of the apartment house and joined them. . . .

A woman's voice sounded loudly over the public address system. There was instant silence everywhere. . . .

"Children," said the voice, "we are going to call out your names. As each child is called, he or she is to go to one of the men waiting along the side walls. Do you see them? They are wearing red uniforms so they will be easy to find. The girls will go to the right. The boys will go to the left. Now look about and see which man in red is nearest to you—"

George found his man at a glance and waited for his name to be called off. He had not been introduced before this to the sophistications of the alphabet, and the length of time it took to reach his own name grew disturbing.

The crowd of children thinned; little rivulets made their way to each of the red-clad guides.

When the name "George Platen" was finally called, his sense of relief was exceeded only by the feeling of pure gladness at the fact that Trevelyan still stood in his place, uncalled. . . .

He was herded into a line and directed down corridors in the company of strange children. They all looked at one another, large-eyed and concerned, but beyond a snuffling, "Quitcher pushing" and "Hey, watch out" there was no conversation.

They were handed little slips of paper which they were told must remain with them. George stared at his curiously. Little black marks of different shapes. He knew it to be printing but how could anyone make words out of it? He couldn't imagine.

He was told to strip; he and four other boys who were all that now remained together. All the new clothes came shucking off and four eight-year-olds stood naked and small, shivering more out of embarrassment than cold. Medical technicians came past, probing them, testing them with odd instruments, pricking them for blood. Each took the little cards and made additional marks on them with little black rods that produced the marks, all neatly lined up, with great speed. George stared at the new marks, but they were no more comprehensible than the old. The children were ordered back into their clothes.

They sat on separate little chairs then and waited again. Names were called again and "George Platen" came third.

He moved into a large room, filled with frightening instruments with knobs and glassy panels in front. There was a desk in the very centre, and behind it a man sat, his eyes on the papers piled before him.

He said, "George Platen?"

"Yes, sir," said George, in a shaky whisper. All this waiting and all this going here and there was making him nervous. He wished it were over.

The man behind the desk said, "I am Dr. Lloyd, George. How are you?"

The doctor didn't look up as he spoke. It was as though he had said those words over and over again and didn't have to look up any more.

"I'm all right."

"Are you afraid, George?"

"N-no, sir," said George, sounding afraid even in his own ears.

"That's good," said the doctor, "because there's nothing to be afraid of, you know. Let's see, George. It says here on your card that your father is named Peter and that he's a Registered Pipe Fitter and your mother is named Amy and is a Registered Home Technician. Is that right?"

"Y-yes, sir."

And your birthday is February 13, and you had an ear infection about a year ago. Right?"

"Yes, sir."

"Do you know how I know all these things?"

"It's on the card, I think, sir."

"That's right." The doctor looked up at George for the first time and smiled. He showed even teeth and looked much younger than George's father. Some of George's nervousness vanished.

The doctor passed the card to George. "Do you know what all those things there mean, George?"

Although George knew he did not he was startled by the sudden request into looking at the card as though he might understand now through some sudden stroke of fate. But they were just marks as before and he passed the card back. "No, sir."

"Why not?"

George felt a sudden pang of suspicion concerning the sanity of this doctor. Didn't he know why not?

George said, "I can't read, sir."

"Would you like to read?"

"Yes, sir."

"Why, George?"

George stared, appalled. No one had ever asked him that. He had no answer, He said falteringly, "I don't know, sir."

"Printed information will direct you all through your life. There is so much you'll have to know even after Education Day. Cards like this one will tell you. Books will tell you. Television screens will tell you. Printing will tell you such useful things and such interesting things that not being able to read would be as bad as not being able to see. Do you understand?"

"Yes, sir."

"Are you afraid, George?"

"No, sir."

"Good. Now I'll tell you exactly what we'll do first. I'm going to put these wires on your forehead just over the corners of your eyes. They'll stick there but they won't hurt at all. Then, I'll turn on something that will make a buzz. It will sound funny and it may tickle you, but it won't hurt. Now if it does hurt, you tell me, and I'll turn it off right away, but it won't hurt. All right?"

George nodded and swallowed.

"Are you ready?"

George nodded. He closed his eyes while the doctor busied himself. His parents had explained this to him. They, too, had said it wouldn't hurt, but then there were always the older children. There were the ten- and twelve-year-olds who howled after the eight-year-olds waiting for Reading Day, "Watch out for the needle." There were the others who took you off in confidence and said, "They got to cut your head open. They use a sharp knife that big with a hook on it," and so on into horrifying details.

George had never believed them but he had had nightmares, and now he closed his eyes and felt pure terror.

He didn't feel the wires at his temple. The buzz was a distant thing, and there was the sound of his own blood in his ears, ringing hollowly as though it and he were in a large cave. Slowly he chanced opening his eyes.

The doctor had his back to him. From one of the instruments a strip of paper unwound and was covered with a thin, wavy purple line. The doctor tore off pieces and put them into a slot in another machine. He did it over and over again. Each time a little piece of film came out, which the doctor looked at. Finally, he turned toward George with a queer frown between his eyes.

The buzzing stopped.

George said breathlessly, "Is it over?"

The doctor said, "Yes," but he was still frowning.

"Can I read now?" asked George. He felt no different.

The doctor said, "What?" then smiled very suddenly and briefly. He said, "It works fine, George. You'll be reading in fifteen minutes. Now we're going to use another machine this time and it will take longer. I'm going to cover your whole head, and when I turn it on you won't be able to see or hear anything for a while, but it won't hurt. Just to make sure I'm going to give you a little switch to hold in your hand. If anything hurts, you press the little button and everything shuts off. All right?"

In later years, George was told that the little switch was strictly a dummy; that it was introduced solely for confidence. He never did know for sure, however, since he never pushed the button.

A large smoothly curved helmet with a rubbery inner lining was placed over his head and left there. Three or four little knobs seemed to grab at him and bite into his skull, but there was only a little pressure that faded. No pain.

The doctor's voice sounded dimly. "Everything all right, George?"

And then, with no real warning, a layer of thick felt closed down all about him. He was disembodied, there was no sensation, no universe, only himself and a distant murmur at the very ends of nothingness telling him something—telling him—telling him—

He strained to hear and understand but there was all that thick felt between.

Then the helmet was taken off his head, and the light was so bright that it hurt his eyes while the doctor's voice drummed at his ears.

The doctor said, "Here's your card, George. What does it say?"

George looked at his card again and gave out a strangled shout. The marks weren't just marks at all. They made up words. They were words just as clearly as though something were whispering them in his ears. He could *hear* them being whispered as he looked at them.

"What does it say, George?"

"It says—it says—'Platen, George. Born 13 February 6492 of Peter and Amy Platen in . . .' " He broke off.

"You can read, George," said the doctor. "It's all over."

"For good? I won't forget how?"

"Of course not." The doctor leaned over to shake hands gravely. "You will be taken home now."

It was days before George got over this new and great talent of his. He read for his father with such facility that Platen, Senior wept and called relatives to tell the good news.

George walked about town, reading every scrap of printing he could find and wondering how it was that none of it had ever made sense to him before.

He tried to remember how it was not to be able to read and he couldn't. As far as his feeling about it was concerned, he had always been able to read. Always.

At eighteen, George was rather dark, of medium height, but thin enough to look taller. Trevelyan, who was scarcely an inch shorter, had a stockiness of build that made "Stubby" more than even appropriate, but in his last year he had grown self-conscious. The nickname could no longer be used without reprisal. And since Trevelyan disapproved of his proper first name even more strongly, he was called Trevelyan or any decent variant of that. As though to prove his manhood further, he had most persistently grown a pair of sideburns and a bristly moustache. . . .

They were in the same large hall they had been in ten years before (and not since). It was as if a vague dream of the past had come to sudden reality. In the first few minutes George had been distinctly surprised at finding everything seem smaller and more cramped than his memory told him; then he made allowance for his own growth.

The crowd was smaller than it had been in childhood. It was exclusively male this time. The girls had another day assigned them.

Trevelyan leaned over to say, "Beats me the way they make you wait."

"Red tape," said George. "You can't avoid it."

Trevelyan said, "What makes *you* so damned tolerant about it?"

"I've got nothing to worry about."

"Oh, brother, you make me sick. I hope you end up Registered Manure Spreader just so I can see your face when you do." His sombre eyes swept the crowd anxiously.

George looked about, too. It wasn't quite the system they used on the children. Matters went slower, and instructions had been given out at the start in print (an advantage over the pre-Readers). The names Platen and Trevelyan were well down the alphabet still, but this time the two knew it.

Young men came out of the education rooms, frowning and uncomfortable, picked up their clothes and belongings, then went off to analysis to learn the results.

Each, as he came out, would be surrounded by a clot of the thinning crowd. "How was it?" "How'd it feel?" "Whacha think ya made?" "Ya feel any different?"

Answers were vague and noncommittal.

George forced himself to remain out of those clots. You only raised your own blood pressure. Everyone said you stood the best chance if you remained calm. Even so, you could feel the palms of your hands grow cold. Funny that new tensions came with the years.

For instance, high-specialty professionals heading out for an Outworld were accompanied by a wife (or husband). It was important to keep the sex ratio in good balance on all worlds. And if you were going out to a Grade A world, what girl would refuse you? George had no specific girl in mind yet; he wanted none. Not now! Once he made Programmer; once he could add to his name, Registered Computer Programmer, he could take his pick, like a sultan in a harem. The thought excited him and he tried to put it away. Must stay calm.

Trevelyan muttered, "What's it all about anyway? First they say it works best if you're relaxed and at ease. Then they put you through this and make it impossible for you to be relaxed and at ease."

"Maybe that's the idea. They're separating the boys from the men to begin with. Take it easy, Trev."

"Shut up."

George's turn came. His name was not called. It appeared in glowing letters on the notice-board.

He waved at Trevelyan. "Take it easy. Don't let it get you."

He was happy as he entered the test "George Platen?"

For a fleeting instant there was a razor-sharp picture in George's mind of another man, ten years earlier, who had asked the same question, and it was almost as though this were the same man and he, George, had turned eight again as he had stepped across the threshold.

But the man looked up and, of course, the face matched that of the sudden memory not at all. The nose was bulbous, the hair thin and stringy, and the chin wattled as though its owner had once been grossly overweight and had reduced.

The man behind the desk looked annoyed. "Well?"

George came to Earth. "I'm George Platen, sir."

"Say so, then. I'm Dr. Zachary Amtonelli, and we're going to be intimately acquainted in a moment."

He stared at small strips of film, holding them up to the light owlishly.

George winced inwardly. Very hazily, he remembered that other doctor (he had forgotten the name) staring at such film. Could these be the same? The other doctor had frowned and this one was looking at him now as though he were angry.

His happiness was already just about gone.

Dr. Antonelli spread the pages of a thickish file out before him now and put the films carefully to one side. "It says here you want to be a Computer Programmer."

"Yes, doctor."

"Still do?"

"Yes, sir."

"It's a responsible and exacting position. Do you feel up to it?"

"Yes, sir."

"Most pre-Educates don't put down any specific profession. I believe they are afraid of queering it."

"I think that's right, sir."

"Aren't you afraid of that?"

"I might as well be honest, sir."

Dr. Antonelli nodded, but without any noticeable lightening of his expression. "Why do you want to be a Programmer?"

"It's a responsible and exacting position as you said, sir. It's an important job and an exciting one. I like it and I think I can do it."

Dr. Antonelli put the papers away, and looked at George sourly. He said, "How do you know you like it? Because you think you'll be snapped up by some Grade A planet?"

George thought uneasily: He's trying to rattle you. Stay calm and stay frank.

He said, "I think a Programmer has a good chance, sir, but even if I were left on Earth, I know I'd like it." (That was true enough. I'm not lying, thought George.)

"All right, how do you know?"

He asked it as though he knew there was no decent answer and George almost smiled. He had one.

He said, "I've been reading about Programming, sir."

"You've been *what?*" Now the doctor looked genuinely astonished and George took pleasure in that.

"Reading about it, sir. I bought a book on the subject and I've been studying it."

"A book for Registered Programmers?"

"Yes, sir."

"But you couldn't understand it."

"Not at first. I got other books on mathematics and electronics. I made out all I could. I still don't know much, but I know enough to know I like it and to know I can make it." (Even his parents never found that secret cache of books or knew why he spent so much time in his own room or exactly what happened to the sleep he missed.)

The doctor pulled at the loose skin under his chin. "What was your idea in doing that, son?"

"I wanted to make sure I would be interested, sir."

"Surely you know that being interested means nothing. You could be devoured by a subject and if the physical make-up of your brain makes it more efficient for you to be something else, something else you will be. You know that, don't you?"

"I've been told that," said George cautiously.

"Well, believe it. It's true."

George said nothing.

Dr. Antonelli said, "Or do you believe that studying some subject will bend the brain cells in that direction, like that other theory that a pregnant woman need only listen to great music persistently to make a composer of her child. Do you believe that?"

George flushed. That had certainly been in his mind. By forcing his intellect constantly in the desired direction, he had felt sure that he would be getting a head start. Most of his confidence had rested on exactly that point.

"I never—" he began, and found no way of finishing.

"Well, it isn't true. Good Lord, youngster, your brain pattern is fixed at birth. It can be altered by a blow hard enough to damage the cells or by a burst blood vessel or by a tumour or by a major infection—each time, of course, for the worse. But it certainly can't be affected by your thinking special thoughts." He stared at George thoughtfully, then said, "Who told you to do this?"

George, now thoroughly disturbed, swallowed and said, "No one, doctor. My own idea."

"Who knew you were doing it after you started?"

"No one. Doctor, I meant to do no wrong."

"Who said anything about wrong? Useless is what I would say. Why did you keep it to yourself?"

"I-I thought they'd laugh at me." (He thought abruptly of a recent exchange with Trevelyan. George had very cautiously broached the thought as of something merely circulating distantly in the very outermost reaches of his mind, concerning the possibility of learning something by ladling it into the mind by hand, so to speak, in bits and pieces. Trevelyan had hooted,

"George, you'll be tanning your own shoes next and weaving your own shirts." He had been thankful then for his policy of secrecy.)

Dr. Antonelli shoved the bits of film he had first looked at from position to position in morose thought. Then he said, "Let's get you analysed. This is getting me nowhere."

The wires went to George's temples. There was the buzzing. Again there came a sharp memory of ten years ago.

George's hands were clammy; his heart pounded. He should never have told the doctor about his secret reading.

It was his damned vanity, he told himself. He had wanted to show how enterprising he was, how full of initiative. Instead, he had showed himself superstitious and ignorant and aroused the hostility of the doctor. (He could tell the doctor hated him for a wise guy on the make.)

And now he had brought himself to such a state of nervousness, he was sure the analyser would show nothing that made sense.

He wasn't aware of the moment when the wires were removed from his temples. The sight of the doctor, staring at him thoughtfully, blinked into his consciousness and that was that; the wires were gone. George dragged himself together with a tearing effort. He had quite given up his ambition to be a Programmer. In the space of ten minutes, it had all gone.

He said dismally, "I suppose no?"

"No what?"

"No Programmer?"

The doctor rubbed his nose and said, "You get your clothes and whatever belongs to you and go to room 15-C. Your files will be waiting for you there. So will my report."

George said in complete surprise. "Have I been Educated already? I thought this was just to—"

Dr. Antonelli stared down at his desk. "It will all be explained to you. You do as I say."

George felt something like panic. What was it they couldn't tell him? He wasn't fit for anything but Registered Labourer. They were going to prepare him for that; adjust him to it.

He was suddenly certain of it and he had to keep from screaming by main force.

He stumbled back to his place of waiting. Trevelyan was not there, a fact for which he would have been thankful if he had had enough self-possession to be meaningfully aware of his surroundings. Hardly anyone was left, in fact, and the few who were looked as though they might ask him questions were it not that they were too worn out by their tail-of-the-alphabet waiting to buck the fierce, hot look of anger and hate he cast at them.

What right had *they* to be technicians and he, himself, a Labourer? Labourer! He was *certain*!

He was led by a red-uniformed guide along the busy corridors lined with separate rooms each containing its groups, here two, there five: the Motor Mechanics, the Construction Engineers, the Agronomists—there were hundreds of specialized Professions and most of them would be represented in this small town by one or two anyway.

He hated them all just then: the Statisticians, the Accountants, the lesser breeds and the higher. He hated them because they owned their smug knowledge now, knew their fate, while he himself, empty still, had to face some kind of further red tape.

He reached 15-C, was ushered in and left in an empty room. For one moment, his spirits bounded. Surely, if this were the Labour classification room, there would be dozens of youngsters present.

A door sucked into its recess on the other side of a waist-high partition and an elderly, white-haired man stepped out. He smiled and showed even teeth that were obviously false, but his face was still ruddy and his voice had vigour.

He said, "Good evening, George. Our own sector has only one of you this time, I see."

"Only one?" said George blankly.

"Thousands over the Earth, of course. Thousands. You're not alone."

George felt exasperated. He said, "I don't understand, sir. What's my classification? What's happening?"

"Easy, son. You're all right. It could happen to anyone." He held out his hand and George took it mechanically. It was warm and it pressed George's hand firmly. "Sit down, son. I'm Sam Ellenford."

George nodded impatiently. "I want to know what's going on, sir."

"Of course. To begin with, you can't be a Computer Programmer, George. You've guessed that, I think."

"Yes, I have," said George bitterly. "What will I be, then?"

"That's the hard part to explain, George." He paused, then said with careful distinctness, "Nothing."

"*What!*"

"Nothing!"

"But what does that mean? Why can't you assign me a profession?"

"We have no choice in the matter, George. It's the structure of your mind that decides that."

George went a sallow yellow. His eyes bulged. "There's something wrong with my mind?"

"There's *something* about it. As far as professional classification is concerned, I suppose you can call it wrong."

"But why?"

Ellenford shrugged. "I'm sure you know how Earth runs its Educational programme, George. Practically any human being can absorb practically any body of knowledge, but each individual brain pattern is better suited to receiving some types of knowledge than others. We try to match mind to knowledge as well as we can within the limits of the quota requirements for each profession."

George nodded. "Yes, I know."

"Every once in a while, George, we come up against a young man whose mind is not suited to receiving a superimposed knowledge of any sort."

"You mean I can't be Educated?"

"That is what I mean."

"But that's crazy. I'm intelligent. I can understand—" He looked helplessly about as though trying to find some way of proving that he had a functioning brain.

"Don't misunderstand me, please," said Ellenford gravely. "You're intelligent. There's no question about that. You're even above average in intelligence. Unfortunately that has nothing to do with whether the mind ought to be allowed to accept superimposed knowledge or not. In fact, it is almost always the intelligent person who comes here."

"You mean I can't even be a Registered Labourer?" babbled George. Suddenly even that was better than the blank that faced him. "What's there to know to be a Labourer?"

"Don't underestimate the Labourer, young man. There are dozens of subclassifications and each variety has its own corpus of fairly detailed knowledge. Do you think there's no skill in knowing the proper manner of lifting a weight? Besides, for the Labourer, we must select not only minds suited to it, but bodies as well. You're not the type, George, to last long as a Labourer."

George was conscious of his slight build. He said, "But I've never heard of anyone without a profession."

"There aren't many," conceded Ellenford. "And we protect them."

"Protect them?" George felt confusion and fright grow higher inside him.

"You're a ward of the planet, George. From the time you walked through that door, we've been in charge of you." And he smiled.

It was a fond smile. To George it seemed the smile of ownership; the smile of a grown man for a helpless child.

He said, "You mean, I'm going to be in prison?"

"Of course not. You will simply be with others of your kind."

Your kind. The words made a kind of thunder in George's ear.

Ellenford said, "You need special treatment. We'll take care of you."

To George's own horror, he burst into tears. Ellenford walked to the other end of the room and faced away as though in thought.

George fought to reduce the agonized weeping to sobs and then to strangle those. He thought of his father and mother, of his friends, of Trevelyan, of his own shame—

He said rebelliously, "I learned to read."

"Everyone with a whole mind can do that. We've never found exceptions. It is at this stage that we discover—exceptions. And when you learned to read, George, we were concerned about your mind pattern. Certain peculiarities were reported even then by the doctor in charge."

"Can't you try Educating me? You haven't even tried. I'm willing to take the risk."

"The law forbids us to do that, George. But look, it will not be bad. We will explain matters to your family so they will not be hurt. At the place to which you'll be taken, you'll be allowed privileges. We'll get you books and you can learn what you will."

"Dab knowledge in by hand," said George bitterly. "Shred by shred. Then, when I die I'll know enough to be a Registered Junior Office Boy, Paper-Clip Division."

"Yet I understand you've already been studying books."

George froze. He was struck devastatingly by sudden understanding. "That's it. . ."

"What is?"

"That fellow Antonelli. He's knifing me."

"No, George. You're quite wrong."

"Don't tell me that." George was in an ecstasy of fury. "That lousy bastard is selling me out because he thought I was a little too wise for him. I read books and tried to get a head start toward programming. Well, what do you want to square things? Money? You won't get it. I'm getting out of here and when I finish broadcasting this—"

He was screaming.

Ellenford shook his head and touched a contact.

Two men entered on catfeet and got on either side of George. They pinned his arms to his sides. One of them used an air-spray hypodermic in the hollow of his right elbow and the hypnotic entered his vein and had an almost immediate effect.

His screams cut off and his head fell forward. His knees buckled and only the men on either side kept him erect as he slept.

II Conducting Efficient Elections

Two criteria of pure democracy are that power rest with the people and that they be able to exercise it directly. The distinction between pure democracy and representative democracy is that in the representative form the populace selects representatives who exercise power on their behalf. One essential aspect of representative democracy is that the governed participate in the selection of those who carry out the business of government.

What, precisely, does it mean to participate in the selection of representatives? The concept of participation could take a number of different forms in practice and still result in a satisfactory set of procedures. In most societies, to participate in the selection of a representative means to vote. Usually, however, all members of a society do not vote for all the representatives who constitute the government. Therefore, it might be argued, each member of the populace is participating only in the selection of a small subset of those who govern.

The concept of participation in most societies usually extends only to the act of voting. If, however, a man votes for a losing candidate, he has still participated. One can imagine an alternative form of selection in which the man who is chosen to represent a group must be agreeable to every single member of the group. Although such a system might be unworkable for groups of any size, it has been used, and it is currently used, for instance, by Quaker meetings and by the College of Cardinals when it selects a pope. At one time (though probably no longer) the rations given to members of the College were systematically reduced over the period of their deliberations (sometimes several weeks). The theory was that if you set a task that requires the group to reach consensus and reduce their food supply to bread and water, one member is more likely to see merit in the proposals of another.

If we recognize that the major consideration in satisfying the definition of participation is that the electorate feel it has participated, a number of variations on our present method of choosing a government might be considered. For example, as long as representatives are chosen to represent geographic areas or units of population within geographic areas, as are United States senators and representatives, the argument could be made that a great many people are not being represented. If a number of people holding similar political opinions are to have a representative in Congress, they must constitute a majority in a geographic area. For instance, assume that in one state 55 percent of the population belongs to party *X* and 45 percent belongs to party *Y*. If each congressional district of the state were divided into the same proportions, and everybody voted along party lines, party *X* would win every congressional election and the members of party *Y* would have no representative of their choosing. If, however, the state's congressional seats were simply divided among parties on the basis of the proportion of the registered electorate that belonged to each party on election day, then all varieties of political opinion would be represented in the proportions in which they were held by the electorate.

Even without altering the relationship between the electorate and their representatives, numerous possibilities still appear for modifying the methods by which officials are selected and for determining the population's preference on issues to be decided. "Franchise" by Isaac Asimov, considers one such innovation. In many respects the electoral procedures used in Asimov's future society are extrapolations of practices now in their infancy.

Franchise

Isaac Asimov

Linda said, "Grandpa," and stood with her chin down and her hands behind her back until his newspaper lowered itself to the point where shaggy eyebrows and eyes, nested in fine wrinkles, showed themselves. It was Friday, October 31.

He said, "Yes?"

Linda came closer and put both her forearms on one of the old man's knees so that he had to discard his newspaper altogether.

She said, "Grandpa, did you really once vote?"

He said, "You heard me say I did, didn't you? Do you think I tell fibs?"

"N-no, but Mamma says everybody voted then."

"So they did."

"But how could they? How could *everybody* vote?"

Matthew stared at her solemnly, then lifted her and put her on his knee. He even moderated the tonal qualities of his voice. He said, "You see, Linda, till about forty years ago, everybody always voted. Say we wanted to decide who was to be the new President of the United States. The Democrats and Republicans would both nominate someone, and everybody would say who they wanted. When Election Day was over, they would count how many people wanted the Democrat and how many wanted the Republican. Whoever had more votes was elected. You see?"

Linda nodded and said, "How did all the people know who to vote for? Did Multivac tell them?"

Matthew's eyebrows hunched down and he looked severe. "They just used their own judgment, girl."

She edged away from him, and he lowered his voice again, "I'm not angry at you, Linda. But, you see, sometimes it took all night to count what everyone said and people were impatient. So they invented special machines which could look at the first few votes and compare them with the votes from the same places in previous years. That way the machine could compute how the total vote would be and who would be elected. You see?"

She nodded. "Like Multivac."

"The first computers were much smaller than Multivac. But the machines grew bigger and they could tell how the election would go from fewer and fewer votes. Then, at last, they built Multivac and it can tell from just one voter."

Linda smiled at having reached a familiar part of the story and said, "That's nice."

Matthew frowned and said, "No, it's not nice. I don't want a machine telling me how I would have voted just because some joker in Milwaukee says he's against higher tariffs. Maybe I want to vote cock-eyed just for the pleasure of it. Maybe I don't want to vote. Maybe—"

But Linda had wriggled from his knee and was beating a retreat.

She met her mother at the door. Her mother, who was still wearing her coat and had not even had time to remove her hat, said breathlessly, "Run along, Linda. Don't get in Mother's way."

Then she said to Matthew, as she lifted her hat from her head and patted her hair back into place, "I've been at Agatha's."

Matthew stared at her censoriously and did not even dignify that piece of information with a grunt as he groped for his newspaper.

Sarah said, as she unbuttoned her coat, "Guess what she said?"

Matthew flattened out his newspaper for reading purposes with a sharp crackle and said, "Don't much care."

Sarah said, "Now, Father—" But she had no time for anger. The news had to be told and Matthew was the only recipient handy, so she went on, "Agatha's Joe is a policeman, you know, and he says a whole truckload of secret service men came into Bloomington last night."

"They're not after me."

"Don't you see, Father? Secret service agents, and its almost election time. In *Bloomington.*"

"Maybe they're after a bank robber."

"There hasn't been a bank robbery in town in ages. . . . Father, you're hopeless."

She stalked away.

Nor did Norman Muller receive the news with noticeably greater excitement.

"Now, Sarah, how did Agatha's Joe know they were secret service agents?" he asked calmly. "They wouldn't go around with identification cards pasted on their foreheads."

But by next evening, with November a day old, she could say triumphantly, "It's just everyone in Bloomington that's waiting for someone local to be the voter. The Bloomington *News* as much as said so on video."

Norman stirred uneasily. He couldn't deny it, and his heart was sinking. If Bloomington was really to be hit by Multivac's lightning, it would mean newspapermen, video shows, tourists, all sorts of—strange upsets. Norman liked the quiet routine of his life, and the distant stir of politics was getting uncomfortably close.

He said, "It's all rumor. Nothing more."

"You wait and see, then. You just wait and see."

As things turned out, there was very little time to wait, for the doorbell rang insistently, and when Norman Muller opened it and said "Yes?" a tall, grave-faced man said, "Are you Norman Muller?"

Norman said, "Yes," again, but in a strange dying voice. It was not difficult to see from the stranger's bearing that he was one carrying authority, and the nature of his errand suddenly became as inevitably obvious as it had, until the moment before, been unthinkably impossible.

The man presented credentials, stepped into the house, closed the door behind him and said ritualistically, "Mr. Norman Muller, it is necessary for me to inform you on the behalf of the President of the United States that you have been chosen to represent the American electorate on Tuesday, November 4, 2008."

Norman Muller managed, with difficulty, to walk unaided to his chair. He sat there, white-faced and almost insensible, while Sarah brought water, slapped his hands in panic, and moaned to her husband between clenched teeth, "Don't be sick, Norman. *Don't* be sick. They'll pick someone else."

When Norman could manage to talk, he whispered, "I'm sorry, sir."

The secret service agent had removed his coat, unbuttoned his jacket and was sitting at ease on the couch.

"It's all right," he said, and the mark of officialdom seemed to have vanished with the formal announcement and leave him simply a large and rather friendly man. "This is the sixth time I've made the announcement and I've seen all kinds of reactions. Not one of them was the kind you see on the video. You know what I mean? A holy, dedicated look, and a character who says, 'It will be a great privilege to serve my country.' That sort of stuff." The agent laughed comfortingly.

Sarah's accompanying laugh held a trace of hysteria.

The agent said, "Now you're going to have me with you for a while. My name is Phil Handley. I'd appreciate it if you call me Phil. Mr. Muller can't leave the house any more till Election Day. You'll have to inform the department store that he's sick, Mrs. Muller. You can go about your business for a while, but you'll have to agree not to say a word about this. Right, Mrs. Muller?"

Sarah nodded vigorously. "No, sir. Not a word."

"All right. But, Mrs. Muller," Handley looked grave, "we're not kidding now. Go out only if you must and you'll be followed when you do. I'm sorry but that's the way we must operate."

"Followed?"

"It won't be obvious. Don't worry. And it's only for two days till the formal announcement to the nation is made. Your daughter—"

"She's in bed," said Sarah hastily.

"Good. She'll have to be told I'm a relative or friend staying with the family. If she does find out the truth, she'll have to be kept in the house. Your father had better stay in the house in any case."

"He won't like that," said Sarah.

"Can't be helped. Now, since you have no others living with you—"

"You know all about us apparently," whispered Norman.

"Quite a bit," agreed Handley. "In any case, those are all my instructions to you for the moment. I'll try to co-operate as much as I can and be as little of a nuisance as possible. The government will pay for my maintenance so I won't be an expense to you. I'll be relieved each night by someone who will sit up in this room, so there will be no problem about sleeping accommodations. Now Mr. Muller—"

"Sir?"

"You can call me Phil," said the agent again. "The purpose of the two-day preliminary before formal announcement is to get you used to your position. We prefer to have you face Multivac in as normal a state of mind as possible. Just relax and try to feel this is all in a day's work. Okay?"

"Okay," said Norman, and then shook his head violently. "But I don't want the responsibility. Why me?"

"All right," said Handley, "let's get that straight to begin with. Multivac weighs all sorts of known factors, billions of them. One factor isn't known, though, and won't be known for a long time. That's the reaction pattern of the human mind. All Americans are subjected to the molding pressure of what other Americans do and say, to the things that are done to him and the things he does to others. Any American can be brought to Multivac to have the bent of his mind surveyed. From that the bent of all other minds in the country can be estimated. Some Americans are better for the purpose than others at some given time, depending upon the happenings of that year. Multivac picked you as most representative this year. Not the smartest, or the strongest, or the luckiest, but just the most representative. Now we don't question Multivac, do we?"

"Couldn't it make a mistake?" asked Norman.

Sarah, who listened impatiently, interrupted to say, "Don't listen to him, sir. He's just nervous, you know. Actually, he's very well read and he always follows politics very closely."

Handley said, "Multivac makes the decisions, Mrs. Muller. It picked your husband."

"But does it know everything?" insisted Norman wildly. "Couldn't it have made a mistake?"

"Yes, it can. There's no point in not being frank. In 1993, a selected Voter died of a stroke two hours before it was time for him to be notified. Multivac didn't predict that; it couldn't. A Voter might be mentally unstable, morally unsuitable, or, for that matter, disloyal. Multivac can't know everything about everybody until he's fed all the data there is. That's why alternate selections are always held in readiness. I don't think we'll be using one this time. You're in good health, Mr. Muller, and you've been carefully investigated. You qualify."

Norman buried his face in his hands and sat motionless.

"By tomorrow morning, sir," said Sarah, "he'll be perfectly all right. He just has to get used to it, that's all."

"Of course," said Handley.

In the privacy of their bedchamber, Sarah Muller expressed herself in other and stronger fashion. The burden of her lecture was, "So get hold of yourself, Norman. You're trying to throw away the chance of a lifetime."

Norman whispered desperately, "It frightens me, Sarah. The whole thing."

"For goodness' sake, why? What's there to it but answering a question or two?"

"The responsibility is too great. I couldn't face it."

"What responsibility? There isn't any. Multivac picked you. It's Multivac's responsibility. Everyone knows that."

Norman sat up in bed in a sudden access of rebellion and anguish. "Everyone is *supposed* to know that. But they don't. They—"

"Lower your voice," hissed Sarah icily. "They'll hear you downtown."

"They don't," said Norman, declining quickly to a whisper. "When they talk about the Ridgely administration of 1988, do they say he won them over with pie-in-the-sky promises and racist baloney? No! They talk about the 'goddam MacComber vote,' as though Humphrey MacComber was the only man who had anything to do with it because he faced Multivac. I've said it myself—only now I think the poor guy was just a truck farmer who didn't ask to be picked. Why was it his fault more than anyone else's? Now his name is a curse."

"You're just being childish," said Sarah.

"I'm being sensible. I tell you, Sarah, I won't accept. They can't make me vote if I don't want to. I'll say I'm sick. I'll say—"

But Sarah had had enough. "Now you listen to me," she whispered in a cold fury. "You don't have only yourself to think about. You know what it means to be Voter of the Year. A presidential year at that. It means publicity and fame and, maybe, buckets of money."

"And then I go back to being a clerk."

"You will *not*. You'll have a branch managership at the least if you have any brains at all, and you *will* have, because I'll tell you what to do. You control this kind of publicity, if you play your cards right, and you can force Kennell Stores, Inc., into a tight contract *and* an escalator clause in connection with your salary *and* a decent pension plan."

"That's not the point in being Voter, Sarah."

"That will be your point. If you don't owe anything to yourself or to me—I'm not asking for myself—you owe something to Linda."

Norman groaned.

"Well, don't you?" snapped Sarah.

"Yes, dear," murmured Norman.

On November 3, the official announcement was made and it was too late for Norman to back out even if he had been able to find the courage to make the attempt.

Their house was sealed off. Secret service agents made their appearance in the open, blocking off all approach.

At first the telephone rang incessantly, but Philip Handley with an engagingly apologetic smile took all calls. Eventually, the exchange shunted all calls directly to the police station.

Norman imagined that, in that way, he was spared not only the bubbling (and envious) congratulations of friends, but also the egregious pressure of salesmen scenting a prospect and the designing smoothness of politicians from all over the nation. . . . Perhaps even death threats from the inevitable cranks.

Newspapers were forbidden to enter the house now in order to keep out weighted pressures, and television was gently but firmly disconnected, over Linda's loud protests.

Matthew growled and stayed in his room; Linda, after the first flurry of excitement, sulked and whined because she could not leave the house; Sarah divided her time between preparation of meals for the present and plans for the future; and Norman's depression lived and fed upon itself.

And the morning of Tuesday, November 4, 2008, came at last, and it was Election Day.

It was early breakfast, but only Norman Muller ate, and that mechanically. Even a shower and shave had not succeeded in either restoring him to reality or removing his own conviction that he was as grimy without as he felt grimy within.

Handley's friendly voice did its best to shed some normality over the gray and unfriendly dawn. (The weather prediction had been for a cloudy day with prospects of rain before noon.)

Handley said, "We'll keep this house insulated till Mr. Muller is back, but after that we'll be off your necks." The secret service agent was in full uniform now, including sidearms in heavily brassed holsters.

"You've been no trouble at all, Mr. Handley," simpered Sarah.

Norman drank through two cups of black coffee, wiped his lips with a napkin, stood up and said haggardly, "I'm ready."

Handley stood up, too. "Very well, sir. And thank you, Mrs. Muller, for your very kind hospitality."

The armored car purred down empty streets. They were empty even for that hour of the morning.

Handley indicated that and said, "They always shift traffic away from the line of drive ever since the attempted bombing that nearly ruined the Leverett Election of '92."

When the car stopped, Norman was helped out by the always polite Handley into an underground drive whose walls were lined with soldiers at attention.

He was led into a brightly lit room, in which three white-uniformed men greeted him smilingly.

Norman said sharply, "But this is the hospital."

"There's no significance to that," said Handley at once. "It's just that the hospital has the necessary facilities."

"Well, what do I do?"

Handley nodded. One of the three men in white advanced and said, "I'll take over now, agent."

Handley saluted in an offhand manner and left the room.

The man in white said, "Won't you sit down, Mr. Muller? I'm John Paulson, senior Computer. These are Samson Levine and Peter Dorogobuzh, my assistants."

Norman shook hands numbly all about. Paulson was a man of middle height with a soft face that seemed used to smiling and a very obvious toupee. He wore plastic-rimmed glasses of an old-fashioned cut, and he lit a cigarette as he talked. (Norman refused his offer of one.)

Paulson said, "In the first place, Mr. Muller, I want you to know we are in no hurry. We want you to stay with us all day if necessary, just so that you get used to your surroundings and get over any thought you might have that there is anything unusual in this, anything clinical, if you know what I mean."

"It's all right," said Norman. "I'd just as soon this were over."

"I understand your feelings. Still, we want you to know exactly what's going on. In the first place, Multivac isn't here."

"It isn't?" Somehow through all his depression, he had still looked forward to seeing Multivac. They said it was half a mile long and three stories high, that fifty technicians walked the corridors *within* its structure continuously. It was one of the wonders of the world.

Paulson smiled. "No. It's not portable, you know. It's located underground, in fact, and very few people know exactly where. You can understand that, since it is our greatest natural resource. Believe me, elections aren't the only things it's used for."

Norman thought he was being deliberately chatty and found himself intrigued all the same. "I thought I'd see it. I'd like to."

"I'm sure of that. But it takes a presidential order and even then it has to be countersigned by Security. However, we are plugged into Multivac right here by beam transmission. What Multivac says can be interpreted here and what we say is beamed directly to Multivac, so in a sense we're in its presence."

Norman looked about. The machines within the room were all meaningless to him.

"Now let me explain, Mr. Muller," Paulson went on. "Multivac already has most of the information it needs to decide all the elections, national, state and local. It needs only to check certain imponderable attitudes of mind and it will use you for that. We can't predict what questions it will ask, but they may not make much sense to you, or even to us. It may ask you how you feel about garbage disposal in your town; whether you favour central incinerators. It might ask you whether you have a doctor of your own or whether you make use of National Medicine, Inc. Do you understand?"

"Yes, sir."

"Whatever it asks, you answer in your own words in any way you please. If you feel you must explain quite a bit, do so. Talk an hour, if necessary."

"Yes, sir."

"Now, one more thing. We will have to make use of some simple devices which will automatically record your blood pressure, heartbeat, skin conductivity and brain-wave pattern while you speak. The machinery will seem formidable, but it's all absolutely painless. You won't even know it's going on."

The other two technicians were already busying themselves with smooth-gleaming apparatus on oiled wheels.

Norman said, "Is that to check on whether I'm lying or not?"

"Not at all, Mr. Muller. There's no question of lying. It's only a matter of emotional intensity. If the machine asks you your opinion of your child's school, you may say, 'I think it is overcrowded.' Those are only words. From the way your brain and heart and hormones and sweat glands work, Multivac can judge exactly how intensely you feel about the matter. It will understand your feelings better than you yourself."

"I never heard of this," said Norman.

"No, I'm sure you didn't. Most of the details of Multivac's workings are top secret. For instance, when you leave, you will be asked to sign a paper swearing that you will never reveal the nature of the questions you were asked, the nature of your responses, what was done, or how it was done. The less is known about the Multivac, the less chance of attempted outside pressures upon the men who service it." He smiled grimly. "Our lives are hard enough as it is."

Norman nodded. "I understand."

"And now would you like anything to eat or drink?"

"No. Nothing right now."

"Do you have any questions?"

Norman shook his head.

"Then you tell us when you're ready."

"I'm ready right now."

"You're certain?"

"Quite."

Paulson nodded, and raised his hand in a gesture to the others.

They advanced with their frightening equipment, and Norman Muller felt his breath come a little quicker as he watched.

The ordeal lasted nearly three hours, with one short break for coffee and an embarrassing session with a chamber pot. During all this time, Norman Muller remained encased in machinery. He was bone-weary at the close.

He thought sardonically that his promise to reveal nothing of what had passed would be an easy one to keep. Already the questions were a hazy mishmash in his mind.

Somehow he had thought Multivac would speak in a sepulchral, superhuman voice, resonant and echoing, but that, after all, was just an idea he had from seeing too many television shows, he now decided. The truth was distressingly undramatic. The questions were slips of a kind of metalic foil patterned with numerous punctures. A second machine converted the pattern into words and Paulson read the words to Norman, then gave him the question and let him read it for himself.

Norman's answers were taken down by a recording machine, played back to Norman for confirmation, with emendations and added remarks also taken down. All that was fed into a pattern-making instrument and that, in turn, was radiated to Multivac.

The one question Norman could remember at the moment was an incongruously gossipy: "What do you think of the price of eggs?"

Now it was over, and gently they removed the electrodes from various portions of his body, unwrapped the pulsating band from his upper arm, moved the machinery away.

He stood up, drew a deep, shuddering breath and said, "Is that all? Am I through?"

"Not quite." Paulson hurried to him, smiling in reassuring fashion. "We'll have to ask you to stay another hour."

"Why?" asked Norman sharply.

"It will take that long for Multivac to weave its new data into the trillions of items it has. Thousands of elections are concerned, you know. It's very complicated. And it may be that an odd contest here or there, a comptrollership in Phoenix, Arizona, or some council seat in Wilkesboro, North Carolina, may be in doubt. In that case, Multivac may be compelled to ask you a deciding question or two."

"No," said Norman. "I won't go through this again."

"It probably won't happen," Paulson said soothingly. "It rarely does. But, just in case, you'll have to stay." A touch of steel, just a touch, entered his voice. "You have no choice, you know. You must."

Norman sat down wearily. He shrugged.

Paulson said, "We can't let you read a newspaper, but if you'd care for a murder mystery, or if you'd like to play chess, or if there's anything we can do for you to help pass the time, I wish you'd mention it."

"It's all right. I'll just wait."

They ushered him into a small room just next to the one in which he had been questioned. He let himself sink into a plastic-covered armchair and closed his eyes.

As well as he could, he must wait out this final hour.

He sat perfectly still and slowly the tension left him. His breathing grew less ragged and he could clasp his hands without being quite so conscious of the trembling of his fingers.

Maybe there would be no questions. Maybe it was all over.

If it *were* over, then the next thing would be torchlight processions and invitations to speak at all sorts of functions. The Voter of the Year!

He, Norman Muller, ordinary clerk of a small department store in Bloomington, Indiana, who had neither been born great nor achieved greatness would be in the extraordinary position of having had greatness thrust upon him.

The historians would speak soberly of the Muller Election of 2008. That would be its name, the Muller Election.

The publicity, the better job, the flash flood of money that interested Sarah so much, occupied only a corner of his mind. It would all be welcome, of course. He couldn't refuse it. But at the moment something else was beginning to concern him.

A latent patriotism was stirring. After all, he was representing the entire electorate. He was the focal point for *them.* He was, in his own person, for this one day, all of America!

The door opened, snapping him to open-eyed attention. For a moment, his stomach constricted. Not more questions!

But Paulson was smiling. "That will be all, Mr. Muller."

"No more questions, sir?"

"None needed. Everything was quite clear-cut. You will be escorted back to your home and then you will be a private citizen once more. Or as much so as the public will allow."

"Thank you. Thank you." Norman flushed and said, "I wonder—who was elected?"

Paulson shook his head. "That will have to wait for the official announcement. The rules are quite strict. We can't even tell you. You understand."

"Of course. Yes." Norman felt embarrassed.

"Secret service will have the necessary papers for you to sign."

"Yes." Suddenly, Norman Muller felt proud. It was on him now in full strength. He was proud.

In this imperfect world, the sovereign citizens of the first and greatest Electronic Democracy had, through Norman Muller (through *him!*), exercised once again its free, untrammelled franchise.

PART THREE
Social Organization

12 The Psycho-Engineering of Personalities

The psychologist B. F. Skinner created a utopian community called Walden Two. An excerpt from his book, *Walden Two,* describes the community's educational institutions and the procedures used to socialize children into the community. Because Skinner is an eminent psychologist and because some principles of his reinforcement-based psychology have been obviously applied in the design of the community's procedures for socializing and educating its members, the plan for Walden Two may be regarded as the most serious attempt by any designer of possible societies whose work is represented in this book to specify how social-science knowledge might be applied. Even Skinner's outline for Walden Two should, however, be viewed as an oversimplified sketch of a small segment of a social system that utilized the procedures he proposed. Walden Two does not provide a detailed plan that could be put directly into operation.

One fear that is often voiced about the effects of the development of a powerful social science (it is frequently echoed in the work of writers of science fiction) is that once the processes of socialization and education are understood and can be controlled, human automatons will be produced whose "free wills" have been destroyed, or at least men will be shaped to fit into their societies. The fear is that knowledge will permit control, and that control will destroy the "natural" process whereby children become adults. In order to see the issue in perspective we have to recognize that two separate components must be considered. The first is the extent to which an individual's *self* is the result of a sequence of socializing experiences. The second is the consequences of controlling this set of experiences.

Proposals for a revision of educational systems or for the introduction of conscious methods of socialization frequently generate great controversy. One reason for controversy is that such proposals occasion some thought about the tremendous effects of socialization and education. Giving serious thought to how much one's personality, personal preferences, beliefs, and opinions are determined by his socialization and his educational experiences makes it difficult to maintain certain cherished myths about freedom of the individual will.

For most people in our society the socialization process is a set of experiences that are unique to each person. Even educational experiences introduce only a minimum core of common experiences; because educational environments are enormously diverse, only relatively small numbers of people have even this much of a common set of experiences. A young man attending an Eastern prep school, one attending a military school which advertises that it will produce *men of character,* another attending a suburban, middle-class high school, and a fourth attending an urban ghetto school can hardly be considered to be experiencing equivalent socializations even with regard to their educational experiences. It could be argued that even when class differences are held constant, regional variations are sufficiently great to destroy comparability across school settings. It is unlikely that the social environment of a middle-class school in Georgia is indistinguishable from the social environment of a middle-class school in Los Angeles, or even that a Los Angeles school is interchangeable with one in San Francisco in terms of social environment. The products of each of these socializing environments are usually more like each other than they are like the products of different environments, and this demonstrates that the particular environment has a substantial effect on the end-product.

The great diversity of socialization patterns (experiences within families, experiences within schools, and so on) in our society makes it difficult to identify the causes of variations in adult personality and belief systems. Therefore, the myth remains that our *social selves* are something other than simply the products of our society, our social-class positions within that society, and the specific set of experiences that mark our personal histories. Attempts to identify the causal forces involved in personality development, and proposals to adopt specified sets of socializing experiences designed to create adults with certain personal characteristics, make clear the cause-and-effect nature of social development. This threatens the myth of essential individuality.

Productive objections to the proposals could be made in terms of whether the innovations would produce the intended effects, or whether some other end-product was more desirable. But objections are rarely productive in this sense; rather, they simply suggest that the designer is touching on a taboo subject.

In addition to a certain unwillingness to admit that those aspects of a person's *self* that seem most personal and unique are merely the result of largely accidental experiences, objections are frequently raised on the grounds that up to the limits of assault and battery and other treatment generally recognized as inhumane, parents have the right to do with their children as they please. If a man is a racist, he will object quite strenuously to his society's taking action to prevent him from passing on this social perspective to his children. A second objection is that parents do not like anyone to say, or even to imply, that they are unfit and are producing disturbed children. In every generation a large number of people are more or less destroyed in the process of being socialized. One result ensured by our not trying to control the socialization process more than we do is that the casualties of one generation will produce casualties in the next generation.

The psychologist Harry Harlow carried out a series of interesting experiments on this point.[1] His research dealt with the effects of rearing infant monkeys in socially abnormal environments. Some monkeys were reared with hostile surrogate mothers,

[1] Harry Harlow and Margaret Harlow, "A Study of Animal Affection," *Natural History,* 70, 10 (December 1961), 48-55.

some with no maternal contact, and some under other unusual conditions. The monkeys reacted to these experiences by behaving, as adults, in ways that could be described as severely disturbed. Some of these monkeys displayed behavior patterns that ranged from periods of complete inactivity to periods of violent self-mutilation. The female monkeys that matured and mated treated their own offspring in a manner more brutal than the manner in which they had been reared. There was little doubt that the second generation would be at least as disturbed as the first.

A great inequity results from society's leaving the socialization process relatively uncontrolled. Parents have certain rights to control their children's minds. Except in the most extreme cases, however, children have virtually no protection from the damage that can be done to them in the process of socialization. Even granting that this damage usually is inflicted accidentally, it would seem that children ought to be protected if possible. Beyond the question of mere protection, it also seems reasonable that if it were possible to help individuals to be put together better, it would be proper to do so. The argument could be made that just as minimum standards of physical health and health practices are required for the protection of the population, minimum standards of socialization should be required for the protection of a person's mental health.

One sense in which fear of a powerful social science is justified is that a greater understanding of the roots of personality and cognitive development could lead to more efficient methods of programing individuals to have specific personality traits and beliefs. Therefore, whoever determines what type of personality traits and beliefs are to be produced has tremendous power. There is some protection in having a hodgepodge of vaguely planned but mainly accidental experiences leading to the production of adult personalities. Such a mixture is very difficult to manipulate, control, and thereby determine what is produced.

When we have enough knowledge about the dynamics of personality formation and the development of belief systems to affect the socialization process in order to generate predictable products, a choice will have to be made. The choice will be: continue to manufacture individuals so that it is not obvious that the manufacturing is being carried out, with each person being handled individually, and with very little idea how the product will turn out; or attempt to introduce some quality control, and at least eliminate the lemons.

The excerpt from *Walden Two* describes how some aspects of a controlled socialization process might be carried out. The group taking part in the discussion includes eight people. Only four of them are frequent speakers—Frazier (the designer of Walden Two and formerly a graduate student with Professor Burris), Professor Burris (a psychologist and a visitor at Walden Two,) Professor Castle (a philosopher, also a visitor), and Mrs. Nash (a worker in the nursery).

Walden Two

B. F. Skinner

A young woman in a white uniform met us in a small waiting room near the entrance. Frazier addressed her as Mrs. Nash.

"I hope Mr. Frazier has warned you," she said with a smile, "that we're going to be rather impolite and give you only a glimpse of our babies. We try to protect them from infection during the first year. It's especially important when they are cared for as a group."

"What about the parents?" said Castle at once. "Don't parents see their babies?"

"Oh, yes, so long as they are in good health. Some parents work in the nursery. Others come around every day or so, for at least a few minutes. They take the baby out for some sunshine, or play with it in a play room." Mrs. Nash smiled at Frazier. "That's the way we build up the baby's resistance," she added.

She opened a door and allowed us to look into a small room, three walls of which were lined with cubicles, each with a large glass window. Behind the windows we could see babies of various ages. None of them wore more than a diaper, and there were no bedclothes. In one cubicle a small red newborn was asleep on its stomach. Some of the older babies were awake and playing with toys. Near the door a baby on all fours pressed its nose against the glass and smiled at us.

"Looks like an aquarium," said Castle.

"And very precious fish they are," said Mrs. Nash, as if the comparison were not unfamiliar.

"Which is yours?" asked Frazier.

"Over there asleep," said Mrs. Nash, pointing to a far corner. "Almost ready to graduate, too. He'll be a year old next month." She drew the door gently shut before we had satisfied out curiosity.

"I can show you one of the units in the isolation room, which isn't being used," she said, leading the way along the corridor. She opened another door and we entered. Two of the cubicles stood against the wall.

"This is a much more efficient way of keeping a baby warm than the usual practice of wrapping it in several layers of cloth," said Mrs. Nash, opening a safety-glass window to permit Barbara and Mary to look inside. "The newborn baby needs moist air at about 88 or 90 degrees. At six months, 80 is about right."

"How do you know that?" said Castle, rather belligerently.

"The baby tells us," said Mrs. Nash pleasantly, as if the question were also familiar.

"You know the story about the bath water, don't you, Mr. Castle?" Frazier interrupted. "The temperature's all right if the baby doesn't turn red or blue."

"But I hope—" Castle began.

"It's only a matter of a degree or two," said Mrs. Nash quickly. "If the baby's too warm, it does turn rather pinkish, and it usually cries. It always stops crying when we lower the temperature." She twisted the dial of a thermostat on the front of a cubicle.

"And I suppose if frost forms around the nose it's too cold," said Castle, getting himself under control.

"The baby turns rather pale," said Mrs. Nash laughing, "and takes a curious posture with its arms along its sides or slightly curled up. With a little practice we can tell at a glance whether the temperature is right or not."

"But why don't you put clothes on them?" said Barbara.

"What for? It would mean laundry for us and discomfort for the child. It's the same with sheets and blankets. Our babies lie on a stretched plastic cloth which doesn't soak up moisture and can be wiped clean in a moment."

'It looks terribly comfortable," I said. "Why don't you all sleep that way?"

"We're working on that," said Frazier, apparently quite seriously. "It would save no end of laundry, and, as you say, it would be comfortable."

"Clothing and blankets are really a great nuisance," said Mrs. Nash. "They keep the baby from exercising, they force it into uncomfortable postures—"

"When a baby graduates from our Lower Nursery," Frazier broke in, "it knows nothing of frustration, anxiety, or fear. It never cries except when sick, which is very seldom, and it has a lively interest in everything."

"But is it prepared for life?" said Castle. "Surely you can't continue to protect it from frustration or frightening situations forever."

"Of course not. But it can be prepared for them. We can build a tolerance for frustration by introducing obstacles gradually as the baby grows strong enough to handle them. But I'm getting ahead of our story. Have you any other point to make, Mrs. Nash?"

"I suppose you'd like to have them know how much work is saved. Since the air is filtered, we only bathe the babies once a week, and we never need to clean their nostrils or eyes. There are no beds to make, of course. And it's easy to prevent infection. The compartments are sound-proofed, and the babies sleep well and don't disturb each other. We can keep them on different schedules, so the nursery runs smoothly. Let me see, is there anything else?"

"I think that's quite enough," said Frazier. "We have a lot of ground to cover this morning.

"Not so fast, if you please," said Castle. "I'm not satisfied yet. Aren't you raising a lot of very inadequate organisms? Controlled temperature, noiseless sleep—aren't these babies going to be completely at the mercy of a normal environment? Can you go on coddling them forever?"

"I can answer that, Mrs. Nash," said Frazier. "The answer is *no*. Our babies are especially resistant. It's true that a constant annoyance may develop a tolerance, but the commoner result is that the baby is worn down or enervated. We introduce annoyances slowly, according to the ability of the baby to take them. It's very much like innoculation."

"Another thing," said Castle. "What about mother love?"

Frazier and Mrs. Nash looked at each other and laughed.

"Are you speaking of mother love as an essence, Mr. Castle?" said Frazier.

"I am not!" said Castle, bristling. "I'm speaking of a concrete thing. I mean the love which the mother gives her baby—the affection—well, to be really concrete, the kisses, the fondling, and so on, I suppose you'd say. You can't expect me to give you the physical dimensions of mother love!" He was confused and flushed. "It's real enough to the baby, I'll bet!" he added blackly.

"Very real," said Frazier quietly. "And we supply it in liberal doses. But we don't limit it to mothers. We go in for father love, too—for everybody's love—community love, if you wish. Our children are treated with affection by everyone—and thoughtful affection too, which isn't marred by fits of temper due to overwork or careless handling due to ignorance."

"But the personal relation between the mother and the child—Isn't there some sort of patterning? I thought the whole personality could be shaped in that way?" Castle appealed to me for professional support, but I failed him.

"You mean what the Freudian calls 'identification' I think," said Frazier. "I agree that it's important, and we use it very effectively in our educational system. But unless you're a strict Freudian, we're talking in the wrong room. Let's wait till we see another age group. Can you come to the Upper Nursery, Mrs. Nash?"

"Let me check my staff," said Mrs. Nash. She disappeared into the "aquarium," returned almost immediately, and led us to another wing.

The quarters for children from one to three consisted of several small playrooms with Lilliputian furniture, a child's lavatory, and a dressing and locker room. Several small sleeping rooms were operated on the same principle as the baby-cubicles. The temperature and the humidity were controlled so that clothes or bedclothing were not needed. The cots were double-decker arrangements of the plastic mattresses we had seen in the cubicles. The children slept unclothed, except for diapers. There were more beds than necessary, so that the children could be grouped according to developmental age or exposure to contagious diseases or need for supervision, or for educational purposes.

We followed Mrs. Nash to a large screened porch on the south side of the building, where several children were playing in sandboxes and on swings and climbing apparatuses. A few wore "training pants"; the rest were naked. Beyond the porch was a grassy play yard enclosed by closely trimmed hedges, where other children, similarly undressed, were at play. Some kind of marching game was in progress.

As we returned, we met two women carrying food hampers. They spoke to Mrs. Nash and followed her to the porch. In a moment five or six children came running into the playrooms and were soon using the lavatory and dressing themselves. Mrs. Nash explained that they were being taken on a picnic.

"What about the children who don't go?" said Castle. "What do you do about the green-eyed monster?"

Mrs. Nash was puzzled.

"Jealousy. Envy." Castle elaborated. "Don't the children who stay home ever feel unhappy about it?"

"I don't understand," said Mrs. Nash.

"And I hope you won't try," said Frazier, with a smile. "I'm afraid we must be moving along."

We said good-bye, and I made an effort to thank Mrs. Nash, but she seemed to be puzzled by that too, and Frazier frowned as if I had committed some breach of good taste.

"I think Mrs. Nash's puzzlement," said Frazier, as we left the building, "is proof enough that our children are seldom envious or jealous. Mrs. Nash was twelve years old when Walden Two was founded. It was a little late to undo her early training, but I think we were successful. She's a good example of the Walden Two product. She could probably recall the experience of jealousy, but it's not part of her present life."

"Surely that's going too far!" said Castle. "You can't be so godlike as all that! You must be assailed by emotions just as much as the rest of us!"

"We can discuss the question of godlikeness later, if you wish," replied Frazier. "As to emotions—we aren't free of them all, nor should we like to be. But the meaner and more annoying—the emotions which breed unhappiness—are almost unknown here, like unhappiness itself. We don't need them any longer in our struggle for existence, and it's easier on our circulatory system, and certainly pleasanter, to dispense with them."

"If you've discovered how to do that, you are indeed a genius," said Castle. He seemed almost stunned as Frazier nodded assent. "We all know that emotions are useless and bad for our peace of mind and our blood pressure," he went on. "But how arrange things otherwise?"

"We arrange them otherwise here," said Frazier. He was showing a mildness of manner which I was coming to recognize as a sign of confidence.

"But emotions are—fun!" said Barbara. "Life wouldn't be worth living without them."

"Some of them, yes," said Frazier. "The productive and strengthening emotions—joy and love. But sorrow and hate—and the high-voltage excitements of anger, fear and rage—are out of proportion with the needs of modern life, and they're wasteful and dangerous. Mr. Castle has mentioned jealousy—a minor form of anger, I think we may call it. Naturally we avoid it. It has served its purpose in the evolution of man; we've no further use for it. If we allowed it to persist, it would only sap the life out of us. In a cooperative society there's no jealousy because there's no need for jealousy."

"That implies that you all get everything you want," said Castle. "But what about social possessions? Last night you mentioned the young man who chose a particular girl or profession. There's still a chance for jealousy there, isn't there?"

"It doesn't imply that we get everything we want," said Frazier. "Of course we don't. But jealousy wouldn't help. In a competitive world there's some point to it. It energizes one to attack a frustrating condition. The impulse and the added energy are an advantage. Indeed, in a competitive world emotions work all too well. Look at the singular lack of success of the complacent man. He enjoys a more serene life, but it's less likely to be a fruitful one. The world isn't ready for simple pacifism or Christian humility, to cite two cases in point. Before you can safely train out the destructive and wasteful emotions, you must make sure they're no longer needed."

"How do you make sure that jealousy isn't needed in Walden Two?" I said.

"In Walden Two problems can't be solved by attacking others," said Frazier with marked finality.

"That's not the same as eliminating jealousy, though," I said.

"Of course it's not. But when a particular emotion is no longer a useful part of a behavioral repertoire, we proceed to eliminate it."

"Yes, but how?"

"It's simply a matter of behavioral engineering," said Frazier.

"Behavioral engineering?"

"You're baiting me, Burris. You know perfectly well what I mean. The techniques have been available for centuries. We use them in education and in the psychological management of the community. But you're forcing my hand," he added. "I was saving that for this evening. But let's strike while the iron is hot."

We had stopped at the door of the large children's building. Frazier shrugged his shoulders, walked to the shade of a large tree, and threw himself on the ground. We arranged ourselves about him and waited.

"Each of us," Frazier began, "is engaged in a pitch battle with the rest of mankind."

"A curious premise for a Utopia," said Castle. "Even a pessimist like myself takes a more hopeful view than that."

"You do, you do," said Frazier. "But let's be realistic. Each of us has interests which conflict with the interests of everybody else. That's our original sin, and it can't be helped. Now, 'everybody else' we call 'society.' It's a powerful opponent, and it always wins. Oh, here and there an individual prevails for a while and gets what he wants. Sometimes he storms the culture of a society and changes it slightly to his own advantage. But society wins in the long run, for it has the advantage of numbers and of age. Many prevail against one, and men against a baby. Society attacks early, when the individual is helpless. It enslaves him almost before he has tasted freedom. The 'ologies' will tell you how it's done. Theology calls it building a conscience or developing a spirit of selflessness. Psychology calls it the growth of the superego.

"Considering how long society has been at it, you'd expect a better job. But the campaigns have been badly planned and the victory has never been secure. The behavior of the individual has been shaped according to revelations of 'good conduct,' never as the result of experimental study. But why not experiment? The questions are simple enough. What's the best behavior for the individual so far as the group is concerned? And how can the individual be induced to behave in that way? Why not explore these questions in a scientific spirit?

"We could do just that in Walden Two. We had already worked out a code of conduct—subject, of course, to experimental modification. The code would keep things running smoothly if everybody lived up to it. Our job was to see that everybody did. Now, you can't get people to follow a useful code by making them into so many jacks-in-the-box. You can't foresee all future circumstances, and you can't specify adequate future conduct. You don't know what will be required. Instead you have to set up certain behavioral processes which will lead the individual to design his own 'good' conduct when the time comes. We call that sort of thing 'self-control.' But don't be misled, the control always rests in the last analysis in the hands of society.

"One of our Planners, a young man named Simmons, worked with me. It was the first time in history that the matter was approached in an experimental way. Do you question that statement, Mr. Castle?"

"I'm not sure I know what you are talking about," said Castle.

"Then let me go on. Simmons and I began by studying the great works on morals and ethics—Plato, Aristotle, Confucius, the New Testament, the Puritan divines, Machiavelli, Chesterfield, Freud—there were scores of them. We were looking for any and every method of shaping human behavior by imparting techniques of self-control. Some techniques were obvious enough, for they had marked turning points in human history. 'Love your enemies' is an example—a psychological invention for easing the lot of an oppressed people. The severest trial of oppression is the constant rage which one suffers at the thought of the oppressor. What Jesus discovered was how to avoid these inner devastations. His technique was to *practice the opposite emotion.* If a man can succeed in 'loving his enemies' and 'taking no thought for the morrow,' he will no longer be assailed by hatred of the oppressor or rage at the loss of his freedom or possessions. He may not get his freedom or possessions back, but he's less miserable. It's a difficult lesson. It comes late in our program."

"I thought you were opposed to modifying emotions and instincts until the world was ready for it," said Castle. "According to you, the principle of 'love your enemies' should have been suicidal."

"It would have been suicidal, except for an entirely unforeseen consequence. Jesus must have been quite astonished at the effect of his discovery. We are only just beginning to understand the power of love because we are just beginning to understand the weakness of force and aggression. But the science of behavior is clear about all that now. Recent discoveries in the analysis of punishment—but I am falling into one digression after another. Let me save my explanation of why the Christian virtues—and I mean merely the Christian techniques of self-control—have not disappeared from the face of the earth, with due recognition of the fact that they suffered a narrow squeak within recent memory.

"When Simmons and I had collected our techniques of control, we had to discover how to teach them. That was more difficult. Current educational practices were of little value, and religious practices scarcely any better. Promising paradise or threatening hell-fire, we assumed, generally admitted to be unproductive. It is based upon a fundamental fraud which, when discovered, turns the individual against society and nourishes the very thing it tries to stamp out. What Jesus offered in return for loving one's enemies was heaven *on earth,* better known as peace of mind.

"We found a few suggestions worth following in the practices of the clinical psychologist. We undertook to build a tolerance for annoying experiences. The sunshine of midday is extremely painful if you come from a dark room, but take it in easy stages and you can avoid pain altogether. The analogy can be misleading, but in much the same way it's possible to build a tolerance to painful or distasteful stimuli, or to frustration, or to situations which arouse fear, anger or rage. Society and nature throw these annoyances at the individual with no regard for the development of tolerances. Some achieve tolerances, most fail. Where would the science of immunization be if it followed a schedule of accidental dosages?

"Take the principle of 'Get thee behind me, Satan,' for example," Frazier continued. "It's a special case of self-control by altering the environment. Subclass A 3, I believe. We give each child a lollipop which has been dipped in powdered sugar so that a single touch of the tongue can be detected. We tell him he may eat the lollipop later in the day, provided it hasn't already been licked. Since the child is only three or four, it is a fairly diff—"

"Three or four!" Castle exclaimed.

"All our ethical training is completed by the age of six," said Frazier quietly. "A simple principle like putting temptation out of sight would be acquired before four. But at such an early age the problem of not licking the lollipop isn't easy. Now, what would you do, Mr. Castle, in a similar situation?"

"Put the lollipop out of sight as quickly as possible."

"Exactly. I can see you've been well trained. Or perhaps you discovered the principle for yourself. We're in favor of original inquiry wherever possible, but in this case we have a more important goal and we don't hesitate to give verbal help. First of all, the children are urged to examine their own behavior while looking at the lollipops. This helps them to recognize the need for self-control. Then the lollipops are concealed, and the children are asked to notice any gain in happiness or any reduction in tension. Then a strong distraction is arranged—say, an interesting game. Later the children are reminded of the candy and encouraged to examine their reaction. The value of the distraction is generally obvious. Well, need I go on? When the experiment is repeated a day or so later, the children all run with the lollipops to their lockers and do exactly what Mr. Castle would do—a sufficient indication of the success of our training."

"I wish to report an objective observation of my reaction to your story," said Castle, controlling his voice with great precision. "I find myself revolted by this display of sadistic tyrany."

"I don't wish to deny you the exercise of an emotion which you seem to find enjoyable," said Frazier. "So let me go on. Concealing a tempting, but forbidden object is a crude solution. For one thing, it's not always feasible. We want a sort of psychological concealment—covering up the candy by paying no attention. In a later experiment the children wear their lollipops like crucifixes for a few hours."

. . . ."Some of us learn control, more or less by accident. The rest of us go all our lives not even understanding how it is possible, and blaming our failure on being born the wrong way."

"How do you build up a tolerance to an annoying situation?" I said.

"Oh, for example, by having the children 'take' a more and more painful shock, or drink cocoa with less and less sugar in it until a bitter concoction can be savored without a bitter face."

"But jealousy or envy—you can't administer them in graded doses," I said.

"And why not? Remember, we control the social environment, too, at this age. That's why we get our ethical training in early. Take this case. A group of children arrive home after a long walk tired and hungry. They're expecting supper; they find, instead, that it's time for a lesson in self-control: they must stand for five minutes in front of steaming bowls of soup.

"The assignment is accepted like a problem in arithmetic. Any groaning or complaining is a wrong answer. Instead, the children begin at once to work upon themselves to avoid any unhappiness during the delay. One of them may make a joke of it. We encourage a sense of humor as a good way of not taking an annoyance seriously. The joke won't be much, according to adult standards—perhaps the child will simply pretend to empty the bowl of soup into his upturned mouth. Another may start a song with many verses. The rest join in at once, for they've learned that it's a good way to make time pass."

Frazier glanced uneasily at Castle, who was not to be appeased.

"That also strikes you as a form of torture, Mr. Castle?" he asked.

"I'd rather be put on the rack," said Castle.

"Then you have by no means had the thorough training I supposed. You can't imagine how lightly the children take such an experience. It's a rather severe biological frustration, for the children are tired and hungry and they must stand and look at food; but it's passed off as lightly as a five-minute delay at curtain time. We regard it as a fairly elementary test. Much more difficult problems follow."

"I suspected as much," muttered Castle.

"In a later stage we forbid all social devices. No songs, no jokes—merely silence. Each child is forced back upon his own resources—a very important step."

"I should think so," I said. "And how do you know it's successful? You might produce a lot of silently resentful children. It's certainly a dangerous stage."

"It is, and we follow each child carefully. If he hasn't picked up the necessary techniques, we start back a little. A still more advanced stage"—Frazier glanced again at Castle, who stirred uneasily—"brings me to my point. When it's time to sit down to the soup, the children count off—heads and tails. Then a coin is tossed and if it comes up heads, the 'heads' sit down and eat. The 'tails' remain standing for another five minutes."

Castle groaned.

"And you call that envy?" I asked.

"Perhaps not exactly," said Frazier. "At least there's seldom any aggression against the lucky ones. The emotion, if any, is directed against Lady Luck herself, against the toss of the coin. That, in itself, is a lesson worth learning, for it's the only direction in which emotion has a surviving chance to be useful. And resentment toward things in general, while perhaps just as silly as personal aggression, is more easily controlled. Its expression is not socially objectionable."

Frazier looked nervously from one of us to the other. He seemed to be trying to discover whether we shared Castle's prejudice. I began to realize, also, that he had not really wanted to tell this story. He was vulnerable. He was treading on sanctified ground, and I was pretty sure he had not established the value of most of these practices in an experimental fashion. He could scarcely have done so in the short space of ten years. He was working on faith, and it bothered him.

I tried to bolster his confidence by reminding him that he had a professional colleague among his listeners. "May you not inadvertently teach your children some of the very emotions you're trying to eliminate?" I said. "What's the effect, for example, of finding the anticipation of a warm supper suddenly thwarted? Doesn't that eventually lead to feelings of uncertainty, or even anxiety?"

"It might. We had to discover how often our lessons could be safely administered. But all our schedules are worked out experimentally. We watch for undesired consequences just as any scientist watches for disrupting factors in his experiments.

"After all, it's a simple and sensible program," he went on in a tone of appeasement. "We set up a system of gradually increasing annoyances and frustrations against a background of complete serenity. An easy environment is made more and more difficult as the children acquire the capacity to adjust."

"But *why?*" said Castle. "Why these deliberate unpleasantnesses—to put it mildly? I must say I think you and your friend Simmons are really very subtle sadists."

"You've reversed your position, Mr. Castle," said Frazier in a sudden flash of anger with which I rather sympathized. Castle was calling names, and he was also being unaccountably and perhaps intentionally obtuse. "A while ago you accused me of breeding a race of softies," Frazier continued. "Now you object to toughening them up. But what you don't understand is that these potentially unhappy situations are never very annoying. Our schedules make sure of that. You wouldn't understand, however, because you're not so far advanced as our children."

Castle grew black.

"But what do your children get out of it?" he insisted, apparently trying to press some vague advantage in Frazier's anger.

"What do they get out of it!" exclaimed Frazier, his eyes flashing with a sort of helpless contempt. His lips curled and he dropped his head to look at his fingers, which were crushing a few blades of grass.

"They must get happiness and freedom and strength," I said, putting myself in a ridiculous position in attempting to make peace.

"They don't sound happy or free to me, standing in front of bowls of Forbidden Soup," said Castle, answering me parenthetically while continuing to stare at Frazier.

"If I must spell it out," Frazier began with a deep sigh, "what they get is escape from the petty emotions which eat the heart out of the unprepared. They get the satisfaction of pleasant and profitable social relations on a scale almost undreamed of in the world at large. They get immeasurably increased efficiency, because they can stick to a job without suffering the aches and pains which soon beset most of us. They get new horizons, for they are spared the emotions characteristic of frustration and failure. They get—" His eyes searched the branches of the trees. "Is that enough?" he said at last.

"And the community must gain their loyalty," I said, "when they discover the fears and jealousies and diffidences in the world at large."

"I'm glad you put it that way," said Frazier. "You might have said that they must feel superior to the miserable products of our public schools. But we're at pains to keep any feeling of superiority or contempt under control, too. Having suffered most acutely from it myself, I put the subject first on our agenda. We carefully avoid any joy in a personal triumph which means the personal failure of somebody else. We take no pleasure in the sophistical, the disputative, the dialectical." He threw a vicious glance at Castle. "We don't use the motive of domination, because we are always thinking of the whole group. We could motivate a few geniuses that way—it was certainly my own motivation—but we'd sacrifice some of the happiness of everyone else. Triumph over nature and over oneself, yes. But over others, never."

"You've taken the mainspring out of the watch," said Castle flatly.

"That's an experimental question, Mr. Castle, and you have the wrong answer."

Frazier was making no effort to conceal his feeling. If he had been riding Castle, he was now using his spurs. Perhaps he sensed that the rest of us had come round and that he could change his tactics with a single holdout. But it was more than strategy, it was genuine feeling. Castle's undeviating skepticism was a growing frustration.

"Are your techniques really so very new?" I said hurriedly. "What about the primitive practice of submitting a boy to various tortures before granting him a place among adults? What about the disciplinary techniques of Puritanism? Or of the modern school, for that matter?"

"In one sense you're right," said Frazier. "And I think you've nicely answered Mr. Castle's tender concern for our little ones. The unhappinesses we deliberately impose are far milder than the normal unhappinesses from which we offer protection. Even at the height of our ethical training, the unhappiness is ridiculously trivial—to the well-trained child.

"But there's a world of difference in the way we use these annoyances," he continued. "For one thing, we don't punish. We never administer an unpleasantness in the hope of repressing or eliminating undesirable behavior. But there's another difference. In most cultures the child meets up with annoyances and reverses of uncontrolled magnitude. Some are imposed in the name of discipline by persons in authority. Some, like hazings, are condoned though not authorized. Others are merely accidental. No one cares to, or is able to, prevent them.

"We all know what happens. A few hardy children emerge, particularly those who have got their unhappiness in doses that could be swallowed. They become brave men. Others become sadists or masochists of varying degrees of pathology. Not having conquered a painful environment, they become preoccupied with pain and make a devious art of it. Others submit—and hope to inherit the earth. The rest—the cravens, the cowards—live in fear for the rest of their lives. And that's only a single field—the reaction to pain. I could cite a dozen parallel cases. The optimist and the pessimist, the contented and the disgruntled, the loved and the unloved, the ambitious and the discouraged—these are only the extreme products of a miserable system.

"Traditional practices are admittedly better than nothing," Frazier went on. "Spartan or Puritan—no one can question the occasional happy result. But the whole system rests upon the wasteful principle of selection. The English public school of the nineteenth century produced brave men—by setting up almost insurmountable barriers and making the most of the few who came over. But selection isn't education. Its crops of brave men will always be small, and the waste enormous. Like all primitive principles, selection serves in place of education only through a profligate use of material. Multiply extravagantly and select with rigor. It's the philosophy of the 'big litter' as an alternative to good child hygiene.

"In Walden Two we have a different objective. We make every man a brave man. They all come over the barriers. Some require more preparation than others, but they all come over. The traditional use of adversity is to select the strong. We control adversity to build strength. And we do it deliberately, no matter how sadistic Mr. Castle may think us, in order to prepare for adversities which are beyond control. Our children eventually experience the 'heartache and the thousand natural shocks that flesh is heir to.' It would be the cruelest possible practice to protect them as long as possible, especially when we *could* protect them so well."

Frazier held out his hands in an exaggerated gesture of appeal.

"What alternative *had* we?" he said, as if he were in pain. "What else could we do? For four or five years we could provide a life in which no important need would go unsatisfied, a life practically free of anxiety or frustration or annoyance. What would *you* do? Would you let the child enjoy this paradise with no thought for the future—like an idolatrous and pampering mother? Or would you relax control of the environment and let the child meet accidental frustrations? But what is the virtue of accident? No, there was only one course open to us. We had to *design* a series of adversities, so that the child would develop the greatest possible self-control. Call it deliberate, if you like, and accuse us of sadism; there was no other course." Frazier turned to Castle, but he was scarcely challenging him. He seemed to be waiting, anxiously, for his capitulation. But Castle merely shifted his ground.

"I find it difficult to classify these practices," he said. Frazier emitted a disgruntled "Ha!" and sat back. "Your system seems to have usurped the place as well as the techniques of religion."

"Of religion and family culture," said Frazier wearily. "But I don't call it usurpation. Ethical training belongs to the community. As for techniques, we took every suggestion we could find without prejudice as to the source. But not on faith. We disregarded all claims of revealed truth and put every principle to an experimental test. And by the way, I've very much misrepresented the whole system if you suppose that any of the practices I've described are fixed. We try out many different techniques. Gradually we work toward the best possible set. And we don't pay much attention to the apparent success of a principle in the course of history. History is honored in Walden Two only as entertainment. It isn't taken seriously as food for thought. Which reminds me, very rudely, of our original plan for the morning. Have you had enough of emotion? Shall we turn to intellect?"

. . . The living quarters and daily schedules of the older children furnished a particularly good example of behavioral engineering. At first sight they seemed wholly casual, almost haphazard, but as Frazier pointed out their significant features and the consequences of each, I began to make out a comprehensive, almost Machiavellian design.

The children passed smoothly from one age group to another, following a natural process of growth and avoiding the abrupt changes of the home-and-school system. The arrangements were such that each child emulated children slightly older than himself and hence derived motives and patterns for much of his early education without adult aid.

The control of the physical and social environment, of which Frazier had made so much, was progressively relaxed—or, to be more exact, the control was transferred from the authorities to the child himself and to the other members of his group. After spending most of the first year in an air-conditioned cubicle, and the second and third mainly in an air-conditioned room with a minimum of clothing and bedding, the three- or four-year-old was introduced to regular clothes and given the care of a small standard cot in a dormitory. The beds of the five- and six-year-olds were grouped by threes and fours in a series of alcoves furnished like rooms and treated as such by the children. Groups of three or four seven-year-olds occupied small rooms together, and this practice was continued, with frequent change of roommates, until the children were about thirteen, at which time they took temporary rooms in the adult building, usually in pairs. At marriage, or whenever the individual chose, he could participate in building a larger room for himself or refurnishing an old room which might be available.

A similar withdrawal of supervision, proceeding as rapidly as the child acquired control of himself, could be seen in the dining arrangements. From three through six, the children ate in a small dining room of their own. The older children, as we had observed on our first day at Walden Two, took their meals at specified times in the adult quarters. At thirteen all supervision was abandoned, and the young member was free to eat when and where he pleased.

We visited some of the workshops, laboratories, studies, and reading rooms used in lieu of classrooms. They were occupied, but it was not entirely clear that the children were actually in school. I supposed that the few adults to be seen about the building were teachers, but many of them were men, contrary to my conception of schoolteachers at that age level, and more often than not they were busy with some private business. Since Frazier had requested that we avoid questions or discussions in the presence of the children, we proceeded from one room to another in growing puzzlement. I had to admit that an enormous amount of learning was probably going on, but I had never seen a school like it before.

We inspected a well-equipped gymnasium, a small assembly room, and other facilities. The building was. . . very simply decorated, but there was a pleasant "non-institutional" character about it. The doors and many of the windows stood open, and a fair share of the schoolwork, or whatever it was, took place outside. Children were constantly passing in and out. Although there was an obvious excitement about the place, there was little of the boisterous confusion which develops in the ordinary school when discipline is momentarily relaxed. Everyone seemed to be enjoying extraordinary freedom, but the efficiency and comfort of the whole group were preserved.

I was reminded of children on good behavior and was on the point of asking how often the pressure reached the bursting point. But there was a difference, too, and my question slowly evaporated. I could only conclude that this happy and productive atmosphere was probably the usual thing. Here again, so far as I could see, Frazier—or someone—had got things under control.

When we returned to our shade tree, I was primed with questions, and so, I am sure, was Castle. But Frazier had other plans. He had either forgotten how remarkable was the spectacle we had just witnessed, or he was intentionally allowing our wonderment and curiosity to ferment. He began from a very different point of view.

"When we discussed the economics of community life," he said, "I should have mentioned education. Teachers are, of course, workers, and I'm willing to defend all that I said about our economic advantage as specifically applied to education. God knows, the outside world is not exactly profligate in the education of its children. It doesn't spend much on equipment or teachers. Yet in spite of this penny-wise policy, there's still enormous waste. A much better education would cost less if society were better organized.

"We can arrange things more expeditiously here because we don't need to be constantly re-educating. The ordinary teacher spends a good share of her time changing the cultural and intellectual habits which the child acquires from its family and surrounding culture. Or else the teacher duplicates home training, in a complete waste of time. Here we can almost say that the school is the family, and vice cersa.

"We can adopt the best educational methods and still avoid the administrative machinery which schools need in order to adjust to an unfavorable social structure. We don't have to worry about standardization in order to permit pupils to transfer from one school to another, or to appraise or control the work of particular schools. We don't need 'grades.' Everyone knows that talents and abilities don't develop at the same rate in different children. A fourth-grade reader may be a sixth-grade mathematician. The grade is an administrative device which does violence to the nature of the developmental process. Here the child advances as rapidly as he likes in any field. No time is wasted in forcing him to participate in, or be bored by, activities he has outgrown. And the backward child can be handled more efficiently too.

"We also don't require all our children to develop the same abilities or skills. We don't insist upon a certain set of courses. I don't suppose we have a single child who has had a 'secondary school education,' whatever that means. But they've all developed as rapidly as advisable, and they're well educated in many useful respects. By the same token we don't waste time in teaching the unteachable. The fixed education represented by a diploma is a bit of conspicuous waste which has no place in Walden Two. We don't attach an economic or honorific value to education. It has its own value or none at all.

"Since our children remain happy, energetic, and curious, we don't need to teach 'subjects' at all. We teach only the techniques of learning and thinking. As for geography, literature, the sciences—we give our children opportunity and guidance, and they learn them for themselves. In that way we dispense with half the teachers required under the old system, and the education is incomparably better. Our children aren't neglected, but they're seldom, if ever, *taught* anything.

"Education in Walden Two is part of the life of the community. We don't need to resort to trumped-up life experiences. Our children begin to work at a very early age. It's no hardship; it's accepted as readily as sport or play. And a good share of our education goes on in workshops, laboratories, and fields. It's part of the Walden Two Code to encourage children in all the arts and crafts. We're glad to spend time in instructing them, for we know it's important for the future of Walden Two and our own security."

"What about higher education?" I said.

"We aren't equipped for professional training, of course," said Frazier. "Those who want to go on to graduate study in a university are given special preparation. Entrance requirements are always tyrannical, though perhaps inevitable in a mass-production system. So far, we've been able to find graduate schools that will take our young people as special students, and as they continue to make excellent records, we expect fewer difficulties. If worse comes to worst, we shall organize as a college and get ourselves accredited. But can you imagine the stupid changes we should have to make?" Frazier snorted with impatience. "Oh, well. Tongue in cheek. Tongue in cheek."

"Don't you mean 'chin up'?" I asked.

"We'd have to set up a 'curriculum,' require a 'C average,' a 'foreign language,' 'so many years of residence,' and so on, and so on. It would be most amusing. No, 'tongue in cheek' was what I meant."

"Your people don't go to college, then?"

"We have no more reason to distinguish between college and high school than between high school and grade school. What are these distinctions, anyway, once you have separated education from the administration of education? Are there any natural breaks in a child's development? Many of our children naturally study more and more advanced material as they grow older. We help them in every way short of teaching them. We give them new techniques of acquiring knowledge and thinking. In spite of the beliefs of most educators, our children are taught to think. We give them an excellent survey of the methods and techniques of thinking, taken from logic, statistics, scientific method, psychology, and mathematics. That's all the 'college education' they need. They get the rest by themselves in our libraries and laboratories."

"But what about libraries and laboratories, though?"

"As to a library, we pride ourselves on having the best books, if not the most. Have you ever spent much time in a large college library? What trash the librarian has saved up in order to report a million volumes in the college catalogue! Bound pamphlets, old journals, ancient junk that even the shoddiest secondhand bookstore would clear from its shelves—all saved on the flimsy pretext that some day someone will want to study the 'history of a field.' Here we have the heart of a great library—not much to please the scholar or specialist, perhaps, but enough to interest the intelligent reader for life. Two or three thousand volumes will do it."

Frazier challenged me with a stare, but I did not wish to fight on such difficult terrain.

"The secret is this," he continued. "We subtract from our shelves as often as we add to them. The result is a collection that never misses fire. We all get something vital every time we take a book from the shelves. If anyone wants to follow a special interest we arrange for loans. If anyone wants to browse, we have half a barnful of discarded volumes.

"Our laboratories are good because they are real. Our workshops are really small engineering laboratories, and anyone with a genuine bent can go farther in them than the college student. We teach anatomy in the slaughterhouse, botany in the field, genetics in the dairy and poultry house, chemistry in the medical building and in the kitchen and dairy laboratory. What more can you ask?"

"And all this is just for the fun of it? You don't feel that some disciplined study is necessary?" said Castle.

"What for?" asked Frazier in unsuccessfully pretended surprise.

"To provide techniques and abilities which will be valuable later," said Castle. "For example, the study of a language."

"Why 'later'? Why not acquire a language when it's valuable? We acquire our own tongue that way! Of course you're thinking of an educational process which comes to a dead stop sometime around the middle of June in one's last year in college. In Walden Two education goes on forever. It's part of our culture. We can acquire a technique whenever we need it.

"As to languages," Frazier continued, "you must know that even in our largest universities a language department considers itself very well off if two or three students at any one time approach fluency. We can do better than that. A member of Walden Two who once lived in France has interested several of our members, from ten to fifty years old, in the language. You may run into them during your stay. I hear them buzzing around the dining room every now and then, and they add a pleasantly cosmopolitan touch. And I'm told they're developing a good feeling for the French language and French literature. They'll never get any grades or credits, but they're getting French. Is there really any choice? Either French is worth learning, *at the time you learn it,* or it's not. And let's be sensible."

"I'm still skeptical," said Castle. "Of course, I'm still at a disadvantage in arguing against an accomplished fact." Frazier nodded his head violently. "But not everything has been accomplished," Castle went on. "Your pleasant schoolrooms, your industrious and contented children—these we must accept. But it would take us a long time to find out how well-educated your children really are according to our standards." Frazier made a move to speak, but Castle hurried on. "I'll admit these standards won't tell us everything. We couldn't ask your children to take our examinations, because they haven't been learning the same things, even in such a field as French. Your students would probably do no better on a second-year French examination than the average Parisian. I'll admit that, and I confess with all the humility I can muster that the kind of learning you've described is the better—if a comparison is possible. It's the ideal which every college teacher glimpses now and then when he looks up from the dance of death in which he has been caught. But I can't swallow the system you've described because I don't see what keeps the motors running. Why do your children learn anything at all? What are your substitutes for our standard motives?"

"Your 'standard motives'—exactly," said Frazier. "And there's the rub. An educational institution spends most of its time, not in presenting facts or imparting techniques of learning, but in trying to make its students learn. It has to create spurious needs. Have you ever stopped to analyze them? What are the 'standard motives,' Mr. Castle?"

"I must admit they're not very attractive," said Castle. "I suppose they consist of fear of one's family in the event of low grades or expulsion, the award of grades and honors, the snob value of a cap and gown, the cash value of a diploma."

"Very good, Mr. Castle," said Frazier. "You're an honest man. And now to answer your questiom—our substitute is simply the absence of these devices. We have had to *uncover* the worth-while and truly productive motives—the motives which inspire creative work in science and art outside the academies. No one asks how to motivate a baby. A baby naturally explores everything it can get at, unless restraining forces have already been at work. And this tendency doesn't die out, it's *wiped* out.

"We made a survey of the motives of the unhampered child and found more than we could use. Our engineering job was to *preserve* them by fortifying the child against discouragement. We introduce discouragement as carefully as we introduce any other emotional situation, beginning at about six months. Some of the toys in our air-conditioned cubicles are designed to build perseverance. A bit of a tune from a music box, or a pattern of flashing lights, is arranged to follow an appropriate response—say, pulling on a ring. Later the ring must be pulled twice, later still three or five or ten times. It's possible to build up fantastically perseverative behavior without encountering frustration or rage. It may not surprise you to learn that some of our experiments miscarried; the resistance to discouragement became almost stupid or pathological. One takes some risks in work of this sort, of course. Fortunately, we were able to reverse the process and restore the children to a satisfactory level.

"Building a tolerance for discouraging events proved to be all we needed," Frazier continued. "The motives in education, Mr. Castle, are the motives in all human behavior. Education should be only life itself. We don't need to create motives. We avoid the spurious academic needs you've just listed so frankly, and also the escape from threat so widely used in our civil institutions. We appeal to the curiosity which is characteristic of the unrestrained child, as well as the alert and inquiring adult. We appeal to that drive to control the environment which makes a baby continue to crumple a piece of noisy paper and the scientist continue to press forward with his predictive analyses of nature. We don't need to motivate anyone by creating spurious needs."

"I've known a few men with the kind of motivation you mean," I said.

"The contemporary culture produces a few by accident," said Frazier quickly, "just as it produces a few brave or happy men."

"But I've never understood them," I said rather faintly.

"Why should you, any more than unhappy people can understand the happy ones?"

"But isn't there a real need for the spurious satisfactions?" I said. "Little signs of personal success, money—personal domination, too, if you like. Most of what I do, I do to avoid undesirable consequences, to evade unpleasantnesses, or to reject or attack forces which interfere with my freedom."

"All the unhappy motives," said Frazier.

"Unhappy, perhaps, but powerful. I think the very thing which seems most unpromising in your system is its happiness. Your people are going to be too happy, too successful. But why won't they just go to sleep? Can we expect real achievements from them? Haven't the great men of history been essentially unhappy or maladjusted or neurotic?"

"I have little interest in conclusions drawn from history," said Frazier, "but if you must play that game, I'll play it too. For every genius you cite whose greatness seems to have sprung from a neurosis, I will undertake to cite similar acts of greatness without neurosis. Turn it around and I'll agree. A man with a touch of genius will be so likely to attack existing institutions that he'll be called unbalanced or neurotic. The only geniuses produced by the chaos of society are those who do something about it." Frazier paused, and I wondered if he were thinking of himself. "Chaos breeds geniuses. It offers a man something to be a genius about. But here, we have better things to do."

"But what about the cases where unhappiness has led to artistic or scientific achievement?" I asked.

"Oh, I daresay a few first-rate sonnets would have remained unwritten had the lady yielded," said Frazier. "But not so many, at that. Not many works of art can be traced to the lack of satisfaction of the basic needs. It's not plain sex that gives rise to art, but personal relations which are social or cultural rather than biological. Art deals with something less obvious than the satisfaction to be found in a square meal." Frazier laughed explosively, as if he had perhaps said more than he intended.

"We shall never produce so satisfying a world that there will be no place for art," he continued. "On the contrary, Walden Two has demonstrated very nicely that as soon as the simple necessities of life are obtained with little effort, there's an enormous welling up of artistic interest. And least of all do we need to fear that simple satisfactions will detract from the scientific conquest of the world. What scientist worth the name is engaged, as scientist, in the satisfaction of his own basic needs? He may be thinking of the basic needs of others, but his own motives are clearly cultural. There can be no doubt of the survival value of the inquiring spirit—of curiosity, or exploration, of the need to dominate media, of the urge to control the forces of nature. The world will never be wholly known, and man can't help trying to know more and more of it."

The topic seemed to have grown too vague to stimulate further discussion, but Castle soon offered a substitute.

"I'm torn between two questions which seem incompatible yet equally pressing," he said. "What do you do about differences among your children in intellect and talent? And what do you do to avoid producing a lot of completely standardized young people? Which question should I ask, and what's your answer?"

"They're both good questions," said Frazier, "and quite compatible." I made a move to speak and Frazier said, "I see that Mr. Burris wants to help with the answers."

"My guess is," I said, "that differences are due to environmental and cultural factors and that Mr. Frazier has no great problem to solve. Give all your children the excellent care we have just been witnessing and your differences will be negligible."

"No, you're wrong, Burris," said Frazier. "That's one question we have answered to our satisfaction. Our ten-year-olds have all had the same environment since birth, but the range of their IQ's is almost as great as in the population at large. This seems to be true of other abilities and skills as well."

"And of physical prowess, of course," said Castle.

"Why do you say 'of course'?" said Frazier, with marked interest.

"Why, I suppose because physical differences are generally acknowledged."

"All differences are physical, my dear Mr. Castle. We think with our bodies, too. You might have replied that differences in prowess have always been obvious and impossible to conceal, while other differences have customarily been disguised for the sake of prestige and family pride. We accept our gross physical limitations without protest and are reasonably happy in spite of them, but we may spend a lifetime trying to live up to a wholly false conception of our powers in another field, and suffer the pain of a lingering failure. Here we accept ourselves as we are."

"Aren't the untalented going to be unhappy?"

"But we don't go in for personal rivalry; individuals are seldom compared. We never develop a taste much beyond a talent. Our parents have little reason to misrepresent their children's abilities to themselves or others. It's easy for our children to accept their limitations—exactly as they have always accepted the gross differences which Mr. Castle called physical prowess. At the same time our gifted children aren't held back by organized mediocrity. We don't throw our geniuses off balance. The brilliant but unstable type is unfamiliar here. Genius can express itself."

13 Biological and Social Manufacturing for Social Stability

In *Brave New World* Aldous Huxley creates an anti-utopian society designed to have stable social institutions in which individuals are to be free of tension and in which neither warfare nor political change was to occur. One might use several approaches to creating a society with these characteristics. The two extreme strategies would be to design social arrangements to which individuals respond in the desired manner or to design individuals that are ideal for the selected set of social arrangements. Huxley designs a set of procedures intended to carry out the second strategy.

In Huxley's anti-utopia people are manufactured, biologically and socially, to fit into the society. That society provides a workable—though distasteful—solution to a number of social problems. For example, alternative stratification systems can be thought of as attempts to solve the problem of how to motivate individuals who have relatively scarce talents to fill essential social roles, so that the talent available in the population is utilized efficiently and people are willing to exchange their labor for the rewards they are offered. In Huxley's society, no problem arises in supplying needed people to staff essential positions; they are simply manufactured to specification. Since socialization is completely controlled, no question arises, either, of motivating people to participate in the society; motivation, like ability, can be built in. Individuals can be produced to match the requirements of their occupations; a man who is to run an elevator is built with a limited intelligence so that he will not become bored by the job, and he is made to believe that he is performing an important and interesting task.

Brave New World depicts the other side of the coin from Walden Two. It is an extreme case of the danger that arises when control over the manufacturing of men is introduced. However, by introducing biological control Huxley goes one step further in his direction than Skinner went along his path. For Skinner, knowledge of the dynamics of socialization makes it possible to devise procedures that lead to results considered either desirable or undesirable. For Huxley, knowledge of prenatal physical development makes it possible to change a fetus' normal environment in order to protect it from birth defects or to introduce agents that produce desired defects.

The industrialization of reproduction is one of the procedures employed to guarantee a stable society. The excerpt from *Brave New World* describes how the manufacturing process works.

Brave New World

ALDOUS HUXLEY

A squat grey building of only thirty-four stories. Over the main entrance the words, *Central London Hatchery and Conditioning Center,* and, in a shield, the World State's motto, *Community, Identity, Stability.*

The enormous room on the ground floor faced towards the north. . . . The overalls of the workers were white, their hands gloved with a pale corpse-coloured rubber. The light was frozen, dead, a ghost. Only from the yellow barrels of the microscopes did it borrow a certain rich and living substance, lying along the polished tubes like butter, streak after luscious streak in long recession down the work tables.

"And this," said the Director opening the door, "is the Fertilizing room."

Bent over their instruments, three hundred fertilizers were plunged, as the Director of Hatcheries and Conditioning entered the room, in the scarcely breathing silence, the absent-minded, soliloquizing hum or whistle, of absorbed concentration. A troop of newly arrived students, very young, pink and callow, followed nervously, rather abjectly, at the Director's heels. Each of them carried a notebook, in which, whenever the great man spoke, he desperately scribbled. Straight from the horse's mouth. It was a rare privilege. The D.H.C. for Central London always made a point of personally conducting his new students round the various departments.

"Just to give you a general idea," he would explain to them. For of course some sort of general idea they must have if they were to do their work intelligently—though as little of one, if they were to be good and happy members of society, as possible. For particulars, as every one knows, make for virtue and happiness; generalities are intellectually necessary evils. Not philosophers but fret-sawyers and stamp collectors compose the backbone of society.

"To-morrow," he would add, smiling at them with a slightly menacing geniality, "you'll be settling down to serious work. You won't have time for generalities. Meanwhile. . . "

Meanwhile, it was a privilege. Straight from the horse's mouth into the notebook. The boys scribbled like mad. . . .

"I shall begin at the beginning,' said the D.M.C. and the more zealous students recorded his intention in their notebooks: *Begin at the beginning.* "These," he waved his hand, "are the incubators." And opening an insulated door he showed them racks upon racks of numbered test-tubes. "The week's supply of ova. Kept," he explained, "at blood heat; whereas the male gametes," and here he opened another door, "they have to be kept at thirty-five instead of thirty-seven. Full blood heat sterilizes." Rams wrapped in theremogene beget no lambs.

Still leaning against the incubators he gave them, while the pencils scurried illegibly across the pages, a brief description of the modern fertilizing process; spoke first, of course, of its surgical introduction—"the operation undergone voluntarily for the good of Society, not to mention the fact that it carries a bonus amounting to six months' salary"; continued with some account of the technique for preserving the excised ovary alive and actively developing; passed on to a consideration of optimum temperature, salinity, viscosity; referred to the liquor in which the detached and ripened eggs were kept; and, leading his charges to the work tables, actually showed them how this liquid was drawn off from the test-tubes; how it was let out drop by drop onto the specially warmed slides of the microscopes; how the eggs which it contained were inspected for abnormalities, counted and transferred to a porous receptacle; how (and he now took them to watch the operation) this receptacle was immersed in a warm bouillon containing free-swimming spermatozoa—at a minimum concentration of one hundred thousand per cubic centimetre, he insisted; and how, after ten minutes, the container was lifted out of the liquor and its contents re-examined; how, if any of the eggs remained unfertilized, it was again immersed, and, if necessary, yet again; how the fertilized ova went back to the incubators; where the Alphas and Betas remained until definitely bottled; while the Gammas, Deltas and Epsilons were brought out again, after only thirty-six hours, to undergo Bokanovsky's Process.

"Bokanovsky's Process," repeated the Director, and the students underlined the words in their little notebooks.

One egg, one embryo, one adult—normality. But a bokanovskified egg will bud, will proliferate, will divide. From eight to ninety-six buds, and every bud will grow into a perfectly formed embryo, and every embryo into a full-sized adult. Making ninety-six human beings grow where only one grew before. Progress.

"Essentially," the D. H. C. concluded, "bokanovskification consists of a series of arrests of development. We check the normal growth and, paradoxically enough, the egg responds by budding."

Responds by budding. The pencils were busy.

He pointed. On a very slowly moving band a rack-full of test-tubes was entering a large metal box, another rack-full was emerging. Machinery faintly purred. It took eight minutes for the tubes to go through, he told them. Eight minutes of hard X-rays being about as much as an egg can stand. A few died; of the rest, the least susceptible divided into two; most put out four buds; some eight; all were returned to the incubators, where the buds began to develop; then, after two days, were suddenly chilled, chilled and checked. Two, four, eight, the buds in their turn budded; and having budded were dosed almost to death with alcohol; consequently burgeoned again and having budded— bud out of bud out of bud—were thereafter—further arrest being generally fatal—left to develop in peace. By which time the original egg was in a fair way to becoming anything from eight to ninety-six embryos—a prodigious improvement, you will agree, on nature. Identical twins—but not in piddling twos and threes as in the old viviparous days, when an egg would sometimes accidentally divide; actually by dozens, by scores at a time.

"Scores," the Director repeated and flung out his arms, as though he were distributing largesse. "Scores."

But one of the students was fool enough to ask where the advantage lay.

"My good boy!" The Director wheeled sharply round on him. "Can't you see? Can't you *see?*" He raised a hand; his expression was solemn. "Bokanovsky's Process is one of the major instruments of social stability!"

Major instruments of social stability.

Standard men and women; in uniform batches. The whole of a small factory staffed with the products of a single bokanovskified egg.

"Ninety-six identical twins working ninety-six identical machines!" The voice was almost tremulous with enthusiasm. "You really know where you are. For the first time in history." He quoted the planetary motto. "Community, Identity, Stability." Grand words. "If we could bokanovskify indefinitely the whole problem would be solved."

Solved by standard Gammas, unvarying Deltas, uniform Epsilons. Millions of identical twins. The principle of mass production at last applied to biology.

"But, alas," the Director shook his head, "we *can't* bokanovskify indefinitely."

Ninety-six seemed to be the limit; seventy-two a good average. From the same ovary and with gametes of the same male to manufacture as many batches of identical twins as possible—that was the best (sadly a second best) that they could do. And even that was difficult.

"For in nature it takes thirty years for two hundred eggs to reach maturity. But our business is to stabilize the population at this moment, here and now. Dribbling out twins over a quarter of a century—what would be the use of that?

Obviously, no use at all. But Podsnap's Technique had immensely accelerated the process of ripening. They could make sure of at least a hundred and fifty mature eggs within two years. Fertilize and bokanovskify—in other words, multiply by seventy-two—and you get an average of nearly eleven thousand brothers and sisters in a hundred and fifty batches of identical twins, all within two years of the same age.

"And in exceptional cases we can make one ovary yield us over fifteen thousand adult individuals."

Beckoning to a fair-haired, ruddy young man who happened to be passing at the moment, "Mr. Foster," he called. The ruddy young man approached. "Can you tell us the record for a single ovary, Mr. Foster?"

"Sixteen thousand and twelve in this Centre," Mr. Foster replied without hesitation. He spoke very quickly, had a vivacious blue eye, and took an evident pleasure in quoting figures. "Sixteen thousand and twelve; in one hundred and eighty-nine batches of identicals. But of course they've done much better," he rattled on, "in some of the tropical Centres. Singapore has often produced over sixteen thousand five hundred; and Mombasa has actually touched the seventeen thousand mark. But then they have unfair advantages. You should see the way a negro ovary responds to pituitary! It's quite astonishing, when you're used to working with European material. Still," he added, with a laugh (but the light of combat was in his eyes and the lift of his chin was challenging), "still, we mean to beat them if we can. I'm working on a wonderful Delta-Minus ovary at this moment. Only just eighteen months old. Over twelve thousand seven hundred children already, either decanted or in embryo. . . ."

In the Bottling Room all was harmonious bustle and ordered activity. Flaps of fresh sow's peritoneum ready cut to the proper size came shooting up in little lifts from the Organ Store in the sub-basement. Whizz and then, click! the lift-hatches flew open; the bottle-liner had only to reach out a hand, take the flap, insert, smooth-down, and before the lined bottle had had time to travel out of reach along the endless band, whizz, click! another flap of peritoneum had shot up from the depths, ready to be slipped into yet another bottle, the next of that slow interminable procession on the band.

Next to the Liners stood the Matriculators. The procession advanced; one by one the eggs were transferred from their test-tubes to the larger containers; deftly the peritoneal lining was slit, the morula dropped into place, the saline solution poured in. . . and already the bottle had passed, and it was the turn of the labellers. Heredity, date of fertilization, membership of Bokanovsky Group—details were transferred from test-tube to bottle. No longer anonymous, but named, identified, the procession marched slowly on; on through an opening in the wall, slowly on into the Social Predestination Room,

"Eighty-eight cubic metres of card-index," said Mr. Foster with relish, as they entered.

"Containing *all* the relevant information," added the Director.

"Brought up to date every morning."

"And coordinated every afternoon."

"On the basis of which they make their calculations."

"So many individuals, of such and such quality," said Mr. Foster.

"Distributed in such and such quantities."

"The optimum Decanting Rate at any given moment."

"Unforeseen wastages promptly made good."

"Promptly," repeated Mr. Foster. "If you knew the amount of overtime I had to put in after the last Japanese earthquake!" He laughed goodhumouredly and shook his head.

"The Predestinators send in their figures to the Fertilizers."

"Who give them the embryos they ask for."

"And the bottles come in here to be predestinated in detail."

"After which they are sent down to the Embryo Store."

"Where we now proceed ourselves."

And opening a door Mr. Foster led the way down a staircase into the basement.

The temperature was still tropical. They descended into a thickening twilight. Two doors and a passage with a double turn insured the cellar against any possible infiltration of the day.

"Embryos are like photograph film," said Mr. Foster waggishly, as he pushed open the second door. "They can only stand red light."

And in effect the sultry darkness into which the students now followed him was visible and crimson, like the darkness of closed eyes on a summer's afternoon. The bulging flanks of row on receding row and tier above tier of bottles glinted with innumerable rubies, and among the rubies moved the dim red spectres of men and women with purple eyes and all the symptoms of lupus. The hum and rattle of machinery faintly stirred the air.

"Give them a few figures, Mr. Foster," said the Director, who was tired of talking.

Mr. Foster was only too happy to give them a few figures.

Two hundred and twenty metres long, two hundred wide, ten high. He pointed upwards. Like chickens drinking, the students lifted their eyes towards the distant ceiling.

Three tiers of racks: ground floor level, first gallery, second gallery.

The spidery steel-work of gallery above gallery faded away in all directions into the dark. Near them three red ghosts were busily unloading demijohns from a moving staircase.

The escalator from the Social Predestination Room.

Each bottle could be placed on one of the fifteen racks, each rack, though you couldn't see it, was a conveyor travelling at the rate of thirty-three and a third centimetres an hour. Two hundred and sixty-seven days at eight metres a day. Two thousand one hundred and thirty-six metres in all. One circuit of the cellar at ground level, one on the first gallery, half on the second, and on the two hundred and sixty-seventh morning, daylight in the Decanting Room. Independent existence—so called.

"But in the interval," Mr. Foster concluded, "we've managed to do a lot to them. Oh, a very great deal." His laugh was knowing and triumphant.

"That's the spirit I like," said the Director once more. "Let's walk round. You tell them everything, Mr. Foster."

Mr. Foster duly told them.

Told them of the growing embryo on its bed of peritoneum. Made them taste the rich blood surrogate on which it fed. Explained why it had to be stimulated with placentin and thyroxin. Told them of the *corpus luteum* extract. Showed them the jets through which at every twelfth metre from zero to 2040 it was automatically injected. Spoke of those gradually increasing doses of pituitary administered during the final ninety-six metres of their course. Described the artificial maternal circulation installed on every bottle at Metre 112; showed them the reservoir of blood-surrogate, the centrifugal pump that kept the liquid moving over the placenta and drove it through the synthetic lung and waste-product filter. Referred to the embryo's troublesome tendency to anemia, to the massive doses of hog's stomach extract and foetal foal's liver with which, in consequence, it had to be supplied.

Showed them the simple mechanism by means of which, during the last two metres out of every eight, all the embryos were simultaneously shaken into familiarity with movement. Hinted at the gravity of the so-called "trauma of decanting," and enumerated the precautions taken to minimize, by a suitable training of the bottled embryo, that dangerous shock. Told them of the tests for sex carried out in the neighbourhood of metre 200.

Explained the system of labelling—a T for the males, a circle for the females, and for those who were destined to become freemartins a question mark, black on a white ground.

"For of course," said Mr. Foster, "in the vast majority of cases, fertility is merely a nuisance. One fertile ovary in twelve hundred— that would really be quite sufficient for our purposes. But we want to have a good choice. And of course one must always leave an enormous margin of safety. So we allow as many as thirty per cent of the female embryos to develop normally. The others get a dose of male sex-hormone every twenty-four metres for the rest of the course. Result: they're decanted as freemartins—structurally quite normal (except," he had to admit, "that they *do* have just the slightest tendency to grow beards), but sterile. Guaranteed sterile. Which brings us at last," continued Mr. Foster, "out of the realm of mere slavish imitation of nature into the much more interesting world of human invention."

He rubbed his hands. For of course, they didn't content themselves with merely hatching out embryos: any cow could do that.

"We also predestine and condition. We decant our babies as socialized human beings, as Alphas or Epsilons, as future sewage workers or future . . ." He was going to say "future World controllers," but correcting himself, said "future Directors of Hatcheries," instead.

The D.H.C. acknowledged the compliment with a smile.

They were passing Metre 320 on rack 11. A young Beta-Minus mechanic was busy with screwdriver and spanner on the blood-surrogate pump of a passing bottle. The hum of the electric motor deepened by fractions of a tone as he turned the nuts. Down, down . . . A final twist, a glance at the revolution counter, and he was done. He moved two paces down the line and began the same process on the next pump.

"Reducing the number of revolutions per minute," Mr. Foster explained. "The surrogate goes round slower; therefore passes through the lung at longer intervals; therefore gives the embryo less oxygen. Nothing like oxygen-shortage for keeping an embryo below par." Again he rubbed his hands.

"But why do you want to keep the embryo below par?" asked an ingenuous student.

"Ass!" said the Director, breaking a long silence. "Hasn't it occurred to you that an Epsilon embryo must have an Epsilon environment as well as an Epsilon heredity?"

It evidently hadn't occured to him. He was covered with confusion.

"The lower caste," said Mr. Foster, "the shorter the oxygen." The first organ affected was the brain. After that the skeleton. At seventy per cent of normal oxygen you got dwarfs. At less than seventy eyeless monsters.

"Who are no use at all," concluded Mr. Foster.

Whereas (his voice became confidential and eager), if they could discover a technique for shortening the period of maturation what a triumph, what a benefaction to Society!

"Consider the horse."

They considered it.

Mature at six; the elephant at ten. While at thirteen a man is not yet sexually mature; and is only full-grown at twenty. Hence, of course, that fruit of delayed development, the human intelligence.

"But in Epsilons," said Mr. Foster very justly, "we don't need human intelligence."

Didn't need and didn't get it. But though the Epsilon mind was mature at ten, the Epsilon body was not fit to work till eighteen. Long years of superfluous and wasted immaturity. If the physical development could be speeded up till it was as quick, say, as a cow's what an enormous saving to the Community!

"Enormous!" murmured the students. Mr. Foster's enthusiasm was infectious.

He became rather technical; spoke of the abnormal endocrine coordination which made men grow so slowly; postulated a germinal mutation to account for it. Could the effects of this germinal mutation be undone? Could the individual Epsilon embryo be made a revert, by a suitable technique, to the normality of dogs and cows? That was the problem. And it was all but solved.

Pilkington, at Mombasa, had produced individuals who were sexually mature at four and full-grown at six and a half. A scientific triumph. But socially useless. Six-year-old men and women were too stupid to do even Epsilon work. And the process was an all-or-nothing one; either you failed to modify at all, or else you modified the whole way. They were still trying to find the ideal compromise between adults of twenty and adults of six. So far without success. Mr. Foster sighed and shook his head.

Their wanderings through the crimson twilight had brought them to the neighborhood of Matre 170 on Rack 9. From this point onwards Rack 9 was enclosed and the bottles performed the remainder of their journey in a kind of tunnel, interrupted here and there by openings two or three metres wide.

"Heat conditioning," said Mr. Foster.

Hot tunnels alternated with cool tunnels. Coolness was wedded to discomfort in the form of hard X-rays. By the time they were decanted the embryos had a horror of cold. They were predestined to emigrate to the tropics, to be miners and acetate silk spinners and steel workers. Later on their minds would be made to endorse the judgment of their bodies. "We condition them to thrive on heat," concluded Mr. Foster. "Our colleagues upstairs will teach them to love it."

"And that," put in the Director sententiously, "that is the secret of happiness and virtue—liking what you've *got* to do. All conditioning aims at that: making people like their unescapable social destiny."

. . . On Rack 10 rows of next generation's chemical workers were being trained in the toleration of lead, caustic soda, tar, chlorine. The first of a batch of two hundred and fifty embryonic rocket-plane engineers was just passing the eleven hundred metre mark on Rack 3. A special mechanism kept their containers in constant rotation. "To improve their sense of balance," Mr. Foster explained. "Doing repairs on the outside of a rocket in mid-air is a ticklish job. We slacken off the circulation when they're right way up, so that they're half starved, and double the flow of surrogate when they're upside down. They learn to associate topsy-turvydom with well-being; in fact, they're only truly happy when they're standing on their heads.

"And now," Mr. Foster went on, "I'd like to show you some very interesting conditioning for Alpha Plus Intellectuals. We have a big batch of them on Rack 5. First Gallery level," he called to two boys who had started to go down to the ground floor.

"They're round about Metre 900," he explained. "You can't really do any useful intellectual conditioning till the foetuses have lost their tails. Follow me."

Later in the novel the relationship between biological control and social stability is discussed in some depth. The conversation is between Mustapha Mond (resident Controller of Western Europe), the Savage (a man raised in an uncivilized part of the world), and Helmholtz Watson (lecturer in the College of Emotional Engineering).

The Savage shook his head. "It all seems to me quite horrible."

"Of course it does. Actual happiness always looks pretty squalid in comparison with the over-compensations for misery. And, of course, stability isn't nearly so spectacular as instability. And being contented has none of the glamour of a good fight against misfortune, none of the picturesqueness of a struggle with temptation, or a fatal overthrow by passion or doubt. Happiness is never grand."

"I suppose not," said the Savage after a silence. "But need it be quite so bad as those twins?" He passed his hand over his eyes as though he were trying to wipe away the remembered image of those long rows of identical midgets at the assembling tables, those queued-up twin-herds at the entrance to the Brentford monorail station . . . , the endlessly repeated face of his assailants. He looked at his bandaged left hand and shuddered. "Horrible!"

"But how useful! I see you don't like our Bokanovsky Groups; but, I assure you, they're the foundation on which everything else is built. They're the gyroscope that stabilizes the rocket plane of state on its unswerving course." The deep voice thrillingly vibrated; the gesticulating hand implied all space and the onrush of the irresistible machine. Mustapha Mond's oratory was almost up to synthetic standards.

"I was wondering," said the Savage, "why you had them at all—seeing that you can get whatever you want out of those bottles. Why don't you make everybody an Alpha Double Plus while you're about it?"

Mustapha Mond laughed. "Because we have no wish to have our throat cut," he answered. "We believe in happiness and stability. A society of Alphas couldn't fail to be unstable and miserable. Imagine a factory staffed by Alphas—that is to say by separate and unrelated individuals of good heredity and conditioned so as to be capable (within limits) of making a free choice and assuming responsibilities. Imagine it!" he repeated. . . .

"It's an absurdity. An Alpha-decanted, Alpha-conditioned man would go mad if he had to do Epsilon Semi-Moron work —go mad, or start smashing things up. Alphas can be completely socialized—but only on condition that you make them do Alpha work. Only an Epsilon can be expected to make Epsilon sacrifices, for the good reason that for him they aren't sacrifices; they're the line of least resistance. His conditioning has laid down rails along which he's got to run. He can't help himself; he's foredoomed. Even after decanting, he's still inside a bottle—an invisible bottle of infantile and embryonic fixations. Each one of us, of course," the Controller meditatively continued, "goes through life inside a bottle. But if we happen to be Alphas, our bottles are, relatively speaking, enormous. We should suffer acutely if we were confined in a narrower space. You cannot pour upper-caste champagne-surrogate into lower-caste bottles. It's obvious theoretically. But it has also been proved in actual practice. The result of the Cyprus experiment was convincing."

"What was that?" asked the Savage.

Mustapha Mond smiled. "Well, you can call it an experiment in rebottling if you like. It began in A.F. 473. The Controllers had the island of Cyprus cleared of all its existing inhabitants and re-colonized with a specially prepared batch of twenty-two thousand Alphas. All agricultural and industrial equipment was handed over to them and they were left to manage their own affairs. The results exactly fulfilled all the theoretical predictions. The land wasn't properly worked; there were strikes in all the factories; the laws were set at naught, orders disobeyed; all the people detailed for a spell of low-grade work were perpetually intriguing for high-grade jobs, and all the people with high-grade jobs were counter-intriguing at all costs to stay where they were. Within six years they were having a first-class civil war. When nineteen out of the twenty-two thousand had been killed, the survivors unanimously petitioned the World Controllers to resume the government of the island. Which they did. And that was the end of the only society of Alphas that the world has ever seen."

The Savage sighed, profoundly.

"The optimum population," said Mustapha Mond, "is modelled on the iceberg—eight-ninths below the water line, one-ninth above."

"And they're happy below the water line?"

"Happier than above it. Happier than your friend here, for example." He pointed.

"In spite of that awful work?"

"Awful? *They* don't find it so. On the contrary, they like it. It's light, it's childishly simple. No strain on the mind or the muscles. Seven and a half hours of mild, unexhausting labour, and then the *soma* ration[1] and games and unrestricted copulation and the feelies.[2] What more can they ask for? True," he added, "they might ask for shorter hours. And of course, we could

[1][Soma was a drug that provided a convenient method of social control. Variations in dosage could produce a feeling of mild relaxation or a full-blown trip (called a soma-holiday). The drug was rationed to the people and then self-administered. People used it to escape boredom and any form of pain. They could adjust the soma intake to compensate for the disappointments of reality. A large part of the population was tripped-out between period of work.]

[2][The feelies were a form of ultimate movie. In addition to seeing the actors it was possible to experience sensory inputs appropriate to the film. The inputs were transmitted to viewers when they placed their hands on metal knobs fixed to the arms of their chairs.]

give them shorter hours. Technically, it would be perfectly simple to reduce all lower-caste working hours to three or four a day. But would they be any the happier for that? No, they wouldn't. The experiment was tried, more than a century and a half ago. The whole of Ireland was put on to the four-hour day. What was the result? Unrest and a large increase in the consumption of *soma;* that was all. Those three and a half hours of extra leisure were so far from being a source of happiness, that people felt constrained to take a holiday from them. The Inventions Office is stuffed with plans for labour-saving processes. Thousands of them." Mustapha Mond made a lavish gesture. "And why don't we put them into execution? For the sake of the labourers; it would be sheer cruelty to afflict them with excessive leisure. It's the same with agriculture. We could synthesize every morsel of food, if we wanted to. But we don't. We prefer to keep a third of the population on the land. For their own sakes—because it takes *longer* to get food out of the land than out of a factory. Besides, we have our stability to think of. We don't want to change. Every change is a menace to stability. That's another reason why we're so chary of applying new inventions. Every discovery in pure science is potentially subversive; even science must sometimes be treated as a possible enemy. Yes, even science."

". . . Yes," Mustapha Mond was saying, "that's another item in the cost of stability. It isn't only art that's incompatible with happiness; it's also science. Science is dangerous; we have to keep it most carefully chained and muzzled."

"What?" said Helmholtz, in astonishment. "But we're always saying that science is everything. . . . All the science propaganda we do at the College. . ."

"Yes; but what sort of science?" asked Mustapha Mond sarcastically. "You've had no scientific training, so you can't judge. I was a pretty good physicist in my time. Too good—good enough to realize that all our science is just a cookery book, with an orthodox theory of cooking that nobody's allowed to question, and a list of recipes that mustn't be added to except by special permission from the head cook. I'm the head cook now."

The second means through which control is established is socialization. Huxley describes a procedure that is in some respects similar to the procedures Skinner utilizes in *Walden Two.* The end-product of the socialization process is, however, quite different.

Infant Nurseries. Neo-Pavlovian Conditioning Rooms, announced the notice board.

The Director opened a door. They were in a large bare room, very bright and sunny; for the whole of the southern wall was a single window. Half a dozen nurses, trousered and jacketed in the regulation white viscose-linen uniform, their hair asceptically hidden under white caps, were engaged in setting out bowls of roses in a long row across the floor. Big bowls, packed tight with blossom. Thousands of petals, ripe-blown and silkily smooth, like the cheeks of innumerable little cherubs, but of cherubs, in that bright light, not exclusively pink and Aryan, but also luminously Chinese, also Mexican, also apoplectic with too much blowing of celestial trumpets, also pale as death, pale with the posthumous whiteness of marble.

The nurses stiffened to attention as the D.H.C. came in.

"Set out the books," he said curtly.

In silence the nurses obeyed his command. Between the rose bowls the books were duly set out—a row of nursery quartos opened invitingly each at some gaily coloured image of beast or fish or bird.

"Now bring in the children."

They hurried out of the room and returned in a minute or two, each pushing a kind of tall dumb-waiter laden, on all its four wire-netted shelves, with eight-month-old babies, all exactly alike (a Bokanovsky Group, it was evident) and all (since their caste was Delta) dressed in khaki.

"Put them down on the floor."

The infants were unloaded.

"Now turn them so that they can see the flowers and books."

Turned, the babies at once fell silent, then began to crawl towards those clusters of sleek colours, those shapes so gay and brilliant on the white pages. As they approached, the sun came out of a momentary eclipse behind a cloud. The roses flamed up as though with a sudden passion from within; a new and profound significance seemed to suffuse the shining pages of the books. From the ranks of the crawling babies came little squeals of excitement, gurgles and twitterings of pleasure.

The Director rubbed his hands. "Excellent!" he said. "It might almost have been done on purpose."

The swiftest crawlers were already at their goal. Small hands reached out uncertainly, touched, grasped, unpetaling the transfigured roses, crumpling the illuminated pages of the books. The Director waited until all were happily busy. Then, "Watch carefully," he said. And, lifting his hand, he gave the signal.

The Head Nurse, who was standing by a switchboard at the other end of the room, pressed down a little lever.

There was a violent explosion. Shriller and ever shriller, a siren shrieked. Alarm bells maddeningly sounded.

The children started, screamed; their faces were distorted with terror.

"And now," the Director shouted (for the noise was deafening), "now we proceed to rub in the lesson with a mild electric shock."

He waved his hand again, and the Head Nurse pressed a second lever. The screaming of the babies suddenly changed its tone. There was something desperate, almost insane, about the sharp spasmodic yelps to which they now gave utterance. Their little bodies twitched and stiffened; their limbs moved jerkily as if to the tug of unseen wires.

"We can electrify that whole strip of floor," bawled the Director in explanation. "But that's enough," he signalled to the nurse.

The explosions ceased, the bells stopped ringing, the shriek of the siren died down from tone to tone into silence. The stiffly twitching bodies relaxed, and what had become the sob and yelp of infant maniacs broadened out once more into a normal howl of ordinary terror.

"Offer them the flowers and the books again."

The nurses obeyed; but at the approach of the roses, at the mere sight of those gaily-coloured images of pussy and cock-a-doodle-doo and baa-baa black sheep, the infants shrank away in horror; the volume of their howling suddenly increased.

"Observe," said the Director triumphantly, "observe."

Books and loud noises, flowers and electric shocks—already in the infant mind these couples were compromisingly linked; and after two hundred repetitions of the same or a similar lesson would be wedded indissolubly. What man has joined, nature is powerless to put asunder.

"They'll grow up with what the psychologists used to call an 'instinctive' hatred of books and flowers. Reflexes unalterably conditioned. They'll be safe from books and botany all their lives." The Director turned to his nurses. "Take them away again."

Still yelling, the khaki babies were loaded on to their dumb-waiters and wheeled out, leaving behind them the smell of sour milk and a most welcome silence.

One of the students held up his hand; and though he could see quite well why you couldn't have lower-caste people wasting the Community's time over books, and that there was always the risk of their reading something which might undesirably decondition one of their reflexes, yet . . . well, he couldn't understand about the flowers. Why go to the trouble of making it psychologically impossible for Deltas to like flowers?

Patiently the D.H.C. explained. If the children were made to scream at the sight of a rose, that was on grounds of high economic policy. Not so very long ago (a century or thereabouts), Gammas, Deltas, even Epsilons, had been conditioned to like flowers—flowers in particular and wild nature in general. The idea was to make them want to be going out into the country at every available opportunity, and so compel them to consume transport.

"And didn't they consume transport?" asked the student.

"Quite a lot," the D.H.C. replied. "But nothing else."

Primroses and landscapes, he pointed out, have one grave defect: they are gratuitous. A love of nature keeps no factories busy. It was decided to abolish the love of nature, at any rate among the lower classes; to abolish the love of nature, but *not* the tendency to consume transport. For of course it was essential that they should keep on going to the country, even though they hated it. The problem was to find an economically sounder reason for consuming transport than a mere affection for primroses and landscapes. It was duly found.

"We condition the masses to hate the country," concluded the Director. "But simultaneously we condition them to love all country sports. At the same time, we see to it that all country sports shall entail the use of elaborate apparatus. So that they consume manufactured articles as well as transport. Hence those electric shocks."

"I see," said the student, and was silent, lost in admiration.

"There was a silence; then, clearing his throat, "Once upon a time," the Director began, "while our Ford was still on earth, there was a little boy called Reuben Rabinovitch. Reuben was the child of Polish-speaking parents." The Director interrupted himself. "You know what Polish is, I suppose?"

"A dead language."

"Like French and German," added another student, officiously showing off his learning.

"And, 'parent'?" questioned the D.H.C.

There was an uneasy silence. Several of the boys blushed. They had not yet learned to draw the significant but often very fine distinction between smut and pure science. One, at last, had the courage to raise a hand.

"Human beings used to be . . ." he hesitated; the blood rushed to his cheeks. "Well, they used to be viviparous."

"Quite right." The Director nodded approvingly.

"And when the babies were decanted . . ."

"'Born'," came the correction.

"Well, then they were the parents—I mean, not the babies, of course; the other ones." The poor boy was overwhelmed with confusion.

"In brief," the Director summed up, the parents were the father and the mother." The smut that was really science fell with a crash into the boys' eye-avoiding silence. "Mother," he repeated loudly rubbing in the science; and, leaning back in his chair, "These," he said gravely, "are unpleasant facts; I know it. But then most historical facts *are* unpleasant."

He returned to Little Reuben—to Little Reuben in whose room, one evening, by an oversight, his father and mother happened to leave the radio turned on.

("For you must remember that in those days of gross viviparous reproduction, children were always brought up by their parents and not in State Conditioning Centres.")

While the child was asleep, a broadcast programme from London suddenly started to come through; and the next morning, to the astonishment of his [parents] (the more daring of the boys ventured to grin at one another), Little Reuben woke up repeating word for word a long lecture by that curious old writer ("one of the very few whose works have been permitted to come down to us"), George Bernard Shaw, who was speaking, according to a well-authenticated tradition, about his own genius. To Little Reuben's wink and snigger, this lecture was, of course, perfectly incomprehensible and, imagining that their child had suddenly gone mad, they sent for a doctor. He, fortunately, understood English, recognized the discourse as that which Shaw had broadcasted the previous evening, realized the significance of what had happened, and sent a letter to the medical press about it.

"The principle of sleep-teaching, or hypnopedia, had been discovered." The D.H.C. made an impressive pause.

The principle had been discovered; but many, many years were to elapse before that principle was usefully applied. . . .

"These early experimenters," the D.H.C. was saying, "were on the wrong track. They thought that hypnopedia could be made an instrument of intellectual education . . ."

(A small boy asleep on his right side, the right arm stuck out, the right hand hanging limp over the edge of the bed. Through a round grating in the side of a box a voice speaks softly.

"The Nile is the longest river in Africa and the second in length of all the rivers of the globe. Although falling short of the length of the Mississippi-Missouri, the Nile is at the head of all rivers as regards the length of its basin, which extends through 35 degrees of latitude . . ."

At breakfast the next morning, "Tommy," someone says, "do you know which is the longest river in Africa?" A shaking of the head. "But don't you remember something that begins: The Nile is the . . ."

"The-Nile-is-the-longest-river-in-Africa-and-the-second-in-length-of-all-the-rivers-of-the-globe. . . ." The words came rushing out. "Although-falling-short-of . . ."

"Well now, which is the longest river in Africa?"

The eyes are blank. "I don't know."

"But the Nile, Tommy."

"The-Nile-is-the-longest-river-in-Africa-and-second . . ."

"Then which river is the longest, Tommy?"

Tommy bursts into tears. "I don't know," he howls.)

That howl, the Director made it plain, discouraged the earliest investigators. The experiments were abandoned. No further attempt was made to teach children the length of the Nile in their sleep. Quite rightly. You can't learn a science unless you know what it's all about.

"Whereas, if they'd only started on *moral* education," said the Director, leading the way towards the door. The students followed him, desperately scribbling as they walked and all the way up in the lift. "Moral education, which ought never, in any circumstances, to be rational."

"Silence, silence," whispered a loud speaker as they stepped out at the fourteenth floor, and "Silence, silence," the trumpet mouths indefatigably repeated at intervals down every corridor. The students and even the Director himself rose automatically to the tips of their toes. They were Alphas, of course; but even Alphas have been well conditioned. "Silence, silence." All the air of the fourteenth floor was sibilant with the categorical imperative.

Fifty yards of tiptoeing brought them to a door which the Director cautiously opened. They stepped over the threshold into the twilight of a shuttered dormitory. Eighty cots stood in a row against the wall. There was a sound of light regular breathing and a continuous murmur, as of very faint voices remotely whispering.

A nurse rose as they entered and came to attention before the Director.

"What's the lesson this afternoon?" he asked.

"We had Elementary Sex for the first forty minutes," she answered. "But now it's switched over to Elementary Class Consciousness."

The Director walked slowly down the long line of cots. Rosy and relaxed with sleep, eighty little boys and girls lay softly breathing. There was a whisper under every pillow. The D.H.C. halted and, bending over one of the little beds, listened attentively.

"Elementary Class Consciousness, did you say? Let's have it repeated a little louder by the trumpet."

At the end of the room a loud speaker projected from the wall. The Director walked up to it and pressed a switch.

". . . all wear green," said a soft but very distinct voice, beginning in the middle of a sentence, "and Delta children wear Khaki. Oh no, I don't want to play with Delta children. And Epsilons are worse. They're too stupid to be able to read or write. Besides they wear black, which is such a beastly colour. I'm *so* glad I'm a Beta."

There was a pause; then the voice began again.

"Alpha children wear grey. They work much harder than we do, because they're so frightfully clever. I'm really awfully glad I'm a Beta, because I don't work so hard. And then we are much better than the Gammas and Deltas. Gammas are stupid. They all wear green, and Delta children wear Khaki. Oh no, I *don't* want to play with Delta children. And Epsilons are still worse. They're too stupid to be able . . ."

The Director pushed back the switch. The voice was silent. Only its thin ghost continued to mutter from beneath the eighty pillows.

"They'll have that repeated forty or fifty times more before they wake; then again on Thursday, and again on Saturday. A hundred and twenty times three times a week for thirty months. After which they go on to a more advanced lesson"

Roses and electric shocks, the khaki of Deltas and a whiff of asafoetida—wedded indissolubly before the child can speak. But wordless conditioning is crude and wholesale; cannot bring home the finer distinctions, cannot inculcate the more complex courses of behaviour. For that there must be words, but words without reason. In brief, hypnopedia.

"The greatest moralizing and socializing force of all time."

. . . Once more the Director touched the switch.

". . . so frightfully clever," the soft, insinuating, indefatigable voice was saying. "I'm really awfully glad I'm a Beta, because . . ."

Not so much like drops of water, though water, it is true can wear holes in the hardest granite; rather, drops of liquid sealing-wax, drops that adhere, incrust, incorporate themselves with what they fall on, till finally the rock is all one scarlet blob.

"Till at last the child's mind *is* these suggestions, and the sum of the suggestions *is* the child's mind. And not the child's mind only. The adult's mind too—all his life long. The mind that judges and desires and desires and decides—made up of these suggestions. But all these suggestions are *our* suggestions!" The Director almost shouted in his triumph. "Suggestions from the State."

Outside, in the garden, it was playtime. Naked in the warm June sunshine, six or seven hundred little boys and girls were running with shrill yells over the lawns, or playing ball games, or squatting silently in twos and threes among the flowering shrubs. The roses were in bloom, two nightingales soliloquized in the boskage, a cuckoo was just going out of tune among the lime trees. The air was drowsy with the murmur of bees and helicopters.

The Director and his students stood for a short time watching a game of Centrifugal Bumble-puppy. Twenty children were grouped in a circle round a chrome steel tower. A ball thrown up so as to land on the platform at the top of the tower rolled down into the interior, fell on a rapidly revolving disk, was hurled through one or other of the numerous apertures pierced in the cylindrical casing, and had to be caught.

"Strange," mused the Director, as they turned away, "strange to think that even in Our Ford's day most games were played without more apparatus than a ball or two and a few sticks and perhaps a bit of netting. Imagine the folly of allowing people to play elaborate games which do nothing whatever to increase consumption. It's madness. Nowadays the Controllers won't approve of any new game unless it can be shown that it requires at least as much apparatus as the most complicated of existing games." He interrupted himself.

"That's a charming little group," he said, pointing.

In a little grassy bay between tall clumps of Mediterranean heather, two children, a little boy of about seven and a little girl who might have been a year older, were playing, very gravely and with all the focused attention of scientists intent on a labour of discovery, a rudimentary sexual game.

"Charming, charming!" the D.H.C. repeated sentimentally.

"Charming," the boys politely agreed. But their smile was rather patronizing. They had put aside similar childish amusements too recently to be able to watch them now without a touch of contempt. Charming? but it was just a pair of kids fooling about; that was all. Just kids.

"I always think," the Director was continuing in the same rather maudlin tone, when he was interrupted by a loud boo-hooing.

From a neighbouring shrubbery emerged a nurse, leading by the hand a small boy, who howled as he went. An anxious-looking little girl trotted at her heels.

"What's the matter?" asked the Director.

The nurse shrugged her shoulders. "Nothing much," she answered. "It's just that this little boy seems rather reluctant to join in the ordinary erotic play. I'd noticed it once or twice before. And now again to-day. He started yelling just now . . ."

"Honestly," put in the anxious-looking little girl, "I didn't mean to hurt him or anything. Honestly."

"Of course you didn't, dear," said the nurse reassuringly. "And so," she went on, turning back to the Director, "I'm taking him in to see the Assistant Superintendent of Psychology. Just to see if anything's at all abnormal."

"Quite right," said the Director. "Take him in. You stay here, little girl," he added, as the nurse moved away with her still howling charge. "What's your name?"

"Polly Trotsky."

"And a very good name too," said the Director. "Run away now and see if you can find some other little boy to play with." The child scampered off into the bushes and was lost to sight.

"Exquisite little creature!" said the Director, looking after her. Then, turning to his students, "What I'm going to tell you now," he said, "may sound incredible. But then, when you're not accustomed to history, most facts about the past *do* sound incredible."

He let out the amazing truth. For a very long period before the time of Our Ford, and even for some generations afterwards, erotic play between children had been regarded as abnormal (there was a roar of laughter); and not only abnormal, actually immoral (no!): and had therefore been rigorously suppressed.

A look of astonished incredulity appeared on the faces of his listeners. Poor little kids not allowed to amuse themselves? They could not believe it.

"Even adolescents," the D.H.C. was saying, "even adolescents like yourselves . . .

"Not possible!"

"Barring a little surreptitious auto-erotism and homosexuality—absolutely nothing.

"Nothing?"

"In most cases, till they were over twenty years old."

"Twenty years old?" echoed the students in a chorus of loud disbelief.

"Twenty," the Director repeated. "I told you that you'd find it incredible."

"But what happened?" they asked. "What were the results?"

"The results were terrible." A deep resonant voice broke startlingly into the dialogue.

They looked round. On the fringe of the little group stood a stranger—a man of middle height, black-haired, with a hooked nose, full red lips, eyes very piercing and dark. "Terrible," he repeated.

The D.H.C. had at that moment sat down on one of the steel and rubber benches conveniently scattered through the gardens; but at the sight of the stranger, he sprang to his feet and darted forward, his hands outstretched, smiling with all his teeth, effusive.

"Controller! What an unexpected pleasure! Boys, what are you thinking of? This is the Controller; this is his fordship, Mustapha Mond."

. . . His fordship Mustapha Mond! The eyes of the saluting students almost popped out of their heads. Mustapha Mond! The Resident Controller for Western Europe! One of the Ten World Controllers. One of the Ten . . . and he sat down on the bench with the D.H.C., he was going to stay, to stay, yes, and actually talk to them . . . straight from the horse's mouth. Straight from the mouth of Ford himself.

Two shrimp-brown children emerged from a neighbouring shrubbery, stared at them for a moment with large astonished eyes, then returned to their amusements among the leaves.

"You all remember," said the Controller, in his strong deep voice, "you all remember, I suppose, that beautiful and inspired saying of Our Ford's: History is bunk. History," he repeated slowly, "is bunk. . . ."

"That's why you're taught no history," the Controller was saying. "But now the time has come . . ."

The D.H.C. looked at him nervously. There were those strange rumours of old forbidden books hidden in a safe in the Controller's study. Bibles, poetry—Ford knew what.

Mustapha Mond intercepted his anxious glance and the corners of his red lips twitched ironically.

"It's all right, Director," he said in a tone of faint derision, "I won't corrupt them."

The D.H.C. was overwhelmed with confusion. . . .

Mustapha Mond leaned forward, shook a finger at them. "Just try to realize it," he said, and his voice sent a strange thrill quivering along their diaphragms. "Try to realize what it was like to have a viviparous mother."

That smutty word again. But none of them dreamed, this time, of smiling.

"Try to imagine what 'living with one's family' meant."

They tried; but obviously without the smallest success.

"And do you know what a 'home' was?"

They shook their heads. . . .

Home, home—a few small rooms, stiflingly over-inhabited by a man, by a periodically teeming woman, by a rabble of boys and girls of all ages. No air, no space; an understerilized prison; darkness, disease, and smells.

(The Controller's evocation was so vivid that one of the boys, more sensitive than the rest, turned pale at the mere description and was on the point of being sick.) . . .

And home was as squalid psychically as physically. Psychically, it was a rabbit hole, a midden, hot with the frictions of tightly packed life, reeking with emotion. What suffocating intimacies, what dangerous, insane, obscene relationships between the members of the family group! Maniacally, the mother brooded over her children (*her* children) . . . brooded over them like a cat over its kittens; but a cat that could talk, a cat that could say, "My baby, my baby," over and over again. "My baby, and oh, oh, at my breast, the little hands, the hunger, and that unspeakable agonizing pleasure! Till at last my baby sleeps, my baby sleeps with a bubble of white milk at the corner of his mouth. My little baby sleeps . . ."

"Yes," said Mustapha Mond, nodding his head, "you may well shudder.". . .

Our Ford—or Our Freud, as, for some inscrutable reason, he chose to call himself whenever he spoke of psychological matters—Our Freud had been the first to reveal the appalling dangers of family life. The world was full of fathers—was therefore full of misery; full of mothers—therefore of every kind of perversion from sadism to chastity; full of brothers, sisters, uncles, aunts—full of madness and suicide.

"And yet, among the savages of Samoa, in certain islands off the coast of New Guinea . . ."

The tropical sunshine lay like warm honey on the naked bodies of children tumbling promiscuously among the hibiscus blossoms. Home was in any one of twenty palm-thatched houses. In the Trobiands conception was the work of ancestral ghosts; nobody had ever heard of a father.

"Extremes," said the Controller, "meet. For the good reason that they were made to meet.". . .

"Mothers and fathers, brothers and sisters. But there were also husbands, wives, lovers. There were also monogamy and romance."

"Though you probably don't know what those are," said Mustapha Mond.

They shook their heads.

Family, monogamy, romance. Everywhere exclusiveness, everywhere a focussing of interest, a narrow channelling of impulse and energy.

"But every one belongs to every one else," he concluded, citing the hypnopedic proverb.

The students nodded, emphatically agreeing with a statement which upwards of sixty-two thousand repetitions in the dark had made them accept, not merely as true, but as axiomatic, self-evident, utterly indisputable. . . .

"Think of water under pressure in a pipe." They thought of it. "I pierce it once," said the Controller. "What a jet!"

He pierced it twenty times. There were twenty piddling little fountains.

"My baby. My baby . . . !"

"Mother!" The madness is infectious.

"My love, my one and only, precious, precious . . ."

Mother, monogamy, romance. High spurts the fountain; fierce and foamy the wild jet. The urge has but a single outlet. My love, my baby. No wonder those poor pre-moderns were mad and wicked and miserable. Their world didn't allow them to take things easily, didn't allow them to be sane, virtuous, happy. What with mothers and lovers, what with the prohibitions they were not conditioned to obey, what with the temptations and the lonely remorses, what with all the diseases and the endless isolating pain, what with the uncertainties and the poverty—they were forced to feel strongly. And feeling strongly (and strongly, what was more, in solitude, in hopelessly individual isolation), how could they be stable? . . .

"Stability," said the Controller, "stability. No civilization without social stability. No social stability without individual stability." His voice was a trumpet. Listening they felt larger, warmer.

The machine turns, turns and must keep on turning—forever. It is death if it stands still. A thousand millions scrabbled the crust of the earth. The wheels began to turn. In a hundred and fifty years there were two thousand millions. Stop all the wheels. In a hundred and fifty weeks there are once more only a thousand millions; a thousand thousand thousand men and women have starved to death.

Wheels must turn steadily, but cannot turn untended. There must be men to tend them, men as steady as the wheels upon their axles, sane men, obedient men, stable in contentment.

Crying: My baby, my mother, my only, only love; groaning: My sin, my terrible God; screaming with pain, muttering with fever, bemoaning old age and poverty—how can they tend the wheels? And if they cannot tend the wheels . . . The corpses of a thousand thousand thousand men and women would be hard to bury or burn. . . .

"Stability," insisted the Controller, "stability. The primal and the ultimate need. Stability. Hence all this."

With a wave of his hand he indicated the gardens, the huge building of the Conditioning Centre, the naked children furtive in the undergrowth or running across the lawns. . . .

Impulse arrested spills over, and the flood is feeling, the flood is passion, the flood is even madness: it depends on the force of the current, the height and strength of the barrier. The unchecked stream flows smoothly down its appointed channels into a calm well-being. (The embryo is hungry; day in, day out, the blood-surrogate pump unceasingly turns in eight hundred revolutions a minute. The decanted infant howls; at once a nurse appears with a bottle of external secretion. Feeling lurks in that interval of time between desire and its consummation. Shorten that interval, break down all those old unnecessary barriers.

"Fortunate boys!" said the Controller. "No pains have been spared to make your lives emotionally easy—to preserve you, so far as that is possible, from having emotions at all." . . .

"Consider your own lives," said Mustapha Mond. "Has any of you ever encountered an insurmountable obstacle?"

The question was answered by a negative silence.

"Has any of you been compelled to live through a long time-interval between the consciousness of a desire and its fulfillment?"

"Well," began one of the boys, and hesitated.

"Speak up," said the D.H.C. "Don't keep his fordship waiting."

"I once had to wait nearly four weeks before a girl I wanted would let me have her."

"And you felt a strong emotion in consequence?"

"Horrible!"

" Horrible; precisely," said the Controller. "Our ancestors were so stupid and short-sighted that when the first reformers came along and offered to deliver them from those horrible emotions, they wouldn't have anything to do with them." . . .

"Take Ectogenesis. Pfitzner and Kawaguchi had got the whole technique worked out. But would the Governments look at it? No. There was something called Christianity. Women were forced to go on being viviparous.". .

"Sleep teaching was actually prohibited in England. There was something called liberalism. Parliament, if you know what that was, passed a law against it. The records survive. Speeches about liberty of the subject. Liberty to be inefficient and miserable. Freedom to be a round peg in a square hole.". . .

"Or the Caste System. Constantly proposed, constantly rejected. There was something called democracy. As though men were more than physico-chemically equal." . . .

"The Nine Years' War began in A.F. 141." . . .

"The noise of fourteen thousand aeroplanes advancing in open order. But in the Kurfurstendamm and the Eighth Arrondissement, the explosion of the anthrax bombs is hardly louder than the popping of a paper bag." . . .

$Ch_3C_6H_2(NO_2)_3 + Hg(CNO)_2$=well, what? An enormous hole in the ground, a pile of masonry, some bits of flesh and mucus, a foot, with the boot still on it, flying through the air and landing, flop, in the middle of the geraniums—the scarlet ones; such a splendid show that summer!. . .

"The Russian technique for infecting water supplies was particularly ingenious.". . .

"The Nine Years' War, the great Economic Collapse. There was a choice between World Control and destruction. Between stability and.". . .

In the nurseries, the Elementary Class Consciousness lesson was over, the voices were adapting future demand to future industrial supply. "I do love flying," they whispered, "I do love flying, I do love having new clothes, I do love . . ."

"Liberalism, of course, was dead of anthrax, but all the same you couldn't do things by force.". . .

"Government's an affair of sitting, not hitting. You rule with the brains and the buttocks, never with the fists. For example, there was the conscription of consumption." . . .

"Every man, woman and child compelled to consume so much a year. In the interests of industry. The sole result."...

"Conscientious objection on an enormous scale. Anything not to consume. Back to nature."...

"Back to culture. Yes, actually to culture. You can't consume much if you sit still and read books."...

"Eight hundred Simple Lifers were mowed down by machine guns at Golders Green."...

"Then came the famous British Museum Massacre. Two thousand culture fans gassed with dichlorethyl sulphide."...

"In the end," said Mustapha Mond, "the Controllers realized that force was no good. The slower but infinitely surer methods of ectogenesis, neo-Pavlovian conditioning and hypnopedia."...

"The discoveries of Pfitzner and Kawaguchi were at last made use of. An intensive propaganda against viviparous reproduction."...

"Accompanied by a campaign against the Past; by the closing of museums, the blowing up of historical monuments (luckily most of them had already been destroyed during the Nine Years' War); by the suppression of all books published before A.F. 150."...

"There were some things called the pyramids, for example."...

"And a man called Shakespeare. You've never heard of them of course."...

"Such are the advantages of a really scientific education."... The introduction of Our Ford's first T-Model."...

"Chosen as the opening date of the new era."...

"There was a thing, as I've said before, called Christianity."...

"The ethics and philosophy of under-consumption."...

"So essential when there was under-production; but in an age of machines and the fixation of nitrogen—positively a crime against society."...

"All crosses had their tops cut and became T's. There was also a thing called God."...

"We have the World State now. And Ford's Day celebrations, and Community Sings, and Solidarity Services."...

"There was a thing called Heaven; but all the same they used to drink enormous quantities of alcohol." ...

"There was thing called the soul and a thing called immortality."...

"But they used to take morphia and cocaine."...

"Two thousand pharmacologists and bio-chemists were subsidized in A.F. 178."...

"Six years later it was being produced commercially. The perfect drug."...

"Euphoric, narcotic, pleasantly hallucinant."...

"All the advantages of Christianity and alcohol; none of their defects." ...

"Take a holiday from reality whenever you like, and come back without so much as a headache or a mythology."...

"Stability was practically assured."...

"It only remained to conquer old age."...

"Gonadal hormones, transfusion of young blood, magnesium salts."...

"All the physiological stigmata of old age have been abolished. And along with them, of course."...

"Along with them all the old man's mental peculiarities. Characters remain constant throughout a whole lifetime."...

"Work, play—at sixty our powers and tastes are what they were at seventeen. Old men in the bad old days used to renounce, retire, take to religion, spend their time reading, thinking—thinking!...

"Now—such is progress— the old men work, the old men copulate, the old men have no time, no leisure from pleasure, not a moment to sit down and think—or if ever by some unlucky chance such a crevice of time should yawn in the solid substance of their distractions, there is always *soma,* delicious *soma,* half a gramme for a half-holiday, a gramme for a week-end, two grammes for a trip to the gorgeous East, three for a dark eternity on the moon; returning whence they find themselves on the other side of the crevice, safe on the solid ground of daily labour and distraction, scampering from feely to feely, from girl to pneumatic girl, from Electromagnetic Golf course to . . ."

14 The Urban Network

There is a great difference between a cluster of habitable structures that are near one another, and therefore called a village, and a complex of habitable structures that constitute a modern city. The absolute size and density of population per acre are by no means the most socially significant of the variables that distinguish between these two extreme forms of non-nomadic human living arrangements. At one extreme, a small number of functionally independent units might be considered a village. By functionally independent I mean that there are no services necessary for the maintenance of the residents of the village that are shared among them. That is, there are no jointly utilized services such as a sewer or water system or power supply arrangement that serve the inhabitants on either a cooperative basis or are provided by some commercial supplier. At this extreme, if all of the inhabitants of the village except one family were to depart, that family could continue to provide for itself those services necessary for its own maintenance with little disruption. At this extreme of functional independence it could also be true that one family's well might go dry and no other family in the village would necessarily be affected.

A modern city is an example of the opposite end of this continuum of functional independence-dependence. Without even raising the issue of economic interdependence, it is immediately obvious that no urban residence unit has any significant degree of functional independence. Consider, for example, a single high-rise apartment building in Manhattan. Dependence upon a complex of support services is so taken for granted that they become the givens of urban life, the forever present element on which the patterns of life depends—right up to the moment they disappear. All that I need to do is to imagine a building that is centrally air-conditioned (and therefore has sealed windows), uses water supplied from the city system, power from Consolidated Edison, is heated by oil purchased from a commercial supplier and in which the residents of the 44th floor penthouse apartment are accustomed to making their heavenward trip by elevator to make the point that left to their own resources, the residents of the building could not maintain the life style to which they are accustomed or anything even resembling it.

Dependence of this type is to some degree a condition of organized social life. The cause for it is that it yields considerable advantages to those who participate. For example, it is simply more efficient to organize a collective system for power supply than to expect everyone to produce his own power. There are economies of scale that accompany collective organization and efficiencies that result from a division of labor and technical specialization and that cannot be matched by an individual who must provide everything for himself.

All of this makes sense. The fact that there are advantages to specialization and economies of scale does not, however, mean that there are no costs. The costs are somewhat harder to see for several reasons. On the one hand it is possible to segregate the population into those who get most of the benefits and few of the costs and those who get the other end of the stick. Those who get the benefits need not consider those who bear the costs (e.g. those who do the dirty work for little pay). Those who bear the bulk of the costs usually cannot identify the cause of their problems. Both are born into the system and participate in it because it is there. As the system becomes more efficient, everyone gains at least a little.

There are also deeply hidden potential costs that all participants in the system bear in direct proportion to the benefits they derive from participation. One of these potential costs is the amount one would lose if the system were to fail. Material luxuries are some of the benefits of social and technological organization and therefore identify one of the costs if the system dies. A more important cost that becomes obvious upon the system failing is the loss of the ability to survive in a world devoid of technological support systems. Consider for a moment the question of how long you could survive if you had to produce for yourself the necessities of survival or could at best join with a few others, but even jointly could not utilize the technology on which we now depend.

In 1928 E. M. Forster wrote of a world even more dependent upon technological support than the one in which we live. We presently depend upon the knowledge and action of people to operate the systems we take for granted. Therefore, the knowledge of how to build and maintain these systems exists in human minds even if spread out among only a segment of the population. We are also close enough to technologically primitive environments both historically and, still, spacially to see the differences and retain some understanding of how life might be organized in the absence of technology. The time that Forster imagines is one in which variations in the degree of technological dependence has all but disappeared and the system that serves man has becomes so complicated that knowledge of how to operate it is lost. For the inhabitants of Forster's world this knowledge is unnecessary because the system is there—just as a scientific understanding of why the sun appears to rise in the morning is useless to primitive man. The sun rises, it is a given around which life is organized, just as the technology of the world is a given for the society Forster imagines.

Forster's world is one in which people have solved the problem of survival through dependence on technology and have moved on to the development of "ideas." Their world is bounded, however, by the limits of their technology in a much more fundamental way than we are in even the most developed urban centers of today's world. The essential difference is that even the most civilized of the earth's population is on some occasion forced to defer to the environment because they cannot control it. For example, at least for the moment, no one can prevent bad weather from closing an airport, rain falling on a day that one would like to sit in the sun, or cause the wind to blow on a given day and dissipate the concentration of junk that accumulated in the air surrounding a modern city. We are, however, working on ways of controlling these aspects of the physical world, developing substitutes for those experiences that don't depend on aspects of the environment we cannot simply control or finding ways to counteract the problems caused by the physical world. Extend these trends and we arrive at Forster's world.

Perhaps the most subtly dangerous and difficult aspect of total dependence on highly complex technologies to conceptualize is the adjustment of each succeeding human generation to the world into which they are born. People live short lives, civilizations endure for generations and, unless accidentally destroyed, knowledge, together with its concomitant of increasing power, can accumulate forever. In a sense, being born into a highly developed technologically dependent society is like being born on an airplane that has been flying for so long that the landing mechanism has decayed; the knowledge of how to land has been useless for so long that it has been forgotten and no one is sure if the flying manual is even aboard. There are no problems as long as the plane keeps flying. In fact, there is little choice about the matter.

I have a friend who may be the first of the properly adjusted modern urban men. He has a severe allergy to sunlight and cannot bear to be in full sunlight for more than a few minutes. He is also allergic to almost every sort of pollen and cannot go to within three blocks of Golden Gate Park without wheezing, sneezing, and being generally miserable. Large open spaces make him nervous and he detests having to leave an urban area unless by plane so that he can move from one built up environment to another. He also cannot sleep where it is quiet, and unless an occasional car or, better yet, bus goes by, he feels ill at ease. He also believes that everyone else is abnormal.My friend is perhaps the first example of the evolutionary dead-end toward which man is moving.

The Machine Stops

E. M. Forster

Part I: The Air-Ship

Imagine, if you can, a small room, hexagonal in shape, like the cell of a bee. It is lighted neither by window nor by lamp, yet it is filled with a soft radiance. There are no apertures for ventilation, yet the air is fresh. There are no musical instruments, and yet, at the moment that my meditation opens, this room is throbbing with melodious sounds. An arm-chair is in the centre, by its side a reading-desk—that is all the furniture. And in the arm-chair there sits a swaddled lump of flesh—a woman, about five feet high, with a face as white as a fungus. It is to her that the little room belongs.

An electric bell rang.

The woman touched a switch and the music was silent.

"I suppose I must see who it is," she thought, and set her chair in motion. The chair, like the music, was worked by machinery, and it rolled her to the other side of the room, where the bell still rang importunately.

"Who is it?" she called. Her voice was irritable, for she had been interrupted often since the music began. She knew several thousand people; in certain directions human intercourse had advanced enormously.

But when she listened into the receiver, her white face wrinkled into smiles, and she said:

"Very well, let us talk, I will isolate myself. I do not expect anything important will happen for the next five minutes—for I can give you fully five minutes, Kuno. Then I must deliver my lecture on 'Music during the Australian Period.'"

She touched the isolation knob, so that no one else could speak to her. Then she touched the lighting apparatus, and the little room was plunged into darkness.

"Be quick!" she called, her irritation returning. "Be quick, Kuno; here I am in the dark wasting my time."

But it was fully fifteen seconds before the round plate that she held in her hands began to glow. A faint blue light shot across it, darkening to purple, and presently she could see the image of her son, who lived on the other side of the earth, and he could see her.

"Kuno, how slow you are."

He smiled gravely.

"I really believe you enjoy dawdling."

"I have called you before, mother, but you were always busy or isolated. I have something particular to say."

"What is it, dearest boy? Be quick. Why could you not send it by pneumatic post?"

"Because I prefer saying such a thing. I want—"

"Well?"

"I want you to come and see me."

Vashti watched his face in the blue plate.

"But I can see you!" she exclaimed. "What more do you want?"

"I want to see you not through the Machine," said Kuno. "I want to speak to you not through the wearisome Machine."

"Oh, hush!" said his mother, vaguely shocked. "You mustn't say anything against the Machine."

"Why not?"

"One mustn't."

"You talk as if a god had made the Machine," cried the other. "I believe that you pray to it when you are unhappy. Men made it, do not forget that. Great men, but men. The Machine is much, but it is not everything. I see something like you in this plate, but I do not see you. I hear something like you through this telephone, but I do not hear you. That is why I want you to come. Come and stop with me. Pay me a visit, so that we can meet face to face, and talk about the hopes that are in my mind."

She replied that she could scarcely spare the time for a visit.

"The air-ship barely takes two days to fly between me and you."

"I dislike air-ships."

"Why?"

"I dislike seeing the horrible brown earth, and the sea, and the stars when it is dark. I get no ideas in an air-ship."

"I do not get them anywhere else,"

"What kind of ideas can the air give you?"

He paused for an instant.

"Do you not know four big stars that form an oblong, and three stars close together in the middle of the oblong, and hanging from these stars, three other stars?"

"No, I do not. I dislike the stars. But did they give you an idea? How interesting; tell me."

"I had an idea that they were like a man."

"I do not understand."

"The four big stars are the man's shoulders and his knees. The three stars in the middle are like the belts that men wore once, and the three stars hanging are like a sword."

"A sword?"

"Men carried swords about with them, to kill animals and other men."

"It does not strike me as a very good idea, but it is certainly original. When did it come to you first?"

"In the air-ship—" He broke off, and she fancied that he looked sad.She could not be sure, for the Machine did not transmit *nuances* of expression. It only gave a general idea of people—an idea that was good enough for all practical purposes, Vashti thought. The imponderable bloom, declared by a discredited philosophy to be the actual essence of intercourse, was rightly ignored by the Machine, just as the imponderable bloom of the grape was ignored by the manufacturers of artificial fruit. Something "good enough" had long since been accepted by our race.

"The truth is," he continued, "that I want to see these stars again. They are curious stars. I want to see them not from the air-ship, but from the surface of the earth, as our ancestors did, thousands of years ago. I want to visit the surface of the earth."

She was shocked again.

"Mother, you must come, if only to explain to me what is the harm of visiting the surface of the earth."

"No harm," she replied, controlling herself. "But no advantage. The surface of the earth is only dust and mud, no life remains on it, and you would need a respirator, or the cold of the outer air would kill you. One dies immediately in the outer air."

"I know; of course I shall take all precautions."

"And besides—"

"Well?"

She considered, and chose her words with care. Her son had a queer temper, and she wished to dissuade him from the expedition.

"It is contrary to the spirit of the age," she asserted.

"Do you mean by that, contrary to the Machine?"

"In a sense, but—"

His image on the blue plate faded.

"Kuno!"

He had isolated himself.

For a moment Vashti felt lonely.

Then she generated the light, and the sight of her room, flooded with radiance and studded with electric buttons, revived her. There were buttons and switches everywhere—buttons to call for food, for music, for clothing. There was the hot-bath button, by pressure of which a basin of (imitation) marble rose out of the floor, filled to the brim with a warm deodorised liquid. There was the cold-bath button. There was the button that produced literature. And there were of course the buttons by which she communicated with her friends. The room, though it contained nothing, was in touch with all that she cared for in the world.

Vashti's next move was to turn off the isolation-switch, and all the accumulations of the last three minutes burst upon her. The room was filled with the noise of bells, and speaking-tubes. What was the new food like? Could she recommend it? Had she had any ideas lately? Might one tell her one's own ideas? Would she make an engagement to visit the public nurseries at an early date?—say this day month.

To most of these questions she replied with irritation—a growing quality in that accelerated age. She said that the new food was horrible. That she could not visit the public nurseries through press of engagements. That she had no ideas of her own but had just been told one—that four stars and three in the middle were like a man: she doubted there was much in it. Then she switched off her correspondents, for it was time to deliver her lecture on Australian music.

The clumsy system of public gatherings had been long since abandoned; neither Vashti nor her audience stirred from their rooms. Seated in her arm-chair she spoke, while they in their arm-chairs heard her, fairly well, and saw her, fairly well. She opened with a humorous account of music in the pre-Mongolian epoch, and went on to describe the great outburst of song that followed the Chinese conquest. Remote and primaeval as were the methods of I-San-So and the Brisbane school, she yet felt (she said) that study of them might repay the musician of today: they had freshness; they had, above all, ideas.

Her lecture, which lasted ten minutes, was well received, and at its conclusion she and many of her audience listened to a lecture on the sea; there were ideas to be got from the sea; the speaker had donned a respirator and visited it lately. Then she fed, talked to many friends, had a bath, talked again, and summoned for her bed.

The bed was not to her liking. It was too large, and she had a feeling for a small bed. Complaint was useless, for beds were of the same dimension all over the world, and to have had an alternative size would have involved vast alterations in the Machine. Vashti isolated herself—it was necessary, for neither day nor night existed under the ground—and reviewed all that had happened since she had summoned the bed last. Ideas? Scarcely any. Events—was Kuno's invitation an event?

By her side, on the little reading-desk, was a survival from the ages of litter—one book. This was the Book of the Machine. In it were instructions against every possible contingency. If she was hot or cold or dyspeptic or at loss for a word, she went to the book, and it told her which button to press. The Central Committee published it. In accordance with a growing habit, it was richly bound.

Sitting up in the bed, she took it reverently in her hands. She glanced round the glowing room as if some one might be watching her. Then, half ashamed, half joyful, she murmured "O Machine! O Machine!" and raised the volume to her lips. Thrice she kissed it, thrice inclined her head, thrice she felt the delirium of acquiescence. Her ritual performed, she turned to page 1367, which gave the times of the departure of the air-ships from the island in the southern hemisphere, under whose soil she lived, to the island in the northern hemisphere, whereunder lived her son.

She thought, "I have not the time."

She made the room dark and slept; she awoke and made the room light; she ate and exchanged ideas with her friends, and listened to music and attended lectures; she made the room dark and slept. Above her, beneath her, and around her, the Machine hummed eternally; she did not notice the noise, for she had been born with it in her ears. The earth, carrying her, hummed as it sped through silence, turning her now to the invisible sun, now to the invisible stars. She awoke and made the room light.

"Kuno!"

"I will not talk to you," he answered, "until you come."

"Have you been on the surface of the earth since we spoke last?"

His image faded.

Again she consulted the book. She became very nervous and lay back in her chair palpitating. Think of her as without teeth or hair. Presently she directed the chair to the wall, and pressed an unfamiliar button. The wall swung apart slowly. Through the opening she saw a tunnel that curved slightly, so that its goal was not visible. Should she go to see her son, here was the beginning of the journey.

Of course she knew all about the communication-system. There was nothing mysterious in it. She would summon a car and it would fly with her down the tunnel until it reached the lift that communicated with the airship station: the system had been in use for many, many years, long before the universal establishment of the Machine. And of course she had studied the civilisation that had immediately preceded her own—the civilisation that had mistaken the functions of the system, and had used it for bringing people to things, instead of for bringing things to people. Those funny old days, when men went for change of air instead of changing the air in their rooms! And yet—she was frightened of the tunnel: she had not seen it since her last child was born. It curved—but not quite as she remembered; it was brilliant—but not quite as brilliant as a lecturer had suggested. Vashti was seized with the terrors of direct experience. She shrank back into the room, and the wall closed up again.

"Kuno," she said, "I cannot come to see you. I am not well."

Immediately an enormous apparatus fell on to her out of the ceiling, a thermometer was automatically inserted between her lips, a stethoscope was automatically laid upon her heart. She lay powerless. Cool pads soothed her forehead. Kuno had telegraphed to her doctor.

So the human passions still blundered up and down in the Machine. Vashti drank the medicine that the doctor projected into her mouth, and the machinery retired into the ceiling. The voice of Kuno was heard asking how she felt.

"Better." Then with irritation: "But why do you not come to me instead?"

"Because I cannot leave this place."

"Why?"

"Because, any moment, something tremendous may happen."

"Have you been on the surface of the earth yet?"

"Not yet."

"Then what is it?"

"I will not tell you through the Machine."

She resumed her life.

But she thought of Kuno as a baby, his birth, his removal to the public nurseries, her one visit to him there, his visits to her—visits which stopped when the Machine had assigned him a room on the other side of the earth. "Parents, duties of," said the book of the Machine, "cease at the moment of birth. P. 422327483." True, but there was something special about Kuno—indeed there had been something special about all her children—and, after all, she must brave the journey if he desired it. And, "something tremendous might happen." What did that mean? The nonsense of a youthful man, no doubt, but she must go. Again she pressed the unfamiliar button, again the wall swung back, and she saw the tunnel that curved out of sight. Clasping the Book, she rose, tottered on to the platform, and summoned the car. Her room closed behind her: the journey to the northern hemisphere had begun.

Of course it was perfectly easy. The car approached and in it she found arm-chairs exactly like her own. When she signalled, it stopped, and she tottered into the lift. One other passenger was in the lift, the first fellow creature she had seen face to face for months. Few travelled in these days, for, thanks to the advance of science, the earth was exactly alike all over. Rapid intercourse, from which the previous civilisation had hoped so much, had ended by defeating itself. What was the good of going to Pekin when it was just like Shrewsbury? Why return to Shrewsbury when it would be just like Pekin? Men seldom moved their bodies; all unrest was concentrated in the soul.

The air-ship was a relic from the former age. It was kept up, because it was easier to keep it up than to stop it or to diminish it, but it now far exceeded the wants of the population. Vessel after vessel would rise from the vomitories of Rye or of Christchurch (I use the antique names), would sail into the crowded sky, and would draw up at the wharves of the south—empty. So nicely adjusted was the system, so independent of meteorology, that the sky, whether calm or cloudy, resembled a vast kaleidoscope whereon the same patterns periodically recurred. The ship on which Vashti sailed started now at sunset, now at dawn. But always, as it passed above Rheims, it would neighbour the ship that served between Helsingfors and the Brazils, and, every third time it surmounted the Alps, the fleet of Palermo would cross its track behind. Night and day, wind and storm, tide and earthquake, impeded man no longer. He had harnessed Leviathan. All the old literature, with its praise of Nature, and its fear of Nature, rang false as the prattle of a child.

Yet, as Vashti saw the vast flank of the ship, stained with exposure to the outer air, her horror of direct experience returned. It was not quite like the air-ship in the cinematophote. For one thing it smelt—not strongly or unpleasantly, but it did smell, and with her eyes shut she should have known that a new thing was close to her. Then she had to walk to it from the lift, had to submit to glances from the other passengers. The man in front dropped his Book—no great matter, but it disquieted them all. In the rooms, if the Book was dropped, the floor raised it mechanically, but the gangway to the air-ship was not so prepared, and the sacred volume lay motionless. They stopped—the thing was unforeseen—and the man, instead of picking up his property, felt the muscles of his arm to see how they had failed him. Then some one actually said with direct utterance: "We shall be late"—and they trooped on board, Vashti treading on the pages as she did so.

Inside, her anxiety increased. The arrangements were old-fashioned and rough. There was even a female attendant, to whom she would have to announce her wants during the voyage. Of course a revolving platform ran the length of the boat, but she was expected to walk from it to her cabin. Some cabins were better than others, and she did not get the best. She thought the attendant had been unfair, and spasms of rage shook her. The glass valves had closed, she could not go back. She saw, at the end of the vestibule, the lift in which she had ascended going quietly up and down, empty. Beneath those corridors of shining tiles were rooms, tier below tier, reaching far into the earth, and in each room there sat a human being, eating, or sleeping, or producing ideas. And buried deep in the hive was her own room. Vashti was afraid.

"O Machine! O Machine!" she murmured, and caressed her Book, and was comforted.

Then the sides of the vestibule seemed to melt together, as do the passages that we see in dreams, the lift vanished, the Book that had been dropped slid to the left and vanished, polished tiles rushed by like a stream of water, there was a slight jar, and the air-ship, issuing from its tunnel, soared above the waters of a tropical ocean.

It was night. For a moment she saw the coast of Sumatra edged by the phosphorescence of waves, and crowned by lighthouses, still sending forth their disregarded beams. These also vanished, and only the stars distracted her. They were not motionless, but swayed to and fro above her head, thronging out of one skylight into another, as if the universe and not the air-ship was careening. And, as often happens on clear nights, they seemed now to be in perspective, now on a plane; now piled tier beyond tier into the infinite heavens, now concealing infinity, a roof limiting for ever the visions of men. In either case they seemed intolerable. "Are we to travel in the dark?" called the passengers angrily, and the attendant, who had been careless, generated the light, and pulled down the blinds of pliable metal. When the air-ships had been built, the desire to look direct at things still lingered in the world. Hence the extraordinary number of skylights and windows, and the proportionate discomfort to those who were civilised and refined. Even in Vashti's cabin one star peeped through a flaw in the blind, and after a few hours' uneasy slumber, she was disturbed by an unfamiliar glow, which was the dawn.

Quick as the ship had sped westwards, the earth had rolled eastwards quicker still, and had dragged back Vashti and her companions towards the sun. Science could prolong the night, but only for a little, and those high hopes of neutralising the earth's diurnal revolution had passed, together with hopes that were possibly higher. To "keep pace with the sun," or even to outstrip it, had been the aim of the civilisation preceding this. Racing aeroplanes had been built for the purpose, capable of enormous speed, and steered by the greatest intellects of the epoch. Round the globe they went, round and round, westward, westward, round and round, amidst humanity's applause. In vain. The globe went eastward quicker still, horrible accidents occurred, and the Committee of the Machine, at the time rising into prominence, declared the pursuit illegal, unmechanical, and punishable by Homelessness.

Of Homelessness more will be said later.

Doubtless the Committee was right. Yet the attempt to "defeat the sun" aroused the last common interest that our race experienced about the heavenly bodies, or indeed about anything. It was the last time that men were compacted by thinking of a power outside the world. The sun had conquered, yet it was the end of his spiritual dominion. Dawn, midday, twilight, the zodiacal path, touched neither men's lives nor their hearts, and science retreated into the ground, to concentrate herself upon problems that she was certain of solving.

So when Vashti found her cabin invaded by a rosy finger of light, she was annoyed, and tried to adjust the blind. But the blind flew up altogether, and she saw through the skylight small pink clouds, swaying against a background of blue, and as the sun crept higher, its radiance entered direct, brimming down the wall, like a golden sea. It rose and fell with the air-ship's motion, just as waves rise and fall, but it advanced steadily, as a tide advances. Unless she was careful, it would strike her face. A spasm of horror shook her and she rang for the attendant. The attendant too was horrified, but she could do nothing; it was not her place to mend the blind. She could only suggest that the lady should change her cabin, which she accordingly prepared to do.

People were almost exactly alike all over the world, but the attendant of the air-ship, perhaps owing to her exceptional duties, had grown a little out of the common. She had often to address passengers with direct speech, and this had given her a certain roughness and originality of manner. When Vashti swerved away from the sunbeams with a cry, she behaved barbarically—she put out her hand to steady her.

"How dare you!" exclaimed the passenger. "You forget yourself!.

The woman was confused, and apologized for not having let her fall. People never touched one another. The custom had become obsolete, owing to the Machine.

"Where are we now?" asked Vashti haughtily.

"We are over Asia," said the attendant, anxious to be polite.

"Asia?"

"You must excuse my common way of speaking. I have got into the habit of calling places over which I pass by their unmechanical names."

"Oh, I remember Asia. The Mongols came from it."

"Beneath us, in the open air, stood a city that was once called Simla."

"Have you ever heard of the Mongols and of the Brisbane school?"

"No."

"Brisbane also stood in the open air."

"Those mountains to the right—let me show you them." She pushed back a metal blind. The main chain of the Himalayas was revealed. "They were once called the Roof of the World, those mountains."

"What a foolish name!"

"You must remember that, before the dawn of civilisation, they seemed to be an impenetrable wall that touched the stars. It was supposed that no one but the gods could exist above their summits. How we have advanced, thanks to the Machine!"

"How we have advanced, thanks to the Machine!" said Vashti.

"How we have advanced, thanks to the Machine!" echoed the passenger who had dropped his Book the night before, and who was standing in the passage.

"And that white stuff in the cracks?—what is it?"

"I have forgotten its name."

"Cover the window, please. These mountains give me no ideas."

The northern aspect of the Himalayas was in deep shadow; on the Indian slope the sun had just prevailed. The forests had been destroyed during the literature epoch for the purpose of making newspaper-pulp, but the snows were awakening to their morning glory, and clouds still hung on the breasts of Kinchinjunga. In the plain were seen the ruins of cities, with diminished rivers creeping by their walls, and by the sides of these were sometimes the signs of vomitories, marking the cities of today. Over the whole prospect air-ships rushed, crossing and intercrossing with incredible *aplomb*, and rising nonchalantly when they desired to escape the perturbations of the lower atmosphere and to traverse the Roof of the World.

"We have indeed advanced, thanks to the Machine," repeated the attendant, and hid the Himalayas behind a metal blind.

The day dragged wearily forward. The passengers sat each in his cabin, avoiding one another with an almost physical repulsion and longing to be once more under the surface of the earth. There were eight or ten of them, mostly young males, sent out from the public nurseries to inhabit the rooms of those who had died in various parts of the earth. The man who had dropped his Book was on the homeward journey. He had been sent to Sumatra for the purpose of propagating the race. Vashti alone was travelling by her private will.

At midday she took a second glance at the earth. The air-ship was crossing another range of mountains, but she could see little, owing to clouds. Masses of black rock hovered below her, and merged indistinctly into grey. Their shapes were fantastic; one of them resembled a prostrate man.

"No ideas here," murmured Vashti, and hid the Caucasus behind a metal blind.

In the evening she looked again. They were crossing a golden sea, in which lay many small islands and one peninsula.

She repeated, "No ideas here," and hid Greece behind a metal blind.

Part II: The Mending Apparatus

By a vestibule, by a lift, by a tubular railway, by a platform, by a sliding door—by reversing all the steps of her departure did Vashti arrive at her son's room, which exactly resembled her own. She might well declare that the visit was superfluous. The buttons, the knobs, the reading-desk with the Book, the temperature, the atmosphere, the illumination—all were exactly the same. And if Kuno himself, flesh of her flesh, stood close beside her at last, what profit was there in that? She was too well-bred to shake him by the hand.

Averting her eyes, she spoke as follows:

"Here I am. I have had the most terrible journey and greatly retarded the development of my soul. It is not worth it, Kuno, it is not worth it. My time is too precious. The sunlight almost touched me, and I have met with the rudest people. I can only stop a few minutes. Say what you want to say, and then I must return."

"I have been threatened with Homelessness," said Kuno.

She looked at him now.

"I have been threatened with Homelessness, and I could not tell you such a thing through the Machine."

Homelessness means death. The victim is exposed to the air, which kills him.

"I have been outside since I spoke to you last. The tremendous thing has happened, and they have discovered me."

"But why shouldn't you go outside!" she exclaimed.

"It is perfectly legal, perfectly mechanical, to visit the surface of the earth. I have lately been to a lecture on the sea; there is no objection to that; one simply summons a respirator and gets an Egression-permit. It is not the kind of thing that spiritually-minded people do, and I begged you not to do it, but there is no legal objection to it."

"I did not get an Egression-permit."

"Then how did you get out?"

"I found out a way of my own."

The phrase conveyed no meaning to her, and he had to repeat it.

"A way of your own?" she whispered. "But that would be wrong."

"Why?"

The question shocked her beyond measure.

"You are beginning to worship the Machine," he said coldly. "You think it irreligious of me to have found out a way of my own. It was just what the Committee thought, when they threatened me with Homelessness."

At this she grew angry. "I worship nothing!" she cried. "I am most advanced. I don't think you irreligious, for there is no such thing as religion left. All the fear and the superstition that existed once have been destroyed by the Machine. I only meant that to find out a way of your own was— Besides, there is no new way out."

"So it is always supposed."

"Except through the vomitories, for which one must have an Egression-permit, it is impossible to get out. The Book says so."

"Well, the Book's wrong, for I have been out on my feet."

For Kuno was possessed of a certain physical strength.

By these days it was a demerit to be muscular. Each infant was examined at birth, and all who promised undue strength were destroyed. Humanitarians may protest, but it would have been no true kindness to let an athlete live; he would never have been happy in that state of life to which the Machine had called him; he would have yearned for trees to climb, rivers to bathe in, meadows and hills against which he might measure his body. Man must be adapted to his surroundings, must he not? In the dawn of the world our weakly must be exposed on Mount Taygetus, in its twilight our strong will suffer euthanasia, that the Machine may progess, that the Machine may progress, that the Machine may progress eternally.

"You know that we have lost the sense of space. We say 'space is annihilated,' but we have annihilated not space, but the sense thereof. We have lost a part of ourselves. I determined to recover it, and I began by walking up and down the platform of the railway outside my room. Up and down, until I was tired, and so did recapture the meaning of 'near' and 'far.' 'Near' is a place to which I can get quickly *on my feet,* not a place to which the train or the air-ship will take me quickly. 'Far' is a place to which I cannot get quickly on my feet; the vomitory is 'far,' though I could be there in thirty-eight seconds by summoning the train. Man is the measure. That was my first lesson. Man's feet are the measure for distance, his hands are the measure for ownership, his body is the measure for all that is lovable and desirable and strong. Then I went further: it was then that I called to you for the first time, and you would not come.

"This city, as you know, is built deep beneath the surface of the earth, with only the vomitories protruding. Having paced the platform outside my own room, I took the lift to the next platform and paced that also, and so with each in turn, until I came to the topmost, above which begins the earth. All the platforms were exactly alike, and all that I gained by visiting them was to develop my sense of space and my muscles. I think I should have been content with this—it is not a little thing— but as I walked and brooded, it occurred to me that our cities had been built in the days when men still breathed the outer air, and that there had been ventilation shafts for the workmen. I could think of nothing but these ventilation shafts. Had they been destroyed by all the food-tubes and medicine-tubes and music-tubes that the Machine has evolved lately? Or did traces of them remain? One thing was certain. If I came upon them anywhere, it would be in the railway-tunnels of the topmost story. Everywhere else, all space was accounted for.

"I am telling my story quickly, but don't think that I was not a coward or that your answers never depressed me. It is not the proper thing, it is not mechanical, it is not decent to walk along a railway-tunnel. I did not fear that I might tread upon a live rail and be killed. I feared something far more intangible—doing what was not contemplated by the Machine. Then I said to myself, 'Man is the measure,' and I went, and after many visits I found an opening.

"The tunnels, of course, were lighted. Everything is light, artificial light; darkness is the exception. So when I saw a black gap in the tiles, I knew that it was an exception, and rejoiced. I put in my arm—I could put in no more at first—and waved it round and round in ecstasy. I loosened another tile, and put in my head, and shouted into the darkness: 'I am coming, I shall do it yet,' and my voice reverberated down endless passages. I seemed to hear the spirits of those dead workmen who had returned each evening to the starlight and to their wives, and all the generations who had lived in the open air called back to me, 'You will do it yet, you are coming.'"

He paused, and, absurd as he was, his last words moved her. For Kuno had lately asked to be a father, and his request had been refused by the Committee. His was not a type that the Machine desired to hand on.

"Then a train passed. It brushed by me, but I thrust my head and arms into the hole. I had done enough for one day, so I crawled back to the platform, went down in the lift, and summoned my bed. Ah, what dreams! And again I called you, and again you refused."

She shook her head and said:

"Don't. Don't talk of these terrible things. You make me miserable. You are throwing civilisation away."

"But I had got back the sense of space and a man cannot rest then. I determined to get in at the hole and climb the shaft. And so I exercised my arms. Day after day I went through ridiculous movements, until my flesh ached, and I could hang by my hands and hold the pillow of my bed outstretched for many minutes. Then I summoned a respirator, and started.

"It was easy at first. The mortar had somehow rotted, and I soon pushed some more tiles in, and clambered after them into the darkness, and the spirits of the dead comforted me. I don't know what I mean by that. I just say what I felt. I felt, for the first time, that a protest had been lodged against corruption, and that even as the dead were comforting me, so I was comforting the unborn. I felt that humanity existed, and that it existed without clothes. How can I possibly explain this? It was naked, humanity seemed naked, and all these tubes and buttons and machineries neither came into the world with us, nor will they follow us out, nor do they matter supremely while we are here. Had I been strong, I would have torn off every garment I had, and gone out into the outer air unswaddled. But this is not for me, nor perhaps for my generation. I climbed with my respirator and my hygienic clothes and my dietetic tabloids! Better thus than not at all.

"There was a ladder, made of some primæval metal. The light from the railway fell upon its lowest rungs, and I saw that it led straight upwards out of the rubble at the bottom of the shaft. Perhaps our ancestors ran up and down it a dozen times daily, in their building. As I climbed, the rough edges cut through my gloves so that my hands bled. The light helped me for a little, and then came darkness and, worse still, silence which pierced my ears like a sword. The Machine hums! Did you know that? Its hum penetrates our blood, and may even guide our thoughts. Who knows! I was getting beyond its power. Then I thought: 'This silence means that I am doing wrong.' But I heard voices in the silence, and again they strengthened me." He laughed. "I had need of them. The next moment I cracked my head against something."

She sighed.

"I had reached one of those pneumatic stoppers that defend us from the outer air. You may have noticed them on the air-ship. Pitch dark, my feet on the rungs of an invisible ladder, my hands cut; I cannot explain how I lived through this part, but the voices still comforted me, and I felt for fastenings. The stopper, I suppose, was about eight feet across. I passed my hand over it as far as I could reach. It was perfectly smooth. I felt it almost to the centre. Not quite to the centre, for my arm was too short. Then the voice said: 'Jump. It is worth it. There may be a handle in the centre, and you may catch hold of it and so come to us your own way. And if there is no handle, so that you may fall and are dashed to pieces—it is still worth it: you will still come to us your own way.' So I jumped. There was a handle, and—"

He paused. Tears gathered in his mother's eyes. She knew that he was fated. If he did not die today he would die tomorrow. There was not room for such a person in the world. And with her pity disgust mingled. She was ashamed at having borne such a son, she who had always been so respectable and so full of ideas. Was he really the little boy to whom she had taught the use of his stops and buttons, and to whom she had given his first lessons in the Book? The very hair that disfigured his lip showed that he was reverting to some savage type. On atavism the Machine can have no mercy.

"There was a handle, and I did catch it. I hung tranced over the darkness and heard the hum of these workings as the last whisper in a dying dream. All the things I had cared about and all the people I had spoken to through tubes appeared infinitely little. Meanwhile the handle revolved. My weight had set something in motion and I span slowly, and then—

"I cannot describe it. I was lying with my face to the sunshine. Blood poured from my nose and ears and I heard a tremendous roaring. The stopper, with me clinging to it, had simply been blown out of the earth, and the air that we make down here was escaping through the vent into the air above. It burst up like a fountain. I crawled back to it—for the upper air hurts—and, as it were, I took great sips from the edge. My respirator had flown goodness knows where, my clothes were torn. I just lay with my lips close to the hole, and I sipped until the bleeding stopped. You can imagine nothing so curious. This hollow in the grass—I will speak of it in a minute,—the sun shining into it, not brilliantly but through marbled clouds,—the peace, the nonchalance, the sense of space, and, brushing my cheek, the roaring fountain of our artificial air! Soon I spied my respirator, bobbing up and down in the current high above my head, and higher still were many air-ships. But no one ever looks out of air-ships, and in my case they could not have picked me up. There I was, stranded. The sun shone a little way down the shaft, and revealed the topmost rung of the ladder, but it was hopeless trying to reach it. I should either have been tossed up again by the escape, or else have fallen in, and died. I could only lie on the grass, sipping and sipping, and from time to time glancing around me.

"I knew that I was in Wessex, for I had taken care to go to a lecture on the subject before starting. Wessex lies above the room in which we are talking now. It was once an important state. Its kings held all the southern coast from the Andredswald to Cornwall, while the Wansdyke protected them on the north, running over the high ground. The lecturer was only concerned with the rise of Wessex, so I do not know how long it remained an international power, nor would the knowledge have assisted me. To tell the truth I could do nothing but laugh, during this part. There was I, with a pneumatic stopper by my side and a respirator bobbing over my head, imprisoned, all three of us, in a grass-grown hollow that was edged with fern."

Then he grew grave again.

"Lucky for me that it was a hollow. For the air began to fall back into it and to fill it as water fills a bowl. I could crawl about. Presently I stood. I breathed a mixture, in which the air that hurts predominated whenever I tried to climb the sides. This was not so bad. I had not lost my tabloids and remained ridiculously cheerful, and as for the Machine, I forgot about it altogether. My one aim now was to get to the top, where the ferns were, and to view whatever objects lay beyond.

"I rushed the slope. The new air was still too bitter for me and I came rolling back, after a momentary vision of something grey. The sun grew very feeble, and I remembered that he was in Scorpio—I had been to a lecture on that too. If the sun is in Scorpio and you are in Wessex, it means that you must be as quick as you can, or it will get too dark. (This is the first bit of useful information I have ever got from a lecture, and I expect it will be the last.) It made me try frantically to breathe the new air, and to advance as far as I dared out of my pond. The hollow filled so slowly. At times I thought that the fountain played with less vigour. My respirator seemed to dance nearer the earth; the roar was decreasing."

He broke off.

"I don't think this is interesting you. The rest will interest you even less. There are no ideas in it, and I wish that I had not troubled you to come. We are too different, mother."

She told him to continue.

"It was evening before I climbed the bank. The sun had very nearly slipped out of the sky by this time, and I could not get a good view. You, who have just crossed the Roof of the World, will not want to hear an account of the little hills that I saw—low colourless hills. But to me they were living and the turf that covered them was a skin, under which their muscles rippled, and I felt that those hills had called with incalculable force to men in the past, and that men had loved them. Now they sleep—perhaps for ever. They commune with humanity in dreams. Happy the man, happy the woman, who awakes the hills of Wessex. For though they sleep, they will never die."

His voice rose passionately.

"Cannot you see, cannot all your lecturers see, that it is we who are dying, and that down here the only thing that really lives is the Machine? We created the Machine, to do our will, but we cannot make it do our will now. It has robbed us of the sense of space and of the sense of touch, it has blurred every human relation and narrowed down love to a carnal act, it has paralysed our bodies and our wills, and now it compels us to worship it. The Machine develops—but not on our lines. The Machine proceeds—but not to our goal. We only exist as the blood corpuscles that course through its arteries, and if it could work without us, it would let us die. Oh, I have no remedy—or, at least, only one—to tell men again and again that I have seen the hills of Wessex as Ælfrid saw them when he overthrew the Danes.

"So the sun set. I forgot to mention that a belt of mist lay between my hill and other hills, and that it was the colour of pearl."

He broke off for the second time.

"Go on," said his mother wearily.

He shook his head.

"Go on. Nothing that you say can distress me now. I am hardened."

"I had meant to tell you the rest, but I cannot: I know that I cannot: good-bye."

Vashti stood irresolute. All her nerves were tingling with his blasphemies. But she was also inquisitive.

"This is unfair," she complained. "You have called me across the world to hear your story, and hear it I will. Tell me—as briefly as possible, for this is a disastrous waste of time—tell me how you returned to civilisation."

"Oh—that!" he said, starting. "You would like to hear about civilisation. Certainly. Had I got to where my respirator fell down?"

"No—but I understand everything now. You put on your respirator, and managed to walk along the surface of the earth to a vomitory, and there your conduct was reported to the Central Committee."

"By no means."

He passed his hand over his forehead, as if dispelling some strong impression. Then, resuming his narrative, he warmed to it again.

"My respirator fell about sunset. I had mentioned that the fountain seemed feebler, had I not."

"Yes."

"About sunset, it let the respirator fall. As I said, I had entirely forgotten about the Machine, and I paid no great attention at the time, being occupied with other things. I had my pool of air, into which I could dip when the outer keenness became intolerable, and which would possibly remain for days, provided that no wind sprang up to disperse it. Not until it was too late, did I realize what the stoppage of the escape implied. You see—the gap in the tunnel had been mended; the Mending Apparatus; the Mending Apparatus, was after me.

"One other warning I had, but I neglected it. The sky at night was clearer than it had been in the day, and the moon, which was about half the sky behind the sun, shone into the dell at moments quite brightly. I was in my usual place—on the boundary between the two atmospheres—when I thought I saw something dark move across the bottom of the dell, and vanish into the shaft. In my folly, I ran down. I bent over and listened, and I thought I heard a faint scraping noise in the depths.

"At this—but it was too late—I took alarm. I determined to put on my respirator and to walk right out of the dell. But my respirator had gone. I knew exactly where it had fallen—between the stopper and the aperature—and I could even feel the mark that it had made in the turf. It had gone, and I realized that something evil was at work, and I had better escape to the other air, and, if I must die, die running towards the cloud that had been the colour of a pearl. I never started. Out of the shaft—it is too horrible. A worm, a long white worm, had crawled out of the shaft and was gliding over the moonlit grass.

"I screamed. I did everything that I should not have done, I stamped upon the creature instead of flying from it, and it at once curled round the ankle. Then we fought. The worm let me run all over the dell, but edged up my leg as I ran. 'Help!' I cried. (That part is too awful. It belongs to the part that you will never know.) 'Help!' I cried. (Why cannot we suffer in silence?) 'Help! I cried. Then my feet were wound together, I fell, I was dragged away from the dear ferns and the living hills, and past the great metal stopper (I can tell you this part), and I thought it might save me again if I caught hold of the handle. It also was enwrapped, it also. Oh, the whole dell was full of the things. They were searching it in all directions, they were denuding it, and the white snouts of others peeped out of the hole, ready if needed. Everything that could be moved they brought—brushwood, bundles of fern, everything, and down we all went intertwined into hell. The last things that I saw, ere the stopper closed after us, were certain stars, and I felt that a man of my sort lived in the sky. For I did fight, I fought till the very end, and it was only my head hitting against the ladder that quieted me. I woke up in this room. The worms had vanished. I was surrounded by artificial air, artificial light, artificial peace, and my friends were calling to me down speaking-tubes to know whether I had come across any new ideas lately."

Here his story ended. Discussion of it was impossible, and Vashti turned to go.

"It will end in Homelessness," she said quietly.

"I wish it would," retorted Kuno.

"The Machine has been most merciful."

"I prefer the mercy of God."

"By that superstitious phrase, do you mean that you could live in the outer air?"

"Yes."

"Have you ever seen, round the vomitories, the bones of those who were extruded after the Great Rebellion?"

"Yes."

"They were left where they perished for our edification. A few crawled away, but they perished, too—who can doubt it? And so with the Homeless of our own day. The surface of the earth supports life no longer."

"Indeed."

"Ferns and a little grass may survive, but all higher forms have perished. Has any air-ship detected them?"

"No."

"Has any lecturer dealt with them?"

"No."

"Then why this obstinacy?"

"Because I have seen them," he exploded.

"Seen *what*"

"Because I have seen her in the twilight—because she came to my help when I called—because she, too, was entangled by the worms, and, luckier than I, was killed by one of them piercing her throat."

He was mad. Vashti departed, nor, in the troubles that followed, did she ever see his face again.

Part III: The Homeless

During the years that followed Kuno's escapade, two important developments took place in the Machine. On the surface they were revolutionary, but in either case men's minds had been prepared beforehand, and they did but express tendencies that were latent already.

The first of these was the abolition of respirators.

Advanced thinkers, like Vashti, had always held it foolish to visit the surface of the earth. Airships might be necessary, but what was the good of going out for mere curiosity and crawling along for a mile or two in a terrestrial motor? The habit was vulgar and perhaps faintly improper: it was unproductive of ideas, and had no connection with the habits that really mattered. So respirators were abolished, and with them, of course, the terrestrial motors, and except for a few lecturers, who complained that they were debarred access to their subject-matter, the development was accepted quietly. Those who still wanted to know what the earth was like had after all only to listen to some gramophone, or to look into some cinematophote. And even the lecturers acquiesced when they found that a lecture on the sea was none the less stimulating when compiled out of other lectures that had already been delivered on the same subject. "Beware of first-hand ideas!" exclaimed one of the most advanced of them. "First-hand ideas do not really exist. They are but the physical impressions produced by love and fear, and on this gross foundation who could erect a philosophy? Let your ideas be second-hand, and if possible tenth-hand, for then they will be far removed from that disturbing element—direct observation. Do not learn anything about this subject of mine—the French Revolution. Learn instead what I think that Enicharmon thought Urizen thought Gutch thought Ho-Yung thought Chi-Bo-Sing thought Lafcadio Hearn thought Carlyle thought Mirabeau said about the French Revolution. Through the medium of these eight great minds, the blood that was shed at Paris and the windows that were broken at Versailles will be clarified to an idea which you may employ most profitably in your daily lives. But be sure that the intermediates are many and varied, for in history one authority exists to counteract another. Unizen must counteract the scepticism of Ho-Yung and Enicharmon, I must myself counteract the impetuosity of Gutch. You who listen to me are in a better position to judge about the French Revolution than I am. Your descendants will be even in a better position than you, for they will learn what you think I think, and yet another intermediate will be added to the chain. And in time" —his voice rose—"there will come a generation that has got beyond facts, beyond impressions, a generation absolutely colourless, a generation

'seraphically free
From taint of personality,'

which will see the French Revolution not as it happened, nor as they would like it to have happened, but as it would have happened, had it taken place in the days of the Machine."

Tremendous applause greeted this lecture, which did but voice a feeling already latent in the minds of men—a feeling that terrestrial facts must be ignored, and that the abolition of respirators was a positive gain. It was even suggested that air-ships should be abolished too. This was not done, because air-ships had somehow worked themselves into the Machine's system. But year by year they were used less, and mentioned less by thoughtful men.

The second great development was the reestablishment of religion.

This, too, had been voiced in the celebrated lecture. No one could mistake the reverent tone in which the peroration had concluded, and it awakened a responsive echo in the heart of each. Those who had long worshipped silently, now began to talk. They described the strange feeling of peace that came over them when they handled the Book of the Machine, the pleasure that it was to repeat certain numerals out of it, however little meaning those numerals conveyed to the outward ear, the ecstasy of touching a button, however unimportant, or of ringing an electric bell, however superfluously.

"The Machine," they exclaimed, "feeds us and clothes us and houses us; through it we speak to one another, through it we see one another, in it we have our being. The Machine is the friend of ideas and the enemy of superstition: the Machine is omnipotent, eternal; blessed is the Machine." And before long this allocution was printed on the first page of the Book, and in subsequent editions the ritual swelled into a complicated system of praise and prayer. The word "religion" was sedulously avoided, and in theory the Machine was still the creation and the implement of man. But in practice all, save a few retrogrades, worshipped it as divine. Nor was it worshipped in unity. One believer would be chiefly impressed by the blue optic plates, through which he saw other believers; another by the mending apparatus, which sinful Kuno had compared to worms; another by the lifts, another by the Book. And each would pray to this or to that, and ask it to intercede for him with the Machine as a whole. Persecution—that also was present. It did not break out, for reasons that will be set forward shortly. But it was latent, and all who did not accept the minimum known as "undenominational Mechanism" lived in danger of Homelessness, which means death, as we know.

To attribute these two great developments to the Central Committee, is to take a very narrow view of civilisation. The Central Committee announced the developments, it is true, but they were no more the cause of them than were the kings of the imperialistic period the cause of war. Rather did they yield to some invincible pressure, which came no one knew whither, and which, when gratified, was succeeded by some new pressure equally invincible. To such a state of affairs it is convenient to give the name of progress. No one confessed the Machine was out of hand. Year by year it was served with increased efficiency and decreased intelligence. The better a man knew his own duties upon it, the less he understood the duties of his neighbour, and in all the world there was not one who understood the monster as a whole. Those master brains had perished. They had left full directions, it is true, and their successors had each of them mastered a portion of those directions. But Humanity, in its desire for comfort, had over-reached itself. It had exploited the riches of nature too far. Quietly and complacently, it was sinking into decadence, and progress had come to mean the progress of the Machine.

As for Vashti, her life went peacefully forward until the final disaster. She made her room dark and slept; she awoke and made the room light. She lectured and attended lectures. She exchanged ideas with her innumerable friends and believed she was growing more spiritual. At times a friend was granted Euthanasia, and left his or her room for the Homelessness that is beyond all human conception. Vashti did not much mind. After an unsuccessful lecture, she would sometimes ask for Euthanasia herself. But the death-rate was not permitted to exceed the birth-rate, and the Machine had hitherto refused it to her.

The troubles began quietly, long before she was conscious of them.

One day she was astonished at receiving a message from her son. They never communicated, having nothing in common, and she had only heard indirectly that he was still alive, and had been transferred from the northern hemisphere, where he had behaved so mischievously, to the southern—indeed, to a room not far from her own.

"Does he want me to visit him?" she thought. "Never again, never. And I have not the time."

No, it was madness of another kind.

He refused to visualize his face upon the blue plate, and speaking out of the darkness with solemnity said:

"The Machine stops."

"What do you say?"

"The Machine is stopping, I know it, I know the signs."

She burst into a peal of laughter. He heard her and was angry, and they spoke no more.

"Can you imagine anything more absurd?" she cried to a friend. "A man who was my son believes that the Machine is stopping. It would be impious if it was not mad."

"The Machine is stopping?" her friend replied. "What does that mean? The phrase conveys nothing to me."

"Nor to me."

"He does not refer, I suppose, to the trouble there has been lately with the music?"

"Oh, no, of course not. Let us talk about music."

"Have you complained to the authorities?"

"Yes, and they say it wants mending, and referred me to the Committee of the Mending Apparatus. I complained of those curious gasping sighs that disfigure the symphonies of the Brisbane school. They sound like some one in pain. The Committee of the Mending Apparatus say that it shall be remedied shortly."

Obscurely worried, she resumed her life. For one thing, the defect in the music irritated her. For another thing, she could not forget Kuno's speech. If he had known that the music was out of repair—he could not know it, for he detested music—if he had known that it was wrong, "the Machine stops" was exactly the venomous sort of remark he would have made. Of course he had made it at a venture, but the coincidence annoyed her, and she spoke with some petulance to the Committee of the Mending Apparatus.

They replied, as before, that the defect would be set right shortly.

"Shortly! At once!" she retorted. "Why should I be worried by imperfect music? Things are always put right at once. If you do not mend it at once, I shall complain to the Central Committee."

"No personal complaints are received by the Central Committee," the Committee of the Mending Apparatus replied.

"Through whom am I to make my complaint, then?"

"Through us."

"I complain then."

"Your complaint shall be forwarded in its turn."

" Have others complained?"

This question was unmechanical, and the Committee of the Mending Apparatus refused to answer it.

"It is too bad!" she exclaimed to another of her friends. "There never was such an unfortunate woman as myself. I can never be sure of my music now. It gets worse and worse each time I summon it."

"I too have my troubles," the friend replied. "Sometimes my ideas are interrupted by a slight jarring noise."

"What is it?"

"I do not know whether it is inside my head, or inside the wall."

"Complain, in either case."

"I have complained, and my complaint will be forwarded in its turn to the Central Committee."

Time passed, and they resented the defects no longer. The defects had not been remedied, but the human tissues in that latter day had become so subservient, that they readily adapted themselves to every caprice of the Machine. The sigh at the crisis of the Brisbane symphony no longer irritated Vashti; she accepted it as part of the melody. The jarring noise, whether in the head or in the wall, was no longer resented by her friend. And so with the mouldy artificial fruit, so with the bath water that began to stink, so with the defective rhymes that the poetry machine had taken to emit. All were bitterly complained of at first, and then acquiesced in and forgotten. Things went from bad to worse unchallenged.

It was otherwise with the failure of the sleeping apparatus. That was a more serious stoppage. There came a day when over the whole world—in Sumatra, in Wessex, in the innumerable cities of Courland and Brazil—the beds, when summoned by their tired owners, failed to appear. It may seem a ludicrous matter, but from it we may date the collapse of humanity. The Committee responsible for the failure was assailed by complainants, whom it referred, as usual, to the Committee of the Mending Apparatus, who in its turn assured them that their complaints would be forwarded to the Central Committee. But the discontent grew, for mankind was not yet sufficiently adaptable to do without sleeping.

"Some one is meddling with the Machine—" they began.

"Some one is trying to make himself king, to reintroduce the personal element."

"Punish that man with Homelessness."

"To the rescue! Avenge the Machine! Avenge the Machine!"

"War! Kill the man!"

But the Committee of the Mending Apparatus now came forward, and allayed the panic with well-chosen words. It confessed that the Mending Apparatus was itself in need of repair.

The effect of this frank confession was admirable.

"Of course," said a famous lecturer—he of the French Revolution, who gilded each new decay with splendour—"of course we shall not press our complaints now. The Mending Apparatus has treated us so well in the past that we all sympathize with it, and will wait patiently for its recovery. In its own good time it will resume its duties. Meanwhile let us do without our beds, our tabloids, our other little wants. Such, I feel sure, would be the wish of the Machine."

Thousands of miles away his audience applauded. The Machine still linked them. Under the seas, beneath the roots of the mountains, ran the wires through which they saw and heard, the enormous eyes and ears that were their heritage, and the hum of many workings clothed their thoughts in one garment of subserviency. Only the old and the sick remained ungrateful, for it was rumoured that Euthanasia, too, was out of order, and that pain had reappeared among men.

It became difficult to read. A blight entered the atmosphere and dulled its luminosity. At times Vashti could scarcely see across her room. The air, too, was foul. Loud were the complaints, impotent the remedies, heroic the tone of the lecturer as he cried: "Courage, courage! What matter so long as the Machine goes on? To it the darkness and the light are one." And though things improved again after a time, the old brilliancy was never recaptured, and humanity never recovered from its entrance into twilight. There was an hysterical talk of "measures," of "provisional dictatorship," and the inhabitants of Sumatra were asked to familiarize themselves with the workings of the central power station, the said power station being situated in France. But for the most part panic reigned, and men spent their strength praying to their Books, tangible proofs of the Machine's omnipotence. There were gradations of terror—at times came rumours of hope—the Mending Apparatus was almost mended—the enemies of the Machine had been got under—new "nerve-centres" were evolving which would do the work even more magnificently than before. But there came a day when, without the slightest warning, without any previous hint of feebleness, the entire communication-system broke down, all over the world, and the world, as they understood it, ended.

Vashti was lecturing at the time and her earlier remarks had been punctuated with applause. As she proceeded the audience became silent, and at the conclusion there was no sound. Somewhat displeased, she called to a friend who was a specialist in sympathy. No sound: doubtless the friend was sleeping. And so with the next friend whom she tried to summon, and so with the next, until she remembered Kuno's cryptic remark, "The Machine stops."

The phrase still conveyed nothing. If Eternity was stopping it would of course be set going shortly.

For example, there was still a little light and air—the atmosphere had improved a few hours previously. There was still the Book, and while there was the Book there was security.

Then she broke down, for with the cessation of activity came an unexpected terror—silence.

She had never known silence, and the coming of it nearly killed her—it did kill many thousands of people outright. Ever since her birth she had been surrounded by the steady hum. It was to the ear what artificial air was to the lungs, and agonizing pains shot across her head. And scarcely knowing what she did, she stumbled forward and pressed the unfamiliar button, the one that opened the door of her cell.

Now the door of the cell worked on a simple hinge of its own. It was not connected with the central power station, dying far away in France. It opened, rousing immoderate hopes in Vashti, for she thought that the Machine had been mended. It opened, and she saw the dim tunnel that curved far away towards freedom. One look, and then she shrank back. For the tunnel was full of people—she was almost the last in that city to have taken alarm.

People at any time repelled her, and these were nightmares from her worst dreams. People were crawling about, people were screaming, whimpering, gasping for breath, touching each other, vanishing in the dark, and ever and anon being pushed off the platform on to the live rail. Some were fighting round the electric bells, trying to summon trains which could not be summoned. Others were yelling for Euthanasia or for respirators, or blaspheming the Machine. Others stood at the doors of their cells fearing, like herself, either to stop in them or to leave them. And behind all the uproar was silence—the silence which is the voice of the earth and of the generations who have gone.

No—it was worse than solitude. She closed the door again and sat down to wait for the end. The disintegration went on, accompanied by horrible cracks and rumbling. The valves that restrained the Medical Apparatus must have been weakened, for it ruptured and hung hideously from the ceiling. The floor heaved and fell and flung her from her chair. A tube oozed towards her serpent fashion. And at last the final horror approached—light began to ebb, and she knew that civilisation's long day was closing.

She whirled round, praying to be saved from this, at any rate, kissing the Book, pressing button after button. The uproar outside was increasing, and even penetrated the wall. Slowly the brilliancy of her cell was dimmed, the reflections faded from her metal switches. Now she could not see the reading-stand, now not the Book, though she held it in her hand. Light followed the flight of sound, air was following light, and the original void returned to the cavern from which it had been so long excluded. Vashti continued to whirl, like the devotees of an earlier religion, screaming, praying, striking at the buttons with bleeding hands.

It was thus that she opened her prison and escaped—escaped in the spirit: at least so it seems to me, ere my meditation closes. That she escaped in the body—I cannot perceive that. She struck, by chance, the switch that released the door, and the rush of foul air on her skin, the loud throbbing whispers in her ears, told her that she was facing the tunnel again, and that tremendous platform on which she had seen men fighting. They were not fighting now. Only the whispers remained, and the little whimpering groans. They were dying by hundreds out in the dark.

She burst into tears.

Tears answered her.

They wept for humanity, those two, not for themselves. They could not bear that this should be the end. Ere silence was completed their hearts were opened, and they knew what had been important on the earth. Man, the flower of all flesh, the noblest of all creatures visible, man who had once made god in his image, and had mirrored his strength on the constellations, beautiful naked man was dying, strangled in the garments that he had woven. Century after century had he toiled, and here was his reward. Truly the garment had seemed heavenly at first, shot with the colours of culture, sewn with the threads of self-denial. And heavenly it had been so long as it was a garment and no more, so long as man could shed it at will and live by the essence that is his soul, and the essence, equally divine, that is his body. The sin against the body—it was for that they wept in chief; the centuries of wrong against the muscles and the nerves, and those five portals by which we can alone apprehend—glozing it over with talk of evolution, until the body was white pap, the home of ideas as colourless, last sloshy stirrings of a spirit that had grasped the stars.

"Where are you?" she sobbed.

His voice in the darkness said, "Here."

"Is there any hope, Kuno?"

"None for us."

"Where are you?"

She crawled towards him over the bodies of the dead. His blood spurted over her hands.

"Quicker," he gasped, "I am dying—but we touch, we talk, not through the Machine.

He kissed her.

"We have come back to our own. We die, but we have recaptured life, as it was in Wessex, when Ælfrid overthrew the Danes. We know what they know outside, they who dwelt in the cloud that is the colour of a pearl."

"But, Kuno, is it true? Are there still men on the surface of the earth? Is this—this tunnel, this poisoned darkness—really not the end?"

He replied:

"I have seen them, spoken to them, loved them. They are hiding in the mist and the ferns until our civilisation stops. Today they are the Homeless—tomorrow—"

"Oh, tomorrow—some fool will start the Machine again, tomorrow."

"Never," said Kuno, "never. Humanity has learnt its lesson."

As he spoke, the whole city was broken like a honeycomb. An air-ship had sailed in through the vomitory into a ruined wharf. It crashed downwards, exploding as it went, rending gallery after gallery with its wings of steel. For a moment they saw the nations of the dead, and, before they joined them, scraps of the untainted sky.

15 Population, Roles, and Civilization

If an aggregate of people has a minimal social organization, it is possible to imagine a state of affairs in which each unit—for example, a small family or an individual—is self-sufficient in that if all other units were to disappear, life style would be relatively unchanged. The less units depend upon one another, the less a single unit is disrupted if all the others disappear. Insofar as the division of labor exists such that each unit is responsible for a certain subset of the activities necessary to sustain the aggregate, a potential for disruption exists. If even a small proportion of the population were eliminated, those remaining would have to make major adjustments. The advantages of organizing an aggregate of individuals in an interdependent manner are, however, substantially greater than the advantages of a system in which each unit provides itself with all the commodities necessary to its existence. The advantages of basing a social organization on the division of labor lie primarily in the greater efficiency with which each essential task can be carried out by specialists in that job.

A relationship probably exists between a society's level of technological sophistication, the diversity and number of specialized roles that must be performed at that level of development, and the size of the population. As long as a society requires men of certain intellectual abilities and special skills to fill the roles that maintain it at a given technical level, it will require a population of some minimum size in order to produce people with the intellectual ability necessary to complete training for these roles. The size of the minimum population base might be affected in several ways. If, for example, automation or reliance on devices such as computers made it possible to reduce the number of necessary roles, then a smaller population could provide the required number of talented people. An engineer who has access to a computer can probably accomplish as much as five engineers who don't have computers. If the average level of ability in a society could be raised, or available talent used more efficiently, then a smaller population could provide the persons required to maintain a given level of technology.

If we accept the premise that a relationship exists between the technological level, the diversity and number of required roles, and the population size, we may pose some questions: What are the effects of having a population base larger than is required to maintain a certain level of technology? What are the effects of having a population base that is too small to produce the people necessary to fill the required roles? In the first case, society can support activities that will change the technological level at which it operates. If a population produces more talented people than are required to maintain its industry, it is possible for the excess talent to be used to generate innovations in technology or to conduct research in new areas. (This assumes that the technological level of the society is high enough to support its population base. It is easy to imagine societies in which the population is so large and growing so rapidly, and technological levels are so low, that there are more than enough talented people to fill specialized technical roles, but where relatively few such positions exist and talented people must do less challenging work simply to support themselves.)

If the opposite were to occur—that is, if a society were to produce too few talented people to support its technology—what would be the effect? This is the central issue of the novel, *Earth Abides,* by George R. Stewart. In the situation Stewart proposes, the bulk of the earth's human population is killed by a virus sometime between 1940 and 1950. Stewart chronicles the life of a man, Isherwood Williams, who is a student at the University of California at Berkeley when the virus strikes. One of the few who recover from the disease, Williams returns to his family home in the Berkeley hills.

Earth Abides

George R. Stewart

The next morning he settled down to establish his life. Food, he knew already, was no problem at all. In the nearest business district he began looking into store-windows. Rats and mice were making a mess of everything, and the floors were littered with gnawed cartons and spilled food. Through one window, however, he was startled to see the gaily colored piles of fruit and vegetables as fresh and lovely as ever. He stared incredulously, peering through the dust-coated glass. Then, first with irritation and then with amusement, he realized that the bright colors were merely from the papier-mâche oranges, apples, tomatoes, and avacados which the store in the old days had used for a permanent front-window display.

After a while he saw through the windows a grocery which was unlittered. Apparently it must be rodent-proof. Carefully jimmying a window, he got into the store.

The bread was inedible, and weevils were at work even in some of the carefully sealed boxes of crackers. But the dried fruit and everything inside of tin and glass was as good as ever. As he was picking out some cans of olives, he heard an electric motor start; curiously, he opened the refrigerator, and found that the butter was still perfectly preserved. Next he investigated the deep-freeze units, and found fresh meat, frozen vegetables, ice-cream, and even materials for a green salad. When he left with his loot, he closed the window carefully behind him, to keep at least that one store free of rats.

After he had returned to the house, he reflected upon his position again, and decided that as yet the mere maintenance of life would be easy, indefinitely. Food, clothing—the shops were full, and he had only to help himself! Water still gushed from the faucets at full pressure. Gas had failed, and if it had been a country of bitterly cold winters, he might have had to consider laying in some kind of fuel supply. But his gasoline stove served excellently for cooking; if the fireplace was not sufficient in the winter, he could round up a battery of such stoves and supply himself with all the heat he needed. In fact, he soon began to feel so pleasantly self-sufficient that he feared he was turning into a hermit.

One evening shortly afterward, he sat reading, and after a while began to feel hungry. He went to the kitchen, and rummaged in the refrigerator for some cheese. Happening to glance at the electric clock, he was surprised to see that the time was only nine-thirty-seven. He had thought it was later. On his way back to the living-room he took a bite of the cheese, and glanced at his wrist-watch. The watch-hands stood at ten-nine, and he knew that he had set the watch by the clock within twenty-four hours.

"That old clock's going to pieces at last," he thought. "Not surprising!" he remembered how the motion of its hands had startled him when he had first returned to the house.

He sat down to read again. A high wind from the north with the heavy smell of smoke in it blew so hard that it rattled the windows occasionally. By now he was used to the smell of smoke, and did not think about it. At many times he could not even get a good view because of the smoke of the burning forests. After a while he blinked his eyes a little and stared more intently at the page where the letters seemed to have grown strangely indistinct. "This smoke must be making my eyes water," he thought. "I don't seem to see so well." But as he looked closer, it seemed that not only the page before him but the whole room had grown dimmer. With a sudden start he looked at the electric-light bulb in the bridge lamp beside him.

Then quickly, with a jumping heart, he was out of his chair and standing on the front porch looking out over the broad stretches of the city below him. The lights were still burning along the streets. The chains of yellow beads still showed on the great bridge, and at the tops of the towers the red lights were flashing. He looked more carefully. The lights seemed a little dimmer than they should be, but he could be imagining that, or they might be obscured by all the drifting smoke. He went back and sat in his chair again and tried to read, forgetting about it—forgetting what he feared.

But he blinked—and again! Looking at the light beside him, he was puzzled. Then suddenly he remembered the clock!

"Well," he thought, "it had to come!"

His watch now showed ten-fifty-two. He went out to the kitchen, and saw that the clock was at ten-fourteen. He calculated apprehensively. The result was bad. As closely as he could remember, the clock had lost six minutes in about three-quarters of an hour.

The clock was run, he knew, by electrical impulses which were ordinarily timed at sixty to the minute. Now they must be coming less often. An electrical engineer would doubtless have found it an elementary matter to calculate just how much less often. Ish could even have made an attempt at the calculation himself, but he saw no use in it, and he felt suddenly downcast. In any case, once the Power-and-Light system had started to go to pieces, the rate of decline would undoubtedly be progressively faster.

Back in the living-room, he could scarcely doubt now that the light had faded still more. Deep shadows seemed to have moved out from behind the chairs in the corners of the room.

"The lights are going out! The lights of the world!" he thought, and he felt like a child going alone into the dark. . . .

He stood on the porch again. Minute by minute the long chains of street-lights grew less and less luminous, more and more yellow. The high wind, he thought, must be helping, blowing down a power-line here, weakening a switch connection there. The fire too was sweeping across the forested ridges unchecked by men, burning power-lines, perhaps, even power-houses.

After a while the lights seemed to fade no further, but to remain at a constant dimness. He went in again, and pulling another bridge-lamp to the side of his chair, he was able to read comfortably with two lights instead of one. . . . By now it was late, but he did not want to go to sleep. He felt as if he were sitting up by the death-bed of his most treasured and oldest friend. He remembered those great words "Let there be light, and there was light." This seemed the other end of that story.

After a while he went to look at the clock again, and saw that it had stopped with the hands symmetrically upward—at eleven-five.

His watch showed him that by now it was well after midnight. The lights might still continue many hours, or even might burn dimly for days. Yet he did not want to go to bed.

A deep shiver shook him, but he stilled his panic. After all, he thought, the great system of Power-and-Light had held up for an amazingly long time, all its automatic processes functioning though the men were gone. He thought clear back to that first day when he had come down out of the mountains not yet even knowing what had happened. Then he had passed the powerhouse, and felt the reassurance that everything must still be normal because he saw the water pouring out from the tailraces and heard the dim continuous hum of the generators. He felt again a curious touch of local pride in thinking of it. Perhaps no system had lasted so long. These might well be the last electric lights to be left burning in the world, and when they faded, the lights would be out for a long, long time.

No longer sleepy, he sat there, feeling that he should not go to sleep, wishing at least that the end would come quickly and with dignity and not be dragged out too long. Again, he felt the light fading, and he thought. "This is the end!" But still it lingered, the filaments now only a cherry-red.

And then again they faded. As a sled on a hillside, slowly first, then gaining momentum. Just for a moment, he thought (or imagined), they flared more brightly—and then they were gone.

He went outside. "Perhaps," he thought, "that was just the failure of some local line." But he was really sure that it had not been. He peered through the darkness, all the thicker for the smoke that was heavy in the air, changing the moon into an orange ball. He could see no light—not along the streets, nor anywhere on the bridge. This, then, was the end. "Let there be *no* light, and *there was no light!*"

"No use being melodramatic!" he thought. Going inside, he stumbled around until he had found the drawer where his mother kept candles. Putting one into a candlestick, he sat again by its feeble but steady and continuing light. Nevertheless he continued to feel a little shaken.

The next day he went out to see what was happening, still thinking of the drama he was prepared to watch. Not so much had occurred, it seemed at first. But after a while he began to notice things. On San Lupo Drive a drain-pipe had plugged with the washing in of all the unswept leaves that lay in the gutter. After the drain-pipe had plugged the water had swirled across the street to the downhill side and flooded over the curb. The stream of water had worked its way across the tangle of tall grass which had been the Harts' lawn, and seeped under the door. Their floors and rugs must be soaked, and slimy with mud. Below the house the water had broken out, and run through the rose-garden, leaving a small gully behind it, at last disappearing into the drainage of a storm-sewer on the street below. It was just a little matter, and yet it showed what must be happening all over the country.

Men had built roads and drains and walls and thousands of other obstructions to the natural flow of water. These could survive and function only because men were constantly at hand to repair and clean the thousands of little breaks and blockages which showed up at every change of the weather. Ish himself could have cleaned out that clogged drain in two minutes by merely scraping the leaves back from the grating where they had plugged it. But he saw no point to stretching out his hand. There were thousands, millions, of spots where the same thing must be happening. The roads and the drains and the walls had been constructed only for man's convenience, and now that man was gone there was no need of them. The water might just as well follow its natural courses, and cut back, through the rose garden. Soaked and muddy, the Harts' rugs would begin to rot where they lay. No matter! To think of that as something bad, was merely to think in terms of what had once been and no longer existed. . . .

In the spring of the second year. Ish planted his first garden. He had never liked gardening, and that probably explained why, in spite of good resolutions and two half-hearted attempts, he had not grown anything during the first year. Nevertheless, as he turned over the dark moist soil with the spade, he felt a deep satisfaction at being in touch again with primeval things.

That was about all the satisfaction he got from the garden. To begin with, the seed (he had had a hard time to find any at all because of the ravages of the rats) was several years old, and much of it failed to sprout. Snails and slugs soon moved in, but by scattering a box of Snale-Killa he eliminated them, and felt triumphant. Then, just as the lettuce was making a good growth, a buck jumped the fence and wrought havoc. Ish put another layer on the top of the fence. Next, some rabbits burrowed beneath—more destruction, and more work! One evening he heard crashing noises and rushed out just in time to scare off a predatory cow on the point of smashing a way through the fence. More work!

By this time he was waking up at night with thoughts of ravening deer, rabbits, and cattle prowling around his fence and ogling his lettuces with eyes that gleamed like tigers' eyes.

Then, in June, the insects arrived. He sprayed poison until he was afraid he would not dare eat the lettuce even if any lived to be harvested.

The crows were the last to find the garden, but when they arrived in July their numbers made up for their late arrival. He stood guard, and shot some of them. But they seemed to post sentries and swoop down as soon as his back was turned, and he could not watch during all the daylight hours. His scarecrows and dangling mirrors kept them off for a day, but after that they lost their fear.

In the end he actually erected a shelter of fly-screen over the few rows of garden which seemed worth saving, and he harvested a little lettuce, along with some scrawny tomatoes and onions. But he conscientiously let some of the plants go to seed, and saved the fresh seed for the future.

He was as thoroughly discouraged as any amateur gardener had ever been. It was one thing apparently to grow vegetables when thousands of others were doing the same, and quite another when yours was the only plot and so from miles around every vegetable hungry animal and bird and mollusk and insect came galloping or flying or oozing or hopping, and apparently sending out by signals to its fellows the universal shout, "Let's eat!"

What aspects of a society can be maintained when its population is reduced beyond the point at which it is possible to fill the roles necessary to carry on the present form of its division of labor? If a population were reduced as much as Stewart reduces the population of the earth, the most likely outcome would certainly be rapid deterioration of technologically based civilizations as we know them, the development of social systems appropriate to the size, particular talents, and abilities of available populations, and adjustment to the environment in which each aggregate of individuals found itself.

In Stewart's account of the deterioration of American society, Williams and a few other survivors band together and found a small community. Since their community is located in the San Francisco Bay area, they face no severe problems with their environment and are able to survive quite easily on the remnants of their civilization. In some respects, the ease with which they are able to maintain themselves discourages any attempt to reestablish control over their immediate physical environment beyond making minor repairs to their shelters. There are no apparently vital and difficult skills that their children must acquire before the last *civilized* generation dies. Most of the members of the community, the "Tribe," see no need even to try to pass on the knowledge on which their civilization depended, or at least they do not seem overconcerned with this question. Their behavior seems quite appropriate to the individuals with whom Stewart populates the community. They are a reasonable sample of the population of the society they have outlived, and their lack of concern about transmitting the knowledge on which their society depended is understandable. Each had only the most rudimentary understanding of a small proportion of that knowledge, and no real understanding of how much their world had been based on science and technology.

Williams is the one exception. He understands the need and potential advantage to future generations of preserving the ability to read and some idea of what the dead civilization might offer to anyone who took the trouble to look. The following excerpt begins just after Williams has realized that the school he has attempted to start for the children of the Tribe has failed. He is discouraged in part because one of his sons, Joey, has recently died. Joey was clearly the brightest of the Tribe's children and seemed to have a genuine interest in learning.

As Ish had expected, they did nothing. Weeks passed. There was no heaving and grunting of men as they carried the refrigerator up the hill, no click and crunch of spades preparing a garden plot. Ish worried occasionally, but in general life drifted along, and even he could not be much concerned. With his old student's habit of observing even when he did not participate, he often wondered just what might be happening.

Was it really, as he sometimes imagined, that all the individuals were still suffering under a kind of shock as the result of the sudden destruction of their old society? His studies in anthropology supplied him with examples—the head-hunters and the plains Indians, who had lost the will to readjust and even the will to live, after their traditional way of life had rudely been made impossible. If they could no longer go head-hunting or ride out to steal horses and take scalps, they had no desire for anything else either. Or, with a mild climate and food-supplies easy to obtain, was there now simply no stimulus to change? He could recollect possible examples of this kind also—some of the South Sea islanders, or those tropical peoples who lived chiefly on bananas. Or was it something else?

Fortunately, he had enough background of philosophy and history to keep his perspective. He was actually, he realized, struggling to solve a problem which had baffled philosophers from the time when they had first become conscious of problems at all. He was facing the basic question of the dynamics of society. What made a society change? He, as a student, was more fortunate than Koheleth or Plato or Malthus or Toynbee. He saw a society reduced in size until it had attained the simplicity of a laboratory experiment.

Yet, whenever he had arrived at this stage of argument, another thought cut across the disturbed the simplicity. He began to feel himself less scientific but more human, to think more nearly as Em thought. This society along San Lupo Drive was not really a philosopher's neat microcosm, a small dip out of the general ocean of humanity. No—it was a group of individuals. It was Ezra and Em and the boys—yes, and Joey! Change the individuals, and the whole situation changed. Change even one individual!

But in one detail Ish thought that Em was wrong. She did not need to fear that he was worrying too much about the situation and would end up with ulcers or a neurosis. Instead, his observation of what was happening kept him interested in life. At first, just after the Great Disaster, he had devoted himself to observing the changes in the world as the result of the disappearance of man. After twenty-one years, however, the world had fairly well adjusted itself, and further changes were too slow to call for day-to-day or even month-to-month observation. Now, however, the problem of society—its adjustment and reconstituition—had moved to the fore, and become his chief interest.

In any case, he could not help wondering what would happen to The Tribe in the years that were ahead. It worried him. After the Great Disaster, he had thought that the people, if any survived at all, would soon be able to get some things running again and proceed gradually toward re-establishing more and more of civilization. He had even dreamed of a time when electric lights might go on again. But nothing like that had happened, and the community was still dependent upon the leavings of the past.

Now he looked around, as he had often looked before, at the ones who were with him. They were, so to speak, the bricks out of which a new civilization must be fashioned. . . .

Sitting there, on the Library steps, pounding the chip of granite into smaller and smaller grains, he began now to have what seemed a little clearer vision of the future. It was all tied up in that same old question. How much did man strike outward to affect all his surroundings and how much did the surroundings press in upon him? Did the Napoleonic age produce Napoleon or did *he* produce *it?* So, even if Joey had lived, the welter of circumstances, the circumstances that made Jack and Roger and Ralph, would probably have affected Joey too, and one small boy was not much to set up against all of that. Yes, even if Joey had lived, things would probably have continued to move in the way they already seemed to be moving. Now that Joey was dead, it was certain—certain, that is, as far as anyone could reasonably expect, granting always some unforeseeable accident.

The stars in their courses! (The chip of granite was nothing but powder under the blows of the hammer.) *The stars in their courses!* No, he did not believe in astrology, and yet the shifting of the stars showed that the solar system too was changing, and that the earth itself was becoming a more or a less habitable place for man. Thus, at some profounder depth of reality, astrology might be right, and the changes in the sky could be taken as symbol of all the grinding wheels of circumstance. *The stars in their courses!* What was man, little man, to withstand them?

Yes, the future was certain. The Tribe was not going to restore civilization. It did not want civilization. For a while the scavenging would go on—this opening of cans, this expending of cartridges and matches stored up from the past, all this uncreative but happy manner of life. Then at last, sooner or later, there would be more and more people, and the supplies would fail. There would perhaps be no quick catastrophe because many cattle could be had for the taking, and life would go on.

So, he thought, and then a new idea came to him with a sudden impact. Even though cattle were left, though there was much food, what would happen when the ammunition for the rifles was exhausted? When the matches were gone? In fact, one might not even have to wait until the ammunition was exhausted. Powder deteriorated with time. Three or four generations, and all who were left might be merely some groveling primitives who had lost civilization and yet, on the other hand, had not learned all those thousand basic skills which enabled savages to live with some degree of stability and comfort! Possibly, indeed—and perhaps this would be best—in three or four generations the race would not be able to survive at all, would not be able to make the transition between the scavenging, uncreative life, and some new level of life at which they could remain permanently, or from which they could once more begin a slow advance.

Again he pounded heavily on the edge of the step. Another chunk of granite fell off. He looked at it gloomily. He had just decided not to worry, and here he was, hard at it again. What could he know about what would be happening three or four generations from now?

He got up and started to walk home. He was quieter now.

"Yes," he thought, again shaping words, "a leopard can't change its spots, and I'll always be a worrier, even though I've lived with Em for twenty-two years. I look before and after. Relax! Yes, I should relax a little. What I have been trying to do—that has failed. I"ll admit it. Just the same, I'm certain I'll never stop trying a little. Now, perhaps, if I try for something less, I may in the end attain something more."

By the time he had finished the long walk up the hill to the houses, his vague plans had shaped themselves, but he would have to wait until morning to begin.

That night, however, an autumn storm began, and he awoke in the morning to a world of low-lying cloud and steady dropping. He felt surprise, for with all the recent troubles he had failed to realize that time was slipping away. Now, however, when he thought of the matter, he remembered that the sun had been setting well toward the south and that the month, if one could still think in such terms, would be November. The rain interfered with the immediate fulfillment of his plans, but there was plenty of time, and he could mature his ideas with thought.

So completely had his attitudes changed within the last day that the sounds of the assembling children, that morning, came to him as a shock. "Of course!" he thought. "They are expecting to have school again."

He went downstairs to meet with them. They were all there—all except Joey, and two younger ones. He looked into their faces, as they sat on chairs wriggling, or squatted more comfortably on the floor. They were looking back at him, he imagined, with more alertness than usual. Joey was gone, and they must be wondering how this would affect school. Yet the change, he knew, must be only temporary, and behind this alertness must lurk still that basic lack of interest against which he had already struggled.

He let his glance run over the little group, pausing individually upon each face. They were fine children, not really stupid, but they lacked the flair. No, there was not one!

He made his decision, and he felt no pain in it.

"School is dismissed," he said.

There was a momentary look almost as of consternation in all the faces, and then he saw that they were suddenly pleased, although they were making some effort not to show their pleasure.

"School is dismissed!" he repeated, feeling that he was being dramatic about it in spite of himself. "There will be no more school—ever!"

Again he saw a look of consternation come into the faces, and this time no pleasure showed afterwards. They stirred uneasily in their seats. Some of them got up to go. But they knew that something had happened, something deeper than their minds could grasp.

They went out slowly and quietly. During as much as a minute after they had gone out into the dripping of the rain, there was silence. Then he heard them suddenly shout, and they were children again. School had been a passing incident. Probably they would never think of it again; certainly they would never regret it. For a moment Ish felt a heaviness within him. "Joey, Joey!" he thought. But he had no regret for what he had just done, and he knew that he had made the right decision. "School is dismissed!" he thought. "School dismissed!" And he remembered suddenly that he had sat in this same room many years before, and watched the electric lights fade out.

Three days of rain gave him plenty of time to think things over and mature all his plans. At last a morning dawned with blue sky and a chilly wind from the north. The sun came out, the vegetation dried. Now was the time.

He hunted through the deserted and overgrown gardens. This had never been an area where citrus fruits were grown commercially, but lemons had produced well enough, and here and there someone had nursed a lemon tree in his garden. That wood, he remembered, was suitable. Of course he could have read any number of books, but his approach had changed. He would read no books on this matter. He could do well enough by himself.

Two blocks up the street there had once been a large and showy garden. There he found a lemon tree. It was still living, although nearly crowded out by the growth of two pines. Moreover, it had suffered badly in a frost of some years previous. Never having been pruned after the frost, the tree was only a wreck of itself. Long suckers had shot up from its base after the frost, and some of these again had died.

Avoiding the long thorns, Ish pressed his way into the tangle, found a suitable shoot, and took out his pocket-knife. The shoot at its base was nearly as big as his thumb. The dead lemon wood was almost as hard as bone, but after a while he whittled it through with his knife and pulled it out from the tangle. The shoot was seven feet long, straight for four feet before other branches had begun to interfere and it had grown crooked. At his shaking, it was stiff, but when he leaned against it, it bent and straightened sharply as he released the pressure. It would suffice.

"Yes," he thought a little bitterly, "it will be good enough for all my needs."

He carried the lemon-shoot back to the house, and sat on the porch, in the sun, whittling. first he cut off the crooked end of the shoot so that he had four feet of straight wood remaining.

Then he stripped off the dead bark, and began to taper the shoot at both ends. The work was very slow, and he paused frequently to sharpen the knife on a whetstone. The white tough-grained wood seemed to turn the edge after only a few strokes.

Walt and Josey had been off playing with the other children, but at lunch-time they came back.

"What are you doing?" Josey asked him.

"I'm getting ready to play a game," Ish answered her. He would not make the mistake, he had decided, of trying to tie this up with anything practical, as he had with the school. Here he would try to harness that love of play which seemed so deep-seated in the human race.

After lunch the children must have carried the word around. In the afternoon George came over.

"Why don't you come to my place," George said, "and use a vise and my spoke-shave? You could work a lot faster."

Ish thanked him, but continued to work with the knife, even though his hand was getting sore. Nevertheless he thought that he would do all this work with the simplest implements.

By the end of the afternoon his hand was beginning to blister where he held the knife, but he judged that the work was done. A four-foot length of the lemon-shoot was now symmetrically tapered toward both ends. He set one end of it against the ground, pressed it to a half circle, and felt it spring back sharply into straightness. Satisfied, he cut notches close to each end, and gladly put the knife away.

The next morning he continued the work. There was plenty of stout string available, and he considered taking some nylon fish line and braiding it into the proper size.

"No," he thought. "I'll work from things they can always get for themselves."

He found the skin of a recently killed calf. From it he cut a long throng of rawhide. The work went slowly, but he had plenty of time. He shaved the hair from the strip, and shaved the strip itself until it was no larger than a small cord. Then he braided three strips together to make a heavy cord, and estimating the proper length, he tied each end into a little loop.

He held the lemon-shoot in one hand and the braided thong in the other, and looked at them. Either by itself amounted to little. Then, bending the shoot, he hooked the loops of the thong into the notches at the ends of the shoot, and the two became one. Since the thong was shorter, the tapered shoot now bent in a clean symmetrical arc. The thong itself cut straight across between the points of the arc. Stick and cord, joined, had suddenly become something new.

He looked at the bow, and knew that creative force had again returned to the world. He could have gone to any sporting-goods store, and picked out a much better bow—a six-foot toy for archery. But he had not done so. He had made himself a bow from the wood itself carved with the simplest of implements, and a string from the hide of a new-killed calf.

He plucked at the thong. It scarcely twanged, but it gave forth a satisfactory dull throbbing vibration. He considered that his work for the day was finished. He unstrung the bow.

The next day, for an arrow, he cut himself a straight branch of a pine tree. The soft green wood cut easily, and he had shaped the arrow and notched it in half an hour. When he had finished it, he called for the children. Walt and Josey came, and Weston with them.

"Let's see how she works," Ish said.

He drew the arrow back, and loosed it. Unfeathered, it flew with a wobbly flight, but he had pointed it at a high angle, and it covered fifty feet before it struck, by chance, pointing upward from the ground.

Instantly he knew that he had won success. The three children had never seen anything like this before, and they stood wide-eyed for a moment. Then with shouts they broke into a run, and went to retrieve the arrow. Ish shot it for them, again and again.

At last came the inevitable request for which Ish had been waiting.

"Let me try it, Daddy," said Walt.

Walt's first shot wobbled a bare twenty feet, but he was pleased. Then Josey tried it, and then Weston.

Before dinner-time, every child in The Tribe was busy at work whittling on a bow of his own.

Everything worked even better than Ish had dared to hope. Within a week the air around the houses seemed to be full of badly shot arrows. Mothers began to worry about lost eyesight, and two children came in crying after having received arrows in various parts of their anatomies. But since the arrows were headless and shot from weak bows, no real harm resulted.

Rules had to be established. "You mustn't shoot in the direction of anyone." "You mustn't shoot close to the houses."

Competition developed. Having learned the trick from the older boys who shot from rifles, children began to hold contests against a mark. They experimented with different lengths and types of bows. When Josey complained that Walt always beat her at shooting, Ish subtly made the suggestion that she might try fixing some quail pinions to the butt-end of her arrow. She did so, and beat Walt, and then suddenly all the arrows had quail pinions at one end, and they were flying farther and truer. Even the older boys became interested, and some of them made bows although they were allowed to use rifles. But archery still continued to flourish chiefly among the ones who were too young for rifles.

Ish bided his time. The early rains had sprouted the grass seed, and now the land was green. At evening the sun set behind the hills to the south of the Golden Gate.

Walt and Weston, the twelve-year-olds, were now deep in some kind of boyish plot. They worked hard with bows and arrows, shaping and perfecting them. They were gone long hours during the day.

Then one day toward evening Ish heard the sound of excited boys' feet running up the steps outside. Walt and Weston burst into the room.

"Look, Daddy," Walt cried, and he held up for Ish the pathetic-looking body of a big rabbit pierced through the side with a headless wooden arrow.

"Look!" Walt cried again. "I hid behind a bush, and waited till he hopped up close to me, and then I shot him right through."

Ish, as he looked, felt a sympathy and pity for the poor dangling body, even though he knew that it was a symbol of his own triumph. Too bad, he thought, that even creation must make use of death also.

"That's fine!" he said. "That's fine, Walt! That was a good shot!"

One day, so suddenly that you might almost say just at that particular moment it happened, the children became tired of playing with bows and arrows, and went off on some new enthusiasm. Ish did not worry. He knew that after the ways of children they would come back again, perhaps at the same time of year. The making of bows and the shooting of arrows would not be forgotten. During twenty years, during one hundred years if need were, the bow might remain a children's plaything. In the end, after the ammunition had failed, it would still be there. It was the greatest weapon that primitive man had ever known and the most difficult to invent. If he had saved that for the future, he had saved much. After the rifles were useless, his great-grandchildren would not have to meet the bear's rush empty-handed or starve in the midst of the cattle herds. His great-grandchildren would never know civilization, but at least they would not be groveling half-apes, but would walk erect as freemen, bow in hand. Even if they should no longer have metal knives, they could still scrape out bows with sharp stones. . . .

Sometime after the year 43:

Ish looked up, he saw, very clearly, a young man standing in front of him. The young man wore a neat-enough pair of blue jeans with copper rivets shining brightly, and yet over his shoulders he wore a tawny hide with sharp claws dangling from it. In his hand he held a strong bow, and over his shoulder was a quiver with the feathered ends of arrows sticking from it.

Ish blinked, for in his old eyes the sunshine was strong.

"Who are you?" said Ish.

The young man answered respectfully, "I am Jack, Ish, as indeed you yourself well know."

The way he said "Ish" did not indicate that he was trying to be unduly familiar with an old man, thus calling him by a nickname, but rather it carried something of great respect and even of awe, and as if "Ish" stood for much more than merely the name of an old man.

But Ish himself was confused, and he squinted, peering more carefully, because at short distances he no longer saw clearly. But he was sure that Jack should have dark hair, or perhaps turned somewhat gray by now, and this one who called himself Jack had long wavy yellow hair.

"You should not make jokes with an old man," said Ish. "Jack is my oldest son, and I would recognize him. He has dark hair, and he is older than you."

The young man laughed, but politely, and said, "You are talking, Ish, of my grandfather, as indeed you yourself well know." Again the way in which he said "Ish" had a certain strange sound to it, and now Ish noticed also the strangeness of his other repeated words, "as indeed you yourself well know."

Then, as Ish still looked, he was puzzled that the young man, who was certainly not a child, was carrying a bow instead of a rifle.

"Why do you not have a rifle?" he asked.

"Rifles are good for playthings!" the young man said, and he laughed, a little scornfully perhaps. "You cannot be sure of a rifle, as indeed you yourself, Ish, well know. Sometimes the rifle works, and it makes the big noise, but other times you pull the trigger, and it only goes 'click'." Here he snapped his fingers. "So you cannot use the rifles for real hunting, although the older men say that this was not so in the long past years. But now we use the arrow because it is sure, and never refuses to fly and besides," here the young man held himself proudly, "besides, it is a matter of strength and skill to shoot with the bow—but anyone, they say, could shoot with a rifle, as you yourself, Ish, well know."

"Let me see an arrow," said Ish.

The young man took an arrow from the quiver, and looked at it, and then handed it across.

"That is a good arrow," he said. "I made it myself."

Ish looked at the arrow and felt the weight of it. This was no plaything for a child. The shaft was nearly a yard long, split cleanly from a billet of flawless straight-grained wood, and then rounded and smoothed. It was well feathered, with pinions of some kind, although Ish could not see well enough to know what bird had yielded the feathers. By feeling, however, he could tell that they were arranged carefully so that the arrow in flight would spin like a rifle-bullet, and thus keep its true course and carry farther.

Then he observed the arrowhead, again more by feel than by sight. The arrowhead was very sharp both at the point and along the edges. Ish nearly pricked his thumb. It had the bumpy yet slick feel which told him that it was of hammered metal. Though he could not see very clearly, he made the color out as silvery-white.

"What is *that* made of?" he asked.

"It is from one of the little round things. They have faces on them. The old men have a name for them, but I do not remember exactly. It is something like *corns*."

The young man paused, as if to be told the right word, but when he had no reply, he went on again, being obviously eager to show off his knowledge about arrowheads.

"We find these little round things in the old buildings. Often there are many—many—of them in the boxes and drawers. Sometimes they are rolled up together in bundles like short round sticks, but heavier than sticks. Some are red and some are white, like this one, and there are two kinds of the white. The one kind of white—the one that has the picture of the hump-backed bull—we do not use those because they are harder to pound."

Ish considered, and thought that he understood.

"And this white one here?" he asked. "Was there a relief—a picture—on this one?"

The young man took the arrow from Ish, and looked at it, and then handed it back.

"They all have pictures," he said. "But I was looking to see if I could still make out what picture was on this one. It has not quite all gone because of the hammering. This was one of the littlest ones, and it had the picture of the woman with the wings growing out of her head. Some of them have pictures of hawks— but not real hawks." The young man was talking very happily. "Others have men; at least, they look like men—one with a beard, and one with long hair hanging behind him and another with a strong-looking face, without a beard and with short hair, and heavy-jawed."

"And who—who do you think—were all these men?"

The young man glanced both ways, as if a little nervous.

"These—oh, these—yes! These, we think—as you yourself, Ish, well know—these were the Old Ones that were before our Old Ones!"

When there was no thunder from heaven and when the young man could see that Ish was not displeased, he went on:

"Yes, that must be it—as you yourself, Ish, well know. These men, and the hawks, and the bull! Perhaps the woman with the wings growing from her head sprang from the marriage of a hawk and a woman. But, however it is, they do not seem to mind our taking their pictures and hammering them up for arrowheads. I have wondered about it. Perhaps they are too great to care about little things, or perhaps they did their work a long time ago and have now grown old and weak."

He stopped talking, but Ish could see that he was pleased with himself, and liked to talk, and was thinking quickly of something more to say. He, at least, had imagination.

"Yes," the young man continued, "I have an idea. Our Old Ones—they were the Americans— made the houses and the bridges and the little round things that we hammer out for arrowheads. But those others—the Old Ones of the Old Ones—perhaps they made the hills and the sun, and the Americans themselves."

Then, though it was a cheap trick to play on the young man, Ish could not resist talking in double meaning.

"Yes," he said, "I have heard it said that those older Old Ones produced the Americans— but I rather doubt that they made the hills and the sun."

Though he could not have understood, perhaps the young man caught the irony in the tone, and so said nothing.

"But, go on," Ish continued then. "Tell me more about the arrowheads themselves. I am not interested in your cosmogony." He used the last word in good-humored malice, knowing that the other would not understand it, but would be impressed by its length and strange sound.

"Yes, about the arrowheads," the young man said, hesitating a moment, and then regaining confidence. "We use both the red and white. The red are good for shooting cattle and lions. The white are for deer and other game."

"Why is that?" Ish asked sharply, for he felt his old-time rationalism stirring at the thought of all such magic and hocus-pocus. The question, however, seemed only to surprise and confuse the young man.

"Why?" he asked. "Why? How would anyone know *why?* Except you yourself, Ish! This matter of the red and white arrowheads is merely something that *is*. It is like—" He hesitated, and then the sunlight seemed to catch his attention. "Yes, it is like the sun that keeps on going round the earth, but naturally no one knows why, or asks why. *Why* should there be a *why?*"

Having said these last words, the young man was obviously very pleased with himself as if he had propounded some great philosophical dictum, although undoubtedly he had spoken only in great simplicity. But when Ish turned the matter over in his mind, he was not sure. Perhaps even in this simplicity there was a depth. Was there ever an answer to "why"? Did not things just exist in the present?

Yet, Ish was certain, a fallacy lurked somewhere in the argument. A sense of cause-and-effect was necessary for life at the human level, and this matter of the different-colored arrowheads was a proof of it, not the contrary. Only, the sense of causation here was faulty and irrational. The young man was maintaining an absurdity—that cattle and lions could be better killed with copper arrowheads hammered from pennies, whereas deer were better killed with silver ones hammered from dimes or quarters. Yet there could obviously not be enough difference in hardness or sharpness to matter. Only, in these primitive minds, the secondary matter of color had in some way come to be considered—this was rank superstition!—the determining factor.

Deep within him, Ish again felt his old hatred of loose thinking boil up. Though he was an old man, still he might do something.

"*No!*" he said, so sharply that the young man started. "*No!* That is not right. The white arrowheads and the red! One just as well as. . . ."

Then, slowly his voice trailed off. No, he thought, that was not the way it was destined to be. He heard a rich contralto voice saying to him, "Relax!" Perhaps he might persuade this young man named Jack, who was undoubtedly a remarkably intelligent and imaginative young man, possibly even somewhat like that little one named Joey. But what would it accomplish? Only, perhaps to make the young man confused and ill at ease among all the others. And what was really the difference? At least, copper arrowheads were not *less* effective against lions, and if the bowmen thought them *more* effective, the thought gave him courage and steadied his hand.

So Ish said nothing more about the matter, and smiled at the young man reassuringly, and looked again at the arrow.

Another thought came to him, and he asked: "Can you always find plenty of those little round things?"

The young man laughed merrily, as if this were a strange question.

"Oh, yes," he said. "There are so many that if all of us spent all our time pounding out arrowheads, still we should never run short."

Ish considered. Yes, that was probably true. Even if there were a hundred men in The Tribe by now, there must be thousands and thousands of coins to be found in tills and cash-boxes, even in this one corner of the city. And if the coins should be exhausted, there would be thousands of miles of copper telephone wire. When he had first made an arrow, he recollected, he had imagined that The Tribe would revert to stone arrow-heads. Instead they had taken a shortcut, and were already fashioning metal. So perhaps The Tribe, his own descendants, had already passed the turning-point, were no longer forgetting more old things than they were learning new things, and were no longer sinking toward savagery, but were maintaining a stable level or perhaps gradually beginning to win new security. By showing them how to make bows, he had helped, and he felt greatly comforted.

Then, having finished looking at the arrow, Ish handed it back. "It seems to be a very good arrow," he said, although he did not really know much about arrows.

Nevertheless the young man smiled with great happiness at this praise of his arrow, and Ish noted that he made a mark on it before he put it back into the quiver, as if he wished to know it and distinguish it from other arrows after what had happened. Then, as he still looked at the young man, Ish felt a sudden great love for him, and he had not been so moved for a long time since he had been sitting as an old man on the hillside. This Jack, must be Ish's great-grandson in the male line, and he was also Em's great-grandson. So, as Ish looked, his heart yearned outwards, and he asked a strange question:

"Young man," he said, "are you happy?" The young man named Jack look startled at this question, and he glanced in both directions before answering, and then he spoke.

"Yes, I am happy. Things are as they are, and I am part of them."

Ish began to think of what this might mean and to wonder again whether the words had been spoken only in simplicity or whether there was some deep philosophy behind them, but he could not decide. At his trying to think, the fog seemed again to move in at the corners of his brain. But still he recollected vaguely that the words—strange as they were—had a ring of familiarity about them. He had not perhaps ever heard those exact words before, but they were words that someone whom he had once known might well have spoken. For in his words the young man had not questioned, but had accepted. Ish could not recall this person exactly, but he remembered softness and warmth, and warm feelings flowed through him.

When he came out of his reverie and looked up again, no one was standing in front of him. In fact, Ish would have been unable to say surely whether the young man named Jack had been there that same day, or whether this was now some other day, or perhaps even another summer.

16 On the Final Solution to the Question of Sexist Institutions

In the literature of science fiction there are several somewhat similar examples of solutions to problems of a certain type of intergroup conflict. The type of intergroup conflict is one in which there is a history of hostility between two groups so old that its initial cause has been forgotten but which continues because members of the two groups define one another as enemies and build institutional arrangements which systematically advantage one group and disadvantage the other. Typically, the groups are different in religion, race, ethnicity, planet of origin, human or robot status, etc. The solution that is frequently considered is one in which the differentiating factor suddenly vanishes and all humans have a green skin color; or perfect segregation occurs through Black migration to the planet Mars; or some variant on human form is found in which the differentiating characteristic is missing (as in Ursala Leguin's *Left Hand of Darkness* in which human-like creatures have mating periods during which they are capable of taking on the sex characteristics of either gender).

John Wyndham's story *Consider Her Ways* is an example of this type of science fiction speculation. It should not in any sense be considered a *modest proposal* for a solution to the problem of oppression of women either by individual men or by men taken as a class. The reason I urge the story be considered as an exercise in thinking about alternative arrangements rather than as a prescription for a realistic strategy is that I find the scenario personally distasteful. Wyndham's characters argue, however, that it is a quite satisfactory solution and perhaps one of the few, or even, the only possible solution. I leave it to you to decide how pleasant or unpleasant you find the state of affairs Wyndham postulates.

One of the most intriguing aspects of this story is that it is written by a man and is concerned with the workings and ideology of a society controlled by women. Wyndham puts himself in the position of arguing the case against men from a woman's point of view. He also takes on the task of describing the manner in which women would behave in a male-free environment. On both these counts, Wyndham's piece is an interesting document as well as an interesting story. The elements of Wyndham's story are of two distinct types. The first concerns the history of the oppression of women by men and the cause of it in modern times. This sets the conditions which determine the response to changes that permit women to control society. The second element of the story is the structure of the society that Wyndham credits women with developing.

Both of these elements, as presented in the story, become good points against which to consider alternative theories and projections. For example, the argument advanced for the position of women in pre-holocaust modern times is that they are valuable as consumers and social arrangements are designed to keep them as such. While there is a certain logic to this position, it might be interesting to consider the arguments leading to an opposite social response made by Michael Young in *Rise of Meritocracy* (chapter 5). Here are clearly two contrasting exercises in social analysis that are worth comparing, since the theories developed by each author can be applied to the case of women. Both arguments are reasonable in that they make no assumptions about the nature of social organization that are patently absurd. The two arguments are particularly interesting in that they are in essential agreement about the variable that determines the direction in which society will move. Wyndham pictures women's position as being due to their value as consumers. Young would attribute changes in their social position as due to their potential contribution as producers. In both cases it is economic value that is assumed to be the primary variable. As my freshman English teacher would have said, "compare and contrast these arguments."

The second element of Wyndham's story concerns what women might do given a certain set of social conditions that offer them the power to take control. This is simply an exercise in speculation that is interesting because the speculation is complicated and is based upon certain assumptions about the "nature" of the female of the human species. It might be interesting to seek to identify the assumptions upon which the post-holocaust world is created and analyze the extent to which you agree or disagree about the viability of these assumptions. It might also be interesting to consider the extent to which Wyndham displays a male bias in the assumptions he makes about this woman's world and discuss with someone of a gender different than your own the extent to which he or she shares your perceptions.

Consider Her Ways

JOHN WYNDHAM

There was nothing but myself.

I hung in a timeless, spaceless, forceless void that was neither light, nor dark. I had entity, but no form; awareness, but no senses; mind, but no memory. I wondered, is this—this nothingness—my soul? And it seemed that I had wondered that always, and should go on wondering it for ever. . . .

But, somehow, timelessness ceased. I became aware that there was a force: that I was being moved, and that spacelessness had, therefore, ceased, too. There was nothing to show that I moved; I knew simply that I was being drawn. I felt happy because I knew there was something or someone to whom I wanted to be drawn. I had no other wish than to turn like a compass-needle and then fall through the void. . . .

But I was disappointed. No smooth, swift fall followed. Instead, other forces fastened on me. I was pulled this way, and then that. I did not know how I knew it; there was no outside reference, no fixed point, no direction even; yet I could feel that I was tugged hither and thither, as though against the resistance of some inner gyroscope. It was as if one force were in command of me for a time, only to weaken and lose me to a new force. Then I would seem to slide towards some unknown point, until I was arrested, and diverted upon another course. I wafted this way and that, with the sense of awareness continually growing firmer; and I wondered whether rival forces were fighting for me, good and evil, perhaps, or life and death. . . .

The sense of pulling back and forth became more definite until I was almost jerked from one course to another. Then, abruptly, the feeling of struggle finished. I had a sense of travelling faster and faster still, plunging like a wandering meteorite that had been trapped at last. . . .

"All right," said a voice. "Resuscitation was a little retarded, for some reason. Better make a note of that on her card. What's the number? Oh, only her fourth time. Yes, certainly make a note. It's all right. Here she comes.'"

It was a woman's voice speaking, with a slightly unfamiliar accent. The surface I was lying on shook under me. I opened my eyes, saw the ceiling moving along above me, and let them close. Presently, another voice, again with an unfamiliar intonation, spoke to me:

"Drink this," she said.

A hand lifted my head, and a cup was pressed against my lips. After I had drunk the stuff I lay back with my eyes closed again. I dozed for a little while, and came out of it feeling stronger. For some minutes I lay looking up at the ceiling and wondering vaguely where I was. I could not recall any ceiling that was painted just this pinkish shade of cream. Then, suddenly, while I was still gazing up at the ceiling, I was shocked, just as if something had hit my mind a sharp blow. I was frighteningly aware that it was not just the pinkish ceiling that was *unfamiliar*—everything was unfamiliar. Where there should have been memories there was just a great gap. I had no idea who I was, or where I was; I could recall nothing of how or why I came to be here. . . .In a rush of panic I tried to sit up, but a hand pressed me back, and presently held the cup to my lips again.

"You're quite all right. Just relax," the same voice told me, reassuringly.

I wanted to ask questions, but somehow I felt immensely weary, and everything was too much trouble. The first rush of panic subsided, leaving me lethargic. I wondered what had happened to me—had I been in an accident, perhaps? Was this the kind of thing that happened when one was badly shocked? I did not know, and now for the moment I did not care: I was being looked after. I felt so drowsy that the questions could wait.

I suppose I dozed, and it may have been for a few minutes, or for an hour. I know only that when I opened my eyes again I felt calmer—more puzzled than alarmed—and I lay for a time without moving. I had recovered enough grasp now to console myself with the thought that if there had been an accident, at least there was no pain.

Presently I gained a little more energy, and, with it, curiosity to know where I was. I rolled my head on the pillow to see more of the surroundings.

A few feet away I saw a contrivance on wheels, something between a bed and a trolley. On it, asleep with her mouth open, was the most enormous woman I had ever seen. I stared, wondering whether it was some kind of cage over her to take the weight of the covers that gave her the mountainous look, but the movement of her breathing soon showed me that it was not. Then I looked beyond her and saw two more trolleys, both supporting equally enormous women.

I studied the nearest one more closely, and discovered to my surprise that she was quite young—not more than twenty-two, or twenty-three, I guessed. Her face was a little plump, perhaps, but by no means over-fat; indeed, with her fresh, healthy young colouring and her short-cropped gold curls, she was quite pretty. I fell to wondering what curious disorder of the glands could cause such a degree of anomaly at her age.

Ten minutes or so passed, and there was a sound of brisk, business-like footsteps approaching. A voice inquired:

"How are you feeling now?"

I rolled my head to the other side, and found myself looking into a face almost level with my own. For a moment I thought its owner must be a child, then I saw that the features under the white cap were certainly not less than thirty years old. Without waiting for a reply she reached under the bedclothes and took my pulse. Its rate appeared to satisfy her, for she nodded confidently.

"You'll be all right now, Mother," she told me.

I stared at her, blankly.

"The car's only just outside the door there. Do you think you can walk it?" she went on.

Bemusedly, I asked:

"What car?"

"Why, to take you home, of course," she said, with professional patience. "Come along now." And she pulled away the bedclothes.

I started to move, and looked down. What I saw there held me fixed. I lifted my arm. It was like nothing so much as a plump, white bolster with a ridiculous little hand attached at the end. I stared at it in horror. Then I heard a far-off scream as I fainted. . . .

When I opened my eyes again there was a woman—a normal-sized woman—in a white overall with a stethoscope round her neck, frowning at me in perplexity. The white-capped woman I had taken for a child stood beside her, reaching only a little above her elbow.

"—I don't know, Doctor," she was saying. "She just suddenly screamed and fainted."

"What is it? What's happened to me? I know I'm not like this—I'm not, I'm not," I said, and I could hear my own voice wailing the words.

The doctor went on looking puzzled.

"What does she mean?" she asked.

"I've no idea, Doctor," said the small one. "It was quite sudden, as if she'd had some kind of shock—but I don't know why."

"Well, she's been passed and signed-off, and, anyway, she can't stay here. We need the room," said the doctor. "I'd better give her a sedative."

"But what's happened? Who am I? There's something terribly wrong. I know I'm not like this. P-please t-tell me—" I implored her, and then somehow lost myself in a stammer and a muddle.

The doctor's manner became soothing. She laid a hand gently on my shoulder.

"That's all right, Mother. There's nothing to worry about. Just take things quietly. We'll soon have you back home."

Another white-capped assistant, no taller than the first, hurried up with a syringe, and handed it to the doctor.

"No." I protested. "I want to know where I am. Who am I? Who are you? What's happened to me?" I tried to slap the syringe out of her hand, but both the small assistants flung themselves on my arm, and held on to it while she pressed in the needle.

It was a sedative, all right. It did not put me out, but it detached me. An odd feeling: I seemed to be floating a few feet outside myself and considering me with an unnatural calmness. I was able, or felt that I was able, to evaluate matters with intelligent clarity. Evidently I was suffering from amnesia. A shock of some kind had caused me to 'lose my memory', as it is often put. Obviously it was only a very small part of my memory that had gone—just the personal part—who I was, what I was, where I lived—all the mechanism for day-to-day getting along seemed to be intact: I'd not forgotten how to talk, or how to think, and I seemed to have quite a well-stored mind to think with.

On the other hand there was a nagging conviction that everything about me was somehow wrong. I *knew,* somehow, that I'd never before seen the place I was in; I *knew,* too, that there was something queer about the presence of the two small nurses; above all, I *knew,* with absolute certainty, that this massive form lying here was not mine. I could not recall what face I ought to see in a mirror, not even whether it would be dark or fair, or old or young, but there was no shadow of doubt in my mind that, whatever it was like, it had never topped such a shape as I had now.

—And there were the other enormous young women, too. Obviously, it could not be a matter of glandular disorder in all of us, or there'd not be this talk of sending me 'home', wherever that might be. . . .

I was still arguing the situation with myself in, thanks no doubt to the sedative, a most reasonable-seeming manner, though without making any progress at all, when the ceiling above my head began to move again, and I realized I was being wheeled along. Doors opened at the end of the room, and the trolley tilted a little beneath me as we went down a gentle ramp beyond.

At the foot of the ramp, an ambulance-like car, with pink coachwork polished until it gleamed, was waiting with the rear doors open. I observed interestedly that I was playing a part in a routine procedure. A team of eight diminutive attendants carried out the task of transferring me from the trolley to a sprung couch in the ambulance as if it were a kind of drill. Two of them lingered after the rest to tuck in my coverings and place another pillow behind my head. Then they got out, closing the doors behind them, and in a minute or two we started off.

It was at this point—and possibly the sedative helped in this, too—that I began to have an increasing sense of balance and a feeling that I was perceiving the situation. Probably there *had* been an accident, as I had suspected, but obviously my error, and the chief cause of my alarm, proceeded from my assumption that I was a stage further on than I actually was. I had assumed that after an interval I had recovered consciousness in these baffling circumstances, whereas the true state of affairs must clearly be that I had *not* recovered consciousness. I must be still in a suspended state, very likely with concussion, and this was a dream, or hallucination. Presently, I should wake up in conditions that would at least be sensible, if not necessarily familiar.

I wondered now that this consoling and stabilizing thought had not occurred to me before, and decided that it was the alarming sense of detailed reality that had thrown me into panic. It had been astonishingly stupid of me to be taken in to the extent of imagining that I really was a kind of Gulliver among rather over-size Lilliputians. It was quite characteristic of most dreams, too, that I should lack a clear knowledge of my identity, so we did not need to be surprised at that. The thing to do was to take an intelligent interest in all I observed: the whole thing must be chockful of symbolic content which it would be most interesting to work out later.

The discovery quite altered my attitude and I looked about me with a new attention. It struck me as odd right away that here was so much circumstantial detail, and all of it in focus—there was none of that sense of foreground in sharp relief against a muzzy, or even non-existent, background that one usually meets in a dream. Everything was presented with a most convincing, three-dimensional solidity. My own sensations, too, seemed perfectly valid. The injection, in particular, had been quite acutely authentic. The illusion of reality fascinated me into taking mental notes with some care.

The interior of the van, or ambulance, or whatever it was, was finished in the same shell-pink as the outside—except for the roof, which was powder-blue with a scatter of small silver stars. Against the front partition were mounted several cupboards, with plated handles. My couch, or stretcher, lay along the left side: on the other were two fixed seats, rather small, and upholstered in a semi-glazed material to match the colour of the rest. Two long windows on each side left little solid wall. Each of them was provided with curtains of a fine net, gathered back now in pink braid loops, and had a roller blind furled above it. Simply by turning my head on the pillow I was able to observe the passing scenery—though somewhat jerkily, for either the springing of the vehicle scarcely matched its appointments, or the road surface was bad: whichever the cause, I was glad my own couch was independently and quite comfortably sprung.

The external view did not offer a great deal of variety save in its hues. Our way was lined by buildings standing back behind some twenty yards of tidy lawn. Each block was three storeys high, about fifty yards long, and had a tiled roof of somewhat low pitch, suggesting a vaguely Italian influence. Structurally the blocks appeared identical, but each was differently coloured, with contrasting window-frames and doors, and carefully considered, uniform curtains. I could see no one behind the windows; indeed there appeared to be no one about at all except here and there a woman in overalls mowing a lawn, or tending one of the inset flower-beds.

Further back from the road, perhaps two hundred yards away, stood larger, taller, more utilitarian-looking blocks, some of them with high, factory-type chimneys. I thought they might actually be factories of some kind, but at the distance, and because I had no more than fugitive views of them between the foreground blocks, I could not be sure.

The road itself seldom ran straight for more than a hundred yards at a stretch, and its windings made one wonder whether the buildings had not been more concerned to follow a contour line than a direction. There was little other traffic, and what there was consisted of lorries, large or small, mostly large. They were painted in one primary colour or other, with only a five-fold combination of letters and figures on their sides for further identification. In design they might have been any lorries anywhere.

We continued this uneventful progress at a modest pace for some twenty minutes, until we came to a stretch where the road was under repair. The car slowed, and the workers moved to one side, out of our way. As we crawled forward over the broken surface I was able to get a good look at them. They were all women or girls dressed in denim-like trousers, sleeveless singlets and working boots. All had their hair cut quite short, and a few wore hats. They were tall and broad-shouldered, bronzed and healthy-looking. The biceps of their arms were like a man's, and the hafts of their picks and shovels rested in the hard, strong hands of manual toilers.

They watched with concern as the car edged its way on to the rough patch, but when it drew level with them they transferred their attention, and jostled and craned to look inside at me.

They smiled widely, showing strong white teeth in their browned faces. All of them raised their right hands, making some sign to me, still smiling. Their goodwill was so evident that I smiled back. They walked along, keeping pace with the crawling car, looking at me expectantly while their smiles faded into puzzlement. They were saying something but I could not hear the words. Some of them insistently repeated the sign. Their disappointed look made it clear that I was expected to respond with more than a smile. The only way that occurred to me was to raise my own right hand in imitation of their gesture. It was at least a qualified success; their faces brightened though a rather puzzled look remained. Then the car lurched on to the made-up road again and their still somewhat troubled faces slid back as we speeded up to our former sedate pace. More dream symbols, of course—but certainly not one of the stock symbols from the book. What on earth, I wondered, could a party of friendly Amazons, equipped with navvying implements instead of bows, stand for in my subconscious? Something frustrated, I imagined. A suppressed desire to dominate? I did not seem to be getting much further along that line when we passed the last of the variegated but nevertheless monotonous blocks, and ran into open country.

The flower-beds had shown me already that it was spring, and now I was able to look on healthy pastures, and neat arable fields already touched with green; there was a haze-like green smoke along the trim hedges, and some of the trees in the tidily placed spinneys were in young leaf. The sun was shining with a bright benignity upon the most precise countryside I had ever seen; only the cattle dotted about the fields introduced a slight disorder into the careful dispositions. The farmhouses themselves were part of the pattern; hollow squares of neat buildings with an acre or so of vegetable garden on one side, an orchard on another, and a rickyard on a third. There was a suggestion of a doll's landscape about it—Grandma Moses, but tidied up and rationalized. I could see no random cottages, casually sited sheds, or unplanned outgrowths from the farm buildings. And what, I asked myself, should we conclude from this rather pathological exhibition of tidiness? That I was a more uncertain person than I had supposed, one who was subconsciously yearning for simplicity and security? Well, well. . . .

An open lorry which must have been travelling ahead of us turned off down a lane bordered by beautifully laid hedges, towards one of the farms. There were half a dozen young women in it, holding implements of some kind; Amazons, again. One of them, looking back, drew the attention of the rest to us. They raised their hands in the same sign that the others had made, and then waved cheerfully. I waved back.

Rather bewildering, I thought: Amazons for domination and this landscape for passive security: the two did not seem to tie up very well.

We trundled on, at our unambitious pace of twenty miles an hour or so, for what I guessed to be three-quarters of an hour, with the prospect changing very little. The country undulated gently and appeared to continue like that to the foot of a line of low, blue hills many miles away. The tidy farmhouses went by with almost the regularity of milestones, though with something like twice the frequency. Occasionally there were working-parties in the fields; more rarely, one saw individuals busy about the farms, and others hoeing with tractors, but they were all too far off for me to make out any details. Presently, however, came a change.

Off to the left of the road, stretching back at right-angles to it for more than a mile, appeared a row of trees. At first I thought it just a wood, but then I noticed that the trunks were evenly spaced, and the trees themselves topped and pruned until they gave more the impression of a high fence.

The end of it came to within twenty feet of the road, where it turned, and we ran along beside it for almost half a mile until the car slowed, turned to the left and stopped in front of a pair of tall gates. There were a couple of toots on the horn.

The gates were ornamental, and possibly of wrought iron under their pink paint. The archway that they barred was stucco-covered, and painted the same colour.

Why, I inquired of myself, this prevalence of pink, which I regard as a namby-pamby colour, anyway? Flesh-colour? Symbolic of an ardency for the flesh which I had insufficiently gratified? I scarcely thought so. Not pink. Surely a burning red. . . . I don't think I know anyone who can be really ardent in a pink way. . . .

While we waited, a feeling that there was something wrong with the gatehouse grew upon me. The structure was a single-storey building, standing against the left, inner side of the archway, and coloured to match it. The woodwork was pale blue, and there were white net curtains at the windows. The door opened, and a middle-aged woman in a white blouse-and-trouser suit came out. She was bare-headed, with a few grey locks in her short, dark hair. Seeing me, she raised her hand in the same sign the Amazons had used, though perfunctorily, and walked over to open the gates. It was only as she pushed them back to admit us that I suddenly saw how small she was—certainly not over four feet tall. And that explained what was wrong with the gatehouse: it was built entirely to her scale. . . .

I went on staring at her and her little house as we passed. Well, what about that? Mythology is rich in gnomes and 'little people', and they are fairly pervasive of dreams, too. Somebody, I was sure, must have decided that they are a standard symbol of something, but for the moment I did not recall what it was. Would it be repressed philoprogenitiveness, or was that too unsubtle? I stowed that away, too, for later contemplation and brought my attention back to the surroundings.

We were on our way, unhurriedly, along something more like a drive than a road, with surroundings that suggested a compromise between a public garden and a municipal housing estate. There were wide lawns of an unblemished velvet green, set here and there with flower-beds, delicate groups of silver birch, and occasional larger, single trees. Among them stood pink, three-storey blocks, dotted about, seemingly to no particular plan.

A couple of the Amazon-types in singlets and trousers of a faded rust-red were engaged in planting-out a bed close beside the drive, and we had to pause while they dragged their handcart full of tulips on to the grass to let us pass. They gave me the usual salute and amiable grin as we went by.

A moment later I had a feeling that something had gone wrong with my sight, but as we passed one block we came in sight of another. It was white instead of pink, but otherwise exactly similar to the rest—except that it was scaled down by at least one-third. . . .

I blinked at it and stared hard, but it continued to seem just the same size.

A little further on, a grotesquely huge woman in pink draperies was walking slowly and heavily across a lawn. She was accompanied by three of the small, white-suited women looking, in contrast, like children, or very animated dolls: one was involuntarily reminded of tugs fussing round a liner.

I began to feel swamped: the proliferation and combination of symbols was getting well out of my class.

The car forked to the right, and presently we drew up before a flight of steps leading to one of the pink buildings—a normal-sized building, but still not free from oddity, for the steps were divided by a central balustrade; those to the left of it were normal, those to right, smaller and more numerous.

Three toots on the horn announced our arrival. In about ten seconds half a dozen small women appeared in the doorway and came running down the right-hand side of the steps. A door slammed as the driver got out and went to meet them. When she came into my range of view I saw that she was one of the little ones, too, but not in white as the rest were; she wore a shining pink suit like a livery that exactly matched the car.

They had a word together before they came round to open the door behind me, then a voice said brightly:

"Welcome, Mother Orchis. Welcome home."

The couch or stretcher slid back on runners, and between them they lowered it to the ground. One young woman whose blouse was badged with a pink St. Andrew's cross on the left breast leaned over me. She inquired considerately:

"Do you think you can walk, Mother?"

It did not seem the moment to inquire into the form of address. I was obviously the only possible target for the question.

"Walk?" I repeated. "Of course I can walk." And I sat up, with about eight hands assisting me.

'Of course' had been an overstatement. I realized that by the time I had been heaved to my feet. Even with all the help that was going on around me it was an exertion which brought on heavy breathing. I looked down at the monstrous form that billowed under my pink draperies, with a sick revulsion and a feeling that, whatever this particular mass of symbolism disguised, it was likely to prove a distasteful revelation later on. I tried a step. 'Walk' was scarcely the word for my progress. It felt like, and must have looked like, a slow series of forward surges. The women, at little more than my elbow height, fluttered about me like a flock of anxious hens. Once started, I was determined to go on, and I progressed with a kind of wave-motion, first across a few yards of gravel, and then, with ponderous deliberation, up the left-hand side of the steps.

There was a perceptible sense of relief and triumph all round as I reached the summit. We paused there a few moments for me to regain my breath, then we moved on into the building. A corridor led straight ahead, with three or four closed doors on each side; at the end it branched right and left. We took the left arm, and, at the end of it, I came face to face, for the first time since the hallucination had set in, with a mirror.

It took every volt of my resolution not to panic again at what I saw in it. The first few seconds of my stare were spent in fighting down a leaping hysteria.

In front of me stood an outrageous travesty, an elephantine female form, looking the more huge for its pink swathings. Mercifully, they covered everything but the head and hands, but these exposures were themselves another kind of shock, for the hands, though soft and dimpled and looking utterly out of proportion, were not uncomely, and the head and face were those of a girl.

She was pretty, too. She could not have been more than twenty-one, if that. Her curling fair hair was touched with auburn lights, and cut in a kind of bob. The complexion of her face was pink and cream, her mouth was gentle, and red without any artifice. She looked back at me, and at the little women anxiously clustering round me, from a pair of blue-green eyes beneath lightly arched brows. And this delicate face, this little Fragonard, was set upon that monstrous body: no less outrageously might a blossom of freesia sprout from a turnip.

When I moved my lips, hers moved; when I bent my arm, hers bent; and yet, once I got the better of that threatening panic, she ceased to be a reflection. She was nothing like me, so she must be a stranger whom I was observing, though in a most bewildering way. My panic and revulsion gave way to sadness, an aching pity for her. I could weep for the shame of it. I did. I watched the tears brim on her lower lids; mistily, I saw them overflow.

One of the little women beside me caught hold of my hand.

"Mother Orchis, dear, what's the matter?" she asked, full of concern.

I could not tell her: I had no clear idea myself. The image in the mirror shook her head, with tears running down her cheeks. Small hands patted me here and there, small, soothing voices encouraged me onward. The next door was opened for me and, amid concerned fussing, I was led into the room beyond.

We entered a place that struck me as a cross between a boudoir and a ward. The boudoir impression was sustained by a great deal of pink—in the carpet, coverlets, cushions, lampshades, and filmy window curtains; the ward motif, by an array of six divans, or couches, one of which was unoccupied.

It was a large enough room for three couches, separated by a chest, a chair and table for each, to be arranged on each side without an effect of crowding, and the open space in the middle was still big enough to contain several expansive easy chairs and a central table bearing an intricate flower-arrangement. A not displeasing scent faintly pervaded the place, and from somewhere came the subdued sound of a string quartette in a sentimental mood. Five of the bed-couches were already mountainously occupied. Two of my attendant party detached themselves and hurried ahead to turn back the pink satin cover on the sixth.

Faces from all the five other beds were turned towards me. Three of them smiling in welcome, the other two less committal.

"Hallo, Orchis," one of them greeted me in a friendly tone. Then, with a touch of concern, she added: "What's the matter, dear? Did you have a bad time?"

I looked at her. She had a kindly, plumply pretty face, framed by light brown hair as she lay back against a cushion. The face looked about twenty-three or twenty-four years old. The rest of her was a huge mound of pink satin. I couldn't make any reply, but I did my best to return her smile as we passed.

Our convoy hove-to by the empty bed. After some preparation and positioning I was helped into it by all hands, and a cushion was arranged behind my head.

The exertion of my journey from the car had been considerable, and I was thankful to relax. While two of the little women pulled up the coverlet and arranged it over me, another produced a handkerchief and dabbed gently at my cheeks. She encouraged me:

"There you are, dear. Safely home again now. You'll be quite all right when you've rested a bit. Just try to sleep for a little."

"What's the matter with her?" inquired a forthright voice from one of the other beds. "Did she make a mess of it?"

The little woman with the handkerchief—she was the one who wore the St. Andrew's cross and appeared to be in charge of the operation—turned her head sharply.

"There's no need for that tone, Mother Hazel. Of course Mother Orchis had four beautiful babies—didn't you dear?" she added to me. "She's just a bit tired after the journey, that's all."

"H'mph," said the girl addressed, in an unaccommodating tone, but she made no further comment.

A degree of fussing continued. Presently the small woman handed me a glass of something that looked like water, but had unsuspected strength. I spluttered a little at the first taste, but quickly felt the better for it. After a little more tidying and ordering my retinue departed, leaving me propped against my cushion, with the eyes of the five other monstrous women dwelling upon me speculatively.

An awkward silence was broken by the girl who had greeted me as I came in.

"Where did they send you for your holiday, Orchis?"

"Holiday?" I asked blankly.

She and the rest stared at me in astonishment.

"I don't know what you're talking about," I told them.

They went on staring, stupidly, stolidly.

"It can't have been much of a holiday," observed one, obviously puzzled. "I'll not forget my last one. They sent me to the sea, and gave me a little car so that I could get about everywhere. Everybody was lovely to us, and there were only six Mothers there, including me. Did you go by the sea, or in the mountains?"

They were determined to be inquisitive, and one would have to make some answer sooner or later. I chose what seemed the simplest way out for the moment.

"I can't remember," I said. "I can't remember a thing. I seem to have lost my memory altogether."

That was not very sympathetically received, either.

"Oh," said the one who had been addressed as Hazel, with a degree of satisfaction. "I thought there was something. And I suppose you can't even remember for certain whether your babies were Grade One this time, Orchis?"

"Don't be stupid, Hazel," one of the others told her. "Of course they were Grade One. If they'd not been, Orchis wouldn't be back here now—she'd have been re-rated as a Class Two Mother, and sent to Whitewich." In a more kindly tone she asked me: "When did it happen, Orchis?"

"I—I don't know," I said. "I can't remember anything before this morning at the hospital. It's all gone entirely."

"Hospital!" repeated Hazel, scornfully.

"She must mean the Centre," said the other. "But do you mean to say you can't even remember us, Orchis?"

"No," I admitted, shaking my head. "I'm sorry, but everything before I came round in the Hosp—in the Centre, is all blank."

"That's queer," Hazel said, in an unsympathetic tone. "Do they know?"

One of the others took my part.

"Of course they're bound to know. I expect they don't think that remembering or not has anything to do with having Grade One babies. And why should it, anyway? But look, Orchis—"

"Why not let her rest for a bit," another cut in. "I don't suppose she's feeling too good after the Centre, and the journey, and getting in here. I never do myself. Don't take any notice of them, Orchis, dear. You just go to sleep for a bit. You'll probably find it's all quite all right when you wake up."

I accepted her suggestion gratefully. The whole thing was far too bewildering to cope with at the moment; moreover, I did feel exhausted. I thanked her for her advice, and lay back on my pillow. In so far as the closing of one's eyes can be made ostentatious, I made it so. What was more surprising was that, if one can be said to sleep within an hallucination or a dream, I slept. . . .

In the moment of waking, before opening my eyes, I had a flash of hope that I should find the illusion had spent itself. Unfortunately, it had not. A hand was shaking my shoulder gently, and the first thing I saw was the face of the little women's leader, close to mine.

In the way of nurses she said:

"There, Mother Orchis, dear. You'll be feeling a lot better after that nice sleep, won't you?"

Beyond her, two more of the small women were carrying a short-legged bed-tray towards me. They set it down so that it bridged me and was convenient to reach. I stared at the load on it. It was, with no exception, the most enormous and nourishing meal I had ever seen put before one person. The first sight of it revolted me—but then I became aware of a schism within, for it did not revolt the physical form that I occupied: that, in fact, had a watering mouth, and was eager to begin. An inner part of me marvelled in a kind of semi-detachment while the rest consumed two or three fish, a whole chicken, some slices of meat, a pile of vegetables, fruit hidden under mounds of stiff cream, and more than a quart of milk, without any sense of surfeit. Occasional glances showed me that the other 'Mothers' were dealing just as thoroughly with the contents of their similar trays.

I caught one or two curious looks from them, but they were too seriously occupied to take up their inquisition again at the moment. I wondered how to fend them off later, and it occurred to me that if only I had a book or a magazine I might be able to bury myself effectively, if not very politely, in it.

When the attendants returned, I asked the badged one if she could let me have something to read. The effect of such a simple request was astonishing:

the two who were removing my tray all but dropped it. The one beside me gaped for an amazed moment before she collected her wits. She looked at me, first with suspicion and then with concern.

"Not feeling quite yourself yet, dear?" she suggested.

"But I am," I protested. "I'm quite all right now."

The look of concern persisted, however.

"If I were you I'd try to sleep again," she advised.

"But I don't want to. I'd just like to read quietly," I objected.

She patted my shoulder, a little uncertainly.

"I'm afraid you've had an exhausting time, Mother. Never mind, I'm sure it'll pass quite soon."

I felt impatient. "What's wrong with wanting to read?" I demanded.

She smiled a smug, professional-nurse smile.

"There, there, dear. Just you try to rest a little more. Why, bless me, what on earth would a Mother want with knowing how to read?"

With that she tidied my coverlet, and bustled away, leaving me to the wide-eyed stares of my five companions. Hazel gave a kind of contemptuous snigger; otherwise there was no audible comment for several minutes.

I had reached a stage where the persistence of the hallucination was beginning to wear away my detachment. I could feel that under a little more pressure I should be losing my confidence and starting to doubt its unreality. I did not at all care for its calm continuity: inconsequent exaggerations and jumps, foolish perspectives, indeed, any of the usual dream characteristics would have been reassuring; but, instead, it continued to present obvious nonsense, with an alarming air of conviction and consequence. Effects, for instance, were unmistakably following causes. I began to have an uncomfortable feeling that were one to dig deep enough one might begin to find logical causes for the absurdities, too. The integration was far too good for mental comfort—even the fact that I had enjoyed my meal as if I were fully awake, and was consciously feeling the better for it, encouraged the disturbing quality of reality.

"Read!" Hazel said suddenly, with a scornful laugh. "And write, too, I suppose?"

"Well, why not?" I retorted.

They all gazed at me more attentively than ever, and then exchanged meaning glances among themselves. Two of them smiled at one another. I demanded irritably: "What on earth's wrong with that? Am I supposed not to be able to read or write, or something?"

One said kindly, soothingly:

"Orchis, dear. Don't you think it would be better if you were to ask to see the doctor? Just for a check-up?"

"No," I told her flatly. "There's nothing wrong with me. I'm just trying to understand. I simply ask for a book, and you all look at me as if I were mad. Why?"

After an awkward pause the same one said humouringly, and almost in the words of the little attendant:

"Orchis, dear, do try to pull yourself together. What sort of good would reading and writing be to a Mother? How could they help her to have better babies?"

"There are other things in life besides having babies," I said, shortly.

If they had been surprised before, they were thunderstruck now. Even Hazel seemed bereft of suitable comment. Their idiotic astonishment exasperated me and made me suddenly sick of the whole nonsensical business. Temporarily, I did forget to be the detached observer of a dream.

"Damn it," I broke out. "What is all this rubbish? Orchis! Mother Orchis!—for God's sake! Where am I? Is this some kind of lunatic asylum?"

I stared at them, angrily, loathing the sight of them, wondering if they were all in some spiteful complicity against me. Somehow I was quite convinced in my own mind that whoever, or whatever, I was, I was not a mother. I said so, forcibly, and then, to my annoyance, burst into tears.

For lack of anything else to use, I dabbed at my eyes with my sleeve. When I could see clearly again I found that four of them were looking at me with kindly concern. Hazel, however, was not.

"I said there was something queer about her," she told the others, triumphantly. "She's mad, that's what it is."

The one who had been most kindly disposed before, tried again:

"But, Orchis, *of course* you are a Mother. You're a Class One Mother—with three births registered. Twelve fine Grade One babies, dear. You *can't* have forgotten that!"

For some reason I wept again. I had a feeling that something was trying to break through the blankness in my mind; but I did not know what it was, only that it made me feel intensely miserable.

"Oh, this is cruel, cruel! Why can't I stop it? Why won't it go away and leave me?" I pleaded. "There's a horrible cruel mockery here—but I don't understand it. What's wrong with me? I'm not obsessional—I'm not—I—oh, can't somebody help me . . . ?"

I kept my eyes tight shut for a time, willing with all my mind that the whole hallucination should fade and disappear.

But it did not. When I looked again they were still there, their silly, pretty faces gaping stupidly at me across the revolting mounds of pink satin.

"I'm going to get out of this," I said.

It was a tremendous effort to raise myself to a sitting position. I was aware of the rest watching me, wide-eyed, while I made it. I struggled to get my feet round and over the side of the bed, but they were all tangled in the satin coverlet and I could not reach to free them. It was the true, desperate frustration of a dream. I heard my voice pleading: "Help me! Oh, Donald, darling, please help me. . . ."

And suddenly, as if the word 'Donald' had released a spring, something seemed to click in my head. The shutter in my mind opened, not entirely, but enough to let me know who I was. I understood, suddenly, where the cruelty had lain.

I looked at the others again. They were still staring half-bewildered, half-alarmed. I gave up the attempt to move, and lay back on my pillows again.

"You can't fool me any more," I told them. "I know who I am, now."

"But, Mother Orchis—" one began.

"Stop that," I snapped at her. I seemed to have swung suddenly out of self-pity into a kind of masochistic callousness. "I am *not* a mother," I said harshly. "I am just a woman who, for a short time, had a husband, and who hoped—but only hoped—that she would have babies by him."

A pause followed that; a rather odd pause, where there should have been at least a murmur. What I had said did not seem to have registered. The faces showed no understanding; they were as uncomprehending as dolls'.

Presently, the most friendly one seemed to feel an obligation to break up the silence. With a little vertical crease between her brows: "What," she inquired tentatively, "what is a husband?"

I looked hard from one face to another. There was no trace of guile in any of them; nothing but puzzled speculation such as one sometimes sees in a child's eyes. I felt close to hysteria for a moment; then I took a grip on myself. Very well, then, since the hallucination would not leave me alone, I would play it at its own game, and see what came of that. I began to explain with a kind of dead-pan, simple-word seriousness:

"A husband is a man whom a woman takes. . ."

Evidently, from their expressions I was not very enlightening. However, they let me go on for three or four sentences without interruption. Then, when I paused for breath, the kindly one chipped in with a point which she evidently felt needed clearing up:

"But what," she asked, in evident perplexity, "what is a man?"

A cool silence hung over the room after my exposition. I had an impression I had been sent to Coventry, or semi-Coventry, by them, but I did not bother to test it. I was too much occupied trying to force the door of my memory further open, and finding that beyond a certain point it would not budge.

I knew now that I was Jane. I had been Jane Summers, and had become Jane Waterleigh when I had married Donald.

I was—had been—twenty-four when we were married: just twenty-five when Donald was killed, six months later. And there it stopped. It seemed like yesterday, but I couldn't tell. . . .

Before that, everything was perfectly clear. My parents and friends, my home, my schools, my training, my job, as Dr. Summers, at the Wraychester Hospital. I could remember my first sight of Donald when they brought him in one evening with a broken leg—and all that followed. . . .

I could remember now the face that I ought to see in a looking-glass—and it was certainly nothing like that I had seen in the corridor outside—it should be more oval, with a complexion looking faintly sun-tanned; with a smaller, neater mouth; surrounded by chestnut hair that curled naturally; with brown eyes rather wide apart and perhaps a little grave as a rule.

I knew, too, how the rest of me should look—slender, long-legged, with small firm breasts—a nice body but one that I had simply taken for granted until Donald gave me pride in it by loving it. . . .

I looked down at the repulsive mound of pink satin, and shuddered. A sense of outrage came welling up. I longed for Donald to comfort and pet me and love me and tell me it would be all right; that I wasn't as I was seeing myself at all, and that it *really* was a dream. At the same time I was stricken with horror at the thought that he should ever see me gross and obese like this. And then I remembered that Donald would never see me again at all—never any more—and I was wretched and miserable, and the tears trickled down my cheeks again.

The five others just went on looking at me, wide-eyed and wondering. Half an hour passed, still in silence, then the door opened to admit a whole troop of the little women, all in white suits. I saw Hazel look at me, and then at the leader. She seemed about to speak, and then to change her mind. The little women split up, two to a couch. Standing one on each side, they stripped away the coverlet, rolled up their sleeves, and set to work at massage.

At first it was not unpleasant, and quite soothing. One lay back and relaxed. Presently, however, I liked it less: soon I found it offensive.

"Stop that!" I told the one on the right, sharply.

She paused, smiled at me amiably, though a trifle uncertainly, and then continued.

"I said stop it," I told her, pushing her away.

Her eyes met mine. They were troubled and hurt, although a professional smile still curved her mouth.

"I mean it," I added, curtly.

She continued to hesitate, and glanced across at her partner on the further side of the bed.

"You, too," I told the other. "That'll do."

She did not even pause in her rhythm. The one on the right plucked a decision and returned. She restarted just what I had stopped. I reached out and pushed her, harder this time. There must have been a lot more muscle in that bolster of an arm than one would have supposed. The shove carried her half across the room, and she tripped and fell.

All movement in the room suddenly ceased. Everybody stared, first at her, and then at me. The pause was brief. They all set to work again. I pushed away the girl on the left, too, though more gently. The other one picked herself up. She was crying and she looked frightened, but she set her jaw doggedly and started to come back.

"You keep away from me, you little horrors," I told them threateningly.

That checked them. They stood off, and looked miserably at one another. The one with the badge of seniority fussed up.

"What's the trouble, Mother Orchis?" she inquired.

I told her. She looked puzzled.

"But that's quite right," she expostulated.

"Not for me. I don't like it, and I won't have it," I replied.

She stood awkwardly, at a loss.

Hazel's voice came from the other side of the room:

"Orchis is off her head. She's been telling us the most disgusting things. She's quite mad."

The little woman turned to regard her, and then looked inquiringly at one of the others. When the girl confirmed with a nod and an expression of distaste she turned back to me, giving me a searching inspection.

"You two go and report," she told my discomfited masseuses.

They were both crying now, and they went wretchedly down the room together. The one in charge gave me another long, thoughtful look, and then followed them.

A few minutes later all the rest had packed-up and gone. The six of us were alone again. It was Hazel who broke the ensuing silence.

"That was a bitchy piece of work. The poor little devils were only doing their job," she observed.

"If that's their job, I don't like it," I told her.

"So you just get them a beating, poor things. But I suppose that's the lost memory again. You wouldn't remember that a Servitor who upsets a Mother is beaten, would you?" she added sarcastically.

"Beaten?" I repeated, uneasily.

"Yes, beaten," she mimicked. "But you don't care what becomes of them, do you? I don't know what's happened to you while you were away, but whatever it was it seems to have produced a thoroughly nasty result. I never did care for you, Orchis, though the others thought I was wrong. Well, now we all know."

None of the rest offered any comment. The feeling that they shared her opinion was strong, but luckily I was spared confirmation by the opening of the door.

The senior attendant re-entered with half a dozen small myrmidons, but this time the group was dominated by a handsome woman of about thirty. Her appearance gave me immense relief. She was neither little, nor Amazonian, nor was she huge. Her present company made her look a little over-tall, perhaps, but I judged her at about five foot ten; a normal, pleasant-featured young woman with brown hair, cut somewhat short, and a pleated black skirt showing beneath a white overall. The senior attendant was almost trotting to keep up with her longer steps, and was saying something about delusions and 'only from the Centre to-day, Doctor.'

The woman stopped beside my couch while the smaller women huddled together, looking at me with some misgiving. She thrust a thermometer into my mouth and held my wrist. Satisfied on both these counts, she inquired:

"Headache? Any other aches or pains?"

"No," I told her.

She regarded me carefully. I looked back at her.

"What—?" she began.

"She's mad," Hazel put in from the other side of the room. "She says she's lost her memory and doesn't know us."

"She's been talking about horrid, disgusting things," added one of the others.

"She's got delusions. She thinks she can read and write," Hazel supplemented.

The doctor smiled at that.

"Do you?" she asked me.

"I don't see why not—but it should be easy enough to prove," I replied, brusquely.

She looked startled, a little taken aback, then she recovered her tolerant half-smile.

"All right," she said, humouring me.

She pulled a small note-pad out of her pocket and offered it to me, with a pencil. The pencil felt a little odd in my hand; the fingers did not fall into place readily on it, nevertheless I wrote:

"I'm only too well aware that I have delusions—and that you are part of them."

Hazel tittered as I handed the pad back.

The doctor's jaw did not actually drop, but her smile came right off. She looked at me very hard indeed. The rest of the room, seeing her expression, went quiet, as though I had performed some startling feat of magic. The doctor turned towards Hazel.

"What sort of things has she been telling you?" she inquired.

Hazel hesitated, then she blurted out:

"Horrible things. She's been talking about two human sexes—just as if we were like the animals. It was disgusting!"

The doctor considered a moment, then she told the senior attendant:

"Better get her along to the sick-bay. I'll examine her there."

As she walked off there was a rush of little women to fetch a low trolley from the corner to the side of my couch. A dozen hands assisted me on to it, and then wheeled me briskly away.

"Now," said the doctor grimly, "let's get down to it. Who told you all this stuff about two human sexes? I want her name."

We were alone in a small room with a gold-dotted pink wallpaper. The attendants, after transferring me from the trolley to a couch again, had taken themselves off. The doctor was sitting with a pad on her knee and a pencil at the ready. Her manner was that of an unbluffable inquisitor.

I was not feeling tactful. I told her not to be a fool.

She looked staggered, flushed with anger for a moment, and then took a hold on herself. She went on:

"After you left the Clinic you had your holiday, of course. Now, where did they send you?"

"I don't know," I replied. "All I can tell you is what I told the others—that this hallucination, or delusion, or whatever it is, started in that hospital place you call the Centre."

With resolute patience she said:

"Look here, Orchis. You were perfectly normal when you left here six weeks ago. You went to the Clinic and had your babies in the ordinary way. *But* between then and now somebody has been filling your head with all this rubbish—and teaching you to read and write, as well. Now you are going to tell me who that somebody was. I warn you you won't get away with this loss of memory nonsense with me. If you are able to remember this nauseating stuff you told the others, then you're able to remember where you got it from."

"Oh, for heaven's sake, talk sense," I told her. She flushed again.

"I can find out from the Clinic where they sent you, and I can find out from the Rest Home who were your chief associates while you were there, but I don't want to waste time following up all your contacts, so I'm asking you to save trouble by telling me now. You might just as well. We don't want to have to *make* you talk," she concluded, ominously.

I shook my head.

"You're on the wrong track. As far as I am concerned this whole hallucination, including my connection with this Orchis, began somehow at the Centre—how it happened I can't tell you, and what happened to her before that just isn't there to be remembered."

She frowned, obviously disturbed.

"What hallucination?" she inquired, carefully.

"Why this fantastic set-up—and you, too." I waved my hand to include it all. "This revolting great body, all those little women, everything. Obviously it is all some projection of the subconscious—and the state of my subconscious is worrying me, for it's certainly no wish-fulfilment."

She went on staring at me, more worried now.

"Who on earth has been telling you about the subconscious and wish-fulfilments?" she asked uncertainly.

"I don't see why, even in an hallucination, I am expected to be an illiterate moron," I replied.

"But a Mother doesn't know anything about such things. She doesn't need to."

"Listen," I said. "I've told you, as I've told those poor grotesques in the other room, that I am *not* a Mother. What I am is just an unfortunate M.B. who is having some kind of nightmare."

"M.B.?" she inquired, vaguely.

"Bachelor of Medicine. I practise medicine," I told her.

She went on looking at me curiously. Her eyes wandered over my mountainous form, uncertainly.

"You are claiming to be a doctor?" she said, in an odd voice.

"Colloquially—yes," I agreed.

There was indignation mixed with bewilderment as she protested:

"But this is sheer nonsense! You were brought up and developed to be a Mother. You are a Mother. Just look at you!"

"Yes," I said, bitterly. "Just look at me!"

There was a pause.

"It seems to me," I suggested at last, "that, hallucination or not, we shan't get much further simply by going on accusing one another of talking nonsense. Suppose you explain to me what this place is, and who you think I am. It might jog my memory."

She countered that. "Suppose," she said, "that first you tell me what you *can* remember. It would give me more idea of what is puzzling you."

"Very well," I agreed, and launched upon a potted history of myself as far as I could recollect it—up to the time, that is to say, when Donald's aircraft crashed.

It was foolish of me to fall for that one. Of course, she had no intention of telling me anything. When she had listened to all I had to say, she went away, leaving me impotently furious.

I waited until the place quietened down. The music had been switched off. An attendant had looked in to inquire, with an air of polishing-off the day's duties, whether there was anything I wanted, and presently there was nothing to be heard. I let a margin of half an hour elapse, and then struggled to get up—taking it by very easy stages this time. The greatest part of the effort was to get on to my feet from a sitting position, but I managed it at the cost of heavy breathing. Presently I crossed to the door, and found it unfastened. I held it a little open, listening. There was no sound of movement in the corridor, so I pulled it wide open, and set out to discover what I could about the place for myself. All the doors of the rooms were shut. Putting my ear close to them I could hear regular, heavy breathing behind some, but there were no other sounds in the stillness. I kept on, turning several corners, until I recognized the front door ahead of me. I tried the latch, and found that it was neither barred nor bolted. I paused again, listening for some moments, and then pulled it open and stepped outside.

The park-like garden stretched out before me, sharp-shadowed in the moonlight. Through the trees to the right was a glint of water, to the left was a house similar to the one behind me, with not a light showing in any of its windows.

I wondered what to do. Trapped in this huge carcass, all but helpless in it, there was very little I could do, but I decided to go on and at least find out what I could while I had the chance. I went forward to the edge of the steps that I had earlier climbed from the ambulance, and started down them cautiously, holding on to the balustrade.

"Mother," said a sharp, incisive voice behind me. "What are you doing?"

I turned and saw one of the little women, her white suit gleaming in the moonlight. She was alone. I made no reply, but took another step down. I could have wept at the outrage of the heavy, ungainly body, and the caution it imposed on me.

"Come back. Come back at once," she told me.

I took no notice. She came pattering down after me and laid hold of my draperies.

"Mother," she said again, "you must come back. You'll catch cold out here."

I started to take another step, and she pulled at the draperies to hold me back. I leant forward against the pull. There was a sharp tearing sound as the material gave. I swung round and lost my balance. The last thing I saw was the rest of the flight of steps coming up to meet me. . . .

As I opened my eyes a voice said:

"That's better, but it was very naughty of you, Mother Orchis. And lucky it wasn't a lot worse. Such a silly thing to do. I'm ashamed of you—really, I am."

My head was aching, and I was exasperated to find that the whole stupid business was still going on; altogether I was in no mood for reproachful drip. I told her to go to hell. Her small face goggled at me for a moment, and then became icily prim. She applied a piece of lint and plaster to the left side of my forehead, in silence, and then departed, stiffly.

Reluctantly, I had to admit to myself that she was perfectly right. What on earth had I been expecting to do—what on earth *could* I do, encumbered by this horrible mass of flesh? A great surge of loathing for it and a feeling of helpless frustration brought me to the verge of tears again. I longed for my own nice, slim body that pleased me and did what I asked of it. I remembered how Donald had once pointed to a young tree swaying in the wind, and introduced it to me as my twin sister. And only a day or two ago. . . .

Then, suddenly, I made a discovery which brought me struggling to sit up. The blank part of my mind had filled up. I could remember everything. . . . The effort made my head throb, so I relaxed and lay back once more, recalling it all, right up to the point where the needle was withdrawn and someone swabbed my arm. . . .

But what had happened after that? Dreams and hallucinations I had expected . . . but not the sharp-focused, detailed sense of reality . . . not this state which was like a nightmare made solid. . . .

What, what in heaven's name, had they done to me . . . ?

I must have fallen asleep again soon, for when I opened my eyes again there was daylight outside, and a covey of little women had arrived to attend to my toilet.

They spread their sheets dexterously and rolled me this way and that with expert technique as they cleaned me up. I suffered their industry patiently, feeling the fresher for it, and glad to discover that the headache had all but gone.

When we were almost at the end of our ablutions there came a peremptory knock, and without invitation two figures, dressed in black uniforms with silver buttons, entered. They were the Amazon type, tall, broad, well set-up, and handsome. The little women dropped everything and fled with squeaks of dismay into the far corner of the room where they cowered in a huddle.

The two gave me the familiar salute. With an odd mixture of decision and deference one of them inquired:

"You are Orchis—Mother Orchis?"

"That's what they're calling me," I admitted.

The girl hesitated, then in a tone rather more pleading than ordering she said:

"I have orders for your arrest, Mother. You will please come with us."

An excited, incredulous twittering broke out among the little women in the corner. The uniformed girl quelled them with a look.

"Get the Mother dressed and make her ready," she commanded.

The little women came out of their corner hesitantly, directing nervous, propitiatory smiles towards the pair. The second one told them briskly, though not altogether unkindly:

"Come along now. Jump to it."

They jumped.

I was almost swathed in my pink draperies again when the doctor strode in. She frowned at the two in uniform.

"What's all this? What are you doing here?" she demanded.

The leader of the two explained.

"Arrest!" exclaimed the doctor. "Arrest a Mother! I never heard such nonsense. What's the charge?"

The uniformed girl said, a little sheepishly:

"She is accused of Reactionism."

The doctor simply stared at her.

"A Reactionist Mother! What'll you people think of next? Go on, get out, both of you."

The young woman protested:

"We have our orders, Doctor."

"Rubbish. There's no authority. Have you ever heard of a Mother being arrested?"

"No, Doctor."

"Well, you aren't going to make a precedent now. Go on."

The uniformed girl hesitated unhappily, then an idea occurred to her.

"If you would let me have a signed refusal to surrender the Mother . . .?" she suggested helpfully.

When the two had departed, quite satisfied with their piece of paper, the doctor looked at the little women gloomily.

"You can't help tattling, you Servitors, can you? Anything you happen to hear goes through the lot of you like a fire in a cornfield, and makes trouble all round. Well, if I hear any more of this I shall know where it comes from." She turned to me. "And you, Mother Orchis, will in future please restrict yourself to yes-and-no in hearing of these nattering little pests. I'll see you again shortly. We want to ask you some questions," she added, as she went out, leaving a subdued, industrious silence behind her.

She returned just as the tray which had held my gargantuan breakfast was being removed, and not alone. The four women who accompanied her and looked as normal as herself were followed by a number of little women lugging in chairs which they arranged beside my couch. When they had departed, the five women, all in white overalls, sat down and regarded me as if I were an exhibit. One appeared to be much the same age as the first doctor, two nearer fifty, and one sixty, or more.

"Now, Mother Orchis," said the doctor, with an air of opening the proceedings, "it is quite clear that something highly unusual has taken place. Naturally we are interested to understand just what and, if possible, why. You don't need to worry about those police this morning—it was quite improper of them to come here at all. This is simply an inquiry—a scientific inquiry—to establish what has happened."

"You can't want to understand more than I do," I replied. I looked at them, at the room about me, and finally at my massive prone figure. "I am aware that all this must be an hallucination, but what is troubling me most is that I have always supposed that any hallucination must be deficient in at least one dimension—must lack reality to some of the senses. But this does not. I have all my senses, and can use them. Nothing is insubstantial: I am trapped in flesh that is very palpably too, too solid. The only striking deficiency, so far as I can see, is reason—even symbolic reason."

The four other women stared at me in astonishment. The doctor gave them a sort of now-perhaps-you'll-believe-me glance, and then turned to me again.

"We'll start with a few questions," she said.

"Before you begin," I put in, "I have something to add to what I told you last night. It has come back to me."

"Perhaps the knock when you fell," she suggested, looking at my piece of plaster. "What were you trying to do?"

I ignored that. "I think I'd better tell you the missing part—it might help—a bit, anyway."

"Very well," she agreed. "You told me you were—er—married, and that your—er—husband was killed soon afterwards." She glanced at the others; their blankness of expression was somehow studious. "It was the part after that that was missing," she added.

"Yes," I said. "He was a test-pilot," I explained to them. "It happened six months after we were married—only one month before his contract was due to expire.

"After that, an aunt took me away for some weeks. I don't suppose I'll ever remember that part very well—I—I wasn't noticing anything very much . . .

"But then I remember waking up one morning and suddenly seeing things differently, and telling myself that I couldn't go on like that. I knew I must have some work, something that would keep me busy.

"Dr. Hellyer, who is in charge of the Wraychester Hospital, where I was working before I married, told me he would be glad to have me with them again. I went back, and worked very hard, so that I did not have much time to think. That would be about eight months ago, now.

"Then one day Dr. Hellyer spoke about a drug that a friend of his had succeeded in synthesizing. I don't think he was really asking for volunteers, but I offered to try it out. From what he said it sounded as if the drug might have some quite important properties. It struck me as a chance to do something useful. Sooner or later, someone would try it, and as I didn't have any ties and didn't care very much what happened, anyway, I thought I might as well be the one to try it."

The spokesman doctor interrupted to ask:

"What was this drug?"

"It's called chuinjuatin," I told her. "Do you know it?"

She shook her head. One of the others put in:

"I've heard the name. What is it?"

"It's a narcotic," I told her. "The original form is in the leaves of a tree that grows chiefly in the South of Venezuela. The tribe of Indians who live there discovered it somehow, like others did quinine, and mescalin. And in much the same way they use it for orgies. Some of them sit and chew the leaves—they have to chew about six ounces of them—and gradually they go into a zombie-like, trance state. It lasts three or four days during which they are quite helpless and incapable of doing the simplest thing for themselves, so that other members of the tribe are appointed to look after them as if they were children, and to guard them.

"It's necessary to guard them because the Indian belief is that chuinjuatin liberates the spirit from the body, setting it free to wander anywhere in space and time, and the guardian's most important job is to see that no other wandering spirit shall slip into the body while the true owner is away. When the subjects recover they claim to have had wonderful mystical experiences. There seem to be no physical ill-effects, and no craving results from it. The mystical experiences, though, are said to be intense, and clearly remembered.

"Dr. Hellyer's friend had tested his synthesized chuinjuatin on a number of laboratory animals and worked out the dosage, and tolerances, and that kind of thing, but what he could not tell, of course, was what validity, if any, the reports of the mystical experiences had. Presumably they were the product of the drug's influence on the nervous system—but whether that effect produced a sensation of pleasure, ecstasy, awe, fear, horror, or any of a dozen more, it was impossible to tell without a human guinea-pig. So that was what I volunteered for."

I stopped. I looked at their serious, puzzled faces, at the billow of pink satin in front of me. . . .

"In fact," I added, "it appears to have produced a combination of the absurd, the incomprehensible, and the grotesque."

They were earnest women, these, not to be side-tracked. They were there to disprove an anomaly—if they could.

"I see," said the spokeswoman with an air of preserving reasonableness, rather than meaning anything. She glanced down at a paper on which she had made a note from time to time.

"Now, can you give us the time and date at which this experiment took place?"

I could, and did, and after that the questions went on and on and on. . . .

The least satisfactory part of it from my point of view was that even though my answers caused them to grow more uncertain of themselves as we went on, they did at least get them; whereas when I put a question it was usually evaded, or answered perfunctorily, as an unimportant digression.

They went on steadily, and only broke off when my next meal arrived. Then they went away, leaving me thankfully in peace—but little the wiser. I half-expected them to return, but when they did not I fell into a doze from which I was awakened by the incursion of a cluster of the little women once more. They brought a trolley with them, and in a short time were wheeling me out of the building on it—but not by the way I had arrived. This time we went down a ramp where another, or the same, pink ambulance waited at the bottom. When they had me safely loaded aboard three of them climbed in, too, to keep me company. They were chattering as they did so, and they kept it up inconsequentially, and almost incomprehensibly, for the whole hour and a half of the journey that ensued.

The countryside differed little from that I had already seen. Once we were outside the gates there were the same tidy fields and standardized farms.

The occasional built-up areas were not extensive and consisted of the same types of blocks close by, and we ran on the same, not very good, road surfaces. There were groups of the Amazon types, and, more rarely, individuals, to be seen at work in the fields; the sparse traffic was lorries, large or small, and occasional buses, but with never a private car to be seen. My illusion, I reflected, was remarkably consistent in its details. Not a single group of Amazons, for instance, failed to raise its right hands in friendly, respectful greeting to the pink car.

Once, we crossed a cutting. Looking down from the bridge I thought at first that we were over the dried bed of a canal, but then I noticed a post leaning at a crazy angle among the grass and weeds: most of its attachments had fallen off, but there were enough left to identify it as a railway signal.

We passed through one concentration of identical blocks which was in size, though in no other way, quite a town, and then, two or three miles further on, ran through an ornamental gateway into a kind of park.

In one way it was not unlike the estate we had left, for everything was meticulously tended; the lawns like velvet, the flower-beds vivid with spring blossoms, but it differed essentially in that the buildings were not blocks. They were houses, quite small for the most part, and varied in style, often no larger than roomy cottages. The place had a subduing effect on my small companions; for the first time they left off chattering, and gazed about them with obvious awe.

The driver stopped once to inquire the way of an overalled Amazon who was striding along with a hod on her shoulder. She directed us, and gave me a cheerful, respectful grin through the window, and presently we drew up again in front of a neat little two-storey Regency-style house.

This time there was no trolley. The little women, assisted by the driver, fussed over helping me out, and then half-supported me into the house, in a kind of buttressing formation.

Inside, I was manœuvred with some difficulty through a door on the left, and found myself in a beautiful room, elegantly decorated and furnished in the period-style of the house. A white-haired woman in a purple silk dress was sitting in a wing-chair beside a wood fire. Both her face and her hands told of considerable age, but she looked at me from keen, lively eyes.

"Welcome, my dear," she said, in a voice which had no trace of the quaver I half-expected.

Her glance went to a chair. Then she looked at me again, and thought better of it.

"I expect you'd be more comfortable on the couch," she suggested.

I regarded the couch—a genuine Georgian piece, I thought—doubtfully.

"Will it stand it?" I wondered.

"Oh, I think so," she said, but not too certainly.

The retinue deposited me there carefully, and stood by, with anxious expressions. When it was clear that, though it creaked, it was probably going to hold, the old lady shooed them away, and rang a little silver bell. A diminutive figure, a perfect parlourmaid three foot ten in height, entered.

"The brown sherry, please, Mildred," instructed the old lady. "You'll take sherry, my dear?" she added to me.

"Y-yes—yes, thank you," I said, faintly. After a pause I added: "You will excuse me, Mrs.—er—Miss—?"

"Oh, I should have introduced myself. My name is Laura—not Miss, or Mrs., just Laura. You, I know, are Orchis—Mother Orchis."

"So they tell me," I owned, distastefully.

We studied one another. For the first time since the hallucination had set in I saw sympathy, even pity, in someone else's eyes. I looked round the room again, noticing the perfection of details.

"This is—I'm not mad, am I?" I asked.

She shook her head slowly, but before she could reply the miniature parlourmaid returned, bearing a cut-glass decanter and glasses on a silver tray. As she poured out a glass for each of us I saw the old lady glance from her to me and back again, as though comparing us. There was a curious, uninterpretable expression on her face. I made an effort.

"Shouldn't it be madeira?" I suggested.

She looked surprised, and then smiled, and nodded appreciatively.

"I think you have accomplished the purpose of this visit in one sentence," she said.

The parlourmaid left, and we raised our glasses. The old lady sipped at hers and then placed it on an occasional table beside her.

"Nevertheless," she went on, "we had better go into it a little more. Did they tell you why they have sent you to me, my dear?"

"No." I shook my head.

"It is because I am a historian," she informed me. "Access to history is a privilege. It is not granted to many of us nowadays—and then somewhat reluctantly. Fortunately, a feeling that no branches of knowledge should be allowed to perish entirely still exists—though some of them are pursued at the cost of a certain political suspicion." She smiled deprecatingly, and then went on. "So when confirmation is required it is necessary to appeal to a specialist. Did they give you any report on their diagnosis?"

I shook my head again.

"I thought not. So like the profession, isn't it? Well, I'll tell you what they told me on the telephone from the Mother's Home, and we shall have a better idea of what we are about. I was informed that you have been interviewed by several doctors whom you have interested, puzzled—and I suspect, distressed—very much, poor things. None of them has more than a minimum smattering of history, you see. Well, briefly, two of them are of the opinion that you are suffering from delusions of a schizophrenic nature: and three are inclined to think you are a genuine case of projected perception. It is an extremely rare condition. There are not more than three reliably documented cases, and one that is more debatable, they tell me; but of those confirmed two are associated with the drug chuinjuatin, and the third with a drug of very similar properties.

"Now, the majority of three found your answers coherent for the most part, and felt that they were authentically circumstantial. That is to say that nothing you told them conflicted directly with what they know, but, since they know so little outside their professional field, they found a great deal of the rest both hard to believe and impossible to check. Therefore, I, with my better means of checking, have been asked for my opinion."

She paused, and looked me thoughtfully over.

"I rather think," she added, "that this is going to be one of the most curiously interesting things that has happened to me in my quite long life—Your glass is empty, my dear."

"Projected perception," I repeated wonderingly, as I held out my glass. "Now, if that were possible—"

"Oh, there's no doubt about the *possibility*. Those three cases I mentioned are fully authenticated."

"It might be that—almost," I admitted. "At least, in some ways it might be—but not in others. There *is* this nightmare quality. You seem perfectly normal to me, but look at me, myself—and at your little maid! There's certainly an element of delusion. I *seem* to be here, like this, and talking to you—but it can't really be so, so where am I?"

"I can understand, better than most, I think, how unreal this must seem to you. In fact, I have spent so much of my time in books that it sometimes seems unreal to me—as if I did not quite belong anywhere. Now, tell me, my dear, when were you born?"

I told her. She thought for a moment.

"H'm," she said. "George the Sixth—but you'd not remember the second big war?"

"No," I agreed.

"But you might remember the coronation of the next monarch? Whose was that?"

"Elizabeth—Elizabeth the Second. My mother took me to see the procession," I told her.

"Do you remember anything about it?"

"Not a lot really—except that it rained, nearly all day," I admitted.

We went on like that for a little while, then she smiled, reassuringly.

"Well, I don't think we need any more to establish our point. I've heard about that coronation before—at secondhand. It must have been a wonderful scene in the Abbey." She mused a moment, and gave a little sigh. "You've been very patient with me, my dear. It is only fair that you should have your turn—but I'm afraid you must prepare yourself for some shocks."

"I think I must be inured after my last thirty-six hours—or what has appeared to be thirty-six hours," I told her.

"I doubt it," she said, looking at me seriously.

"Tell me," I asked her. "Please, explain it all—if you can."

"Your glass, my dear. Then I'll get the crux of it over." She poured for each of us, then she asked:

"What strikes you as the oddest feature of your experience, so far?"

I considered. "There's so much—"

"Might it not be that you have not seen a single man?" she suggested.

I thought back. I remembered the wondering tone of one of the Mothers asking: "What is a man?"

"That's certainly one of them," I agreed. "Where are they?"

She shook her head, watching me steadily.

"There aren't any, my dear. Not any more. None at all."

I simply went on staring at her. Her expression was perfectly serious and sympathetic. There was no trace of guile there or deception while I struggled with the idea. At last I managed:

"But—but that's impossible! There must be some somewhere. . . .You couldn't—I mean, how—? I mean . . ." My expostulation trailed off in confusion.

She shook her head.

"I know it must seem impossible to you, Jane—may I call you Jane? But it is so. I am an old woman now, nearly eighty, and in all my long life I have never seen a man—save in old pictures and photographs. Drink your sherry, my dear. It will do you good." She paused. "I'm afraid this upsets you."

I obeyed, too bewildered for further comment at the moment, protesting inwardly, yet not altogether disbelieving, for certainly I had not seen one man, nor sign of any. She went on quietly, giving me time to collect my wits:

"I can understand a little how you must feel. I haven't had to learn all my history entirely from books, you see. When I was a girl, sixteen or seventeen, I used to listen a lot to my grandmother. She was as old then as I am now, but her memory of her youth was still very good. I was able almost to see the places she talked about—but they were part of such a different world that it was difficult for me to understand how she felt. When she spoke about the young man she had been engaged to, tears would roll down her cheeks, even then—not just for him, of course, but for the whole world that she had known as a girl. I was sorry for her, although I could not really understand how she felt—How should I? But now that I am old, too, and have read so much I am perhaps a little nearer to understanding her feelings, I think." She looked at me curiously. "And you, my dear. Perhaps you, too were engaged to be married?"

"I was married—for a little time," I told her.

She contemplated that for some seconds, then:

"It must be a very strange experience to be owned," she remarked, reflectively.

"Owned?" I exclaimed, in astonishment.

"Ruled by a husband," she explained, sympathetically.

I stared at her.

"But it—it wasn't like that—it wasn't like that at all," I protested. "It was—" But there I broke off, with tears too close. To steer her away I asked:

"But what happened? What on earth happened to the men?"

"They all died," she told me. "They fell sick. Nobody could do anything for them, so they died. In little more than a year they were all gone—all but a very few."

"But surely—surely everything would collapse?"

"Oh, yes. Very largely it did. It was very bad. There was a dreadful lot of starvation. The industrial parts were the worst hit, of course. In the more backward countries and in rural areas women were able to turn to the land and till it to keep themselves and their children alive, but almost all the large organizations broke down entirely. Transport ceased very soon: petrol ran out, and no coal was being mined. It was quite a dreadful state of affairs because, although there were a great many women, and they had outnumbered the men, in fact, they had only really been important as consumers and spenders of money. So when the crisis came it turned out that scarcely any of them knew how to do any of the important things because they had nearly all been owned by men, and had to lead their lives as pets and parasites."

I started to protest, but her frail hand waved me aside.

"It wasn't their *fault*—not entirely," she explained. "They were caught up in a process, and everything conspired against their escape. It was a long process, going right back to the eleventh century, in Southern France. The Romantic conception started there as an elegant and amusing fashion for the leisured classes. Gradually, as time went on, it permeated through most levels of society, but it was not until the latter part of the nineteenth century that its commercial possibilities were intelligently perceived, and not until the twentieth that it was really exploited.

"At the beginning of the twentieth century women were starting to have their chance to lead useful, creative, interesting lives. But that did not suit commerce: it needed them much more as mass-consumers than as producers—except on the most routine levels. So Romance was adopted and developed as a weapon against their further progress and to promote consumption, and it was used intensively.

"Women must never for a moment be allowed to forget their sex, and compete as equals. Everything had to have a 'feminine angle' which must be different from the masculine angle, and be dinned in without ceasing. It would have been unpopular for manufacturers actually to issue an order 'back to the kitchen,' but there were other ways. A profession without a difference, called 'housewife,' could be invented. The kitchen could be glorified and made more expensive; it could be made to seem desirable, and it could be shown that the way to realize this heart's desire was through marriage. So the presses turned out, by the hundred thousand a week, journals which concentrated the attention of women ceaselessly and relentlessly upon selling themselves to some man in order that they might achieve some small, uneconomic unit of a home upon which money could be spent.

"Whole trades adopted the romantic approach and the glamour was spread thicker and thicker in the articles, the write-ups, and most of all in the advertisements. Romance found a place in everything that women might buy, from underclothes to motor-bicycles, from 'health' foods to kitchen stoves, from deodorants to foreign travel, until soon they were too bemused to be amused any more.

"The air was filled with frustrated moanings. Women maundered in front of microphones yearning only to 'surrender,' and 'give themselves,' to adore and to be adored. The cinema most of all maintained the propaganda, persuading the main and important part of their audience, which was female, that nothing in life was worth achieving but dewy-eyed passivity in the strong arms of Romance. The pressure became such that the majority of young women spent all their leisure time dreaming of Romance, and the means of securing it. They were brought to a state of honestly believing that to be owned by some man and set down in a little brick box to buy all the things that the manufacturers wanted them to buy would be the highest form of bliss that life could offer."

"But—" I began to protest again. The old lady was now well launched, however, and swept on without a check.

"All this could not help distorting society, of course. The divorce-rate went up. Real life simply could not come near to providing the degree of romantic glamour which was being represented as every girl's proper inheritance. There was probably, in the aggregate, more disappointment, disillusion, and dissatisfaction among women than there had ever been before. Yet, with this ridiculous and ornamented ideal grained-in by unceasing propaganda, what could a conscientious idealist do but take steps to break up the short-weight marriage she had made, and seek elsewhere for the ideal which was hers, she understood, by right?

"It was a wretched state of affairs brought about by deliberately promoted dissatisfactions; a kind of rat-race with, somewhere safely out of reach, the glamourized romantic ideal always luring. Perhaps an exceptional few almost attained it, but, for all except those very few, it was a cruel, tantalizing sham on which they spent themselves, and of course their money, in vain."

This time I did get in my protest.

"But it wasn't like that. Some of what you say may be true—but that's all the superficial part. It didn't feel a bit like the way you put it. I was in it. I *know.*"

She shook her head reprovingly.

"There is such a thing as being too close to make a proper evaluation. At a distance we are able to see more clearly. We can perceive it for what it was—a gross and heartless exploitation of the weaker-willed majority. Some women of education and resolution were able to withstand it, of course, but at a cost. There must always be a painful price for resisting majority pressure—even they could not always altogether escape the feeling that they might be wrong, and that the rat-racers were having the better time of it.

"You see, the great hopes for the emancipation of women with which the century had started had been outflanked. Purchasing-power had passed into the hands of the ill-educated and highly suggestible. The desire for Romance is essentially a selfish wish, and when it is encouraged to dominate every other it breaks down all corporate loyalties. The individual woman thus separated from, and yet at the same time thrust into competition with, all other women was almost defenceless; she became the prey of organized suggestion. When it was represented to her that the lack of certain goods or amenities would be fatal to Romance she became alarmed and, thus, eminently exploitable. She could only believe what she was told, and spent a great deal of time worrying about whether she was doing all the right things to encourage Romance. Thus, she became, in a new, subtler way, more exploited, more dependent, and less creative than she had ever been before."

"Well," I said, "this is the most curiously unrecognizable account of my world that I have ever heard—it's like something copied, but with all the proportions wrong. And as for 'less creative'—well, perhaps families were smaller, but women still went on having babies. The population was still increasing."

The old lady's eyes dwelt on me a moment.

"You are undoubtedly a thought-child of your time, in some ways," she observed. "What makes you think there is anything creative about having babies? Would you call a plant-pot creative because seeds grow in it? It is a mechanical operation—and, like most mechanical operations, is most easily performed by the least intelligent. Now, bringing up a child, educating, helping her to become a *person,* that *is* creative. But unfortunately, in the time we are speaking of, women had, in the main, been successfully conditioned into bringing up their daughters to be unintelligent consumers, like themselves."

"But," I said helplessly, "I *know* the time. It's my time. This is all distorted."

"The perspective of history must be truer," she told me again, unimpressed, and went on: "But if what happened *had* to happen, then it chose a fortunate time to happen. A hundred years earlier, even fifty years earlier, it would very likely have meant extinction. Fifty years later might easily have been too late—it might have come upon a world in which all women were profitably restricted to domesticity and consumership. Luckily, however, in the middle of the century women were still entering the professions, and by far the greatest number of professional women was to be found in medicine—which is to say that they were only really numerous in, and skilled in, the very profession which immediately became of vital importance if we were to survive at all.

"I have no medical knowledge, so I cannot give you any details of the steps they took. All I can tell you is that there was intensive research on lines which will probably be more obvious to you than they are to me.

"A species, even our species, has great will to survive, and the doctors saw to it that the will had the means of expression. Through all the hunger, and the chaos, and the other privations, babies somehow continued to be born. That had to be. Reconstruction could wait: the priority was the new generation that would help in the reconstruction, and then inherit it. So babies were born: the girl babies lived, the boy babies died. That was distressing, and wasteful, too, and so, presently, only girl babies were born—again, the means by which that could be achieved will be easier for you to understand than for me.

"It is, they tell me, not nearly so remarkable as it would appear at first sight. The locust, it seems, will continue to produce female locusts without male, or any other kind of assistance; the aphis, too, is able to go on breeding alone and in seclusion, certainly for eight generations, perhaps more. So it would be a poor thing if we, with all our knowledge and powers of research to assist us, should find ourselves inferior to the locust and the aphis in this respect, would it not?"

She paused, looking at me somewhat quizzically for my response. Perhaps she expected amazed—or possibly shocked—disbelief. If so, I disappointed her: technical achievements have ceased to arouse simple wonder since atomic physics showed how barriers fall before the pressure of a good brains-team. One can take it that most things are possible: whether they are desirable, or worth doing, is a different matter—and one that seemed to me particularly pertinent to her question. I asked her:

"And what is it that you have achieved?"

"Survival," she said, simply.

"Materially," I agreed. "I suppose you have. But when it has cost all the rest, when love, art, poetry, excitement, and physical joy have all been sacrificed to mere continued existence, what is left but a soulless waste? What reason is there any longer for survival?"

"As to the reason, I don't know—except that survival is a desire common to all species. I am quite sure that the reason for that desire was no clearer in the twentieth century than it is now. But, for the rest, why should you assume that they are gone? Did not Sappho write poetry? And your assumption that the possession of a soul depends upon a duality of sexes surprises me: it has so often been held that the two are in some sort of conflict, has it not?"

"As a historian who must have studied men, women, and motives you should have taken my meaning better," I told her.

She shook her head, with reproof. "You are so much the conditioned product of your age, my dear. They told you on all levels, from the works of Freud to that of the most nugatory magazines for women, that it was sex, civilized into romantic love, that made the world go round—and you believed them. But the world continues to go round for others, too—for the insects, the fish, the birds, the animals—and how much do you suppose they know of romantic love, even in their brief mating-seasons? They hoodwinked you, my dear. Between them they channelled your interests and ambitions along courses that were socially convenient, economically profitable, and almost harmless."

I shook my head.

"I just don't believe it. Oh, yes, you know something of my world—from the outside. But you don't understand it, or feel it."

"That's your conditioning, my dear," she told me, calmly.

Her repeated assumption irritated me. I asked:

"Suppose I were to believe what you say, what is it, then, that *does* make the world go round?"

"That's simple, my dear. It is the will to power. We have that as babies; we have it still in old age. It occurs in men and women alike. It is more fundamental, and more desirable, than sex; I tell you, you were misled—exploited, sublimated for economic convenience.

"After the disease had struck, women ceased, for the first time in history, to be an exploited class. Without male rulers to confuse and divert them they began to perceive that all true power resides in the female principle. The male had served only one brief useful purpose; for the rest of his life he was a painful and costly parasite.

"As they became aware of power, the doctors grasped it. In twenty years they were in full control. With them were the few women engineers, architects, lawyers, administrators, some teachers, and so on, but it was the doctors who held the keys of life and death. The future was in their hands and, as things began gradually to revive, they, together with the other professions, remained the dominant class and became known as the Doctorate. It assumed authority; it made the laws; it enforced them.

"There was opposition, of course. Neither the memory of the old days, nor the effect of twenty years of lawlessness, could be wiped out at once, but the doctors had the whip-hand—any woman who wanted a child had to come to them, and they saw to it that she was satisfactorily settled in a community. The roving gangs dwindled away, and gradually order was restored.

"Later on, they faced better organized opposition. There was a party which contended that the disease which had struck down the men had run its course, and the balance could, and should, be restored—they were known as Reactionists, and they became an embarrassment.

"Most of the Council of the Doctorate still had clear memories of a system which used every weakness of women, and had been no more than a more civilized culmination of their exploitation through the ages. They remembered how they themselves had only grudgingly been allowed to qualify for their careers. They were now in command: they felt no obligation to surrender their power and authority, and eventually, no doubt, their freedom to a creature whom they had proved to be biologically, and in all other ways, expendable. They refused unanimously to take a step that would lead to corporate suicide, and the Reactionists were proscribed as a subversive criminal organization.

"That, however, was just a palliative. It quickly became clear that they were attacking a symptom and neglecting the cause. The Council was driven to realize that it had an unbalanced society at its hands—a society that was capable of continuity, but was in structure, you might say, little more than the residue of a vanished form. It could not continue in that truncated shape and, as long as it tried to, disaffection would increase. Therefore, if power were to become stable, a new form suitable to the circumstances must be found.

"In deciding the shape it should take, the natural tendencies of the little-educated and uneducated woman were carefully considered—such qualities as her feeling for hierarchical principles and her disposition to respect artificial distinctions. You will no doubt recollect that in your own time any fool of a woman whose husband was ennobled or honoured at once acquired increased respect and envy from other women though she remained the same fool; and also, that any gathering or society of unoccupied women would soon become obsessionally enmeshed in the creation and preservation of social distinctions. Allied to this is the high value they usually place upon a feeling of security. Important, too is the capacity for devoted self-sacrifice, and slavery to conscience within the canons of any local convention. We are naturally very biddable creatures. Most of us are happiest when we are being orthodox, however odd our customs may appear to an outsider; the difficulty in handling us lies chiefly in establishing the required standards of orthodoxy.

"Obviously, the broad outline of a system which was going to stand any chance of success would have to provide scope for these and other characteristic traits. It must be a scheme where the interplay of forces would preserve equilibrium and respect for authority. The details of such an organization, however, were less easy to determine.

"An extensive study of social forms and orders was undertaken, but for several years every plan put forward was rejected as in some way unsuitable. The architecture of that finally chosen was said, though I do not know with how much truth, to have been inspired by the Bible—a book at that time still unprohibited, and the source of much unrest. I am told that it ran something like: 'Go to the ant, thou sluggard; consider her ways.'

"The Council appears to have felt that this advice, suitably modified, could be expected to lead to a state of affairs which would provide most of the requisite characteristics.

"A four-class system was chosen as the basis, and strong differentiations were gradually introduced. These, now that they have become well established, greatly help to ensure stability: there is scope for ambition within one's class, but none for passing from one class to another. Thus, we have the Doctorate—the educated ruling-classes, fifty per cent of whom are actually of the medical profession. The Mothers, whose title is self-explanatory. The Servitors, who are numerous and, for psychological reasons, small. The Workers, who are physically and muscularly strong, to do the heavier work. All the three lower classes respect the authority of the Doctorate. Both the employed classes revere the Mothers. The Servitors consider themselves more favoured in their tasks than the Workers; and the Workers tend to regard the puniness of the Servitors with a semi-affectionate contempt.

"So you see a balance has been struck, and though it works somewhat crudely as yet, no doubt it will improve. It seems likely, for instance, that it would be advantageous to introduce sub-divisions into the Servitor class before long, and the police are thought by some to be put at a disadvantage by having no more than a little education to distinguish them from the ordinary Worker. . . ."

She went on explaining with increasing detail while the enormity of the whole process gradually grew upon me.

"Ants!" I broke in, suddenly. "The ant-nest! You've taken that for your model?"

She looked surprised, either at my tone, or the fact that what she was saying had taken so long to register.

"And why not?" she asked. "Surely it is one of the most enduring social patterns that nature has evolved—though of course some adaptation—"

"You're—are you telling me that only the Mothers have children?" I demanded.

"Oh, members of the Doctorate do, too, when they wish," she assured me.

"But—but."

"The Council decides the ratios," she went on to explain. "The doctors at the clinic examine the babies and allocate them suitably to the different classes. After that, of course, it is just a matter of seeing to their specialized feeding, glandular control, and proper training."

"But," I objected wildly, "what's it *for*? Where's the sense in it? What's the good of being alive, like that?"

"Well, what *is* the sense in being alive? You tell me," she suggested.

"But we're *meant* to love and be loved, to have babies we love by people we love."

"There's your conditioning again; glorifying and romanticizing primitive animalism. Surely you consider that we are superior to the animals?"

"Of course I do, but—"

"Love, you say, but what can you know of the love there can be between mother and daughter when there are no men to introduce jealousy? Do you know of any purer sentiment than the love of a girl for her little sisters?"

"But you don't understand," I protested again. "How should you understand a love that colours the whole world? How it centres in your heart and reaches out from there to pervade your whole being, how it can affect everything you are, everything you touch, everything you hear. . . . It can hurt dreadfully, I know, oh, I know, but it can run like sunlight in your veins. . . . It can make you a garden out of a slum; brocade out of rags; music out of speaking voice. It can show you a whole universe in someone else's eyes. Oh, you don't understand . . . you don't know . . . you can't. . . . Oh, Donald, darling, how can I show her what she's never even guessed at . . . ?"

There was an uncertain pause, but presently she said:

"Naturally, in your form of society it was necessary for you to be given such a conditioned reaction, but you can scarcely expect us to surrender our freedom, to connive at our own re-subjection by calling our oppressors into existence again."

"Oh, you *won't* understand. It was only the more stupid men and women who were continually at war with one another. Lots of us were complementary. We were pairs who formed units."

She smiled. "My dear, either you are surprisingly ill-informed on your own period, or else the stupidity you speak of was astonishingly dominant. Neither as myself, nor as a historian, can I consider that we should be justified in resurrecting such a state of affairs. A primitive stage of our development has now given way to a civilized era. Woman, who is the vessel of life, had the misfortune to find man necessary for a time, but now she does so no longer. Are you suggesting that such a useless and dangerous encumbrance ought to be preserved, out of sheer sentimentality? I will admit that we have lost some minor conveniences—you will have noticed, I expect, that we are less inventive mechanically, and tend to copy the patterns we have inherited; but that troubles us very little; our interests lie not in the inorganic, but in the organic and the sentient. Perhaps men could show us how to travel twice as fast, or how to fly to the moon, or how to kill more people more quickly; but it does not seem to us that such kinds of knowledge would be good payment for re-enslaving ourselves. No, our kind of world suits us better—all of us except a few Reactionists. You have seen our Servitors. They are a little timid in manner, perhaps, but are they oppressed, or sad? Don't they chatter among themselves as brightly and perkily as sparrows? And the Workers—those you called the Amazons—don't they look strong, healthy, and cheerful?"

"But you're robbing them all—robbing them of their birthright."

"You mustn't give me cant, my dear. Did not your social system conspire to rob a woman of her 'birthright' unless she married? You not only let her know it, but socially you rubbed it in: here, our Servitors and Workers do not know it, and they are not worried by a sense of inadequacy. Motherhood is the function of the Mothers, and understood as such."

I shook my head. "Nevertheless, they are being robbed. A woman has a right to love—"

For once she was a little impatient as she cut me short.

"You keep repeating to me the propaganda of your age. The love you talk about, my dear, existed in your little sheltered part of the world by polite and profitable convention. You were scarcely ever allowed to see its other face, unglamourized by Romance. *You* were never openly bought and sold, like livestock; *you* never had to sell yourself to the first comer in order to live; *you* did not happen to be one of the women who through the centuries screamed in agony and suffered and died under invaders in a sacked city—nor were you ever flung into a pit of fire to be saved from them; *you* were never compelled to suttee upon your dead husband's pyre; *you* did not have to spend your whole life imprisoned in a harem; *you* were never part of the cargo of a slave-ship; *you* never retained your own life only at the pleasure of your lord and master. . . .

"That is the other side—the age-long side. There is going to be no more of such things. They are finished at last. Dare you suggest that we should call them back, to suffer them all again?"

"But most of these things had already gone," I protested. "The world was getting better."

"Was it?" she said. "I wonder if the women of Berlin thought so when it fell? Was it, indeed?—or was it on the edge of a new barbarism?"

"But if you can only get rid of evil by throwing out the good, too, what is there left?"

"There is a great deal. Man was only a means to an end. We needed him in order to have babies. The rest of his vitality accounted for all the misery in the world. We are a great deal better off without him."

"So you really consider that you've improved on nature?"

"Tcha!" she said, impatient with my tone. "Civilization *is* improvement on nature. Would you want to live in a cave and have most of your babies die in infancy?"

"There are some things, some fundamental things—" I began, but she checked me, holding up her hand for silence.

Outside, the long shadows had crept across the lawns. In the evening quiet I could hear a choir of women's voices singing some little distance away. We listened for some minutes until the song was finished.

"Beautiful!" said the old lady. "Could angels themselves sing more sweetly? They sound happy enough, don't they? Our own lovely children—two of my granddaughters are there among them. They are happy, and they've reason to be happy: they're not growing up into a world where they must gamble on the goodwill of some man to keep them; they'll never need to be servile before a lord and master; they'll never stand in danger of rape and butchery, either. Listen to them!"

Another song had started and came lilting lightly to us out of the dusk.

"Why are you crying?" the old lady asked me as it ended.

"I know it's stupid—I don't really believe any of this is what it seems to be—so I suppose I'm crying for all you would have lost if it were true," I told her. "There should be lovers out there under the trees; they should be listening hand in hand to that song while they watch the moon rise. But there are no lovers now, there won't be any more. . . ." I looked back at her.

"Did you ever read the lines: 'Full many a flower is born to blush unseen, and waste its sweetness on the desert air'? Can't you feel the forlornness of this world you've made? Do you *really* not understand?" I asked.

"I know you've only seen a little of us, but do you not begin to understand what it can be like when women are no longer forced to fight one another for the favours of men?" she countered.

We talked on while the dusk gave way to darkness and the lights of other houses started to twinkle through the trees. Her reading had been wide. It had given her even an affection for some periods of the past, but her approval of her own era was unshaken. She felt no aridity in it. Always it was my 'conditioning' which prevented me from seeing that the golden age of woman had begun at last.

"You cling to too many myths," she told me. "You speak of a full life, and your instance is some unfortunate woman hugging her chains in a suburban villa. Full life, fiddlesticks! But it was convenient for the traders that she could be made to think so. A truly full life would be an exceedingly short one, in any form of society."

And so on. . . .

At length, the little parlourmaid reappeared to say that my attendants were ready to leave when it should be convenient. But there was one thing I very much wanted to know before I left. I put the question to the old lady.

"Please tell me. How did it—how could it—happen?"

"Simply by accident, my dear—though it was the kind of accident that was entirely the product of its time. A piece of research which showed unexpected, secondary results, that's all."

"But how?"

"Rather curiously—almost irrelevantly, you might say. Did you ever hear of a man called Perrigan?"

"Perrigan?" I repeated. "I don't think so; it's an uncommon name."

"It became very commonly known indeed," she assured me. "Doctor Perrigan was a biologist, and his concern was the extermination of rats—particularly the brown rat, which used to do a great deal of expensive damage.

"His approach to the problem was to find a disease which would attack them fatally. In order to produce it he took as his basis a virus infection often fatal to rabbits—or, rather, a group of virus infections that were highly selective, and also unstable since they were highly liable to mutation. Indeed, there was so much variation in the strains that when infection of rabbits in Australia was tried, it was only at the sixth attempt that it was successful; all the earlier strains died out as the rabbits developed immunity. It was tried in other places, too, though with indifferent success until a still more effective strain was started in France, and ran through the rabbit population of Europe.

"Well, taking some of these viruses as a basis, Perrigan induced new mutations by irradiation and other means, and succeeded in producing a variant that would attack rats. That was not enough, however, and he continued his work until he had a strain that had enough of its ancestral selectivity to attack only the brown rat, and with great virulence.

"In that way he settled the question of a long-standing pest, for there are no brown rats now. But something went amiss. It is still an open question whether the successful virus mutated again, or whether one of his earlier experimental viruses was accidentally liberated by escaped 'carrier' rats, but that's academic. The important thing is that somehow a strain capable of attacking human beings got loose, and that it was already widely disseminated before it was traced—also, that once it was free, it spread with devastating speed; too fast for any effective steps to be taken to check it.

"The majority of women were found to be immune; and of the ten per cent or so whom it attacked over eight per cent recovered. Among men, however, there was almost no immunity, and the few recoveries were only partial. A few men were preserved by the most elaborate precautions, but they could not be kept confined for ever, and in the end the virus, which had a remarkable capacity for dormancy, got them, too."

Inevitably several questions of professional interest occurred to me, but for an answer she shook her head.

"I'm afraid I can't help you there. Possibly the medical people will be willing to explain," she said, but her expression was doubtful.

I manœuvred myself into a sitting position on the side of the couch.

"I see," I said. "Just an accident—yes, I suppose one could scarcely think of it happening any other way."

"Unless," she remarked, "unless one were to look upon it as divine intervention."

"Isn't that a little impious?"

"I was thinking of the Death of the Firstborn," she said, reflectively.

There did not seem to be an immediate answer to that. Instead, I asked:

"Can you honestly tell me that you never have the feeling that you are living in a dreary kind of nightmare?"

"Never," she said. "There was a nightmare—but it's over now. Listen!"

The voices of the choir, reinforced now by an orchestra, reached us distantly out of the darkened garden. No, they were not dreary: they even sounded almost exultant—but then, poor things, how were they to understand . . . ?

My attendants arrived and helped me to my feet. I thanked the old lady for her patience with me and her kindness. But she shook her head.

"My dear, it is I who am indebted to you. In a short time I have learnt more about the conditioning of women in a mixed society than all my books have been able to show me in the rest of my long life. I hope, my dear, that the doctors will find some way of enabling you to forget it and live happily here with us."

At the door I paused and turned, still helpfully shored up by my attendants.

"Laura," I said, using her name for the first time, "so many of your arguments are right—yet, over all, you're, oh, so *wrong*. Did you never read of lovers? Did you never, as a girl, sigh for a Romeo who would say: 'It is the east, and Laura is the sun!'?"

"I think not. Though I have read the play. A pretty, idealized tale—I wonder how much heartbreak it has given to how many would-be Juliets? But I would set a question against yours, my dear Jane. Did you ever see Goya's cycle of pictures called 'The Horrors of War'?"

The pink car did not return me to the 'Home'. Our destination turned out to be a more austere and hospital-like building where I was fussed into bed in a room alone. In the morning, after my massive breakfast, three new doctors visited me. Their manner was more social than professional, and we chatted amiably for half an hour. They had evidently been fully informed on my conversation with the old lady, and they were not averse to answering my questions. Indeed, they found some amusement in many of them, though I found none, for there was nothing consolingly vague in what they told me—it all sounded too disturbingly practicable, once the technique had been worked out. At the end of that time, however, their mood changed. One of them, with an air of getting down to business said:

"You will understand that you present us with a problem. Your fellow Mothers, of course, are scarcely susceptible to Reactionist disaffection—though you have in quite a short time managed to disgust and bewilder them considerably—but on others less stable your influence might be more serious. It is not just a matter of what you may say; your difference from the rest is implicit in your whole attitude. You cannot help that, and, frankly, we do not see how you, as a woman of education, could possibly adapt yourself to the placid, unthinking acceptance that is expected of a Mother. You would quickly feel frustrated beyond endurance. Furthermore, it is clear that the conditioning you have had under your system prevents you from feeling any goodwill towards ours."

I took that straight; simply as a judgment without bias. Moreover, I could not dispute it. The prospect of spending the rest of my life in pink, scented, soft-musicked illiteracy, interrupted, one gathered, only by the production of quadruplet daughters at regular intervals, would certainly have me violently unhinged in a very short time.

"And so—what?" I asked. "Can you reduce this great carcase to normal shape and size?"

She shook her head. "I imagine not—though I don't know that it has ever been attempted. But even if it were possible, you would be just as much of a misfit in the Doctorate—and far more of a liability as a Reactionist influence."

I could understand that, too.

"What, then?" I inquired.

She hesitated, then she said gently:

"The only practicable proposal we can make is that you should agree to a hypnotic treatment which will remove your memory."

As the meaning of that came home to me I had to fight off a rush of panic. After all, I told myself, they were being reasonable with me. I must do my best to respond sensibly. Nevertheless, some minutes must have passed before I answered, unsteadily.

"You are asking me to commit suicide. My mind is my memories: they are me. If I lose them I shall die, just as surely as if you were to kill my—this body."

They did not dispute that. How could they?

There is just one thing that makes my life worth living—knowing that you loved me, my sweet, sweet Donald. It is only in my memory that you live now. If you ever leave there you will die again—and for ever.

"No!" I told them. "No! No!"

At intervals during the day small servitors staggered in under the weight of my meals. In between their visits I had only my thoughts to occupy me, and they were not good company.

"Frankly," one of the doctors had put it to me, not unsympathetically, "we can see no alternative. For years after it happened the annual figures of mental breakdowns were our greatest worry. Even though the women then could keep themselves fully occupied with the tremendous amount of work that had to be done, so many of them could not adjust. And we can't even offer you work."

I knew that it was a fair warning she was giving me—and I knew that, unless the hallucination which seemed to grow more real all the time could soon be induced to dissolve, I was trapped.

During the long day and the following night I tried my hardest to get back to the objectivity I had managed earlier, but I failed. The whole dialectic was too strong for me now; my senses too consciously aware of my surroundings; the air of consequence and coherence too convincingly persistent. . . .

When they had let me have twenty-four hours to think it over, the same trio visited me again.

"I think," I told them, "that I understand better now. What you are offering me is painless oblivion, in place of a breakdown followed by oblivion—and you see no other choice."

"We don't," admitted the spokeswoman, and the other two nodded. "But, of course, for the hypnosis we shall need your co-operation."

"I realize that," I told her, "and I also see now that in the circumstances it would be obstinately futile to withhold it. So I—I—yes, I'm willing to give it—but on one condition."

They looked at me questioningly.

"It is this," I explained, "that you will try one other course first. I want you to give me an injection of chuinjuatin. I want it in precisely the same strength as I had it before—I can tell you the dose.

"You see, whether this is an intense hallucination, or whether it is some kind of projection which makes it seem very similar, it must have something to do with that drug. I'm sure it must—nothing remotely like this has ever happened to me before. So, I thought that if I could repeat the condition—or, would you say, believe myself to be repeating the condition?—there may be just a chance . . . I don't know. It may be simply silly . . . but even if nothing comes of it, it can't make things worse in any way now, can it? So, if you will let me try it. . . ?"

The three of them considered for some moments.

"I can see no reason why not . . ." said one.

The spokeswoman nodded.

"I shouldn't think there'll be any difficulty with authorization in the circumstances," she agreed. "If you want to try, well, it's fair to let you, but—I'd not count on it too much. . . ."

In the afternoon half a dozen small servitors arrived, bustling round, making me and the room ready, with anxious industry. Presently there came one more, scarcely tall enough to see over the trolley of bottles, trays, and phials which she pushed to my bedside.

The three doctors entered together. One of the little servitors began rolling up my sleeve. The doctor who had done most of the talking looked at me, kindly, but seriously.

"This is a sheer gamble, you know that?" she said.

"I know. But it's my only chance. I'm willing to take it."

She nodded, picked up the syringe, and charged it while the little servitor swabbed my monstrous arm. She approached the bedside, and hesitated.

"Go on," I told her. "What is there for me here, anyway?"

She nodded, and pressed in the needle . . . .

Now, I have written the foregoing for a purpose. I shall deposit it with my bank, where it will remain unread unless it should be needed.

I have spoken of it to no one. The report on the effect of chuinjuatin—the one that I made to Dr. Hellyer where I described my sensation as simply one of floating in space—was false. The foregoing was my true experience.

I concealed it because after I came round, when I found that I was back in my own body in my normal world, the experience haunted me as vividly as if it had been actuality. The details were too sharp, too vivid, for me to get them out of my mind. It overhung me all the time, like a threat. It would not leave me alone. . . .

I did not dare to tell Dr. Hellyer how it worried me—he would have put me under treatment. If my other friends did not take it seriously enough to recommend treatment, too, then they would have laughed over it, and amused themselves at my expense interpreting the symbolism. So I kept it to myself.

As I went over parts of it again and again in detail, I grew angry with myself for not asking the old lady for more facts, things like dates, and details that could be verified. If, for instance, the thing should, by her account, have started two or three years ago, then the whole sense of threat would fall to pieces: it would all be discredited. But it had not occurred to me to ask that crucial question. . . . And then, as I went on thinking about it, I remembered that there was one, just one, piece of information that I could check, and I made inquiries. I wish now that I had not, but I felt forced to. . . .

So I have discovered that:

There *is* a Dr. Perrigan, he *is* a biologist, he does work with rabbits and rats. . . .

He is quite well known in his field. He has published papers on pest-control in a number of journals. It is no secret that he is evolving new strains of myxomatosis to attack rats; indeed, he has already developed a group of them and calls them mucosimorbus, though he has not yet succeeded in making them either stable or selective enough for general use. . . .

But I had never heard of this man or his work until his name was mentioned by the old lady in my 'hallucination'. . . .

I have given a great deal of thought to this whole matter. What sort of experience is it that I have recorded above? If it should be a kind of prevision of an inevitable, predestined future, then nothing anyone could do would change it. But this does not seem to me to make sense: it is what has happened, and is happening now, that determines the future. Therefore, there must be a great number of *possible* futures, each a possible consequence of what is being done now. It seems to me that under chuinjuatin I saw one of those futures. . . .

It was, I think, a warning of what *may* happen—unless it is prevented. . . .

The whole idea is so repulsive and misconceived, it amounts to such a monstrous aberration of the normal course, that failure to heed the warning would be neglect of duty to one's kind.

I shall, therefore, on my own responsibility and without taking any other person into my confidence, do my best to ensure that such a state as I have described *cannot* come about.

Should it happen that any other person is unjustly accused of doing, or of assisting me to do, what I intend to do, this document must stand in his defence. That is why I have written it.

It is my own unaided decision that Dr. Perrigan must not be permitted to continue his work.

(Signed) Jane Waterleigh

The solicitor stared at the signature for some moments; then he nodded.

"And so," he said, "she then took her car and drove over to Perrigan's—with this tragic result.

"From the little I do know of her, I'd say that she probably did her best to persuade him to give up his work—though she can scarcely have expected any success with that. It is difficult to imagine a man who would be willing to give up the work of years on account of what must sound to him like a sort of gipsy's warning. So, clearly, she went prepared to fall back on direct action, if necessary. It looks as if the police are quite right when they suppose her to have shot him deliberately; but not so right when they suppose that she burnt the place down to hide evidence of the crime. The statement makes it pretty obvious that her main intention in doing that was to wipe out Perrigan's work."

He shook his head. "Poor girl! There's a clear conviction of duty in her last page or two: the sort of simplified clarity that drives martyrs on, regardless of consequences. She has never denied that she did it. What she wouldn't tell the police is *why* she did it."

He paused again, before he added: "Anyway, thank goodness for this document. It ought at least to save her life. I should be very surprised indeed if a plea of insanity could fail, backed up by this." He tapped the pile of manuscript with his finger. "It's a lucky thing she put off her intention of taking it to her bank."

Dr. Hellyer's face was lined and worried.

"I blame myself most bitterly for the whole thing," he said. "I never ought to have let her try the damned drug in the first place, but I thought she was over the shock of her husband's death. She was trying to keep her time fully occupied, and she was anxious to volunteer. You've met her enough to know how purposeful she can be. She saw it as a chance to contribute something to medical knowledge—which it was, of course. But I ought to have been more careful, and I ought to have seen afterwards that there was something wrong. The real responsibility for this thing runs right back to me."

"H'm," said the solicitor. "Putting that forward as a main line of defence isn't going to do you a lot of good professionally, you know, Hellyer."

"Possibly not. I can look after that when we come to it. The point is that I hold a responsibility for her as a member of my staff, if for no other reason. It can't be denied that, if I had refused her offer to take part in the experiment, this would not have happened. Therefore it seems to me that we ought to be able to argue a state of temporary insanity; that the balance of her mind was disturbed by the effects of the drug which I administered. And if we can get that as a verdict it will result in detention at a mental hospital for observation and treatment—perhaps quite a short spell of treatment."

"I can't say. We can certainly put it up to counsel and see what he thinks of it."

"It's valid, too," Hellyer persisted. "People like Jane don't do murder if they are in their right minds, not unless they're really in a corner, then they do it more cleverly. Certainly they don't murder perfect strangers. Clearly, the drug caused an hallucination sufficiently vivid to confuse her to a point where she was unable to make a proper distinction between the actual and the hypothetical. She got into a state where she believed the mirage was real, and acted accordingly."

"Yes. Yes, I suppose one might put it that way," agreed the solicitor. He looked down again at the pile of paper before him. "The whole account is, of course, unreasonable," he said, "and yet it is pervaded throughout with such an air of reasonableness. I wonder . . ." He paused pensively, and went on: "This expendability of the male, Hellyer. She doesn't seem to find it so much incredible, as undesirable. That seems odd in itself to a layman who takes the natural order for granted, but would you, as a medical scientist, say it was—well, not impossible, in theory?"

Dr. Hellyer frowned.

"That's very much the kind of question one wants more notice of. It would be very rash to proclaim it *impossible*. Considering it purely as an abstract problem, I can see two or three lines of approach. . . . Of course, if an utterly improbable situation were to arise calling for intensive research—research, that is, on the sort of scale they tackled the atom—well, who can tell . . . ?" He shrugged.

The solicitor nodded again.

"That's just what I was getting at," he observed. "Basically it is only just such a little way off the beam; quite near enough to possibility to be faintly disturbing. Mind you, as far as the defence is concerned, her air of thorough conviction, taken in conjunction with the near-plausibility of the thing, will probably help. But as far as I am concerned it is just that nearness that is enough to make me a trifle uneasy."

The doctor looked at him rather sharply.

"Oh, come! Really now! A hard-boiled solicitor, too! Don't tell me you're going in for fantasy-building. Anyway, if you are, you'll have to conjure up another one. If Jane, poor girl, has settled one thing, it is that there's no future in this particular fantasy. Perrigan's finished with, and all his work's gone up in smoke."

"H'm," said the solicitor again. "All the same, it would be more satisfactory if we knew of some way other than this"—he tapped the pile of papers—"some other way in which she is likely to have acquired a knowledge of Perrigan and his work. There is, as far as one knows, no other way in which he can have come into her orbit at all—unless, perhaps, she takes an interest in veterinary subjects?"

"She doesn't. I'm sure of that," Hellyer told him, shaking his head.

"Well, that, then, remains one slightly disturbing aspect. And there is another. You'll think it foolish of me, I'm sure—and no doubt time will prove you right to do so—but I have to admit I'd be feeling easier in my mind if Jane had been just a bit more thorough in her inquiries before she went into action."

"Meaning—?" asked Dr. Hellyer, looking puzzled.

"Only that she does not seem to have found out that there is a son. But there is, you see. He appears to have taken quite a close interest in his father's work, and is determined that it shan't be wasted. In fact he has already announced that he will do his best to carry it on with the very few specimens that were saved from the fire. . . .

"Laudably filial, no doubt. All the same it does disturb me a little to find that he, also happens to be D.Sc., a biochemist; and that very naturally, his name, too, is Perrigan. . . ."

PART FOUR
Culture

17 Ideology, Cognitive Consistency, and Crucial Experiment

Social psychologists have long been interested in the dynamics of cognitive organization, particularly in the manner in which individuals integrate new ideas or facts with existing belief systems. Knowledge of this process could provide a basis for understanding the manner in which attitudes and beliefs initially develop; it is certainly the key to understanding how cognitive structures are modified by new information. The problem of accounting for the way in which individuals assimilate new information is particularly intriguing, for some evidence suggests that individuals strive for a certain consistency among their cognitions, and other evidence indicates that they frequently maintain sets of beliefs that are psychologically inconsistent.

Considerable research has been done on the manner in which beliefs about a certain topic—say, beliefs about the qualities possessed by a friend or an acquaintance—are interrelated and on the extent to which the evaluation of one facet of an issue, or one aspect of a person's character, determines expectations about other facets of the issue or aspects of his character. If, for example, a person's experience with another leads him to believe that the other is honest in his business dealings, he will be more likely to expect the other to possess additional positive attributes, rather than negative ones. If additional information indicates that the person is miserly and treats his family badly, it will cause considerable discomfort for the person who at first possessed only positive information about his acquaintance. An attempt to attain cognitive consistency will typically follow receipt of the new information. Under these circumstances, it is likely that some thought will be given to the question of whether the initial impression of honesty was erroneous. Usually, the individual will seek some way of reconciling the psychological inconsistency of a person's being both honest and miserly.

The various strategies that individuals use in attempting to reconcile distressing cognitive inconsistencies have been only minimally charted, and even less is known about the conditions under which two or more inconsistent beliefs, belief systems, or sets of beliefs and actions can be maintained. It is, for example, not clearly understood how a man is able to feel no great psychological stress when he claims to be committed to the revolution of a society and the abolition of economic capitalism and yet permits himself to be supported by the income from stock investments made for him by his parents. In the same vein, little is understood of the psychological mechanisms that permit a man to claim to adhere to a value system in which material possessions are considered irrelevant and yet define his life in terms of his possessions.

Harry Harrison's story "The Streets of Ashkelon" deals with the effects on a nonhuman species of the introduction of two sets of beliefs that are commonly held by humans and that contradict one another.

The Streets of Ashkelon

HARRY HARRISON

Somewhere above, hidden by the eternal clouds of Wesker's World, a thunder rumbled and grew. Trader John Garth stopped when he heard it. . . .

"That noise is the same as the noise of your sky-ship," Itin said, with stolid Wesker logicality, slowly pulverizing the idea in his mind and turning over the bits one by one for closer examination. "But your ship is still sitting where you landed it. It must be, even though we cannot see it, because you are the only one who can operate it. And even if anyone else could operate it we would have heard it rising into the sky. Since we did not, and if this sound is a sky-ship sound, then it must mean. . ."

"Yes, another ship," Garth said, too absorbed in his own thoughts to wait for the laborious Weskerian chains of logic to clank their way through to the end. . . .

"You better go ahead, Itin," he said. "Use the water so you can get to the village quickly. Tell everyone to get back into the swamps, well clear of the hard ground. That ship is landing on instruments and anyone underneath at touchdown is going to be cooked."

This immediate threat was clear enough to the little Wesker amphibian. Before Garth finished speaking Itin's ribbed ears had folded like a bat's wing and he slipped silently into the nearby canal. Garth squelched on through the mud, making as good time as he could over the clinging surface. He had just reached the fringes of the village clearing when the rumbling grew to a head-splitting roar and the spacer broke through the low-hanging layer of clouds above. Garth shielded his eyes from the down-reaching tongue of flame and examined the growing form of the grey-black ship with mixed feelings.

After almost a standard year on Wesker's World he had to fight down a longing for human companionship of any kind. While this buried fragment of herd-spirit chattered for the rest of the monkey tribe, his trader's mind was busily drawing a line under a column of figures and adding up the total. This could very well be another trader's ship, and if it were his monopoly of the Wesker trade was at an end. Then again, this might not be a trader at all, which was the reason he stayed in the shelter of the giant fern and loosened his gun in its holster.

The ship baked dry a hundred square metres of mud, the roaring blast died, and the landing feet crunched down through the crackling crust. Metal creaked and settled into place while the cloud of smoke and steam slowly drifted lower in the humid air.

"Garth, where are you?" the ship's speaker boomed. The lines of the spacer had looked only slightly familiar, but there was no mistaking the rasping tones of that voice. Garth wore a smile when he stepped out into the open and whistled shrilly through two fingers. A directional microphone ground out of its casing on the ship's fin and turned in his direction.

"What are you doing here, Singh?" he shouted towards the mike. . . .

"I am on course to a more fairly atmosphered world where a fortune is waiting to be made. I only stopped here since an opportunity presented to turn an honest credit by running a taxi service. I bring you friendship, the perfect companionship, a man in a different line of business who might help you in yours. I'd come out and say hello myself, except I would have to decon for biologicals. I'm cycling the passenger through the lock so I hope you won't mind helping with his luggage."

At least there would be no other trader on the planet now, that worry was gone. But Garth still wondered what sort of passenger would be taking one-way passage to an uninhabited world. And what was behind that concealed hint of merriment in Singh's voice? He walked around to the far side of the spacer where the ramp had dropped, and looked up at the man in the cargo lock who was wrestling ineffectually with a large crate. The man turned towards him and Garth saw the clerical dog-collar and knew just what it was Singh had been chuckling about.

"What are you doing here?" Garth asked; in spite of his attempt at self control he snapped the words. If the man noticed this he ignored it, because he was still smiling and putting out his hand as he came down the ramp.

"Father Mark," he said. "Of the Missionary Society of Brothers. I'm very pleased to . . ."

"I said what are you doing here." Garth's voice was under control now, quiet and cold. He knew what had to be done, and it must be done quickly or not at all.

"That should be obvious," Father Mark said, his good nature still unruffled. "Our missionary society has raised funds to send spiritual emissaries to alien worlds for the first time. I was lucky enough . . . "

"Take your luggage and get back into the ship. You're not wanted here and have no permission to land. You'll be a liability and there is no one on Wesker to take care of you. Get back into the ship."

"I don't know who you are sir, or why you are lying to me," the priest said. He was still calm but the smile was gone. "But I have studied galactic law and the history of this planet very well. There are no diseases or beasts here that I should have any particular fear of. It is also an open planet, and until the Space Survey changes that status I have as much right to be here as you do."

The man was of course right, but Garth couldn't let him know that. He had been bluffing, hoping the priest didn't know his rights. But he did. There was only one distasteful course left for him, and he had better do it while there was still time.

"Get back in that ship," he shouted, not hiding his anger now. With a smooth motion his gun was out of the holster and the pitted black muzzle only inches from the priest's stomach. The man's face turned white, but he did not move.

"What the hell are you doing, Garth!" Singh's shocked voice grated from the speaker. "The guy paid his fare and you have no rights at all to throw him off the planet."

"I have this right," Garth said, raising his gun and sighting between the priest's eyes. "I give him thirty seconds to get back aboard the ship or I pull the trigger."

"Well I think you are either off your head or playing a joke," Singh's exasperated voice rasped down at them. "If a joke, it is in bad taste, and either way you're not getting away with it. Two can play at that game, only I can play it better."

There was the rumble of heavy bearings and the remote-controlled four-gun turret on the ship's side rotated and pointed at Garth. "Now—down gun and give Father Mark a hand with the luggage," the speaker commanded, a trace of humour back in the voice now. "As much as I would like to help, Old Friend, I cannot. I feel it is time you had a chance to talk to the father; after all, I have had the opportunity of speaking with him all the way from Earth."

Garth jammed the gun back into the holster with an acute feeling of loss. Father Mark stepped forward, the winning smile back now and a bible taken from a pocket of his robe, in his raised hand. "My son," he said.

"I'm not your son," was all Garth could choke out as defeat welled up in him. His fist drew back as the anger rose, and the best he could do was open the fist so he struck only with the flat of his hand. Still the blow sent the priest crashing to the ground and fluttered the pages of the book splattering into the thick mud.

Itin and the other Weskers had watched everything with seemingly emotionless interest, and Garth made no attempt to answer their unspoken questions. He started towards his house, but turned back when he saw they were still unmoving.

"A new man has come," he told them. "He will need help with the things he has brought. If he doesn't have any place for them, you can put them in the big warehouse until he has a place of his own."

He watched them waddle across the clearing towards the ship, then went inside and gained a certain satisfaction from slamming the door hard enough to crack one of the panes. There was an equal amount of painful pleasure in breaking out one of the remaining bottles of Irish whiskey that he had been saving for a special occasion. Well this was special enough, though not really what he had had in mind. The whiskey was good and burned away some of the bad taste in his mouth, but not all of it. If his tactics had worked, success would have justified everything. But he had failed and in addition to the pain of failure there was the acute feeling that he had made a horse's ass out of himself. Singh had blasted off without any good-byes. There was no telling what sense he had made of the whole matter, though he would surely carry some strange stories back to the trader's lodge. Well, that could be worried about the next time Garth signed in. Right now he had to go about setting things right with the missionary. Squinting out through the rain he saw the man struggling to erect a collapsible tent while the entire population of the village stood in ordered ranks and watched. Naturally none of them offered to help.

By the time the tent was up and the crates and boxes stowed inside it the rain had stopped. The level of fluid in the bottle was a good bit lower and Garth felt more like facing up to the unavoidable meeting. In truth, he was looking forward to talking to the man. This whole nasty business aside, after an entire solitary year any human companionship looked good. *Will you join me now for dinner. John Garth,* he wrote on the back of an old invoice. But maybe the guy was too frightened to come? Which was no way to start any kind of relationship. Rummaging under the bunk, he found a box that was big enough and put his pistol inside. Itin was of course waiting outside the door when he opened it, since this was his tour as Knowledge Collector. He handed him the note and the box.

"Would you take these to the new man," he said.

"Is the new man's name New Man?" Itin asked.

"No, it's not!" Garth snapped. "His name is Mark. But I'm only asking you to deliver this, not get involved in conversation."

As always when he lost his temper, the literal minded Weskers won the round. "You are not asking for conversation," Itin said slowly, "but Mark may ask for conversation. And others will ask me his name, if I do not know his na . . ." The voice cut off as Garth slammed the door. This didn't work in the long run either because next time he saw Itin—a day, a week, or even a month later—the monologue would be picked up on the very word it had ended and the thought rambled out to its last frayed end. Garth cursed under his breath and poured water over a pair of the tastier concentrates that he had left.

"Come in," he said when there was a quiet knock on the door. The priest entered and held out the box with the gun.

"Thank you for the loan, Mr. Garth, I appreciate the spirit that made you send it. I have no idea of what caused the unhappy affair when I landed, but I think it would be best forgotten if we are going to be on this planet together for any length of time."

"Drink?" Garth asked, taking the box and pointing to the bottle on the table. He poured two glasses full and handed one to the priest. "That's about what I had in mind, but I still owe you an explanation of what happened out there." He scowled into his glass for a second, then raised it to the other man. "It's a big universe and I guess we have to make out as best we can. Here's to Sanity."

"God be with you," Father Mark said, and raised his glass as well.

"Not with me or with this planet," Garth said firmly. "And that's the crux of the matter." He half-drained the glass and sighed.

"Do you say that to shock me?" the priest asked with a smile. "I assure you it doesn't."

"Not intended to shock. I meant it quite literally. I suppose I'm what you would call an atheist, so revealed religion is no concern of mine. While these natives, simple and unlettered stone-age types that they are, have managed to come this far with no superstitions or traces of deism whatsoever. I had hoped that they might continue that way."

"What are you saying?" the priest frowned. "Do you mean they have no gods, no belief in the hereafter? They must die . . . ?"

"Die they do, and to dust returneth like the rest of the animals. They have thunder, trees, and water without having thunder-gods, tree sprites, or water nymphs. They have no ugly little gods, taboos, or spells to hag-ride and limit their lives. They are the only primitive people I have ever encountered that are completely free of superstition and appear to be much happier and sane because of it. I just wanted to keep them that way."

"You wanted to keep them from God—from salvation?" The priest's eyes widened and he recoiled slightly.

"No," Garth said. "I wanted to keep them from superstition until they knew more and could think about it realistically without being absorbed and perhaps destroyed by it."

"You're being insulting to the Church, sir, to equate it with superstition . . ."

"Please," Garth said, raising his hand. "No theological arguments. I don't think your society footed the bill for this trip just to attempt a conversion on me. Just accept the fact that my beliefs have been arrived at through careful thought over a period of years, and no amount of undergraduate metaphysics will change them. I'll promise not to try and convert you—if you will do the same for me."

"Agreed, Mr. Garth. As you have reminded me, my mission here is to save these souls, and that is what I must do. But why should my work disturb you so much that you try and keep me from landing? Even threaten me with your gun and . . ." the priest broke off and looked into his glass.

"And even slug you?" Garth asked, suddenly frowning. "There was no excuse for that, and I would like to say that I'm sorry. Plain bad manners and an even worse temper. Live alone long enough and you find yourself doing that kind of thing." He brooded down at his big hands where they lay on the table, reading memories into the scars and callouses patterned there. "Let's just call it frustration, for lack of a better word. In your business you must have had a lot of chance to peep into the darker places in men's minds and you should know a bit about motives and happiness. I have had too busy a life to ever consider settling down and raising a family, and right up until recently I never missed it. Maybe leakage radiation is softening up my brain, but I had begun to think of these furry and fishy Weskers as being a little like my own children, that I was somehow responsible to them."

"We are all His children," Father Mark said quietly.

"Well, here are some of His children that can't even imagine His existence," Garth said, suddenly angry at himself for allowing gentler emotions to show through. Yet he forgot himself at once, leaning forward with the intensity of his feelings. "Can't you realize the importance of this? Live with these Weskers awhile and you will discover a simple and happy life that matches the state of grace you people are always talking about. They get *pleasure* from their lives—and cause no one pain. By circumstances they have evolved on an almost barren world, so have never had a chance to grow out of a physical stone age culture. But mentally they are our match—or perhaps better. They have all learned my language so I can easily explain the many things they want to know. Knowledge and the gaining of knowledge gives them real satisfaction. They tend to be exasperating at times because every new fact must be related to the structure of all other things, but the more they learn the faster this process becomes. Someday they are going to be man's equal in every way, perhaps surpass us. If—would you do me a favour?"

"Whatever I can."

"Leave them alone. Or teach them if you must—history and science, philosophy, law, anything that will help them face the realities of the greater universe they never even knew existed before. But don't confuse them with your hatreds and pain, guilt, sin, and punishment. Who knows the harm. . ."

"You are being insulting, sir!" the priest said, jumping to his feet. The top of his grey head barely came to the massive spaceman's chin, yet he showed no fear in defending what he believed. Garth, standing now himself, was no longer the penitent. They faced each other in anger, as men have always stood, unbending in the defence of that which they think right.

"Yours is the insult," Garth shouted. "The incredible egotism to feel that your derivative little mythology, differing only slightly from the thousands of others that still burden men, can do anything but confuse their still fresh minds! Don't you realize that they believe in truth—and have never heard of such a thing as a lie. They have not been trained yet to understand that other kinds of minds can think differently from theirs. Will you spare them this . . . ?"

"I will do my duty which is His will, Mr. Garth. These are God's creatures here, and they have souls. I cannot shirk my duty, which is to bring them His word, so that they may be saved and enter into the kingdom of heaven."

When the priest opened the door the wind caught it and blew it wide. He vanished into the stormswept darkness and the door swung back and forth and a splatter of raindrops blew in. Garth's boots left muddy footprints when he closed the door, shutting out the sight of Itin sitting patiently and uncomplaining in the storm, hoping only that Garth might stop for a moment and leave with him some of the wonderful knowledge of which he had so much.

By unspoken consent that first night was never mentioned again. After a few days of loneliness, made worse because each knew of the other's proximity, they found themselves talking on carefully neutral grounds. Garth slowly packed and stowed away his stock and never admitted that his work was finished and he could leave at any time. He had a fair amount of interesting drugs and botanicals that would fetch a good price. And the Wesker Artifacts were sure to create a sensation in the sophisticated galactic market. Crafts on the planet here had been limited before his arrival, mostly pieces of carving painfully chipped into the hard wood with fragments of stone. He had supplied tools and a stock of raw metal from his own supplies, nothing more than that. In a few months the Weskers had not only learned to work with the new materials, but had translated their own designs and forms into the most alien—but most beautiful—artifacts that he had ever seen. All he had to do was release these on the market to create a primary demand, then return for a new supply. The Weskers wanted only books and tools and knowledge in return, and through their own efforts he knew they would pull themselves into the galactic union.

This is what Garth had hoped. But a wind of change was blowing through the settlement that had grown up around his ship. No longer was he the centre of attention and focal point of the village life. He had to grin when he thought of his fall from power; yet there was very little humour in the smile. Serious and attentive Weskers still took turns of duty as Knowledge Collectors, but their recording of dry facts was in sharp contrast to the intellectual hurricane that surrounded the priest.

Where Garth had made them work for each book and machine, the priest gave freely. Garth had tried to be progressive in his supply of knowledge, treating them as bright but unlettered children. He had wanted them to walk before they could run, to master one step before going on the next.

Father Mark simply brought them the benefits of Christianity. The only physical work he required was the construction of a church, a place of worship and learning. More Weskers had appeared out of the limitless planetary swamps and within days the roof was up, supported on a framework of poles. Each morning the congregation worked a little while on the walls, then hurried inside to learn the all-promising, all-encompassing, all-important facts about the universe.

Garth never told the Weskers what he thought about their new interest, and this was mainly because they never asked him. Pride or honour stood in the way of his grabbing a willing listener and pouring out his grievances. Perhaps it would have been different if Itin was on Collecting duty; he was the brightest of the lot; but Itin had been rotated the day after the priest had arrived and Garth had not talked to him since.

It was a surprise then when after seventeen of the trebly-long Wesker days, he found a delegation at his doorstep when he emerged after breakfast. Itin was their spokesman, and his mouth was open slightly. Many of the other Weskers had their mouths open as well, one even appearing to be yawning, clearly revealing the double row of sharp teeth and the purple-black throat. The mouths impressed Garth as to the seriousness of the meeting: this was the one Wesker expression he had learned to recognize. An open mouth indicated some strong emotion; happiness, sadness, anger, he could never be really sure which. The Weskers were normally placid and he had never seen enough open mouths to tell what was causing them. But he was surrounded by them now.

"Will you help us, John Garth," Itin said. "We have a question."

"I'll answer any question you ask," Garth said, with more than a hint of misgiving. "What is it?"

"Is there a God?"

"What do you mean by 'God'?" Garth asked in turn. What should he tell them?

"God is our Father in Heaven, who made us all and protects us. Whom we pray to for aid, and if we are saved will find a place . . ."

"That's enough," Garth said. "There is no God."

All of them had their mouths open now, even Itin, as they looked at Garth and thought about his answer. The rows of pink teeth would have been frightening if he hadn't known these creatures so well. For one instant he wondered if perhaps they had been already indoctrinated and looked upon him as a heretic, but he brushed the thought away.

"Thank you," Itin said, and they turned and left.

Though the morning was still cool, Garth noticed that he was sweating and wondered why.

The reaction was not long in coming. Itin returned that same afternoon. "Will you come to the church?" he asked. "Many of the things that we study are difficult to learn, but none as difficult as this. We need your help because we must hear you and Father talk together. This is because he says one thing is true and you say another is true and both cannot be true at the same time. We must find out what is true."

"I'll come, of course," Garth said, trying to hide the sudden feeling of elation. He had done nothing, but the Weskers had come to him anyway. There could still be grounds for hope that they might yet be free.

It was hot inside the church, and Garth was surprised at the number of Weskers who were there, more than he had seen gathered at any one time before. There were many open mouths. Father Mark sat at a table covered with books. He looked unhappy but didn't say anything when Garth came in. Garth spoke first.

"I hope you realize this is their idea—that they came to me of their own free will and asked me to come here?"

"I know that," the priest said resignedly. "At times they can be very difficult. But they are learning and want to believe, and that is what is important."

"Father Mark, Trader Garth, we need your help," Itin said. "You both know many things that we do not know. You must help us come to religion which is not an easy thing to do." Garth started to say something, then changed his mind. Itin went on. "We have read the bibles and all the books that Father Mark gave us, and one thing is clear. We have discussed this and we are all agreed. These books are very different from the ones that Trader Garth gave us. In Trader Garth's books there is the universe which we have not seen, and it goes on without God, for he is mentioned nowhere; we have searched very carefully. In Father Mark's books He is everywhere and nothing can go without Him. One of these must be right and the other must be wrong. We do not know how this can be, but after we find out which is right then perhaps we will know. If God does not exist . . ."

"Of course He exists, my children," Father Mark said in a voice of heartfelt intensity. "He is our Father in Heaven who has created us all . . ."

"Who created God?" Itin asked and the murmur ceased and every one of the Weskers watched Father Mark intensely. He recoiled a bit under the impact of their eyes, then smiled.

"Nothing created God, since He is the Creator. He always was . . ."

"If He always was in existence—why cannot the universe have always been in existence? Without having had a creator?" Itin broke in with a rush of words. The importance of the question was obvious. The priest answered slowly, with infinite patience.

"Would that the answers were that simple, my children. But even the scientists do not agree about the creation of the universe. While they doubt—we who have seen the light *know*. We can see the miracle of creation all about us. And how can there be a creation without a Creator? That is He, our Father, our God in Heaven. I know you have doubts; that is because you have souls and free will. Still, the answer is so simple. Have faith, that is all you need. Just believe."

"How can we believe without proof?"

"If you cannot see that this world itself is proof of His existence, then I say to you that belief needs no proof—if you have faith!"

A babble of voices arose in the room and more of the Wesker mouths were open now as they tried to force their thoughts through the tangled skein of words and separate the thread of truth.

"Can you tell us, Garth?" Itin asked, and the sound of his voice quieted the hubbub.

"I can tell you to use the scientific method which can examine all things—including itself—and give you answers that can prove the truth or falsity of any statement."

"That is what we must do," Itin said, "we had reached the same conclusion." He held a thick book before him and a ripple of nods ran across the watchers. "We have been studying the bible as Father Mark told us to do, and we have found the answer. God will make a miracle for us, thereby proving that He is watching us. And by this sign we will know Him and go to Him."

"That is the sin of false pride," Father Mark said. "God needs no miracles to prove His existence."

"But *we* need a miracle!" Itin shouted, and though he wasn't human there was need in his voice. "We have read here of many smaller miracles—loaves, fishes, wine, snakes—many of them, for much smaller reasons. Now all He need do is make a miracle and He will bring us all to Him—the wonder of an entire new world worshipping at His throne as you have told us, Father Mark. And you have told us how important this is. We have discussed this and find that there is only one miracle that is best for this kind of thing."

His boredom at the theological wrangling drained from Garth in an instant. He had not been really thinking or he would have realized where all this was leading. He could see the illustration in the bible where Itin held it open, and knew in advance what picture it was. He rose slowly from his chair, as if stretching, and turned to the priest behind him.

"Get ready!" he whispered. "Get out the back and get to the ship; I'll keep them busy here. I don't think they'll harm me."

"What do you mean . . . ?" Father Mark asked, blinking in surprise.

"Get out, you fool!" Garth hissed. "What miracle do you think they mean? What miracle is supposed to have converted the world to Christianity?"

"No!" Father Mark said. "It cannot be. It just cannot be . . .!"

"GET MOVING!" Garth shouted, dragging the priest from the chair and hurling him towards the rear wall. Father Mark stumbled to a halt, turned back. Garth leaped for him, but it was already too late. The amphibians were small, but there were so many of them. Garth lashed out and his fist struck Itin, hurling him back into the crowd. The others came on as he fought his way towards the priest. He beat at them but it was like struggling against waves. The furry, musky bodies washed over and engulfed him. He fought until they tied him, and he still struggled until they beat on his head until he stopped. Then they pulled him outside where he could only lie in the rain and curse and watch.

Of course the Weskers were marvellous craftsmen, and everything had been constructed down to the last detail, following the illustration in the bible. There was the cross, planted firmly on the top of a small hill, the gleaming metal spikes, the hammer. Father Mark was stripped and draped in a carefully pleated loincloth. They led him out of the church.

At the sight of the cross he almost fainted. After that he held his head high and determined to die as he had lived, with faith.

Yet this was hard. It was unbearable even for Garth, who only watched. It is one thing to talk of crucifixion and look at the gentle carved bodies in the dim light of prayer. It is another to see a man naked, ropes cutting into his skin where he hangs from a bar of wood. And to see the needle-tipped spike raised and placed against the soft flesh of his palm, to see the hammer come back with the calm deliberation of an artisan's measured stroke. To hear the thick sound of metal penetrating flesh.

Then to hear the screams.

Few are born to be martyrs; Father Mark was not one of them. With the first blows, the blood ran from his lips where his clenched teeth met. Then his mouth was wide and his head strained back and the guttural horror of his screams sliced through the susurration of the falling rain. It resounded as a silent echo from the masses of watching Weskers, for whatever emotion opened their mouths was now tearing at their bodies with all its force, and row after row of gaping jaws reflected the crucified priest's agony.

Mercifully he fainted as the last nail was driven home. Blood ran from the raw wounds, mixing with the rain to drip faintly pink from his feet as the life ran out of him. At this time, somewhere at this time, sobbing and tearing at his own bonds, numbed from the blows on the head, Garth lost consciousness.

He awoke in his own warehouse and it was dark. Someone was cutting away the woven ropes they had bound him with. The rain still dripped and splashed outside.

"Itin," he said. It could be no one else.

"Yes," the alien voice whispered back. "The others are all talking in the church. Lin died after you struck his head, and Inon is very sick. There are some that say you should be crucified too, and I think that is what will happen. Or perhaps killed by stoning on the head. They have found in the bible where it says . . ."

"I know." With infinite weariness. "An eye for an eye. You'll find lots of things like that once you start looking. It's a wonderful book." His head ached terribly.

"You must go, you can get to your ship without anyone seeing you. There has been enough killing." Itin as well, spoke with a new-found weariness.

Garth experimented, pulling himself to his feet. He pressed his head to the rough wood of the wall until the nausea stopped. "He's dead." He said it as a statement, not a question.

"Yes, some time ago. Or I could not have come away to see you."

"And buried of course, or they wouldn't be thinking about starting on me next."

"And buried!" There was almost a ring of emotion in the alien's voice, an echo of the dead priest's. "He is buried and he will rise on High. It is written and that is the way it will happen. Father Mark will be so happy that it has happened like this." The voice ended in a sound like a human sob.

Garth painfully worked his way towards the door, leaning against the wall so he wouldn't fall.

"We did the right thing, didn't we?" Itin asked. There was no answer. "He will rise up, Garth, won't he rise?"

Garth was at the door and enough light came from the brightly lit church to show his torn and bloody hands clutching at the frame. Itin's face swam into sight close to his, and Garth felt the delicate, many fingered hands with the sharp nails catch at his clothes.

"He will rise, won't he, Garth?"

"No," Garth said, "he is going to stay buried right where you put him. Nothing is going to happen because he is dead and he is going to stay dead."

The rain runnelled through Itin's fur and his mouth was opened so wide that he seemed to be screaming into the night. Only with effort could he talk, squeezing out the alien thoughts in an alien language.

"Then we will not be saved? We will not become pure?"

"You were pure," Garth said, in a voice somewhere between a sob and a laugh. "That's the horrible ugly dirty part of it. You were pure. Now you are . . ."

"Murderers," Itin said, and the water ran down from his lowered head and streamed away into the darkness.

18 From the Secular to the Sacred

In his novel *A Canticle for Leibowitz* Walter M. Miller, Jr., chronicles the regeneration of a civilization following nuclear war. As in the Middle Ages, the one organized attempt to preserve knowledge is carried on by a religious institution. In Miller's future the only major institution to survive the war (the "Flame Deluge," in the novel) is a mutated form of the Roman Catholic church.

After the holocaust, even the continued existence of religion itself is in doubt for a time. Most of the population who survive the Flame Deluge are, for understandable reasons, violently opposed to preserving anything from the past. In the eyes of those who experienced the war, nothing is to be despised more greatly than a scientist or a scholar; even the merely literate are suspect. For these are the men whose knowledge and energies created the instruments necessary to the conduct of nuclear warfare.

The excerpts from Miller's novel treat two important events in the history of the Albertian Order of Leibowitz. The order takes responsibility for the preservation of some "pre-Deluge" scienfific knowledge. This charge makes the Order, in fact, responsible for preserving a more important matter—the fundamentals of a belief system conducive to scientific and scholarly activity. Bits and pieces of "pre-Deluge" science—two pages of a text on Lebesque equations, half a blueprint for a gun turret—are hardly sufficient to lead to the rapid regeneration of a technological society sophisticated enough to destroy itself through nuclear war. The preservation of a system of beliefs supporting scientific investigation could, however, provide the social conditions necessary to the development of a technological society in a shorter time than it took originally.

The first excerpt tells how the Order of Leibowitz was founded. The history of the period is written in the style of a religious-historical account.

A Canticle for Leibowitz

WALTER M. MILLER, JR.

It was said that God, in order to test mankind which had become swelled with pride as in the time of Noah, had commanded the wise men of that age, among them the Blessed Leibowitz, to devise great engines of war such as had never before been upon the Earth, weapons of such might that they contained the very fires of Hell, and that God had suffered these magi to place the weapons in the hands of princes, and to say to each prince: "Only because the enemies have such a thing have we devised this for thee, in order that they may know that thou hast it also, and fear to strike. See to it, m'Lord, that thou fearest them as much as they shall now fear thee, that none may unleash this dread thing which we have wrought."

But the princes, putting the words of their wise men to naught, thought each to himself: If I but strike quickly enough, and in secret, I shall destroy those others in their sleep, and there will be none to fight back; the earth shall be mine.

Such was the folly of princes, and there followed the Flame Deluge.

Within weeks—some said days—it was ended, after the first unleashing of the hell-fire. Cities had become puddles of glass, surrounded by vast acreages of broken stone. While nations had vanished from the earth, the lands littered with bodies, both men and cattle, and all manner of beasts together with the birds of the air and all things that flew, all things that swam in the rivers, crept in the grass, or burrowed in holes; having sickened and perished, they covered the land, and yet where the demons of the Fallout covered the countryside, the bodies for a time would not decay, except in contact with fertile earth. The great clouds of wrath engulfed the forests and the fields, withering trees and causing the crops to die. There were great deserts where once life was, and in those places of the Earth where men still lived, all were sickened by the poisoned air, so that, while some escaped death, none was left untouched; and many died even in those lands where the weapons had not struck, because of the poisoned air.

In all parts of the world men fled from one place to other places, and there was a confusion of tongues. Much wrath was kindled against the princes and the servants of the princes and against the magi who had devised the weapons. Years passed, and yet the Earth was not cleansed. So it was clearly recorded in the Memorabilia.

From the confusion of tongues, the intermingling of the remnants of many nations, from fear, the hate was born. And the hate said: *Let us stone and disembowel and burn the ones who did this thing. Let us make a holocaust of those who wrought this crime, together with their hirelings and their wise men; burning, let them perish, and all their works, their names, and even their memories. Let us destroy them all, and teach our children that the world is new, that they may know nothing of the deeds that went before. Let us make a great simplification, and then the world shall begin again.*

So it was that, after the Deluge, the Fallout, the plagues, the madness, the confusion of tongues, the rage, there began the bloodletting of the Simplification, when remants of mankind had torn other remnants limb from limb, killing rulers, scientists, leaders, technicians, teachers, and whatever persons the leaders of the maddened mobs said deserved death for having helped to make the Earth what it had become. Nothing had been so hateful in the sight of these mobs as the man of learning, at first because they had served the princes, but then later because they refused to join in the bloodletting and tried to oppose the mobs, calling the crowds "bloodthirsty simpletons."

Joyfully the mobs accepted the name, took up the cry: *Simpletons! Yes, yes! I'm a simpleton! Are you a simpleton? We'll build a town and we'll name it Simple Town, because by then all the smart bastards that caused all this, they'll be dead! Simpletons! Let's go! This ought to show 'em! Anybody here not a simpleton? Get the bastard, if there is!*

To escape the fury of the simpleton packs, such learned people as still survived fled to any sanctuary that offered itself. When Holy Church received them, she vested them in monks' robes and tried to hide them in such monasteries and convents as had survived and could be reoccupied, for the religious were less despised by the mob except when they openly defied it and accepted martyrdom. Sometimes such sanctuary was effective, but more often it was not. Monasteries were invaded, records and sacred books were burned, refugees were seized and summarily hanged or burned. The Simplification had ceased to have plan or purpose soon after it began, and became an insane frenzy of mass murder and destruction such as can occur only when the last traces of social order are gone. The madness was transmitted to the children, taught as they were—not merely to forget—but to hate, and surges of mob fury recurred sporadically even through the fourth generation after the Deluge. By then, the fury was directed not against the learned, for there were none, but against the merely literate.

Isaac Edward Leibowitz, after a fruitless search for his wife, had fled to the Cistercians where he remained in hiding during the early post-Deluge years. After six years, he had gone once more to search for Emily or her grave, in the far southwest. There he had become convinced at last of her death, for death was unconditionally triumphant in that place. There in the desert he quietly made a vow. Then he went back to the Cistercians, took their habit, and after more years became a priest. He gathered a few companions about him and made some quiet proposals. After a few more years, the proposals filtered to "Rome," which was no longer Rome (which was no longer a city), having moved elsewhere, moved again, and still again—in less than two decades, after staying in one place for two millennia. Twelve years after the proposals were made, Father Isaac Edward Leibowitz had won permission from the Holy See to found a new community of religious, to be named after Albertus Magnus, teacher of Saint Thomas, and patron of men of science. Its task, unannounced, and at first only vaguely defined, was to preserve human history for the great-great-great-grandchildren of the children of the simpletons who wanted it destroyed. Its earliest habit was burlap rags and bindlestiffs—the uniform of the simpleton mob. Its members were either "bookleggers" or "memorizers," according to the tasks assigned. The bookleggers smuggled books to the southwest desert and buried them there in kegs. The memorizers committed to rote memory entire volumes of history, sacred writings, literature, and science, in case some unfortunate book smuggler was caught, tortured, and forced to reveal the location of the kegs. Meanwhile, other members of the new Order located a water hole about three days' journey from the book cache and began the building of a monastery. The project, aimed at saving a small remnant of human culture from the remnant of humanity who wanted it destroyed, was then underway.

Leibowitz, while taking his own turn at booklegging, was caught by a simpleton mob; a turncoat technician, whom the priest swiftly forgave, identified him as not only a man of learning, but also a specialist in the weapons field. Hooded in burlap, he was martyred forthwith, by strangulation with a hangman's noose not tied for neck-breaking, at the same time being roasted alive—thus settling a dispute in the crowd concerning the method of execution.

The memorizers were few, their memories limited.

Some of the book kegs were found and burned, as well as several other bookleggers. The monastery itself was attacked thrice before the madness subsided.

From the vast store of human knowledge, only a few kegs of original books and a pitiful collection of hand-copied texts, rewritten from memory, had survived in the possession of the Order by the time the madness had ended.

Now, after six centuries of darkness, the monks still preserved this Memorabilia, studied it, copied and recopied it, and patiently waited. At the beginning, in the time of Leibowitz, it had been hoped—and even anticipated as probable—that the fourth of fifth generation would begin to want its heritage back. But the monks of the earliest days had not counted on the human ability to generate a new cultural inheritance in a couple of generations if an old one is utterly destroyed, to generate it by virtue of lawgivers and prophets, geniuses or maniacs; through a Moses, or through a Hitler, or an ignorant but tyrannical grandfather, a cultural inheritance may be acquired between dusk and dawn, and many have been so acquired. But the new "culture" was an inheritance of darkness, wherein "simpleton" meant the same thing as "citizen" meant the same thing as "slave." The monks waited. It mattered not at all to them that the knowledge they saved was useless, that much of it was not really knowledge now, was as inscrutable to the monks in some instances as it would be to an illiterate wild-boy from the hills; this knowledge was empty of content, its subject matter long since gone. Still, such knowledge had a symbolic structure that was peculiar to itself, and at least the symbol interplay could be observed. To observe the way a knowledge-system is knit together is to learn at least a minimum knowledge-of-knowledge, until someday—someday, or some century—an Integrator would come, and things would be fitted together again. So time mattered not at all. The Memorabilia was there, and it was given to them by duty to preserve, and preserve it they would if the darkness in the world lasted ten more centuries, or even ten thousand years, for they, though born in that darkest of ages, were still the very bookleggers and memorizers of the Beatus Leibowitz; and when they wandered abroad from their abbey, each of them, the professed of the Order—whether stable-hand or Lord Abbot—carried as part of his habit a book, usually a Breviary these days, tied up in a bindlestiff.

About 600 years after the founding of the order, the question of canonizing Leibowitz is being considered by the church. The major stumbling block to his elevation is that available information is inadequate to determine when Leibowitz' wife died; he cannot be canonized unless it can be proved that his wife had died before he took vows.

At the start of this excerpt, Brother Francis, a novice performing a vigil in the desert near the abbey, has just discovered an opening in the ground. To understand his reactions to his discoveries, we must remember that knowledge of "pre-Deluge" America is at best vague; no written records survive, and for the first few generations after the war "pre-Deluge" science and history were actively suppressed. To complicate matters further, the war has come to be viewed in terms of a set of religious beliefs and to be interpreted as punishment for the sins of civilization. Keeping these facts in mind, consider how some remnants of America *circa* 1970 might be understood by a man attempting to integrate them with a set of vague and distorted images of the past and an interpretation of history that is bound up with a well established set of religious beliefs.

A dust column which had plumed up from the site of the cave-in was tapering away on the breeze. He hoped someone would see it from the abbey's watchtowers and come to investigate. At his feet, a square opening yawned in the earth, where one flank of the mound had collapsed into the pit below. Stairs led downward, but only the top steps remained unburied by the avalanche which had paused for six centuries in mid-fall to await the assistance of Brother Francis before completing its roaring descent.

On one wall of the stair well a half-buried sign remained legible. Mustering his modest command of pre-Deluge English, he whispered the words haltingly:

FALLOUT SURVIVAL SHELTER
Maximum Occupancy: 15

> Provision limitations, single occupant: 180 days; divide by actual number of occupants. Upon entering shelter, see that First Hatch is securely locked and sealed, that the intruder shields are electrified to repel contaminated persons attempting entry, that the warning lights are ON outside the enclosure. . . .

The rest was buried, but first word was enough for Francis. He had never seen a "Fallout," and he hoped he'd never see one. A consistent description of the monster had not survived, but Francis had heard the legends. He crossed himself and backed away from the hole. Tradition told that the Beatus Leibowitz himself had encountered a Fallout, and had been possessed by it for many months before the exorcism which accompanied his Baptism drove the fiend away.

Brother Francis visualized a Fallout as half-salamander, because, according to tradition, the thing was born in the Flame Deluge, and as half-incubus who despoiled virgins in their sleep, for, were not the monsters of the world still called "children of the Fallout"? That the demon was capable of inflicting all the woes which descended upon Job was recorded fact, if not an article of creed.

The novice stared at the sign in dismay. Its meaning was plain enough. He had unwittingly broken into the abode (deserted, he prayed) of not just one, but fifteen of the dreadful beings! He groped for his phial of holy water. . . .

Brother Francis lowered himself gingerly into the stair well of the ancient Fallout Shelter, armed as he was only with holy water and an improvised torch lighted from the banked embers of last night's fire. He had waited more than an hour for someone from the abbey to come investigate the dust plume. No one had come.

To abandon his vocational vigil even briefly, unless seriously ill or unless ordered to return to the abbey, would be regarded as an *ipso facto* renunciation of his claim of a true vocation to life as a monk of the Albertian Order of Leibowitz. Brother Francis would have preferred death. He was faced, therefore, with the choice of investigating the fearsome pit before sunset, or of spending the night in his burrow in ignorance of whatever might lurk in the shelter and might reawaken to prowl in darkness. . . .

The debris which had crashed down into the shelter formed a hill with its crest near the head of the stairs, and there was only a narrow squeeze-way between the rocks and the ceiling. He went through it feet first and found himself forced to continue feet first, because of the steepness of the slope. Thus confronting the Unknown face-to-backside, he groped for footholds in the loose heap of broken stone and gradually worked his way downward. Occasionally, when his torch flickered low, he paused to tilt its flame downward, letting the fire spread further along the wood; during such pauses, he tried to appraise the danger about him and below. There was little to be seen. He was in an underground room, but at least one third of its volume was filled by the mound of debris that had fallen through the stair well. The cascade of stone had covered all the floor, crushed several pieces of furniture that he could see, and perhaps had completely buried others. He saw battered metal lockers leaning awry, waist-deep in rubble. At the far end of the room was a metal door, hinged to swing toward him, and tightly sealed by the avalanche. Still legible in flaking paint on the door were the stenciled letters:

INNER HATCH
SEALED ENVIRONMENT

Evidently the room into which he was descending was only an antechamber. But whatever lay beyond "Inner Hatch" was sealed there by several tons of rock against the door. Its environment was "Sealed" indeed, unless it had another exit.

Having made his way to the foot of the slope, and after assuring himself that the antechamber contained no obvious menace, the novice went cautiously to inspect the metal door at closer range by torchlight. Printed under the stenciled letters of "Inner Hatch" was a smaller rust-streaked sign:

WARNING: This hatch must not be sealed before all personnel have been admitted, or before all steps of safety procedure prescribed by Technical Manual CD-Bu-83A have been accomplished. When Hatch is sealed, air within shelter will be pressurized 2.0 p.s.i. above ambient barometic level to minimize inward diffusion. Once sealed, the hatch will be automatically unlocked by the servomoniter system when, but not before, any of the following conditions prevail: (1) when the exterior radiation count falls below the danger level, (2) when the air and water repurification system fails, (3) when the food supply is exhausted, (4) when the internal power supply fails. See CD-Bu-83A for further instructions.

Brother Francis found himself slightly confused by the Warning, but he intended to heed it by not touching the door at all. The miraculous contraptions of the ancients were not to be carelessly tampered with, as many a dead excavator-of-the-past had testified with his dying gasp.

Brother Francis noticed that the debris which had been lying in the antechamber for centuries was darker in color and rougher in texture than the debris which had weathered under the desert sun and in the sandy wind before today's cave-in. One could tell by a glance at the stones that Inner Hatch had been blocked not by today's rockslide but by one more ancient than the abbey itself. If Fallout Shelter's Sealed Environment contained a Fallout, the demon had obviously not opened Inner Hatch since the time of the Flame Deluge, before the Simplification. And, if it had been sealed beyond the metal door for so many centuries, there was small reason, Francis told himself, to fear that it might come bursting through the hatch today.

His torch burned low. Having found a splintered chair leg, he set it ablaze with his waning flame, then began gathering bits of broken furniture with which to build a dependable fire, meanwhile pondering the meaning of that ancient sign: *Fallout Survival Shelter.*

As Brother Francis readily admitted, his mastery of pre-Deluge English was far from masterful yet. The way nouns could sometimes modify other nouns in that tongue had always been one of his weak points. In Latin, as in most simple dialects of the region, a construction like *servus puer* meant about the same thing as *puer servus,* and even in English *slave boy* meant *boy slave*. But there the similarity ended. He had finally learned that *house cat* did not mean *cat house*, and that a dative of purpose or possession, as in *mihi amicus*, was somehow conveyed by *dog food* or *sentry box* even without inflection. But what of a triple appositive like *fallout survival shelter*? Brother Francis shook his head. The Warning on Inner Hatch mentioned food, water, and air, and yet surely these were not necessities for the fiends of Hell. At times, the novice found pre-Deluge English more perplexing that either Intermediate Angelology or Saint Leslie's theological calculus.

He built his fire on the slope of the rubble pile, where it could brighten the darker crannies of the antechamber. Then he went to explore whatever might remain uncovered by debris. The ruins above ground had been reduced to archaeological ambiguity by generations of scavengers, but this underground ruin had been touched by no hand but the hand of impersonal disaster. The place seemed haunted by the presences of another age. A skull, lying among the rocks in a darker corner, still retained a gold tooth in its grin—clear evidence that the shelter had never been invaded by wanderers. The gold incisor flickered when the fire danced high.

More than once in the desert had Brother Francis encountered, near some parched arroyo, a small heap of human bones, picked clean and whitening in the sun. He was not especially squeamish, and one expected such things. He was, therefore, not startled when he first noticed the skull in the corner of the antechamber, but the flicker of gold in its grin kept catching his eye while he pried at the doors (locked or stuck) of the rusty lockers and tugged at the drawers (also stuck) of a battered metal desk. The desk might prove to be a priceless find, if it contained documents or a small book or two that had survived the angry bonfires of the Age of Simplification. While he kept trying to open the drawers, the fire burned low; he fancied that the skull began emitting a faint glow of its own. Such a phenomenon was not especially uncommon, but in the gloomy crypt, Brother Francis found it somehow most disturbing. He gathered more wood for the fire, returned to jerk and tug at the desk, and tried to ignore the skull's flickering grin. While a little wary yet of lurking Fallouts, Francis had sufficiently recovered from his initial fright to realize that the shelter, notably the desk and the lockers, might well be teeming with rich relics of an age which the world had, for the most part, deliberately chosen to forget.

Providence had bestowed a blessing here. To find a bit of the past which had escaped both the bonfires and the looting scavengers was a rare stroke of luck these days. There was, however, always a risk involved. Monastic excavators, alert for ancient treasures, had been known to emerge from a hole in the ground, triumphantly carrying a strange cylindrical artifact, and then—while cleaning it or trying to ascertain its purpose—press the wrong button or twist the wrong knob, thereby ending the matter without benefit of clergy. Only eighty years ago the Venerable Boedullus had written with obvious delight to his Lord Abbot that his small expedition had uncovered the remains of, in his own words, "the site of an intercontinental launching pad, complete with several fascinating subterranean storage tanks." No one at the abbey ever knew what the Venerable Boedullus meant by "intercontinental launching pad," but the Lord Abbot who had reigned at that time sternly decreed that monastic antiquarians must, on pain of excommunication, avoid such "pads" thenceforth. For his letter to the abbot was the last that anyone ever saw of the Venerable Boedullus, his party, his "launching pad" site, and the small village which had grown up over that site; an interesting lake now graced the landscape where the village had been, thanks to some shepherds who diverted the course of a creek and caused it to flow into the crater to store water for their flocks in time of drought. A traveler who had come from that direction about a decade ago reported excellent fishing in that lake, but the shepherds thereabouts regarded the fish as the souls of the departed villagers and excavators; they refused to fish there because of Bo'dollos, the giant catfish that brooded in the deep.

. . . nor shall any other excavation be initiated which does not have as its primary purpose the augmentation of the Memorabilia, the Lord Abbot's decree had

added—meaning that Brother Francis should search the shelter only for books and papers, not tampering with interesting hardware.

The gold-capped tooth kept winking and glittering at the corner of his eye while Brother Francis heaved and strained at the desk drawers. The drawers refused to budge. He gave the desk a final kick and turned to glare impatiently at the skull: *Why don't you grin at something else for a change?*

The grin remained. The gold-toothed residuum lay with its head pillowed between a rock and a rusty metal box. Quitting the desk, the novice picked his way across the debris at last for a closer inspection of the mortal remains. Clearly, the person had died on the spot, struck down by the torrent of stones and half buried by the debris. Only the skull and the bones of one leg had not been covered. The femur was broken, the back of the skull was crushed.

Brother Francis breathed a prayer for the departed, then very gently lifted the skull from its resting place and turned it around so that it grinned toward the wall. Then his eye fell on the rusty box. . . .

Minutes later, seated on a cracked foundation slab, he began removing the tidbits of metal and glass that filled the trays he found in the box. Most of them were small tubular things with a wire whisker at each end of each tube. These, he had seen before. The abbey's small museum had a few of them, of various size, shape, and color. Once he had seen a shaman of the hill-pagan people wearing a string of them as a ceremonial necklace. The hill people thought of them as "parts of the body of the god"—of the fabled *Machina analytica,* hailed as the wisest of their gods. By swallowing one of them, a shaman could acquire "Infallibility," they said. He certainly acquired Indisputability that way, among his own people—unless he swallowed one of the poison kind. The similar tidbits in the museum were connected together too—not in the form of a necklace, but as a complex and rather disorderly maze in the bottom of a small metal box, exhibited as "Radio Chassis: Application Uncertain."

Inside the lid of the carrying case, a note had been glued; the glue had powdered, the ink had faded, and the paper was so darkened by rusty stains that even good handwriting would have been hard enough to read, but this was written in a hasty scrawl. He studied it intermittenly while emptying the trays. It seemed to be English, of a sort, but half an hour passed before he deciphered most of the message:

Carl—

Must grab plane for [*undecipherable*] in twenty minutes. For God's sake, keep Em there till we know if we're at war. Please! try to get her on the alternate list for the shelter. Can't get her a seat my plane. Don't tell her why I sent her over with this box of junk, but try to keep her there till we know [*undecipherable*] at worst, one of the alternates not show.

I.E.L.

P.S. I put the seal on the lock and put TOP SECRET on the lid just to keep Em from looking inside. First tool box I happened to grab. Shove it in my locker or something.

The note seemed hasty gibberish to Brother Francis, who was at the moment too excited to concentrate on any single item more than the rest. After a final sneer at the note-writer's hasty scrawl, he began the task of removing the tray-racks to get at the papers in the bottom of the box. The trays were mounted on a swinging linkage which was obviously meant to swing the trays out of the box in stair-step array, but the pins were rusted fast, and Francis found it necessary to pry them out with a short steel tool from one of the tray compartments.

When Brother Francis had removed the last tray, he touched the papers reverently: only a handful of folded documents here, and yet a treasure; for they had escaped the angry flames of the Simplification, wherein even sacred writings had curled, blackened, and withered into smoke while ignorant mobs howled and hailed it a triumph. He handled the papers as one might handle holy things, shielding them from the wind with his habit, for all were brittle and cracked from age. There was a sheaf of rough sketches and diagrams. There were hand-scribbled notes, two large folded papers, and a small book entitled *Memo.*

First he examined the jotted notes. They were scrawled by the same hand that had written the note glued to the lid, and the penmanship was no less abominable. *Pound pastrami,* said one note, *can kraut, six bagels—bring home for Emma.* Another reminded: *Remember—pick up Form 1040, Uncle Revenue.* Another was only a column of figures with a circled total from which a second amount was subtracted and finally a percentage taken, followed by the word *damn!* Brother Francis checked the figures: he could find no fault with the abominable penman's arithmetic, at least, although he could deduce nothing about what the quantities might represent.

Memo, he handled with special reverence, because its title was suggestive of "Memorabilia." Before opening it, he crossed himself and murmured the Blessing of Texts. But the small book proved a disappointment. He had expected printed matter, but found only a hand-written list of names, places, numbers and dates. The dates ranged throughout the latter part of the fifth decade, and earlier part of the sixth decade, twentieth century. Again it was affirmed!—the contents of the shelter came from the twilight period of the Age of Enlightenment. An important discovery indeed. . . .

He turned to a second folded document; its creases were so brittle that he dared inspect only a little of it, by parting the folds slightly and peering between them.

A diagram it seemed, but—a diagram of white lines on dark paper!

Again he felt the thrill of discovery. It was clearly a blueprint!—and there was not a single original blueprint left at the abbey, but only inked facsimiles of several such prints. Never before had Francis seen an original, although he had seen enough hand-painted reproductions to recognize it as a blueprint, which, while stained and faded, remained legible after so many centuries because of the total darkness and low humidity in the shelter. He turned the document over—and felt brief fury. What idiot had desecrated the priceless paper? Someone had sketched absentminded geometrical figures and childish cartoon faces all over the back. What thoughtless vandal—

The anger passed after a moment's reflection. At the time of the deed, blueprints had probably been as common as weeds, and the owner of the box the probable culprit. He shielded the print from the sun with his own shadow while trying to unfold it further. In the lower right-hand corner was a printed rectangle containing, in simple block letters, various titles, dates, "patent numbers," reference numbers, and names. His eye traveled down the list until it encountered: "CIRCUIT DESIGN BY: Leibowitz, I.E."

He closed his eyes tightly and shook his head until it seemed to rattle. Then he looked again. There it was quite plainly:

CIRCUIT DESIGN BY: Leibowitz, I.E.

He flipped the paper over again. Among the geometric figures and childish sketches, clearly stamped in purple ink, was the form:

THIS FILE COPY TO:

Supv. ______________

Pint. ______________

Dsgn. ______________

Engr. ______________

Army ______________

The name was written in a clear feminine hand, not in the hasty scrawl of the other notes. He looked again at the initialed signature of the note in the lid of the box: I. E. L.—and again at "Circuit Design by . . ." And the same initials appeared elsewhere throughout the notes.

There had been argument, all highly conjectural, about whether the beatified founder of the Order, if finally canonized, should be addressed as Saint Isaac or as Saint Edward. Some even favored Saint Leibowitz as the proper address, since the Beatus had, until the present, been referred to by his surname.

"Beate Leibowitz, ora pro me!" whispered Brother Francis. His hands were trembling so violently that they threatened to ruin the brittle documents.

He had uncovered relics of the Saint.

Of course, New Rome had not yet proclaimed that Leibowitz was a saint, but Brother Francis was so convinced of it that he made bold to add: *"Sancte Leibowitz, ora pro me!"*

Brother Francis wasted no idle logic in leaping to his immediate conclusion: he had just been granted a token of his vocation by Heaven itself. He had found what he had been sent into the desert to find, as Brother Francis saw it. He was called to be a professed monk of the Order.

Forgetting his abbot's stern warning against expecting a vocation to come in any spectacular or miraculous form, the novice knelt in the sand to pray his thanks and to offer a few decades of the rosary for the intentions of the old pilgrim who had pointed out the rock leading to the shelter. *May you find your Voice soon, boy,* the wanderer had said. Not until now did the novice suspect that the pilgrim meant Voice with a capital V.

"Ut solius tuae voluntatis mihi cupidus sim, et vocationis tuae conscius, si digneris me vocare. . ."

19 The Creation of a Perfect Society

Recorded sociological thought precedes the coining of the word "sociology" by more than 2,000 years. One of the earliest and most famous long discourses on the dynamics and effects of social organization is Socrates' description of a utopian society. Recorded in Plato's *Republic,* the society that Socrates described was designed to produce conditions under which "man might realize the best that was in him."[1]

The designer of a utopian society is faced with a task of enormous magnitude. It is virtually impossible for a single person to take a social void and describe in minute detail how it is to be filled with a functioning social system. To succeed at this task calls for creating sociological blueprints that specify *precisely* how the society's stratification system is to operate, how the economic sphere is to be controlled, what norms are to regulate social interaction, how new members of the society are to be socialized, what sort of political institutions will operate, and so on. Consider that it takes about two tons of blueprints to tell a work force how to build an ocean liner; then try to imagine how many volumes of codes and specifications it would take to design completely a social system.

In Socrates' utopia, as in every other utopia ever created, about 99 percent of the social system is expected to be just like the one in which the writer lives, and about 1 percent is to be changed. You can identify the 99 percent by listing all those aspects of the created society that are never discussed. The 1 percent is easily recognized, for it is with this portion of the utopia that the designer concerns himself.

It is hardly likely that the issues a designer raises are selected in some haphazard fashion. The designer of a utopia is himself a member of a real society, and there exist within the set of social arrangements which describe that society the causes of the social problems with which the designer is familiar. It seems likely that the alterations in the social structure of a designer's utopia represent a set of arrangements that he believes would correct some of the problems he understands to exist within his own social world. In some cases writers—Orwell in *1984* and Huxley in *Brave New World*—have created anti-utopias in which undesirable aspects of an existing society are used to focus attention on their possible consequences. For these

[1]*The Republic of Plato,* translated with an introduction by Francis M. Cornford (Oxford at the Clarendon Press, 1941), p. xv. The text reprinted here is Cornford's translation.

reasons, the proposals of creators of utopian societies will be viewed as the proposals of social engineers for the solutions to contemporary problems, some of which still exist.

The sections from *The Republic* deal with a number of issues in the construction of a social system. Material was chosen to shed some light on the principles by which Socrates' utopia was to be constructed, on his thinking about the reasons society is necessary, on the ideal set of social arrangements, and on the manner in which to produce an ideal society. Much of the material attacks a single issue: how to construct a system in which those with power will use it for the good of those they govern, not for their own enhancement. No modern society has come up with a solution that is clearly better than the one proposed by Socrates.[2]

To understand the social order Socrates creates in *The Republic,* it is necessary to understand his assumptions about the nature of man. Socrates assumes that men are inherently different from one another to the extent that their different natures lead necessarily to different occupations. A man's nature is a property, a characteristic, with which he is born and which should determine his occupation and hence his social position. In our day, Socrates' view of men's natures would be identified as an extreme genetic position. The modern counterposition, an extreme environmental position, is that what individuals inherit varies little from one person to another and that most of the differences we observe in adults can be explained as a function of the physical and social environments in which they matured. Recognition of Socrates' position is important because the stratification system of *The Republic* is designed to ensure that men occupy the positions for which they are best suited by their natures. Therefore, the system is one in which some attention is given to discovering precisely what a man's nature suits him for, and virtually no possibility exists of changing one's social position in adult life. In a stratification system designed to be optimal for a society peopled by men who are believed to be substantially affected by their environments, greater attention would probably be given to problems of socially affected opportunities to obtain education and to the mechanisms whereby men are trained to fill social roles that are recognized as being important. In addition, considerably more attention would probably be given to the possibility of change in an individual's social position.

From a modern viewpoint, one of the most interesting aspects of Socrates' utopia is that he attempted to design a system in which there was virtually no expectation of or provision for social change. The system Socrates designed was intended to bring about a state of affairs that would perpetuate itself indefinitely.[3] One can easily understand how the creator of a utopian social system might not consider the management of social change an important issue if his own were pre-scientific, pre-industrial, and pre-technological. It is difficult to imagine the modern designer of a large-scale social system failing to consider how to manage innovations generated by the science and technology of the society. Even if the designer wished to create a social system in which no change was permitted, as does Huxley in *Brave New World,* he would have to incorporate elaborate mechanisms designed to prevent innovations from being made and to prevent their diffusion within the society.

[2]Bellamy considers this same problem in the selection from *Looking Backward.* He postulates the same causation of the problem but proposes a different solution.

[3]This is not the first comment on the static aspect of Socrates' utopia; Plato also noticed it.

The Republic

PLATO

Socrates: My notion is, said I, that a state comes into existence because no individual is self-sufficing; we all have many needs. But perhaps you can suggest some different origin for the foundation of a community?

Adeimantus: No, I agree with you.

So, having all these needs, we call in one another's help to satisfy our various requirements; and when we have collected a number of helpers and associates to live together in one place, we call that settlement a state.

Yes.

So if one man gives another what he has to give in exchange for what he can get, it is because each finds that to do so is for his own advantage.

Certainly.

Very well, said I. Now let us build up our imaginary state from the beginning. Apparently, it will owe its existence to our needs, the first and greatest need being the provision of food to keep us alive. Next we shall want a house; and thirdly, such things as clothing.

True.

How will our state be able to supply all these demands? We shall need at least one man to be a farmer, another a builder, and a third a weaver. Will that do, or shall we add a shoemaker and one or two more to provide for our personal wants?

By all means.

The minimum state, then, will consist of four or five men.

Apparently.

Now here is a further point. Is each one of them to bring the product of his work into a common stock? Should our one farmer, for example, provide food enough for four people and spend the whole of his working time in producing corn, so as to share with the rest; or should he take no notice of them and spend only a quarter of his time on growing just enough corn for himself, and divide the other three-quarters between building his house, weaving his clothes, and making his shoes, so as to save the trouble of sharing with others and attend himself to all his own concerns?

The first plan might be the easier, replied Adeimantus.

That may very well be so, said I; for, as you spoke, it occurred to me, for one thing, that no two people are born exactly alike. There are innate differences which fit them for different occupations.

I agree.

And will a man do better working at many trades, or keeping to one only?

Keeping to one.

And there is another point: obviously work may be ruined, if you let the right time go by. The workman must wait upon the work; it will not wait upon his leisure and allow itself to be done in a spare moment. So the conclusion is that more things will be produced and the work be more easily and better done, when every man is set free from all other occupations to do, at the right time, the one thing for which he is naturally fitted.

That is certainly true.

We shall need more than four citizens, then, to supply all those necessaries we mentioned. You see, Adeimantus, if the farmer is to have a good plough and spade and other tools, he will not make them himself. No more will the builder and weaver and shoemaker make all the many implements they need. So quite a number of carpenters and smiths and other craftsmen must be enlisted. Our miniature state is beginning to grow.

It is.

Still, it will not be very large, even when we have added cowherds and shepherds to provide the farmers with oxen for the plough, and the builders as well as the farmers with draught-animals, and the weavers and shoemakers with wool and leather.

No; but it will not be so very small either.

And yet, again, it will be next to impossible to plant our city in a territory where it will need no imports. So there will have to be still another set of people, to fetch what it needs from other countries.

There will.

Moreover, if these agents take with them nothing that those other countries require in exchange, they will return as empty-handed as they went. So, besides everything wanted for consumption at home, we must produce enough goods of the right kind for the foreigners whom we depend on to supply us. That will mean increasing the number of farmers and craftsmen.

Yes.

And then, there are these agents who are to import and export all kinds of goods—merchants, as we call them. We must have them; and if they are to do business overseas, we shall need quite a number of ship-owners and others who know about that branch of trading.

We shall.

Again, in the city itself how are the various sets of producers to exchange their products? That was our object, you will remember, in forming a community and so laying the foundation of our state.

Obviously, they must buy and sell.

That will mean having a market-place, and a currency to serve as a token for purposes of exchange.

Certainly.

Now suppose a farmer, or an artisan, brings some of his produce to market at a time when no one is there who wants to exchange with him. Is he to sit there idle, when he might be at work?

No, he replied; there are people who have seen an opening here for their services. In well-ordered communities they are generally men not strong enough to be of use in any other occupation. They have to stay where they are in the market-place and take goods for money from those who want to sell, and money for goods from those who want to buy.

That, then, is the reason why our city must include a class of shopkeepers—so we call these people who sit still in the market-place to buy and sell, in contrast with merchants who travel to other countries.

Quite so.

There are also the services of yet another class, who have the physical strength for heavy work, though on intellectual grounds they are hardly worth including in our society—hired labourers, as we call them, because they sell the use of their strength for wages. They will go to make up our population. . . .

Let us [consider] a picture of our citizens' manner of life, with the provision we have made for them. They will be producing corn and wine, and making clothes and shoes. When they have built their houses, they will mostly work without their coats or shoes in summer, and in winter be well shod and clothed. For their food, they will prepare flour and barley-meal for kneading and baking, and set out a grand spread of loaves and cakes on rushes or fresh leaves. Then they will lie on beds of myrtleboughs and bryony and make merry with their children, drinking their wine after the feast with garlands on their heads and singing the praises of the gods. So they will live pleasantly together; and a prudent fear of poverty or war will keep them from begetting children beyond their means.

Here Glaucon interrupted me: You seem to expect your citizens to feast on dry bread.

True, I said; I forgot that they will have something to give it a relish, salt, no doubt, and olives, and cheese, and country stews of roots and vegetables. And for dessert we will give them figs and peas and beans; and they shall roast myrtle-berries and acorns at the fire while they sip their wine. Leading such a healthy life in peace, they will naturally come to a good old age, and leave their children to live after them in the same manner.

That is just the sort of provender you would supply, Socrates, if you were founding a community of pigs.

Well, how are they to live, then, Glaucon?

With the ordinary comforts. Let them lie on couches and dine off tables on such dishes and sweets as we have nowadays.

Ah, I see, said I; we are to study the growth, not just of a state, but of a luxurious one. Well, there may be no harm in that; the consideration of luxury may help us to discover how justice and injustice take root in society. The community I have described seems to me the ideal one, in sound health as it were: but if you want to see one suffering from inflammation, there is nothing to hinder us. So some people, it seems, will not be satisfied to live in this simple way; they must have couches and tables and furniture of all sorts; and delicacies too, perfumes, unguents, courtesans, sweetmeats, all in plentiful variety. And besides, we must not limit ourselves now to those bare necessaries of house and clothes and shoes; we shall have to set going the arts of embroidery and painting, and collect rich materials, like gold and ivory.

Yes.

Then we must once more enlarge our community. The healthy one will not be big enough now; it must be swollen up with a whole multitude of callings not ministering to any bare necessity: hunters and fishermen, for instance; artists in sculpture, painting, and music; poets with their attendant train of professional reciters, actors, dancers, producers; and makers of all sorts of household gear, including everything for women's adornment. And we shall want more servants: children's nurses and attendants, lady's maids, barbers, cooks and confectioners. And then swineherds—there was no need for them in our original state, but we shall want them now; and a great quantity of sheep and cattle too, if people are going to live on meat.

Of course.

And with this manner of life physicians will be in much greater request.

No doubt.

The country, too, which was large enough to support the original inhabitants, will now be too small. If we are to have enough pasture and plough land, we shall have to cut off a slice of our neighbours' territory; and if they too are not content with necessaries, but give themselves up to getting unlimited wealth, they will want a slice of ours.

That is inevitable, Socrates.

So the next thing will be, Glaucon, that we shall be at war.

No doubt.

We need not say yet whether war does good or harm, but only that we have discovered its origin in desires which are the most fruitful source of evils both to individuals and to states.[1]

Quite true.

This will mean a considerable addition to our community—a whole army, to go out to battle with any invader, in defence of all this property and of the citizens we have been describing.

Why so? Can't they defend themselves?

Not if the principle was right, which we all accepted in framing our society. You remember we agreed that no one man can practise many trades or arts satisfactorily.

True.

Well, is not the conduct of war an art, quite as important as shoemaking?

Yes.

But we would not allow our shoemaker to try to be also farmer or weaver or builder, because we wanted our shoes well made. We gave each man one trade, for which he was naturally fitted; he would do good work, if he confined himself to that all his life, never letting the right moment slip by. Now in no form of work is efficiency so important as in war; and fighting is not so easy a business that a man can follow another trade, such as farming or shoemaking, and also be an efficient soldier. Why, even a game like draughts or dice must be studied from childhood; no one can become a fine player in his spare moments. Just taking up a shield or other weapon will not make a man capable of fighting that very day in any sort of warfare, any more than taking up a tool or implement of some kind will make a man a craftsman or an athlete, if he does not understand its use and has never been properly trained to handle it.

[1] "All wars are made for the sake of getting money" *(Phaedo)*.

No, if that were so, tools would indeed be worth having.

These guardians of our state, then, inasmuch as their work is the most important of all, will need the most complete freedom from other occupations and the greatest amount of skill and practice.

I quite agree.

And also a native aptitude for their calling.

Certainly.

So it is our business to define, if we can, the natural gifts that fit men to be guardians of a commonwealth, and to select them accordingly. It will certainly be a formidable task; but we must grapple with it to the best of our power.

Yes. . . .

Don't you think then, said I, that, for the purpose of keeping guard, a young man should have much the same temperament and qualities as a well-bred watch-dog? I mean, for instance, that both must have quick senses to detect an enemy, swiftness in pursuing him, and strength, if they have to fight when they have caught him.

Yes, they will need all those qualities.

And also courage, if they are to fight well.

Of course.

And courage, in dog or horse or any other creature, implies a spirited disposition. You must have noticed that a high spirit is unconquerable. Every soul possessed of it is fearless and indomitable in the face of any danger.

Yes, I have noticed that.

So now we know what physical qualities our Guardian must have, and also that he must be of a spirited temper.

Yes.

Then, Glaucon, how are men of that natural disposition to be kept from behaving pugnaciously to one another and to the rest of their countrymen?

It is not at all easy to see.

And yet they must be gentle to their own people and dangerous only to enemies; otherwise they will destroy themselves without waiting till others destroy them.

True.

What are we to do, then? If gentleness and a high temper are contraries, where shall we find a character to combine them? Both are necessary to make a good Guardian, but it seems they are incompatible. So we shall never have a good Guardian.

It looks like it.

Here I was perplexed, but on thinking over what we had been saying, I remarked that we deserved to be puzzled, because we had not followed up the comparison we had just drawn.

What do you mean? he asked.

We never noticed that, after all, there are natures in which these contraries are combined. They are to be found in animals, and not least in the kind we compared to our Guardian. Well-bred dogs, as you know, are by instinct perfectly gentle to people whom they know and are accustomed to, and fierce to strangers. So the combination of qualities we require for our Guardian is, after all, possible and not against nature.

Evidently.

Do you further agree that, besides this spirited temper, he must have a philosophical element in his nature?

I don't see what you mean.

This is another trait you will see in the dog. It is really remarkable how the creature gets angry at the mere sight of a stranger and welcomes anyone he knows, though he may never have been treated unkindly by the one or kindly by the other. Did that never strike you as curious?

I had not thought of it before; but that certainly is how a dog behaves.

Well, but that shows a fine instinct, which is philosophic in the true sense.

How so?

Because the only mark by which he distinguishes a friendly and an unfriendly face is that he knows the one and does not know the other; and if a creature makes that the test of what it finds congenial or otherwise, how can you deny that it has a passion for knowledge and understanding?

Of course, I cannot.

And that passion is the same thing as philosophy—the love of wisdom.

Yes.

Shall we boldly say, then, that the same is true of human beings? If a man is to be gentle towards his own people whom he knows, he must have an instinctive love of wisdom and understanding.

Agreed.

So the nature required to make a really noble Guardian of our commonwealth will be swift and strong, spirited, and philosophic.

Quite so.

Given those natural qualities, then, how are these Guardians to be brought up and educated? . . .

Socrates devotes considerable attention to the manner in which the population of the Republic is to be educated. His proposals for an educational program are not reproduced here because several such proposals are treated in other selections (chapters 10 and 12). But certain aspects of Socrates' proposed educational system and its relationship to society require comment.

In most discussions of social stability, innovation, and change, Socrates' interest is focused primarily on the Guardian class. The members of this class are thought of as crucial to the stability of the society. Socrates' assumption differs from the assumptions of many modern designers who expend great effort in creating mechanisms to control the masses. Ever since Marx, considerably more attention has been given to the possibility of social change generated by the lower classes.

Socrates argues that once the institutions of a society have been *properly* established, the growth and development of the society will proceed without much need, if any, to modify the basic institutions. (Socrates' society *develops* in terms of the greater acceptance of its unchanging institutions by the population.) He suggests, in fact, that the destruction of a society can usually be explained in terms of a slow erosion of its initial ideals through change.[4] Education is thought of as a method of controlling and thereby holding constant the content of the culture transmitted to each new generation of the population. Since the society is itself virtually unchanging, a set of educational procedures can be designed to teach the answers to the problems with which the person will be confronted during his lifetime; with no innovation there are no new problems, and hence no need to search for new solutions.

The educational system of *The Republic* was a variation on the system in operation in Athens when *The Republic* was written. At that time the family, not the state, was responsible for the education of Athenian boys. Education was usually accomplished in private day-schools, which boys attended until the age of 17. Their education consisted primarily of learning to read and write ("gramatic"); learning and reciting epic and dramatic poetry, playing the lyre and singing lyric poetry, the rudiments of arithmetic and geometry ("music," which included all the arts over which the Muses presided: music, art, letters, culture, and philosophy) and athletic exercises ("gymnastic").

The major modifications Socrates proposed for this system was to make the state responsible for education and for educating both boys and girls. The other changes were designed to assist in the production of Guardians of a certain type. Socrates was concerned with eliminating certain personal characteristics from members of the Guardian class and fostering the development of other attributes. For example, Socrates proposed to eliminate learning of epics and myths that had to do with warfare, intrigue, and battles of god against god, and any stories of self-indulgence and lamentation. Children, it was argued, could not distinguish between allegorical meaning and literal meaning, and hence it was necessary to prevent their exposure to ideas they might misunderstand. Similarly, in his playacting, the young Guardian was to act only certain appropriate roles, since playing the role of an objectionable character might lead to the development of personality traits similar to those of the character.

. . . What is the next point to be settled? Is it not the question, which of these Guardians are to be rulers and which are to obey?

No doubt.

Well, it is obvious that the elder must have authority over the young, and that the rulers must be the best.

Yes.

And as among farmers the best are those with a natural turn for farming, so, if we want the best among our Guardians, we must take those naturally fitted to watch over a commonwealth. They must have the right sort of intelligence and ability; and also they must look upon the commonwealth as their special concern—the sort of concern that is felt for something so closely bound up with oneself that its interests and fortunes, for good or ill, are held to be identical with one's own.

Exactly.

So the kind of men we must choose from among the Guardians will be

[4]This idea is not completely without present day acceptance. Much of the propaganda of a number of extreme right-wing political groups is based on this premise.

those who, when we look at the whole course of their lives, are found to be full of zeal to do whatever they believe is for the good of the commonwealth and never willing to act against its interest.

Yes, they will be the men we want.

We must watch them, I think, at every age and see whether they are capable of preserving this conviction that they must do what is best for the community, never forgetting it or allowing themselves to be either forced or bewitched into throwing it over.

How does this throwing over come about?

I will explain. When a belief passes out of the mind, a man may be willing to part with it, if it is false and he has learnt better, or unwilling, if it is true.

I see how he might be willing to let it go; but you must explain how he can be unwilling.

Where is your difficulty? Don't you agree that men are unwilling to be deprived of good, though ready enough to part with evil? Or that to be deceived about the truth is evil, to possess it good? Or don't you think possessing truth means thinking of things as they really are?

You are right. I do agree that men are unwilling to be robbed of a true belief.

When that happens to them, then, it must be by theft, or violence, or bewitchment.

Again I do not understand.

Perhaps my metaphors are too high-flown. I call it theft when one is persuaded out of one's belief or forgets it. Argument in the one case, and time in the other, steal it away without one's knowing what is happening. You understand now?

Yes.

And by violence I mean being driven to change one's mind by pain or suffering.

That too I understand, and you are right.

And bewitchment, as I think you would agree, occurs when a man is beguiled out of his opinion by the allurements of pleasure or scared out of it under the spell of panic.

Yes, all delusions are like a sort of bewitchment.

As I said just now, then, we must find out who are the best guardians of this inward conviction that they must always do what they believe to be best for the commonwealth. We shall have to watch them from earliest childhood and set them tasks in which they would be most likely to forget or to be beguiled out of this duty. We shall then choose only those whose memory holds firm and who are proof against delusion.

Yes.

We must also subject them to ordeals of toil and pain and watch for the same qualities there. And we must observe them when exposed to the test of yet a third kind of bewitchment. As people lead colts up to alarming noises to see whether they are timid, so these young men must be brought into terrifying situations and then into scenes of pleasure, which will put them to severer proof than gold tried in the furnace. If we find one bearing himself well in all these trials and resisting every enchantment, a true guardian of himself, preserving always that perfect rhythm and harmony of being which he has acquired from his training in music and poetry, such a one will be of the greatest service to the commonwealth as well as to himself. Whenever we find one who has come unscathed through every test in childhood, youth, and manhood, we shall set him as a Ruler to watch over the commonwealth; he will be honoured in life, and after death receive the highest tribute of funeral rites and other memorials. All who do not reach this standard we must reject. And that, I think, my dear Glaucon, may be taken as an outline of the way in which we shall select Guardians to be set in authority as Rulers.

I am very much of your mind.

These, then, may properly be called Guardians in the fullest sense, who will ensure that neither foes without shall have the power, nor friends within the wish, to do harm. Those young men whom up to now we have been speaking of as Guardians, will be better described as Auxiliaries, who will enforce the decisions of the Rulers.

I agree.

Now, said I, can we devise something in the way of those convenient fictions we spoke of earlier, a single bold flight of invention,[2] which we may induce the community in general, and if possible the Rulers themselves, to accept?

What kind of fiction?

Nothing new; something like an Eastern tale of what, according to the poets, has happened before now in more than one part of the world. The poets have been believed; but the thing has not happened in our day, and it would be hard to persuade anyone that it could ever happen again.

You seem rather shy of telling this story of yours.

With good reason, as you will see when I have told it.

Out with it; don't be afraid.

Well, here it is; though I hardly know how to find the courage or the words to express it. I shall try to convince, first the Rulers and the soldiers,[3] and then the whole community, that all that nurture and education which we gave them was only something they seemed to experience as it were in a dream. In reality they were the whole time down inside the earth, being moulded and fostered while their arms and all their equipment were being fashioned also; and at last, when they were complete, the earth sent them up from her womb into the light of day. So now they must think of the land they dwell in as a mother and nurse, whom they must take thought for and defend against any attack, and of their fellow citizens as brothers born of the same soil.

You might well be bashful about coming out with your fiction.

No doubt; but still you must hear the rest of the story. It is true, we shall tell our people in this fable, that all of you in this land are brothers; but the god

[2]This phrase is commonly rendered by "noble lie," a self-contradictory expression no more applicable to Plato's harmless allegory than to a New Testament parable or the Pilgrim's Progress, and liable to suggest that he would countenance the lies, for the most part ignoble, now called propaganda.

[3]Note that the Guardians themselves are to accept this allegory, if possible. It is not "propaganda" foisted on the masses by the Rulers.

who fashioned you mixed gold in the composition of those among you who are fit to rule, so that they are of the most precious quality; and he put silver in the Auxiliaries, and iron and brass in the farmers and craftsmen. Now, since you are all of one stock, although your children will generally be like their parents, sometimes a golden parent may have a silver child or a silver parent a golden one, and so on with all the other combinations. So the first and chief injunction laid by heaven upon the Rulers is that, among all the things of which they must show themselves good guardians, there is none that needs to be so carefully watched as the mixture of metals in the souls of the children. If a child of their own is born with an alloy of iron or brass, they must, without the smallest pity, assign him the station proper to his nature and thrust him out among the craftsmen or the farmers. If, on the contrary, these classes produce a child with gold or silver in his composition, they will promote him, according to his value, to be a Guardian or an Auxiliary. They will appeal to a prophecy that ruin will come upon the state when it passes into the keeping of a man of iron or brass. Such is the story; can you think of any device to make them believe it?

Not in the first generation; but their sons and descendants might believe it, and finally the rest of mankind.

Well, said I, even so it might have a good effect in making them care more for the commonwealth and for one another; for I think I see what you mean.

So, I continued, we will leave the success of our story to the care of popular tradition; and now let us arm these sons of Earth and lead them, under the command of their Rulers, to the site of our city. There let them look round for the best place to fix their camp, from which they will be able to control any rebellion against the laws from within and to beat off enemies who may come from without like wolves to attack the fold. When they have pitched their camp and offered sacrifice to the proper divinities, they must arrange their sleeping quarters; and these must be sufficient to shelter them from winter cold and summer heat.

Naturally. You mean they are going to live there?

Yes, said I; but live like soldiers, not like men of business.

What is the difference?

I will try to explain. It would be very strange if a shepherd were to disgrace himself by keeping, for the protection of his flock, dogs who were so ill-bred and badly trained that hunger or unruliness or some bad habit or other would set them worrying the sheep and behaving no better than wolves. We must take every precaution against our Auxiliaries treating the citizens in any such way and, because they are stronger, turning into savage tyrants instead of friendly allies; and they will have been furnished with the best of safeguards, if they have really been educated in the right way.

But surely there is nothing wrong with their education..

We must not be too positive about that, my dear Glaucon; but we can be sure of what we said not long ago, that if they are to have the best chance of being gentle and humane to one another and to their charges, they must have the right education, whatever that may be.

We were certainly right there.

Then besides that education, it is only common sense to say that the dwellings and other belongings provided for them must be such as will neither make them less perfect Guardians nor encourage them to maltreat their fellow citizens.

True.

With that end in view, let us consider how they should live and be housed. First, none of them must possess any private property beyond the barest necessaries. Next, no one is to have any dwelling or store-house that is not open for all to enter at will. Their food, in the quantities required by men of temperance and courage who are in training for war, they will receive from the other citizens as the wages of their guardianship, fixed so that there shall be just enough for the year with nothing over; and they will have meals in common and all live together like soldiers in a camp. Gold and silver, we shall tell them, they will not need, having the divine counterparts of those metals always in their souls as a god-given possession, whose purity it is not lawful to sully by the acquisition of that mortal dross, current among mankind, which has been the occasion of so many unholy deeds. They alone of all the citizens are forbidden to touch and handle silver or gold, or to come under the same roof with them, or wear them as ornaments, or drink from vessels made of them. This manner of life will be their salvation and make them the saviours of the commonwealth. If ever they should come to possess land of their own and houses and money, they will give up their guardianship for the management of their farms and households and become tyrants at enmity with their fellow citizens instead of allies. And so they will pass all their lives in hating and being hated, plotting and being plotted against, in much greater fear of their enemies at home than of any foreign foe, and fast heading for the destruction that will soon overwhelm their country with themselves. For all these reasons let us say that this is how our Guardians are to be housed and otherwise provided for, and let us make laws accordingly.

By all means, said Glaucon.

Here Adeimantus interposed. Socrates, he said, how would you meet the objection that you are not making these people particularly happy? It is their own fault too, if they are not; for they are really masters of the state, and yet they get no good out of it as other rulers do, who own lands, build themselves fine houses with handsome furniture, offer private sacrifices to the gods, and entertain visitors from abroad; who possess, in fact, that gold and silver you spoke of, with everything else that is usually thought necessary for happiness. These people seem like nothing so much as a garrison of mercenaries posted in the city and perpetually mounting guard.

Yes, I said, and what is more they will serve for their food only without getting a mercenary's pay, so that they will not be able to travel on their own account or to make presents to a mistress or to spend as they please in other ways, like the people who are commonly thought happy. You have forgotten to include these counts in your indictment, and many more to the same effect.

Well, take them as included now.

And you want to hear the answer?

Yes.

We shall find one, I think, by keeping to the line we have followed so far. We shall say that, though it would not be surprising if even these people were perfectly happy under such conditions, our aim in founding the commonwealth was not to make any one class specially happy, but to secure the greatest possible happiness for the community as a whole. We thought we should have the best chance of finding justice in a state so constituted, just as we should find injustice where the consititution was of the worst possible type; we could then decide the question which has been before us all this time. For the moment, we are constructing, as we believe, the state which will be happy as a whole, not trying to secure the well-being of a select few; we shall study a state of the opposite kind presently. It is as if we were colouring a statue[4] and someone came up and blamed us for not putting the most beautiful colours on the noblest parts of the figure; the eyes, for instance, should be painted crimson, but we had made them black. We should think it a fair answer to say: Really, you must not expect us to paint eyes so handsome as not to look like eyes at all. This applies to all the parts: the question is whether, by giving each its proper colour, we make the whole beautiful. So too, in the present case, you must not press us to endow our Guardians with a happiness that will make them anything rather than guardians. We could quite easily clothe our farmers in gorgeous robes, crown them with gold, and invite them to till the soil at their pleasure; or we might set our potters to lie on couches by their fire, passing round the wine and making merry, with their wheel at hand to work at whenever they felt so inclined. We could make all the rest happy in the same sort of way, and so spread this well-being through the whole community. But you must not put that idea into our heads; if we take your advice, the farmer will be no farmer, the potter no longer a potter; none of the elements that make up the community will keep its character. In many cases this does not matter so much: if a cobbler goes to the bad and pretends to be what he is not, he is not a danger to the state; but, as you must surely see, men who make only a vain show of being guardians of the laws and of the commonwealth bring the whole state to utter ruin, just as, on the other hand, its good government and well-being depend entirely on them. We, in fact, are making genuine Guardians who will be the last to bring harm upon the commonwealth; if our critic aims rather at producing a happiness like that of a party of peasants feasting at a fair, what he has in mind is something other than a civic community. So we must consider whether our aim in establishing Guardians is to secure the greatest possible happiness for them, or happiness is something of which we should watch the development in the whole commonwealth. If so, we must compel these Guardians and Auxiliaries of ours to second our efforts; and they, and all the rest with them, must be induced to make themselves perfect masters each of his own craft. In that way, as the community grows into a well-ordered whole, the several classes may be allowed such measure of happiness as their nature will compass.

I think that is an admirable reply. . . .

[4]Greek statues were commonly tinted, wholly or in part.

. . . In my judgment, then, the question under what conditions people born and educated as we have described should possess wives and children, and how they should treat them, can be rightly settled only by keeping to the course on which we started them at the outset. We undertook to put these men in the position of watch-dogs guarding a flock. Suppose we follow up the analogy and imagine them bred and reared in the same sort of way. We can then see if that plan will suit our purpose.

How will that be?

In this way. Which do we think right for watch-dogs: should the females guard the flock and hunt with the males and take a share in all they do, or should they be kept within doors as fit for no more than bearing and feeding their puppies, while all the hard work of looking after the flock is left to the males?

They are expected to take their full share, except that we treat them as not quite so strong.

Can you employ any creature for the same work as another, if you do not give them both the same upbringing and education?

No.

Then, if we are to set women to the same tasks as men, we must teach them the same things. They must have the same two branches of training for mind and body and also be taught the art of war, and they must receive the same treatment.

That seems to follow.

Possibly, if these proposals were carried out, they might be ridiculed as involving a good many breaches of custom.

They might indeed.

The most ridiculous—don't you think?—being the notion of women exercising naked along with the men in the wrestling-schools; some of them elderly women too, like the old men who still have a passion for exercise when they are wrinkled and not very agreeable to look at.

Yes, that would be thought laughable, according to our present notions.

Now we have started on this subject, we must not be frightened of the many witticisms that might be aimed at such a revolution, not only in the matter of bodily exercise but in the training of women's minds, and not least when it comes to their bearing arms and riding on horseback. Having begun upon these rules, we must not draw back from the harsher provisions. The wits may be asked to stop being witty and try to be serious; and we may remind them that it is not so long since the Greeks, like most foreign nations of the present day, thought it ridiculous and shameful for men to be seen naked. When gymnastic exercises were first introduced in Crete and later at Sparta, the humorists had their chance to make fun of them; but when experience had shown that nakedness is better uncovered than muffled up, the laughter died down and a practice which the reason approved ceased to look ridiculous to the eye. This shows how idle it is to think anything ludicrous but what is base. One who tries to raise a laugh at any spectacle save that of baseness and folly will also, in his serious moments, set before himself some other standard than goodness of what deserves to be held in honour.

Most assuredly.

The first thing to be settled, then, is whether these proposals are feasible; and it must be open to anyone, whether a humorist or serious-minded, to raise the question whether, in the case of mankind, the feminine nature is capable of taking part with the other sex in all occupations, or in none at all, or in some only; and in particular under which of these heads this business of military service falls. Well begun is half done, and would not this be the best way to begin?

Yes.

Shall we take the other side in this debate and argue against ourselves? We do not want the adversary's position to be taken by storm for lack of defenders.

I have no objection.

Let us state his case for him. 'Socrates and Glaucon,' he will say, 'there is no need for others to dispute your position; you yourselves, at the very outset of founding your commonwealth, agreed that everyone should do the one work for which nature fits him.' Yes, of course; I suppose we did. 'And isn't there a very great difference in nature between man and woman?' Yes, surely. 'Does not that natural difference imply a corresponding difference in the work to be given to each?' Yes. 'But if so, surely you must be mistaken now and contradicting yourselves when you say that men and women, having such widely divergent natures, should do the same things?' What is your answer to that, my ingenious friend?

It is not easy to find one at the moment. I can only appeal to you to state the case on our own side, whatever it may be.

This, Glaucon, is one of many alarming objections which I foresaw some time ago. That is why I shrank from touching upon these laws concerning the possession of wives and the rearing of children.

It looks like anything but an easy problem.

True, I said; but whether a man tumbles into a swimming-pool or into mid-ocean, he has to swim all the same. So must we, and try if we can reach the shore, hoping for some Arion's dolphin or other miraculous deliverance to bring us safe to land.[5]

I suppose so.

Come then, let us see if we can find the way out. We did agree that different natures should have different occupations, and that the natures of man and woman are different; and yet we are now saying that these different natures are to have the same occupations. Is that the charge against us?

Exactly.

It is extraordinary, Glaucon, what an effect the practice of debating has upon people.

Why do you say that?

Because they often seem to fall unconsciously into mere disputes which they mistake for reasonable argument, through being unable to draw the distinctions proper to their subject; and so, instead of a philosophical ex-

[5]The musician Arion, to escape the treachery of Corinthian sailors, leapt into the sea and was carried ashore at Taenarum by a dolphin, Herod.

change of ideas, they go off in chase of contradictions which are purely verbal.

I know that happens to many people; but does it apply to us at this moment?

Absolutely. At least I am afraid we are slipping unconsciously into a dispute about words. We have been strenuously insisting on the letter of our principle that different natures should not have the same occupations, as if we were scoring a point in a debate; but we have altogether neglected to consider what sort of sameness of difference we meant and in what respect these natures and occupations were to be defined as different or the same. Consequently, we might very well be asking one another whether there is not an opposition in nature between bald and long-haired men, and, when that was admitted, forbid one set to be shoemakers, if the other were following that trade.

That would be absurd.

Yes, but only because we never meant any and every sort of sameness or difference in nature, but the sort that was relevant to the occupations in question. We meant, for instance, that a man and a woman have the same nature if both have a talent for medicine; whereas two men have different natures if one is a born physician, the other a born carpenter.

Yes, of course.

If, then, we find that either the male sex or the female is specially qualified for any particular form of occupation, then that occupation, we shall say, ought to be assigned to one sex or the other. But if the only difference appears to be that the male begets and the female brings forth, we shall conclude that no difference between man and woman has yet been produced that is relevant to our purpose. We shall continue to think it proper for our Guardians and their wives to share in the same pursuits.

And quite rightly.

The next thing will be to ask our opponent to name any profession or occupation in civic life for the purposes of which woman's nature is different from man's.

That is a fair question.

He might reply, as you did just now, that it is not easy to find a satisfactory answer on the spur of the moment, but that there would be no difficulty after a little reflection.

Perhaps.

Suppose, then, we invite him to follow us and see if we can convince him that there is no occupation concerned with the management of social affairs that is peculiar to women. We will confront him with a question: When you speak of a man having a natural talent for something, do you mean that he finds it easy to learn, and after a little instruction can find out much more for himself; whereas a man who is not so gifted learns with difficulty and no amount of instruction and practise will make him even remember what he has been taught? Is the talented man one whose bodily powers are readily at the service of his mind, instead of being a hindrance? Are not these the marks by which you distinguish the presence of a natural gift for any pursuit?

Yes, precisely.

Now do you know of any human occupation in which the male sex is not superior to the female in all these respects? Need I waste time over exceptions like weaving and watching over saucepans and batches of cakes, though women are supposed to be good at such things and get laughed at when a man does them better?

It is true, he replied, in almost everything one sex is easily beaten by the other. No doubt many women are better at many things than many men; but taking the sexes as a whole, it is as you say.

To conclude, then, there is no occupation concerned with the management of social affairs which belongs either to woman or to man, as such. Natural gifts are to be found here and there in both creatures alike; and every occupation is open to both, so far as their natures are concerned, though woman is for all purposes the weaker.

Certainly.

Is that a reason for making over all occupations to men only?

Of course not.

No, because one woman may have a natural gift for medicine or for music, another may not.

Surely.

Is it not also true that a woman may, or may not, be warlike or athletic?

I think so.

And again, one may love knowledge, another hate it; one may be high-spirited, another spiritless?

True again.

It follows that one woman will be fitted by nature to be a Guardian, another will not; because these were the qualities for which we selected our men Guardians. So for the purpose of keeping watch over the commonwealth, woman has the same nature as man, save in so far as she is weaker.

So it appears.

It follows that women of this type must be selected to share the life and duties of Guardians with men of the same type, since they are competent and of a like nature, and the same natures must be allowed the same pursuits.

Yes.

We come round, then, to our former position, that there is nothing contrary to nature in giving our Guardians' wives the same training for mind and body. The practice we proposed to establish was not impossible or visionary, since it was in accordance with nature. Rather, the contrary practice which now prevails turns out to be unnatural.

So it appears.

Well, we set out to inquire whether the plan we proposed was feasible and also the best. That it is feasible is now agreed; we must next settle whether it is the best.

Obviously.

Now, for the purpose of producing a woman fit to be a Guardian, we shall not have one education for men and another for women, precisely because the nature to be taken in hand is the same.

True.

What is your opinion on the question of one man being better than another? Do you think there is no such difference?

Certainly I do not.

And in this commonwealth of ours which will prove the better men—the Guardians who have received the education we described, or the shoemakers who have been trained to make shoes?

It is absurd to ask such a question.

Very well. So these Guardians will be the best of all the citizens?

By far.

And these women the best of all the women?

Yes.

Can anything be better for a commonwealth than to produce in it men and women of the best possible type?

No.

And that result will be brought about by such a system of mental and bodily training as we have described?

Surely.

We may conclude that the institution we proposed was not only practicable, but also the best for the commonwealth.

Yes.

The wives of our Guardians, then, must strip for exercise, since they will be clothed with virtue, and they must take their share in war and in the other social duties of guardianship. They are to have no other occupation; and in these duties the lighter part must fall to the women, because of the weakness of their sex. The man who laughs at naked women, exercising their bodies for the best of reasons, is like one that 'gathers fruit unripe,' for he does not know what it is that he is laughing at or what he is doing. There will never be a finer saying than the one which declares that whatever does good should be held in honour, and the only shame is in doing harm.

That is perfectly true. . . .

So far, then, in regulating the position of women, we may claim to have come safely through with one hazardous proposal, that male and female Guardians shall have all occupations in common. The consistency of the argument is an assurance that the plan is a good one and also feasible. We are like swimmers who have breasted the first wave without being swallowed up.

Not such a small wave either.

You will not call it large when you see the next.

Let me have a look at the next one, then.

Here it is: a law which follows from that principle and all that has gone before, namely that, of these Guardians, no one man and one woman are to set up house together privately: wives are to be held in common by all; so too are the children, and no parent is to know his own child, nor any child his parent.

It will be much harder to convince people that that is either a feasible plan or a good one.

As to its being a good plan, I imagine no one would deny the immense advantage of wives and children being held in common, provided it can be done. I should expect dispute to arise chiefly over the question whether it is possible.

There may well be a good deal of dispute over both points.

You mean, I must meet attacks on two fronts. I was hoping to escape one by running away: if you agreed it was a good plan, then I should only have had to inquire whether it was feasible.

No, we have seen through that manoeuvre. You will have to defend both positions.

Well, I must pay the penalty for my cowardice. But grant me one favour. Let me indulge my fancy, like one who entertains himself with idle day-dreams on a solitary walk. Before he has any notion how his desires can be realized, he will set aside that question, to save himself the trouble of reckoning what may or may not be possible. He will assume that his wish has come true, and amuse himself with settling all the details of what he means to do then. So a lazy mind encourages itself to be lazier than ever; and I am giving way to the same weakness myself. I want to put off till later that question, how the thing can be done. For the moment, with your leave, I shall assume it to be possible, and ask how the Rulers will work out the details in practice; and I shall argue that the plan, once carried into effect, would be the best thing in the world for our commonwealth and for its Guardians. That is what I shall now try to make out with your help, if you will allow me to postpone the other question.

Very good; I have no objection.

Well, if our Rulers are worthy of the name, and their Auxiliaries likewise, these latter will be ready to do what they are told, and the Rulers, in giving their commands, will themselves obey our laws and will be faithful to their spirit in any details we leave to their discretion.

No doubt.

It is for you, then, as their lawgivers, who have already selected the men, to select for association with them women who are so far as possible of the same natural capacity. Now since none of them will have any private home of his own, but they will share the same dwelling and eat at common tables, the two sexes will be together; and meeting without restriction for exercise and all through their upbringing, they will surely be drawn towards union with one another by a necessity of their nature—necessity is not too strong a word, I think?

Not too strong for the constraint of love, which for the mass of mankind is more persuasive and compelling than even the necessity of mathematical proof.

Exactly. But in the next place, Glaucon, anything like unregulated unions would be a profanation in a state whose citizens lead the good life. The Rulers will not allow such a thing.

No, it would not be right.

Clearly, then, we must have marriages, as sacred as we can make them; and this sanctity will attach to those which yield the best results.

Certainly.

How are we to get the best results? You must tell me, Glaucon, because I see you keep sporting dogs and a great many game birds at your house; and there is something about their mating and breeding that you must have noticed.

What is that?

In the first place, though they may all be of good stock, are there not some that turn out to be better than the rest?

There are.

And do you breed from all indiscriminately? Are you not careful to breed from the best so far as you can?

Yes.

And from those in their prime, rather than the very young or the very old?

Yes.

Otherwise, the stock of your birds or dogs would deteriorate very much, wouldn't it?

It would.

And the same is true of horses or of any animal?

It would be very strange if it were not.

Dear me, said I; we shall need consummate skill in our Rulers, if it is also true of the human race.

Well, it is true. But why must they be so skilful?

Because they will have to administer a large dose of that medicine we spoke of earlier.[6] An ordinary doctor is thought good enough for a patient who will submit to be dieted and can do without medicine; but he must be much more of a man if drugs are required.

True, but how does that apply?

It applies to our Rulers: it seems they will have to give their subjects a considerable dose of imposition and deception for their good. We said, if you remember, that such expedients would be useful as a sort of medicine.

Yes, a very sound principle.

Well, it looks as if this sound principle will play no small part in this matter of marriage and child-bearing.

How so?

It follows from what we have just said that, if we are to keep our flock at the highest pitch of excellence, there should be as many unions of the best of both sexes, and as few of the inferior, as possible, and that only the offspring of the better unions should be kept.[7] And again, no one but the Rulers must know how all this is being effected; otherwise our herd of Guardians may become rebellious.

Quite true.

We must, then, institute certain festivals at which we shall bring together

[6]In the *Laws* "Plato's view of marriage is very far from being merely physical. It has its moral and even its religious side."

[7]That is, "kept as *Guardians*." The inferior children of Guardians were to be "thrust out among the craftsmen and farmers."

the brides and the bridegrooms. There will be sacrifices, and our poets will write songs befitting the occasion. The number of marriages we shall leave to the Rulers' discretion. They will aim at keeping the number of the citizens as constant as possible, having regard to losses caused by war, epidemics, and so on; and they must do their best to see that our state does not become either great or small.[8]

Very good.

I think they will have to invent some ingenious system of drawing lots, so that, at each pairing off, the inferior candidate may blame his luck rather than the Rulers.

Yes, certainly.

Moreover, young men who acquit themselves well in war and other duties, should be given, among other rewards and privileges, more liberal opportunities to sleep with a wife,[9] for the further purpose that, with good excuse, as many as possible of the children may be begotten of such fathers.

Yes.

As soon as children are born, they will be taken in charge by officers appointed for the purpose, who may be men or women or both, since offices are to be shared by both sexes. The children of the better parents they will carry to the crèche to be reared in the care of nurses living apart in a certain quarter of the city. Those of the inferior parents and any children of the rest that are born defective will be hidden away, in some appropriate manner that must be kept secret.[10]

They must be, if the breed of our Guardians is to be kept pure.

These officers will also superintend the nursing of the children. They will bring the mothers to the crèche when their breasts are full, while taking every precaution that no mother shall know her own child; and if the mothers have not enough milk, they will provide wet-nurses. They will limit the time during which the mothers will suckle their children, and hand over all the hard work and sitting up at night to nurses and attendants.

That will make child-bearing an easy business for the Guardians' wives.

[8]Plato seems to forget that these rules apply only to Guardians. If the much larger third class is to breed without restriction, a substantial rise in their numbers might entail suspension of all childbirth among Guardians, with a dysgenic effect. Plato, however, feared a decline, rather than a rise, in the birth rate. (The state described in the *Laws* is always to have 5,040 citizens, each holding one inalienable lot of land.)

The "number of marriages" may include both the number of candidates admitted at each festival and the frequency of the festival. But it is perhaps likely that the festivals are to be annual, so that women who had borne children since the last festival would be re-marriageable. If so, at each festival a fresh group will be called up, consisting of all who have reached the age of 25 for men or 20 for women since the previous festival. Some or all of these will be paired with one another or with members of older groups. The couples will cohabit during the festival, which might last (say) for a month. The marriages will then be dissolved and the partners remain celibate until the next festival at earliest.

[9]Not to have several wives at once, but to be admitted at more frequent intervals to the periodic marriage festivals, not necessarily with a different wife each time.

[10]Infanticide of defective children was practised at Sparta; but the vague expression used does not imply that all children of inferior Guardians are to be destroyed. Those not defective would be relegated to the third class.

So it should be. To go on with our scheme: we said that children should be born from parents in the prime of life. Do you agree that this lasts about twenty years for a woman, and thirty for a man? A woman should bear children for the commonwealth from her twentieth to her fortieth year; a man should begin to beget them when he has passed "the racer's prime in swiftness,"[11] and continue till he is fifty-five.

Those are certainly the years in which both the bodily and the mental powers of man and woman are at their best.

If a man either above or below this age meddles with the begetting of children for the commonwealth, we shall hold it an offence against divine and human law. He will be begetting for his country a child conceived in darkness and dire incontinence, whose birth, if it escape detection, will not have been sanctioned by the sacrifices and prayers offered at each marriage festival, when priests and priestesses join with the whole community in praying that the children to be born may be even better and more useful citizens than their parents.

You are right.

The same law will apply to any man within the prescribed limits who touches a woman also of marriageable age when the Ruler has not paired them. We shall say that he is foisting on the commonwealth a bastard, unsanctioned by law or by religion.

Perfectly right.

As soon, however, as the men and the women have passed the age prescribed for producing children, we shall leave them free to form a connexion with whom they will, except that a man shall not take his daughter or daughter's daughter or mother or mother's mother, nor a woman her son or father or her son's son or father's father; and all this only after we have exhorted them to see that no child, if any be conceived, shall be brought to light, or, if they cannot prevent its birth, to dispose of it on the understanding that no such child can be reared.[12]

That too is reasonable. But how are they to distinguish fathers and daughters and those other relations you mentioned?

They will not, said I. But, reckoning from the day when he becomes a bridegroom, a man will call all children born in the tenth or the seventh month sons and daughters, and they will call him father. Their children again he will call grandchildren, and they will call his group grandfathers and grandmothers; and all who are born within the period during which their mothers and fathers were having children will be called brothers and

[11]A poetical quotation, which may, in its original context, have referred to a racehorse, brought to the stud when he had ceased to run.

[12]The unofficial unions might be permanent. The only unions barred as incestuous are between parents and children, or grandparents and grandchildren (all such are included, since, if a woman cannot marry her father's father, a man cannot marry his son's daughter). It seems to follow that Plato did not regard the much more probable connexions of brothers and sisters as incestuous; and if so, he would see no reason against legal marriage of real brothers and sisters, who would not know they were so related. Such unions were regular in Egypt; and some modern authorities deny that they are dysgenic. Greek law allowed marriage between brother and half-sister by a different mother.

sisters. This will provide for those restrictions on unions that we mentioned; but the law will allow brothers and sisters to live together, if the lot so falls out and the Delphic oracle also approves.[13]

Very good.

This, then, Glaucon, is the manner in which the Guardians of your commonwealth are to hold their wives and children in common. Must we not next find arguments to establish that it is consistent with our other institutions and also by far the best plan?

Yes, surely.

We had better begin by asking what is the greatest good at which the lawgiver should aim in laying down the constitution of a state, and what is the worst evil. We can then consider whether our proposals are in keeping with that good and irreconcilable with the evil.

By all means.

Does not the worst evil for a state arise from anything that tends to rend it asunder and destroy its unity, while nothing does it more good than whatever tends to bind it together and make it one?

That is true.

And are not citizens bound together by sharing in the same pleasures and pains, all feeling glad or grieved on the same occasions of gain or loss; whereas the bond is broken when such feelings are no longer universal, but

[13]This last speech deals with two distinct questions: (1) avoidance of incestuous unions as above defined; (2) legal marriage of brothers and sisters.

(1) Since the elderly people forming unofficial unions are not to know who are their parents or children, they must avoid all persons who could possibly be so related to them. This is easy, if cohabitation in legal marriage is confined to the duration of a marriage festival and the children of any parent must therefore belong to a batch born in the seventh or tenth month after any festival at which that parent has been married. (Most ancient authorities denied that a child could be born in the eighth month.) If a register was kept, a man could be told all the dates in question without being told who were his real children.

(2) After explaining how incestuous unions can be avoided by a man treating certain whole groups as his parents or children or grandparents or grandchildren, Plato adds that all persons "born within the period during which their mothers and fathers (not *his* father and mother) were having children" will be called "brothers" and "sisters." If unions of real brothers and sisters are not incestuous, this clause has nothing to do with avoidance of incest. It only adds to the definition of nominal parents and children and grandparents and grandchildren, a definition of those who will call one another "brothers" and "sisters," whether they are really so related or not. Probably, it is meant that these will be all the Guardians born in the same generation (in a vague sense). Since there is no question of incest, these persons will never need to inquire about dates of marriage and birth, if they wish to form a union.

The last sentence refers to both topics of the previous one: (1) avoidance of incestuous unions, (2) legal marriage of real brothers and sisters. It has been held that Plato regarded such marriages as incestuous and that the Oracle was to guard against them. But either the Rulers knew how all Guardians were related or they did not. If (as seems likely) they did know, they could avoid arranging such marriages without invoking an oracle to negative their own proposals. If they did not (though it would be folly to keep no registers if *any* incest was to be avoided), then how could the Oracle know? Granted that Plato did not hold marriage of brothers and sisters to be incestuous, the Rulers could sometimes knowingly arrange such marriages. The Oracle might be asked once for all to approve the whole scheme of marriage laws, or it might be formally invoked at each festival. If it raised no objection, the Rulers would be protected from any charge of violating religious law.

any event of public or personal concern fills some with joy and others with distress?

Certainly.

And this disunion comes about when the words "mine" and "not mine," "another's" and "not another's" are not applied to the same things throughout the community. The best ordered state will be the one in which the largest number of persons use these terms in the same sense, and which accordingly most nearly resembles a single person. When one of us hurts his finger, the whole extent of those bodily connexions which are gathered up in the soul and unified by its ruling element is made aware and it all shares as a whole in the pain of the suffering part; hence we say that the man has a pain in his finger. The same thing is true of the pain or pleasure felt when any other part of the person suffers or is relieved.

Yes; I agree that the best organized community comes nearest to that condition.

And so it will recognize as a part of itself the individual citizen to whom good or evil happens, and will share as a whole in his joy or sorrow.

It must, if the constitution is sound.

It is time now to go back to our own commonwealth and see whether these conclusions apply to it more than to any other type of state. In all alike there are rulers and common people, all of whom will call one another fellow citizens.

Yes.

But in other states the people have another name as well for their rulers, haven't they?

Yes; in most they call them masters; in democracies, simply the government.

And in ours?

The people will look upon their rulers as preservers and protectors.

And how will our rulers regard the people?

As those who maintain them and pay them wages.

And elsewhere?

As slaves.

And what do rulers elsewhere call one another?

Colleagues.

And ours?

Fellow Guardians.

And in other states may not a ruler regard one colleague as a friend in whom he has an interest, and another as a stranger with whom he has nothing in common?

Yes, that often happens.

But that could not be so with your Guardians? None of them could ever treat a fellow Guardian as a stranger.

Certainly not. He must regard everyone whom he meets as brother or sister, father or mother, son or daughter, grandchild or grandparent.

Very good; but here is a further point. Will you not require them, not merely to use these family terms, but to behave as a real family? Must they not show towards all whom they call "father" the customary reverence, care, and obedience due to a parent, if they look for any favour from gods or men, since to act otherwise is contrary to divine and human law? Should not all the citizens constantly reiterate in the hearing of the children from their earliest years such traditional maxims of conduct towards those whom they are taught to call father and their other kindred?

They should. It would be absurd that terms of kinship should be on their lips without any action to correspond.

In our community, then, above all others, when things go well or ill with any individual everyone will use that word "mine" in the same sense and say that all is going well or ill with him and his.

Quite true.

And, as we said, this way of speaking and thinking goes with fellow-feeling; so that our citizens, sharing as they do in a common interest which each will call his own, will have all their feelings of pleasure or pain in common.

Assuredly.

A result that will be due to our institutions, and in particular to our Guardians' holding their wives and children in common.

Very much so.

But you will remember how, when we compared a well-ordered community to the body which shares in the pleasures and pains of any members, we saw in this unity the greatest good that a state can enjoy. So the conclusion is that our commonwealth owes to this sharing of wives and children by its protectors its enjoyment of the greatest of all goods.

Yes, that follows.

Moreover, this agrees with our principle that they were not to have houses or lands or any property of their own, but receive sustenance from the other citizens, as wages for their guardianship, and to consume it in common. Only so will they keep to their true character; and our present proposals will do still more to make them genuine Guardians. They will not rend the community asunder by each applying that word "mine" to different things and dragging off whatever he can get for himself into a private home, where he will have his separate family, forming a centre of exclusive joys and sorrows. Rather they will all, so far as may be, feel together and aim at the same ends, because they are convinced that all their interests are identical.

Quite so.

Again, if a man's person is his only private possession, lawsuits and prosecutions will all but vanish, and they will be free of those quarrels that arise from ownership of property and from having family ties. Nor would they be justified even in bringing actions for assault and outrage; for we shall pronounce it right and honourable for a man to defend himself against an assailant of his own age, and in that way they will be compelled to keep themselves fit.

That would be a sound law.

And it would also have the advantage that, if a man's anger can be satisfied in this way, a fit of passion is less likely to grow into a serious quarrel.

True.

But an older man will be given authority over all younger persons and power to correct them; whereas the younger will, naturally, not dare to strike the elder or do him any violence, except by command of a Ruler. He will not show him any sort of disrespect. Two guardian spirits, fear and reverence, will be enough to restrain him—reverence forbidding him to lay hands on a parent, and fear of all those others who as sons or brothers or fathers would come to the rescue.

Yes, that will be the result.

So our laws will secure that these men will live in complete peace with one another; and if they never quarrel among themselves, there is no fear of the rest of the community being divided either against them or against itself.[14]

No.

There are other evils they will escape, so mean and petty that I hardly like to mention them: the poor man's flattery of the rich, and all the embarrassments and vexations of rearing a family and earning just enough to maintain a household; now borrowing and now refusing to repay, and by any and every means scraping together money to be handed over to wife and servants to spend. These sordid troubles are familiar and not worth describing.

Only too familiar.

Rid of all these cares, they will live a more enviable life than the Olympic victor, who is counted happy on the strength of far fewer blessings than our Guardians will enjoy. Their victory is the nobler, since by their success the whole commonwealth is preserved; and their reward of maintenance at the public cost is more complete, since their prize is to have every need of life supplied for themselves and for their children; their country honours them while they live, and when they die they receive a worthy burial.

Yes, they will be nobly rewarded.

Do you remember, then, how someone who shall be nameless reproached us for not making our Guardians happy: they were to possess nothing, though all the wealth of their fellow citizens was within their grasp? We replied, I believe, that we would consider that objection later, if it came in our way: for the moment we were bent on making our Guardians real guardians, and moulding our commonwealth with a view to the greatest happiness, not of one section of it, but of the whole.

Yes, I remember.

Well, it appears now that these protectors of our state will have a life better and more honourable than that of any Olympic victor; and we can hardly rank it on a level with the life of a shoemaker or other artisan or of a farmer.

I should think not.

However, it is right to repeat what I said at the time: if ever a Guardian tries to make himself happy in such a way that he will be a guardian no longer; if, not content with the moderation and security of this way of living which we think the best, he becomes possessed with some silly and childish

[14]"Revolution always starts from the outbreak of internal dissension in the ruling class."

notion of happiness, impelling him to make his power a means to appropriate all the citizens' wealth, then he will learn the wisdom of Hesiod's saying that the half is more than the whole.

My advice would certainly be that he should keep to his own way of living.

You do agree, then, that women are to take their full share with men in education, in the care of children, and in the guardianship of the other citizens; whether they stay at home or go out to war, they will be like watch-dogs which take their part either in guarding the fold or in hunting and share in every task so far as their strength allows. Such conduct will not be unwomanly, but all for the best and in accordance with the natural partnership of the sexes.

Yes, I agree. . . .

Here, then, are some more evils which must not elude the vigilance of our Guardians and find their way into the commonwealth: riches and poverty. The one produces luxury and idelness, the other low standards of conduct and workmanship; and both have a subversive tendency.

True enough. But I should like to know, Socrates, how our state will be able to go to war, if it has no money, especially if it is forced to fight a rich and powerful enemy.

Obviously it would be hard to fight one such enemy, but easier to deal with two.

What do you mean by that?

In the first place, if they have to fight, they will be highly trained soldiers matched against rich men.

True, so far as that goes.

Well then, Adeimantus, would not a single boxer in perfect training easily be a match for two wealthy and corpulent antagonists who could not box?

Not for both at once perhaps.

Not even if he could give ground and then turn and plant a blow on whichever came up first? Suppose he kept on doing that under a burning sun, would he not get the better of even more than two?

It would certainly not be surprising.

Well, don't you think that rich people know more of the theory and practice of boxing than of the art of war?

I am sure they do.

In that case it will probably be an easy matter for our trained warriors to fight twice or three times their number.

I will grant you that; I believe you are right.

And now suppose they sent envoys to one of the two enemy countries to tell them what is in fact the truth: "We have no use for gold and silver; we are not allowed to possess them. But you are allowed; so join forces with us, and you may have the spoils of the other country."[15] After such an offer would anyone choose to fight against tough, wiry dogs sooner than join the dogs in attacking the fat and tender sheep?

[15]This message is in the "laconic" style of Spartan diplomacy.

I should say not. But if a single state amasses the wealth of all the others, will not that be a danger to a state that has none?

I congratulate you on your idea that any state other than the one we are constructing deserves the name.

Why, what should the others be called?

By some grander name, for each of them is not one state, but many: two at least, which are at war with one another, one of the rich, the other of the poor, and each of these is divided into many more. To treat them all as a single state is a complete mistake. If you treat them as many and offer to make over to one class the wealth and power and even the persons of the others, you will always find that your allies outnumber your enemies. Consequently, so long as your commonwealth is ordered wisely on the lines we have laid down, it will be the greatest of all; I do not mean the most famous, but greatest in the literal sense, even though it have no more than a thousand men to fight in its defence. You will not easily find in Hellas or elsewhere a state of that size which is really one, though there are plenty which look like single states and are many times as large. Don't you agree?

I do indeed.

Here, then, our Rulers will find the best principle for determining the size of the state and the proportionate amount of territory, beyond which they will not go: the state should be allowed to grow only so far as it can increase in size without loss of unity.

An excellent rule.

So we must lay yet another command on our Guardians: they are to take all possible care that the state shall neither be too small nor yet one that seems great but has no unity.

You think that will be easy!

Not so hard as the duty we mentioned earlier, of moving down any inferior child born to the Guardians into the other classes and promoting from those classes any child who is good enough to be a Guardian. Our intention there was to set the other citizens to work, one man at one task for which his nature fitted him, so that by keeping to that one business he might come to be a single man and not many. In that way the state as a whole would grow to be a single community, and not many.

You may well call that not so easy!

No, but really, my good Adeimantus, we are not laying upon the Guardians a whole number of burdensome duties, as you might suppose. It will all be easy enough, if only they will see to 'the one great thing,' as the saying goes, though I would rather call it the one thing that is sufficient: education and nurture. If a sound education has made them reasonable men, they will easily see their way through all these matters as well as others which we will pass over for the moment, such as the possession of wives, marriage, and child-bearing, and the principle that here we should follow, as far as possible, the proverb which says that friends have all things in common.

Yes, all should go well then.

Moreover, when a community has once made a good start, its growth proceeds in a sort of cycle. If a sound system of nurture and education is maintained, it produces men of a good disposition; and these in their turn, taking advantage of such education, develop into better men than their forebears, and their breeding qualities improve among the rest, as may be seen in animals.

That is likely enough.

In short, then, those who keep watch over our commonwealth must take the greatest care not to overlook the least infraction of the rule against any innovation upon the established system of education either of the body or of the mind. When the poet says that men care most for "the newest air that hovers on the singer's lips," they will be afraid lest he be taken not merely to mean new songs, but to be commending a new style of music. Such innovation is not to be commended, nor should the poet be so understood. The introduction of novel fashions in music is a thing to beware of as endangering the whole fabric of society, whose most important conventions are unsettled by any revolution in that quarter. So Daman declares, and I believe him.

You may count me too among his supporters, said Adeimantus.

It seems, then, said I, that it is here, in the field of music and poetry, that our Guardians must build their watch-tower.

It is certainly there that lawlessness easily creeps in unobserved.

Yes, I said, in the guise of a pastime, which seems so harmless.

It would be harmless, he replied, were it not that, little by little, this lawless spirit gains a lodgement and spreads imperceptibly to manners and pursuits; and from thence with gathering force invades men's dealings with one another, and next goes on to attack the laws and the constitution with wanton recklessness, until it ends by overthrowing the whole structure of public and private life.

Really? said I. Is all that true?

So I believe, he replied.

Our children's pastimes, then, as I began by saying, must be kept from the first within stricter bounds; if any licence be admitted, they will catch the spirit and will never grow into law-abiding and well-conducted men. And so, when children have made a good beginning in their play and musical education has instilled a spirit of order, this reverence for law, in complete contrast to the licence you were describing just now, will attend them in all their doings and foster their growth, restoring any institutions that may earlier have fallen into decay.[16]

That is true.

As a consequence, they will rediscover rules of behaviour which their predecessors have let fall into disuse, including matters supposed to be of little importance: how the young should be silent in the presence of their elders, give up their seats to them, and take dutiful care of their parents; not to mention details of personal appearance, such as the way their hair is cut and the clothes and shoes they wear. It would be silly, I think, to make laws on

[16]Plato is here thinking of a reformed Athens, rather than of the ideal state.

these matters; such habits cannot be established or kept up by written legislation. It is probable, at any rate, that the bent given by education will determine the quality of later life, by that sort of attraction which like things always have for one another, till they finally mount up to one imposing result, whether for good or ill. For that reason I should not myself be inclined to push legislation to that length.

With good reason.

But now look here, what are we to do about business transactions, dealings between buyers and sellers, contracts with tradesmen, actions for foul language and assault, legal proceedings and the impanelling of juries, collection and payment of any market or harbour dues that may be needed, and generally regulations for markets, police, custom houses, and all that sort of thing? Can we go so far as to legislate on any of these matters?

No; there will be no need to dictate to men of good breeding. They will soon find out for themselves what regulations are needed.

Yes, my friend, I replied, provided that, by the grace of heaven, they preserve the institutions we have already described.

Quite so, he agreed. Otherwise they will spend their lives making a host of petty regulations and amending them in the hope of reaching perfection.

Living, in fact, like those invalids who are too self-indulgent to give up their unwholesome habits.

Exactly.

And a pretty sort of life they have of it. All they gain from being doctored is that their ailments grow more severe and complicated, though they are always expecting to be cured by every fresh remedy that someone recommends.

Yes, that is a good description of a certain type of invalid.

And another amusing thing about them is that they take for their worst enemy anyone who tells them frankly that until they give up eating and drinking too much and idleness and debauchery, no medicine or surgery and no charms or amulets will do them any good.

I see nothing very amusing in being in a rage with good advice.

You don't seem to be an admirer of people like that.

I certainly am not.

Then neither will you admire the same sort of behaviour in a whole society. You will find something very like those invalids in some states with a bad form of government, which forbid their citizens, under pain of death, to make any radical change in the constitution, and at the same time honour as a good and profoundly wise person any obsequious flatterer who, without attempting such drastic treatment, can minister agreeable to their humours, which he is clever enough to anticipate.

The resemblance is very close, and I have nothing to say for them.

And what of the men who are willing and eager to minister to these invalid states? Have you no admiration for such cool temerity?

Yes, except when they are deluded by popular applause into fancying themselves to be real statesmen.

Why, said I, can't you make some allowances for them? When a man who cannot measure is told by a lot of equally ignorant people that he is six feet high, you cannot expect him not to believe them.

No, not in that instance.

Don't be so hard upon them, then. Surely there is something very amusing in the way they go on enacting their petty laws and amending them, always imagining they will find some way to put an end to fraud in business and in all those other transactions I was speaking of. They have no idea that really they are cutting off the heads of a hydra.

It is true; that is all they are doing.

I should have thought that laws and institutions of that order do not deserve the attention of a law-giver worthy of the name, no matter whether the constitution be good or bad. If it is bad, they are useless and effect nothing; if good, some are such as anyone could devise, and the rest will follow of themselves from the practices we have already instituted.

Then, what is there left for us to do in the way of legislation?

For us, nothing; but there are institutions of the highest worth and importance that must be left to the Delphian Apollo.

What are they?

The founding of temples, sacrifices, and the cults of gods, demigods, and heroes; the burial of the dead, and services to propitiate the powers of the other world. These are matters we do not understand ourselves, and in founding our commonwealth we shall be wise to consult no other religious authority than our national divinity. Indeed in religious matters, the authority of this god, from his seat at the very navel of the earth, may be said to extend to all mankind.[17]

Good. Let us do so.

[17]Excavation at Delphi has brought to light in the temple of Apollo the *omphalos ("navel"), a conical stone which had been supposed to mark the centre of the earth when the earth was imagined to be a circular disk surrounded by the stream of Ocean. The oracle was in fact sometimes consulted by non-Greek states.*

20 A Utopia Under Conditions of Affluence

Edward Bellamy's *Looking Backward,* written in 1888, describes a post-Industrial-Revolution world system of the year 2000. Bellamy's society is based on forms of industrial, economic, and social organization that differ substantially from the structure of any real modern society. When coupled with the production power of an industrialized economy, Bellamy's radical form of social organization results in a society in which the population is truly affluent.

Although present-day American society is frequently called "affluent," it is the *average* level of wealth in the country that is being acknowledged. Variations in the life styles of members of the society are so great that to use the term "affluent society" in any but a statistical sense is absurd. For example, in 1965 the average size of a household in the United States was between three and four persons. If the part of the country's gross national product devoted to personal consumption had been divided equally among all households, the average buying power of each household would have been about $8,000.[1] This figure hardly describes the economic condition of the poor in American society. In 1969 President Nixon proposed a new welfare system for the United States. Under this system, a family of four would be guaranteed a minimum yearly income of $1,600. While it might be reasonable to assert that the United States as a society is affluent, it is certainly incorrect to assert that the population of the society is necessarily affluent.

Based on the present rate of population growth and a reasonable estimate of the United States' rate of economic development, the share for each household of the personal consumption portion of the gross national product will be approximately $28,000 (1965 dollars) in the year 2000, the year in which Bellamy's society is described.[2] What this means is that if in the year 2000 the part of the country's gross national product devoted to personal consumption were *divided equally* among all families in the society, each would have the buying power of a 1965 family with an income of $28,000. However, will an accurate description of the economic condition of large numbers of families in the country come from a statistic based on an equal

[1]This calculation is based on figures reported in Herman Kahn and Anthony J. Wiener, *The Year 2000* (New York: The Macmillan Company, 1967), p. 168.

[2]The projections of gross national product and population growth are from *ibid.,* p. 168.

division of the available gross national product? Given our present social arrangements, it will probably be no more appropriate to do this in the year 2000 than it is to do so today. Under the set of social arrangements outlined by Bellamy, this statistic would be appropriate.

The social system Bellamy creates incorporates the principles that an individual should not benefit from or be disadvantaged for his entire life by his ancestors, and that there should be equality in the contribution a man is expected to make to his society and equality in the share of its rewards that he receives. The first principle was intended to lead to rules that would eliminate the effects of two variables known to have pervasive influences on major aspects of an individual's life in all real societies: class origins and inherited abilities. Although much attention has recently focused on the effects of one's parents' socioeconomic status on a person's chances for success in American society, no serious question has ever been raised concerning the legitimacy of the social effects that follow from genetic factors. Certainly there is acceptance of the idea that a society has a responsibility to provide some minimum care for members who are born with severe disabilities and even some recognition that a man should not be discriminated against because of a physical deformity. Bellamy raises a question about the other end of the spectrum—that is, about the justification for the advantages that accrue to those whose unusual, genetically determined characteristics are socially valuable. Is it any more reasonable to reward a man relatively well because he has the good fortune to have been born with high intelligence than it is to punish another who is born mentally deficient?

The second principle, equal contribution and equal return, focused attention on the relationship between an individual's abilities and his efforts, and was the basis for determining work load and payment. It is easy to understand why men who possess scarce and valuable abilities and are willing to use them have come to command greater shares of the products of their societies than those who possess less unusual and less valuable personal characteristics. If the norms of a society do not prevent a man from doing so, he will attempt to exchange his labor for the maximal return. If a job requires special abilities or skills that are rare in the population, the person who has these abilities or skills can refuse to accept a job unless he is paid more than he could get by filling another job that also requires special characteristics or a job that could be filled by most people. Bellamy attempts to design a society in which the norms do not permit this type of free labor-reward market. It is, of course, easy to design a society in which all individuals share equally in the goods and services that the society is able to provide. The difficult problem is to design one that does not appear certain to collapse.

Bellamy develops a conception of the relationship between ability and effort that is used to define "work." He then proceeds to elaborate the mechanisms whereby work loads can be equalized in the society. How is it possible to compare the work done by two men and devise a method of adjusting work load so that each will be satisfied to receive the same pay as the other, even though one is an administrator who sits at a desk for eight hours a day, makes decisions, and worries, and the other is a laborer who spends six hours a day digging ditches. This is one problem that Bellamy must solve if the society he creates is to have any chance of survival.

As a vehicle for presenting his ideas on social organization, Bellamy uses the device of moving an adult male from Boston in 1887 to the same city in 2000. Although the method Bellamy uses to accomplish movement is not as interesting as the methods used by writers of straight science fiction to accomplish the same end, it provides a satisfactory device for comparing Mr. West's 1887 American society to Dr. Leete's American Society of 2000.

The discussion of differences in social organization between the two societies begins with an account of the transformation of West's society into Leete's.

Looking Backward

EDWARD BELLAMY

"I am impatient to know by what contradiction of natural sequence the peace and prosperity which you now seem to enjoy could have been the outcome of an era like my own," [I said].

"Since you are in the humor to talk rather than to sleep" [replied my host], "as I certainly am, perhaps I cannot do better than to try to give you enough idea of our modern industrial system to dissipate at least the impression that there is any mystery about the process of its evolution. The Bostonians of your day had the reputation of being great askers of questions, and I am going to show my descent by asking you one to begin with. What should you name as the most prominent feature of the labor troubles of your day?"

"Why, the strikes, of course," I replied.

"Exactly. But what made the strikes so formidable?"

"The great labor organizations."

"And what was the motive of these great organizations?"

"The workmen claimed they had to organize to get their rights from the big corporations," I replied.

"That is just it," said Doctor Leete. "The organization of labor and the strikes were an effect, merely, of the concentration of capital in greater masses than had ever been known before. Before this concentration began, while as yet commerce and industry were conducted by innumerable petty concerns with small capital, instead of a small number of great concerns with vast capital, the individual workman was relatively important and independent in his relations to the employer. Moreover, when a little capital or a new idea was enough to start a man in business for himself, workingmen were constantly becoming employers and there was no hard and fast line between the two classes. Labor unions were needless then, and general strikes out of the question. But when the era of small concerns with small capital was succeeded by that of the great aggregations of capital, all this was changed. The individual laborer, who had been relatively important to the small employer, was reduced to insignificance and powerlessness against the great corporation, while at the same time the way upward to the grade of employer was closed to him. Self-defense drove him to union with his fellows.

"The records of the period show that the outcry against the concentration of capital was furious. Men believed that it threatened society with a form of tyranny more abhorrent than it had ever endured. They believed that the great corporations were preparing for them the yoke of a baser servitude than had ever been imposed on the race, servitude not to men but to soulless machines incapable of any motive but insatiable greed. Looking back, we cannot wonder at their desperation, for certainly humanity was never confronted with a fate more sordid and hideous than would have been the era of corporate tyranny which they anticipated.

"Meanwhile, without being in the smallest degree checked by the clamor against it, the absorption of business by ever-larger monopolies continued. In the United States there was not, after the beginning of the last quarter of the century, any opportunity whatever for individual enterprise in any important field of industry, unless backed by a great capital. During the last decade of the century, such small businesses as still remained were fast-failing survivals of a past epoch, or mere parasites on the great corporations, or else existed in fields too small to attract the great capitalists. Small businesses, as far as they still remained, were reduced to the condition of rats and mice, living in holes and corners, and counting on evading notice for the enjoyment of existence. The railroads had gone on combining till a few great syndicates controlled every rail in the land. In manufactories, every important staple was controlled by a syndicate. These syndicates, pools, trusts, or whatever their name, fixed prices and crushed all competition except when combinations as vast as themselves arose. Then a struggle, resulting in a still greater consolidation, ensued. The great city bazaar crushed its country rivals with branch stores, and in the city itself absorbed its smaller rivals till the business of a whole quarter was concentrated under one roof, with a hundred former proprietors of shops serving as clerks. Having no business of his own to put his money in, the small capitalist, at the same time that he took service under the corporation, found no other investment for his money but its stocks and bonds, thus becoming doubly dependent upon it.

"The fact that the desperate popular opposition to the consolidation of business in a few powerful hands had no effect to check it proves that there must have been a strong economical reason for it. The small capitalists, with their innumerable petty concerns, had in fact yielded the field to the great aggregations of capital because they belonged to a day of small things and were totally incompetent to the demands of an age of steam and telegraphs and the gigantic scale of its enterprises. To restore the former order to things, even if possible, would have involved returning to the day of stagecoaches. Oppressive and intolerable as was the regime of the great consolidations of capital, even its victims, while they cursed it, were forced to admit the prodigious increase of efficiency which had been imparted to the national industries, the vast economies effected by concentration of management and unity of organization, and to confess that since the new system had taken the place of the old the wealth of the world had increased at a rate before undreamed of. To be sure this vast increase had gone chiefly to make the rich richer, increasing the gap between them and the poor; but the fact remained that, as a means merely of producing wealth, capital had been proved efficient in proportion to its consolidation. The restoration of the old system with the subdivision of capital, if it were possible, might indeed bring back a greater equality of conditions, with more individual dignity and freedom, but it would be at the price of general poverty and the arrest of material progress.

"Was there, then no way of commanding the services of the mighty wealth-producing principle of consolidated capital without bowing down to a plutocracy like that of Carthage? As soon as men began to ask themselves these questions, they found the answer ready for them. The movement toward the conduct of business by larger and larger aggregations of capital, the tendency toward monopolies, which had been so desperately and vainly resisted, was recognized at last, in its true significance, as a process which only needed to complete its logical evolution to open a golden future to humanity.

"Early in the last century the evolution was completed by the final consolidation of the entire capital of the nation. The industry and commerce of the country, ceasing to be conducted by a set of irresponsible corporations and syndicates of private persons at their caprice and for their profit, were entrusted to a single syndicate representing the people, to be conducted in the common interest for the common profit. The nation, that is to say, organized as the one great business corporation in which all other corporations were absorbed; it became the one capitalist in place of all other capitalists, the sole employer, the final monopoly in which all previous and lesser monopolies were swallowed up, a monopoly in the profits and economies of which all citizens shared. The epoch of trusts had ended in The Great Trust. In a word, the people of the United States concluded to assume the conduct of their own business, just as one hundred-odd years before they had assumed the conduct of their own government, organizing now for industrial purposes on precisely the same grounds that they had then organized for political purposes. At last, strangely late in the world's history, the obvious fact was perceived that no business is so essentially the public business as the industry and commerce on which the people's livelihood depends, and that to entrust it to private persons to be managed for private profit is a folly similar in kind, though vastly greater in magnitude, to that of surrendering the functions of political government to kings and nobles to be conducted for their personal glorification."

"Such a stupendous change as you describe," said I, "did not, of course, take place without great bloodshed and terrible convulsions."

"On the contrary," replied Doctor Leete, "there was absolutely no violence. The change had been long foreseen. Public opinion had become fully ripe for it, and the whole mass of the people was behind it. There was no more possibility of opposing it by force than by argument. On the other hand the popular sentiment toward the great corporations and those identified with them had ceased to be one of bitterness, as they came to realize their necessity as a link, a transition phase, in the evolution of the true industrial system. The most violent foes of the great private monopolies were now forced to recognize how invaluable and indispensable had been their office in educating the people up to the point of assuming control of their own business. Fifty years before, the consolidation of the industries of the country under national control would have seemed a very daring experiment to the most sanguine. But by a series of object lessons, seen and studied by all men, the great corporations had taught the people an entirely new set of ideas on this subject. They had seen for many years syndicates handling revenues greater than those of states, and directing the labors of hundreds of thousands of men with an efficiency and economy unattainable in smaller operations. It had come to be recognized as an axiom that the larger the business the simpler the principles that can be applied to it; that, as the machine is truer than the hand, so the system, which in a great concern does the work of the master's eye in a small business, turns out more accurate results. Thus it came about that, thanks to the corporations themselves, when it was proposed that the nation should assume their functions, the suggestion implied nothing which seemed impracticable even to the timid. To be sure, it was a step beyond any yet taken, a broader generalization, but the very fact that the nation would be the sole corporation in the field would, it was seen, relieve the undertaking of many difficulties with which the partial monopolies had contended."

Doctor Leete ceased speaking, and I remained silent, endeavoring to form some general conception of the changes in the arrangements of society implied in the tremendous revolution which he had described.

Finally I said, "The idea of such an extension of the function of government is, to say the least, rather overwhelming."

"Extension!" he repeated. "Where is the extension?"

"In my day," I replied, "it was considered that the proper functions of government, strictly speaking, were limited to keeping the peace and defending the people against the public enemy, that is, to the military and police powers."

"And, in heaven's name, who are the public enemies?" exclaimed Doctor Leete. "Are they France, England, Germany or hunger, cold, and nakedness? In your day governments were accustomed, on the slightest international misunderstanding, to seize upon the bodies of citizens and deliver them over by hundreds of thousands to death and mutilation, wasting their treasures the while like water; and all this often for no imaginable profit to the victims. We have no wars now, and our governments no war powers, but in order to protect every citizen against hunger, cold, and nakedness, and provide for all his physical and mental needs, the function is assumed of directing his industry for a term of years. No, Mr. West, I am sure on reflection you will perceive that it was in your age, not in ours, that the extension of the functions of governments was extraordinary. Not even for the best ends would men now allow their governments such powers as were then used for the most maleficent."

"Leaving comparisons aside," I said, "the demagoguery and corruption of our public men would have been considered, in my day, insuperable objections to any assumption by government of the charge of the national industries. We should have thought that no arrangement could be worse than to entrust the politicians with control of the wealth-producing machinery of the country. Its material interests were quite too much the football of parties as it was."

"No doubt you were right," rejoined Doctor Leete, "but all that is changed now. We have no parties or politicians, and as for demagoguery and corruption, they are words having only an historical significance."

"Human nature itself must have changed very much," I said.

"Not at all," was Doctor Leete's reply, "but the conditions of human life have changed, and with them the motives of human action. The organization of society with you was such that officials were under a constant temptation to misuse their power for the private profit of themselves or others. Under such circumstances it seems almost strange that you dared entrust them with any of your affairs. Nowadays, on the contrary, society is so constituted that there is absolutely no way in which an official, however ill-disposed, could possibly make any profit for himself or any one else by a misuse of his power. Let him be as bad an official as you please, he cannot be a corrupt one. There is no motive to be. The social system no longer offers a premium on dishonesty. But these are matters which you can only understand as you come, with time, to know us better."

"But you have not yet told me how you have settled the labor problem. It is the problem of capital which we have been discussing," I said. "After the nation had assumed conduct of the mills, machinery, railroads, farms, mines, and capital in general of the country, the labor question still remained. In assuming the responsibilities of capital the nation had assumed the difficulties of the capitalist's position."

"The moment the nation assumed the responsibilities of capital those difficulties vanished," replied Doctor Leete. "The national organization of labor under one direction was the complete solution of what was, in your day and under your system, justly regarded as the insoluble labor problem. When the nation became the sole employer, all the citizens, by virtue of their citizenship, became employees, to be distributed according to the needs of industry."

"That is," I suggested, "you have simply applied the principle of universal military service, as it was understood in our day, to the labor question."

"Yes," said Doctor Leete, "that was something which followed as a matter of course as soon as the nation had become the sole capitalist. The people were already accustomed to the idea that the obligation of every citizen, not physically disabled, to contribute his military services to the defense of the nation was equal and absolute. That it was equally the duty of every citizen to contribute his quota of industrial or intellectual services to the maintenance of the nation was equally evident, though it was not until the nation became the employer of labor that citizens were able to render this sort of service with any pretense either of universality or equity. No organization of labor was possible when the employing power was divided among hundreds or thousands of individuals and corporations, between which concert of any kind was neither desired, nor indeed feasible. It constantly happened then that vast numbers who desired to labor could find no opportunity, and on the other hand, those who desired to evade a part or all of their debt could easily do so."

"Service, now, I suppose, is compulsory upon all," I suggested.

"It is rather a matter of course than of compulsion," replied Doctor Leete. "It is regarded as so absolutely natural and reasonable that the idea of its being compulsory has ceased to be thought of. He would be thought to be an incredibly contemptible person who should need compulsion in such a case. Nevertheless, to speak of service being compulsory would be a weak way to state its absolute inevitableness. Our entire social order is so wholly based upon and deduced from it that if it were conceivable that a man could escape it, he would be left with no possible way to provide for his existence. He would have excluded himself from the world, cut himself off from his kind, in a word, committed suicide."

"Is the term of service in this industrial army for life?"

"Oh, no; it both begins later and ends earlier than the average working period in your day. Your workshops were filled with children and old men, but we hold the period of youth sacred to education, and the period of maturity, when the physical forces begin to flag, equally sacred to ease and aggreable relaxation. The period of industrial service is twenty-four years, beginning at the close of the course of education at twenty-one and terminating at forty-five. After forty-five, while discharged from labor, the citizen still remains liable to special calls, in case of emergencies causing a sudden great increase in the demand for labor, till he reaches the age of fifty-five, but such calls are rarely, in fact almost never, made. The fifteenth day of October of every year is what we call Muster Day, because those who have reached the age of twenty-one are then mustered into the industrial service, and at the same time those who, after twenty-four years' service, have reached the age of forty-five are honorably mustered out. It is the great day of the year with us, whence we reckon all other events, our Olympiad, save that it is annual."

"It is after you have mustered your industrial army into service," I said, "that I should expect the difficulty to arise, for there its analogy with a military army must cease. Soldiers have all the same thing, and a very simple thing, to do, namely, to practice the manual of arms, to march and stand guard. But the industrial army must learn and follow two or three hundred diverse trades and avocations. What administrative talent can be equal to determine wisely what trade or business every individual in a great nation shall pursue?"

"The administration has nothing to do with determining that point."

"Who does determine it, then?" I asked.

"Every man for himself in accordance with his natural aptitude, the utmost pains being taken to enable him to find out what his natural aptitude really is. The principle on which our industrial army is organized is that a man's natural endowments, mental and physical, determine what he can work at most profitably to the nation and most satisfactorily to himself. While the obligation of service in some form is not to be evaded, voluntary election, subject only to necessary regulation, is depended on to determine the particular sort of service every man is to render. As an individual's satisfaction during his term of service depends on his having an occupation to his taste, parents and teachers watch from early years for indications of special aptitudes in children. A thorough study of the national industrial system, with the history and rudiments of all the great trades, is an essential part of our educational system. While manual training is not allowed to encroach on the general intellectual culture to which our schools are devoted, it is carried far enough to give our youth, in addition to their theoretical knowledge of the national industries, mechanical and agricultural, a certain familiarity with their tools and methods. Our schools are constantly visiting our workshops, and often are taken on long excursions to inspect particular industrial enterprises. In your day a man was not ashamed to be grossly ignorant of all trades except his own, but such ignorance would not be consistent with our idea of placing everyone in a position to select intelligently the occupation for which he has most taste. Usually long before he is mustered into service a young man has found out the pursuit he wants to follow, has acquired a great deal of knowledge about it, and is waiting impatiently the time when he can enlist in its ranks."

"Surely," I said, "it can hardly be that the number of volunteers for any trade is exactly the number needed in that trade. It must be generally either under or over the demand."

"The supply of volunteers is always expected to fully equal the demand," replied Doctor Leete. "It is the business of the administration to see that this is the case. The rate of volunteering for each trade is closely watched. If there be a noticeably greater excess of volunteers over men needed in any trade, it is inferred that the trade offers greater attractions than others. On the other hand, if the number of volunteers for a trade tends to drop below the demand, it is inferred that it is thought more arduous. It is the business of the administration to seek constantly to equalize the attractions of the trades, so far as the conditions of labor in them are concerned, so that all trades shall be equally attractive to persons having natural tastes for them. This is done by making the hours of labor in different trades to differ according to their arduousness. The lighter trades, prosecuted under the most agreeable circumstances, have in this way the longest hours, while an arduous trade, such as mining, has very short hours. There is no theory, no a priori rule, by which the respective attractiveness of industries is determined. The administration, in taking burdens off one class of workers and adding them to other classes, simply follows the fluctuations of opinion among the workers themselves as indicated by the rate of volunteering. The principle is that no man's work ought to be, on the whole, harder for him than any other man's for him, the workers themselves to be the judges. There are no limits to the application of this rule. If any particular occupations is in itself so arduous or so oppressing that, in order to induce volunteers, the day's work in it had to be reduced to ten minutes, it would be done. If, even then, no man was willing to do it, it would remain undone. But of course, in point of fact, a moderate reduction in the hours of labor or addition of other privileges suffices to secure all needed volunteers for any occupation necessary to men. If, indeed, the unavoidable difficulties and dangers of such a necessary pursuit were so great that no inducement of compensating advantages would overcome men's repugnance to it, the administration would only need to take it out of the common order of occupations by declaring it 'extra hazardous,' and those who pursued it especially worthy of the national gratitude, to be overrun with volunteers. Our young men are very greedy of honor, and do not let slip such opportunities. Of course you will see that dependence on the purely voluntary choice of avocations involves the abolition in all of anything like unhygienic conditions or special peril to life and limb. Health and safety are conditions common to all industries. The nation does not maim and slaughter its workmen by thousands, as did the private capitalists and corporations of your day."

"When there are more who want to enter a particular trade than there is room for, how do you decide between the applicants?" I inquired.

"Preference is given to those who have acquired the most knowledge of the trade they wish to follow. No man, however, who through successive years remains persistent in his desire to show what he can do at any particular trade, is in the end denied an opportunity. Meanwhile, if a man cannot at first win entrance into the business he prefers, he has usually one or more alternative preferences, pursuits for which he has some degree of aptitude, although not the highest. Everyone, indeed, is expected to study his aptitudes so as to have not only a first choice as to occupation, but a second or third, so that if, either at the outset of his career or subsequently, owing to the progress of invention or changes in demand, he is unable to follow his first vocation, he can still find reasonably congenial employment. This principle of secondary choices as to occupation is quite important in our system. I should add, in reference to the counterpossibility of some sudden failure of volunteers in a particular trade, or some sudden necessity of an increased force, that the administration, while depending on the voluntary system for filling up the trades as a rule, holds always in reserve the power to call for special volunteers, or draft any force needed from any quarter. Generally, however, all needs of this sort can be met by details from the class of unskilled or common laborers."

"How is this class of common laborers recruited?" I asked. "Surely nobody voluntarily enters that."

"It is the grade to which all new recruits belong for the first three years of their service. It is not till after this period, during which he is assignable to do any work at the discretion of his superiors, that the young man is allowed to elect a special avocation. These three years of stringent discipline none are exempt from, and very glad our young men are to pass from this severe school into the comparative liberty of the trades. If a man were so stupid as to have no choice as to occupation, he would simply remain a common laborer; but such cases, as you may suppose, are not common."

"Having once elected and entered on a trade or occupation," I remarked, "I suppose he has to stick to it the rest of his life."

"Not necessarily," replied Doctor Leete. "While frequent and merely capricious changes of occupation are not encouraged or even permitted, every worker is allowed, of course, under certain regulations and in accordance with the exigencies of the service, to volunteer for another industry which he thinks would suit him better than his first choice. In this case his application is received just as if he were volunteering for the first time, and on the same terms. Not only this, but a worker may likewise, under suitable regulations and not too frequently, obtain a transfer to an establishment of the same industry in another part of the country which for any reason he may prefer. Under your system a discontented man could indeed leave his work at will, but he left his means of support at the same time, and took his chances as to future livelihood. We find that the number of men who wish to abandon an accustomed occupation for a new one, and old friends and associations for strange ones, is small. It is only the poorer sort of workmen who desire to change even as frequently as our regulations permit. Of course, transfers or discharges, when health demands them, are always given."

"As an industrial system, I should think this might be extremely efficient," I said, "but I don't see that it makes any provision for the professional classes, the men who serve the nation with brains instead of hands. Of course you can't get along without the brain workers. How, then, are they selected from those who are to serve as farmers and mechanics? That must require a very delicate sort of sifting process, I should say."

"So it does," replied Doctor Leete. "The most delicate possible test is needed here, and so we leave the question whether a man shall be a brain or hand worker entirely to him to settle. At the end of the term of three years as a common laborer, which every man must serve, it is for him to choose, in accordance to his natural tastes, whether he will fit himself for an art or profession, or be a farmer or mechanic. If he feels that he can do better work with his brains than his muscles, he finds every facility for testing the reality of his supposed bent, of cultivating it, and, if fit, of pursuing it as his avocation. The schools of technology, of medicine, of art, of music, of histrionics, and of higher liberal learning are always open to aspirants without condition."

"Are not the schools flooded with young men whose only motive is to avoid work?"

Doctor Leete smiled a little grimly.

"No one is at all likely to enter the professional schools for the purpose of avoiding work, I assure you," he said. "They are intended for those with special aptitude for the branches they teach, and anyone without it would find it easier to do double hours at his trade than try to keep up with the classes. Of course many honestly mistake their vocation, and, finding themselves unequal to the requirements of the schools, drop out and return to the industrial service; no discredit attaches to such persons, for the public policy is to encourage all to develop suspected talents which only actual tests can prove the reality of. The professional and scientific schools of your day depended on the patronage of their pupils for support, and the practice appears to have been common of giving diplomas to unfit persons, who afterward found their way into the professions. Our schools are national institutions, and to have passed their tests is a proof of special abilities not to be questioned.

"This opportunity for a professional training," the doctor continued, "remains open to every man till the age of thirty is reached, after which students are not received, as there would remain too brief a period before the age of discharge in which to serve the nation in their professions. In your day young men had to choose their professions very young, and therefore, in a large proportion of instances, wholly mistook their vocations. It is recognized nowadays that the natural aptitudes of some are later than those of others in developing, and therefore, while the choice of professions may be made as early as twenty-four, it remains open for six years longer."

A question which had a dozen times before been on my lips now found utterance, a question which touched upon what, in my time, had been regarded the most vital difficulty in the way of any final settlement of the industrial problem. "It's an extraordinary thing," I said, "that you should not yet have said a word about the method of adjusting the wages. Since the nation is the sole employer, the government must fix the rate of wages and determine just how much everybody shall earn, from the doctors to the diggers. All I can say is, that this plan would never have worked with us, and I don't see how it can now unless human nature has changed. In my day, nobody was satisfied with his wages or salary. Even if he felt he received enough, he was sure his neighbor had too much, which was as bad. If the universal discontent on this subject, instead of being dissipated in curses and strikes directed against innumerable employers, could have been concentrated upon one, and that the government, the strongest ever devised would not have seen two pay days."

Doctor Leete laughed heartily.

"Very true, very true," he said, "a general strike would most probably have followed the first pay day, and a strike directed against a government is a revolution. . . ."

"How . . . can you adjust satisfactorily the comparative wages or remuneration of the multitude of avocations, so unlike and so incommensurable, which are necessary for the service of society? In our day the market rate determined the price of labor of all sorts, as well as of goods. The employer paid as little as he could, and the worker got as much. It was not a pretty system ethically, I admit; but it did, at least, furnish us a rough-and-ready formula for settling a question which must be settled ten thousand times a day if the world was ever going to get forward. There seemed to us no other practicable way of doing it."

"Yes," replied Doctor Leete, "it was the only practicable way under a system which made the interests of every individual antagonistic to those of every other; but it would have been a pity if humanity could never have devised a better plan, for yours was simply the application to the mutual relations of men of the devil's maxim, 'Your necessity is my opportunity.' The reward of any service depended not upon its difficulty, danger, or hardship, for throughout the world it seems that the most perilous, severe, and repulsive labor was done by the worst-paid classes, but solely upon the straits of those who needed the service."

"All that is conceded," I said. "But, with all its defects, the plan of settling prices by the market rate was a practical plan; and I cannot conceive what satisfactory substitute you can have devised for it. The government being the only possible employer, there is of course no labor market or market rate. Wages of all sorts must be arbitrarily fixed by the government. I cannot imagine a more complex and delicate function than that must be, or one, however performed, more certain to breed universal dissatisfaction."

"I beg your pardon," replied Doctor Leete, "but I think you exaggerate the difficulty. Suppose a board of fairly sensible men were charged with settling the wages for all sorts of trades under a system which, like ours, guaranteed employment to all, while permitting the choice of avocations. Don't you see that, however unsatisfactory the first adjustment might be, the mistakes would soon correct themselves? The favored trades would have too many volunteers, and those discriminated against would lack them till the errors were set right. But this is aside from the purpose, for, though this plan would, I fancy, be practicable enough, it is no part of our system."

"How, then, do you regulate wages?" I once more asked.

Doctor Leete did not reply till after several moments of meditative silence. "I know, of course," he finally said, "enough of the old order of things to understand just what you mean by that question; and yet the present order is so utterly different at this point that I am a little at a loss how to answer you best. You ask me how we regulate wages; I can only reply that there is no idea in the modern social economy which at all corresponds with what was meant by wages in your day."

"I suppose you mean that you have no money to pay wages in," said I. "But the credit given the worker at the government storehouse answers to his wages with us. How is the amount of the credit given respectively to the workers in different lines determined? By what title does the individual claim his particular share? What is the basis of allotment?"

"His title," replied Doctor Leete, "is his humanity. The basis of his claim is the fact that he is a man."

"The fact that he is a man!" I repeated, incredulously. "Do you possibly mean that all have the same share?"

"Most assuredly."

"You see," he said, smiling, "that it is not merely that we have no money to pay wages in, but, as I said, we have nothing at all answering to your idea of wages."

By this time I had pulled myself together sufficiently to voice some of the criticisms which, man of the nineteenth century as I was, came upper most in my mind, upon this, to me, astounding arrangement. "Some men do twice the work of others!" I exclaimed. "Are the clever workmen content with a plan that ranks them with the indifferent?"

"We leave no possible ground for any complaint of injustice," replied Doctor Leete, "by requiring precisely the same measure of service from all."

"How can you do that, I should like to know, when no two men's powers are the same?"

"Nothing could be simpler," was Doctor Leete's reply. "We require of each that he shall make the same effort; that is, we demand of him the best service it is in his power to give."

"And supposing all do the best they can," I answered, "the amount of the produce resulting is twice greater from one man than from another."

"Very true," replied Doctor Leete, "but the amount of the resulting product has nothing whatever to do with the question, which is one of desert. Desert is a moral question, and the amount of the product a material quantity. It would be an extraordinary sort of logic which should try to determine a moral question by a material standard. The amount of the effort alone is pertinent to the question of desert. All men who do their best, do the same. A man's endowments, however godlike, merely fix the measure of his duty. The man of great endowments who does not do all he might, though he may do more than a man of small endowments who does his best, is deemed a less deserving worker than the latter, and dies a debtor to his fellows. The Creator sets men's tasks for them by the faculties he gives them; we simply exact their fulfillment."

"No doubt that is very fine philosophy," I said. "Nevertheless it seems hard that the man who produces twice as much as another, even if both do their best, should have only the same share."

"Does it, indeed, seem so to you?" responded Doctor Leete. "Now, do you know, that seems very curious to me? The way it strikes people nowadays is that a man who can produce twice as much as another with the same effort, instead of being rewarded for doing so, ought to be punished if he does not do so. In the nineteenth century, when a horse pulled a heavier load than a goat, I suppose you rewarded him. Now, we should have whipped him soundly if he had not, on the ground that, being much stronger, he ought to. It is singular how ethical standards change." The doctor said this with such a twinkle in his eye that I was obliged to laugh.

"I suppose," I said, "that the real reason that we rewarded men for their endowments, while we considered those of horses and goats merely as fixing the service to be severally required of them was that the animals, not being reasoning beings, naturally did the best they could, whereas men could only be induced to do so by rewarding them according to the amount of their product. That brings me to ask why, unless human nature has mightily changed in a hundred years, you are not under the same necessity."

"We are," replied Doctor Leete. "I don't think there has been any change in human nature in that respect since your day. It is so constituted still that special incentives in the form of prizes, and advantages to be gained, are requisite to call out the best endeavors of the average man in any direction."

"But what inducement," I asked, "can a man have to put forth his best endeavors when, however much or little he accomplishes, his income remains the same? High characters may be moved by devotion to the common welfare under such a system, but does not the average man tend to rest back on his oar, reasoning that it is of no use to make a special effort, since the effort will not increase his income, nor its withholding diminish it?"

"Does it then really seem to you," answered my companion, "that human nature is insensible to any motives save fear of want and love of luxury, that you should expect security and equality of livelihood to leave them without possible incentives to effort? Your contemporaries did not really think so, though they might fancy they did. When it was a question of the grandest class of efforts, the most absolute self-devotion, they depended on quite other incentives. Not higher wages, but honor and the hope of men's gratitude, patriotism and the inspiration of duty, were the motives which they set before their soldiers when it was a question of dying for the nation, and never was there an age of the world when those motives did not call out what is best and noblest in men. And not only this, but when you come to analyze the love of money which was the general impulse to effort in your day, you find that the dread of want and desire of luxury was but one of several motives which the pursuit of money represented; the others, and with many the more influential, being desire of power, of social position, and reputation for ability and success. So you see that though we have abolished poverty and the fear of it, and inordinate luxury with the hope of it, we have not touched the greater part of the motives which underlay the love of money in former times, or any of those which prompted the supremer sorts of effort. The coarser motives, which no longer move us, have been replaced by higher motives wholly unknown to the mere wage earners of your age. Now that industry, of whatever sort, is no longer self-service, but service of the nation, patriotism, passion for humanity, impel the worker as in your day they did the soldier. The army of industry is an army, not alone by virtue of its perfect organization, but by reason also of the ardor of self-devotion which animates its members.

"But as you used to supplement the motives of patriotism with the love of glory, in order to stimulate the valor of your soldiers, so do we. Based as our industrial system is on the principle of requiring the same unit of effort from every man, that is, the best he can do, you will see that the means by which we spur the workers to do their best must be a very essential part of our scheme. With us, diligence in the national service is the sole and certain way to public repute, social distinction, and official power. The value of a man's services to society fixes his rank in it. Compared with the effort of our social arrangements in impelling men to be zealous in business, we deem the object lessons of biting poverty and wanton luxury on which you depended a device as weak and uncertain as it was barbaric. The lust of honor even in your sordid day notoriously impelled men to more desperate effort than the love of money could."

"I should be extremely interested," I said, "to learn something of what these social arrangements are. . . ."

"You must understand in the first place," replied the doctor, "that the supply of incentives to effort is but one of the objects sought in the organization we have adopted for the army. The other, and equally important, is to secure for the file leaders and captains of the force, and the great officers of the nation, men of proved abilities, who are pledged by their own careers to hold their followers up to their highest standard of performance and permit no lagging. With a view to these two ends the industrial army is organized. First comes the unclassified grade of common laborers, men of all work, to which all recruits during their first three years belong. This grade is a sort of school and a very strict one, in which the young men are taught habits of obedience, subordination, and devotion to duty. While the miscellaneous nature of the work done by this force prevents the systematic grading of the workers which is afterward possible, yet individual records are kept, and excellence receives distinction corresponding with the penalties that negligence incurs. It is not, however, policy with us to permit youthful recklessness or indiscretion, when not deeply culpable, to handicap the future careers of young men, and all who have passed through the unclassified grade without serious disgrace have an equal opportunity to choose the life employment they have most liking for. Having selected this, they enter upon it as apprentices. The length of the apprenticeship naturally differs in different occupations. At the end of it the apprentice becomes a full workman, and a member of his trade or guild. Now not only are the individual records of the apprentices for ability and industry strictly kept, and excellence distinguished by suitable distinctions, but upon the average of his record during apprenticeship the standing given the apprentice among the full workmen depends.

"While the internal organizations of different industries, mechanical and agricultural, differ according to their peculiar conditions, they agree in a general division of their workers into first, second, and third grades, according to ability, and these grades are in many cases subdivided into first and second classes. According to his standing as an apprentice, a young man is assigned his place as a first-, second-, or third-grade worker. Of course only young men of unusual ability pass directly from apprenticeship into the first grade of the workers. The most fall into the lower grades, working up as they grow more experienced, at the periodical regradings. These regradings take place in each industry at intervals corresponding with the length of the apprenticeship to that industry, so that merit never need wait long to rise, nor can any rest on past achievements unless they would drop into a lower rank. One of the notable advantages of a high grading is the privilege it gives the worker in electing which of the various branches or processes of his industry he will follow as his specialty. Of course it is not intended that any of the processes shall be disproportionately arduous, but there is often much difference between them, and the privilege of election is accordingly highly prized. So far as possible, indeed, the preferences even of the poorest workmen are considered in assigning them their line of work, because not only their happiness but their usefulness is thus enhanced. While, however, the wish of the lower-grade man is consulted so far as the exigencies of the service permit, he is considered only after the upper-grade men have been provided for, and often he has to put up with second or third choice, or even with an arbitrary assignment when help is needed. This privilege of election attends every regrading, and when a man loses a grade he also risks having to exchange the sort of work he likes for some other less to his taste. The results of each regrading, giving the standing of every man in his industry, are gazetted in the public prints, and those who have won promotion since the last regrading receive the nation's thanks and are publicly invested with the badge of their new rank."

"What may this badge be?" I asked.

"Every industry has its emblematic device," replied Doctor Leete, "and this, in the shape of a metallic badge so small that you might not see it unless you knew where to look, is all the insignes which the men of the army wear, except where public convenience demands a distinctive uniform. This badge is the same in form for all grades of industry, but while the badge of the third grade is iron, that of the second grade is silver, and that of the first is gilt.

"Apart from the grand incentive to endeavor afforded by the fact that the high places in the nation are open only to the highest-class men, and that rank in the army constitutes the only mode of social distinction for the vast majority who are not aspirants in art, literature, and the professions, various incitements of a minor, but perhaps equally effective, sort are provided in the form of special privileges and immunities in the way of discipline, which the superior-class men enjoy. These, while intended to be as little as possible invidious to the less successful, have the effect of keeping constantly before every man's mind the great desirability of attaining the grade next above his own.

"It is obviously important that not only the good but also the indifferent and poor workmen should be able to cherish the ambition of rising. Indeed, the number of the latter being so much greater, it is even more essential that the ranking system should not operate to discourage them than that it should stimulate the others. It is to this end that the grades are divided into classes. The grades as well as the classes being made numerically equal at each regrading, there is not at any time, counting out the officers and the unclassified and apprentice grades, over one-ninth of the industrial army in the lowest class, and most of this number are recent apprentices, all of whom expect to rise. Those who remain during the entire term of service in the lowest class are but a trifling fraction of the industrial army, and likely to be as deficient in sensibility to their position as in ability to better it.

"It is not even necessary that a worker should win promotion to a higher grade to have at least a taste of glory. While promotion requires a general excellence of record as a worker, honorable mention and various sorts of prizes are awarded for excellence less than sufficient for promotion, and also for special feats and single performances in the various industries. There are many minor distinctions of standing, not only within the grades but within the classes, each of which acts as a spur to the efforts of a group. It is intended that no form of merit shall wholly fail of recognition.

"As for actual neglect of work, positively bad work, or other overt remissness on the part of men incapable of generous motives, the discipline of the industrial army is far too strict to allow anything whatever of the sort. A man able to duty, and persistently refusing, is sentenced to solitary imprisonment on bread and water till he consents.

"The lowest grade of the officers of the industrial army, that of assistant foreman, or lieutenants, is appointed out of men who have held their place for two years in the first class of the first grade. Where this leaves too large a range of choice, only the first group of this class are eligible. No one thus comes to the point of commanding men until he is about thirty years old. After a man becomes an officer, his rating of course no longer depends on the efficiency of his own work, but on that of his men. The foremen are appointed from among the assistant foremen, by the same exercise of discretion limited to a small eligible class. In the appointments to the still higher grades another principle is introduced, which it would take too much time to explain now.

"Of course such a system of grading as I have described would have been impracticable applied to the small industrial concerns of your day, in some of which there were hardly enough employees to have left one apiece for the classes. You must remember that, under the national organization of labor, all industries are carried on by great bodies of men, many of your farms or shops being combined as one. It is also owing solely to the vast scale on which industry is organized, with coordinate establishments in every part of the country, that we are able by exchanges and transfers to fit every man so nearly with the sort of work he can do best.

"And now, Mr. West, I will leave it to you, on the bare outline of its features which I have given, if those who need special incentives to do their best are likely to lack them under our system. Does it not seem to you that men who found themselves obliged, whether they wished or not, to work, would under such a system be strongly impelled to do their best?"

I replied that it seemed to me the incentives offered were, if any objection were to be made, too strong; that the pace set for the young men was too hot; and such, indeed, I would add with deference, still remains my opinion, now that by longer residence among you I have become better acquainted with the whole subject.

Doctor Leete, however, desired me to reflect, and I am ready to say that it is perhaps a sufficient reply to my objection, that the worker's livelihood is in no way dependent on his ranking, and anxiety for that never embitters his disappointments; that the working hours are short, the vacations regular, and that all emulation ceases at forty-five, with the attainment of middle life.

"There are two or three other points I ought to refer to," he added, "to prevent your getting mistaken impressions. In the first place, you must understand that this system of preferment given the most efficient workers over the less so, in no way contravenes the fundamental idea of our social system, that all who do their best are equally deserving, whether the best be great or small. I have shown that the system is arranged to encourage the weaker as well as the stronger with the hope of rising, while the fact that the stronger are are selected for the leaders is in no way a reflection upon the weaker, but in the interest of the common weal.

"Do not imagine, either, because emulation is given free play as an incentive under our system, that we deem it a motive likely to appeal to the nobler sort of men, or worthy of them. Such as these find their motives within, not without, and measure their duty by their own endowments, not by those of others. So long as their achievement is proportioned to their powers, they would consider it preposterous to expect praise or blame because it chanced to be great or small. To such natures emulation appears philosophically absurd, and despicable in a moral aspect by its substitution of envy for admiration, and exultation for regret, in one's attitude toward the successes and the failures of others.

"But all men, even in the last year of the twentieth century, are not of this high order, and the incentives to endeavor requisite for those who are not must be of a sort adapted to their inferior natures. For these, then, emulation of the keenest edge is provided as a constant spur. Those who need this motive will feel it. Those who are above its influence do not need it.

"I should not fail to mention," resumed the doctor, "that for those too deficient in mental or bodily strength to be fairly graded with the main body of workers, we have a separate grade, unconnected with the others—a sort of invalid corps, the members of which are provided with a light class of tasks fitted to their strength. All our sick in mind and body, all our deaf and dumb, and lame and blind and crippled, and even our insane, belong to this invalid corps, and bear its insigne. The strongest often do nearly a man's work, the feeblest, of course, nothing; but none who can do anything are willing quite to give up. In their lucid intervals, even our insane are eager to do what they can."

"That is a pretty idea of the invalid corps," I said. "Even a barbarian from the nineteenth century can appreciate that. It is a very graceful way of disguising charity, and must be grateful to the feelings of its recipients."

"Charity!" repeated Doctor Leete. "Did you suppose that we consider the incapable class we are talking of objects of charity?"

"Why, naturally," I said, "inasmuch as they are incapable of self-support."

But here the doctor took me up quickly.

"Who is capable of self-support?" he demand. "There is no such thing in a civilized society as self-support. In a state of society so barbarous as not even to know family cooperation, each individual may possibly support himself, though even then for a part of his life only; but from the moment that men begin to live together, and constitute even the rudest of society, self-support becomes impossible. As men grow more civilized, and the subdivision of occupations and services is carried out, a complex mutual dependence becomes the universal rule. Every man, however solitary may seem his occupation, is a member of a vast industrial partnership, as large as the nation, as large as humanity. The necessity of mutual dependence should imply the duty and guarantee of mutual support; and that it did not in your day constituted the essential cruelty and unreason for your system."

"That may all be so," I replied, "but it does not touch the case of those who are unable to contribute anything to the product of industry."

"Surely I told you [earlier, at] least I thought I did," replied Doctor Leete, "that the right of a man to maintenance at the nation's table depends on the fact that he is a man, and not on the amount of health and strength he may have, so long as he does his best."

"You said so," I answered, "but I supposed the rule applied only to the workers of different ability. Does it also hold of those who can do nothing at all?"

"Are they not also men?"

"I am to understand, then, that the lame, the blind, the sick, and the impotent, are as well off as the most efficient, and have the same income?"

"Certainly," was the reply.

"The idea of charity on such a scale," I answered, "would have made our most enthusiastic philanthropists gasp."

"If you had a sick brother at home," replied Doctor Leete, "unable to work, would you feed him on less dainty food, and lodge and clothe him more poorly, than yourself? More likely far, you would give him the preference; nor would you think of calling it charity. Would not the word, in that connection, fill you with indignation?"

"Of course," I replied, "but the cases are not parallel. There is a sense, no doubt, in which all men are brothers; but this general sort of brotherhood is not to be compared, except for rhetorical purposes, to the brotherhood of blood, either as to its sentiment or its obligations."

"There speaks the nineteenth century!" exclaimed Doctor Leete. "Ah, Mr. West, there is no doubt as to the length of time that you slept. If I were to give you, in one sentence, a key to what may seem the mysteries of our civilization as compared with that of your age, I should say that it is the fact that the solidarity of the race and the brotherhood of man, which to you were but fine phrases, are, to our thinking and feeling, ties as real and as vital as physical fraternity.

"But even setting that consideration aside, I do not see why it so surprises you that those who cannot work are conceded the full right to live on the produce of those who can. Even in your day, the duty of military service for the protection of the nation, to which our industrial service corresponds, while obligatory on those able to discharge it, did not operate to deprive of the privileges of citizenship those who were unable. They stayed at home, and were protected by those who fought, and nobody questioned their right to be, or thought less of them. So, now, the requirement of industrial service from those able to render it does not operate to deprive of the privileges of citizenship, which now implies the citizen's maintenance, him who cannot work. The worker is not a citizen because he works, but works because he is a citizen. As you recognize the duty of the strong to fight for the weak, we, now that fighting is gone by, recognize his duty to work for him.

"A solution which leaves an unaccounted-for residuum is no solution at all; and our solution of the problem of human society would have been none at all had it left the lame, the sick, and the blind outside with the beasts, to fare as they might. Better far have left the strong and well unprovided for than these burdened ones, toward whom every heart must yearn, and for whom ease of mind and body should be provided, if for no others. Therefore it is, as I told you this morning, that the title of every man, woman, and child to the means of existence rests on no basis less plain, broad, and simple than the fact that they are fellows of one race—members of one human family. The only coin current is the image of God, and that is good for all we have.

"I think there is no feature of the civilization of your epoch so repugnant to modern ideas as the neglect with which you treated your dependent classes. Even if you had no pity, no feeling of brotherhood, how was it that you did not see that you were robbing the incapable class of their plain right in leaving them unprovided for?"

"I don't quite follow you there," I said. "I admit the claim of this class to our pity, but how could they who produced nothing claim a share of the product as a right?"

"How happened it," was Doctor Leete's reply, "that your workers were able to produce more than so many savages would have done? Was it not wholly on account of the heritage of the past knowledge and achievements of the race, the machinery of society, thousands of years in contriving, found by you ready-made to your hand? How did you come to be possessors of this knowledge and this machinery, which represent nine parts to one contributed by yourself in the value of your product? You inherited it, did you not? And were not these others, these unfortunate and crippled brothers whom you cast out, joint inheritors, coheirs with you? What did you do with their share? Did you not rob them when you put them off with crusts, who were entitled to sit with the heirs, and did you not add insult to robbery when you called the crusts charity?

"Ah, Mr. West," Doctor Leete continued, as I did not respond, "what I do not understand is, setting aside all considerations either of justice or brotherly feeling toward the crippled and defective, how the workers of your day could have had any heart for their work, knowing that their children, or grandchildren, if unfortunate, would be deprived of the comforts and even necessities of life. It is a mystery how men with children could favor a system under which they were rewarded beyond those less endowed with bodily strength or mental power. For, by the same discrimination by which the father profited, the son, for whom he would give his life, being perchance weaker than others, might be reduced to crusts and beggary. How men dared leave children behind them, I have never been able to understand."